Studies in Eighteenth-Century Culture

Volume 54

Studies in Eighteenth-Century Culture

Volume 54

Editor
George E. Boulukos
Southern Illinois University Carbondale

Advisory Board

Benjamin Breen
University of California, Santa Cruz

Sarah R. Cohen
University at Albany, State University of New York

Rebecca Geoffroy-Schwinden
University of North Texas

Jennifer Van Horn
University of Delaware

Published by Johns Hopkins University Press for the
American Society for Eighteenth-Century Studies

Johns Hopkins University Press
Baltimore and London
2025

© 2025 American Society for Eighteenth-Century Studies
All rights reserved.
Printed in the United States of America on acid-free paper.
9 8 7 6 5 4 3 2 1

Johns Hopkins University Press
2715 North Charles Street
Baltimore, Maryland 21218-4363
www.press.jhu.edu

ISBN 978-1-4214-5175-6
ISSN 0360-2370

Articles appearing in this annual series are abstracted and indexed in *America: History and Life, Current Abstracts, Historical Abstracts, MLA International Bibliography, Poetry and Short Story Reference Center, and RILM Abstracts of Music Literature*

EU GPSR Authorized Representative
LOGOS EUROPE, 9 rue Nicolas Poussin, 17000, La Rochelle, France
E-mail: Contact@logoseurope.eu

Contents

Editor's Note viii

Letters "à la Sévigné": A Seventeenth-Century Model for the Eighteenth Century
CHLOE SUMMERS EDMONDSON 1

Emotions, Work, and Form in the Diary of Edmund Harrold, 1712–15
ROBERT STEARN 23

"Not for mere children": Charlotte Smith's Feminist Novels for "Young Persons"
JOANI ETSKOVITZ 47

Richard Coeur de Lion: Fighting Queens, Gothic Politics, and Heterosexual Pleasure on the English Stage
ROBERT W. JONES 69

"Queer Periodical Temporality": Spinsterhood in the Eighteenth-Century English Periodical
FAUVE VANDENBERGHE 93

Close Encounters and Stranger Things: Angelica Kauffman's First Years in London
WENDY WASSYNG ROWORTH 109

Un homme à l'antique: The Visual Vocabulary of Antiquity in Men's Fashion and Democratic Uniforms in Revolutionary France
BRONTË HEBDON 133

Styling Equiano: Accumulation and Conversion in the *Interesting Narrative*
YAN CHE 159

Bartering Knowledge, Imposing Silence: Indigenous Guanche Presence in Thomas Sprat's *History of the Royal Society of London*
ALLISON Y. GIBEILY 181

The Question of Iʻtisam-ud-Din: An Indian Traveler in Eighteenth-Century Europe
  SANJAY SUBRAHMANYAM 199
Turning the Crank: The Performance of Empire through Tipu's Tiger
  VINCENT PHAM 225
The Principle of Neutrality and the Evidentiary Patterns of Conspiratorial Thought in the Early United States
  NAN GOODMAN 239
Contributors 263
Executive Board 2024–25 267
Sponsor Members 269
Institutional Members 269

ASECS Affiliate and Regional Societies

American Antiquarian Society
Aphra Behn Society
Bibliographical Society of America
Burney Society of North America
The Burney Society (UK)
Canadian Society for Eighteenth-Century Studies
Daniel Defoe Society
Early Caribbean Society
East-Central ASECS
Eighteenth-Century Scottish Studies Society
Germaine de Staël Society
German Society for Eighteenth-Century Studies
Goethe Society of North America
Historians of Eighteenth-Century Art and Architecture
Ibero-American Society for Eighteenth-Century Studies
International Adam Smith Society
International Herder Society
Johnson Society of the Central Region
Lessing Society
Midwestern ASECS
Mozart Society of America
North American British Music Studies Association
North American Kant Society
Northeast ASECS
Rousseau Association
Samuel Johnson Society of the West
Samuel Richardson Society
Society of Early Americanists
Society for Eighteenth-Century French Studies
Society for Eighteenth-Century Music
Society for the History of Authorship, Reading and Publishing
South Central Society for Eighteenth-Century Studies
Southeast Asian Society for Eighteenth-Century Studies
Southeastern ASECS
Voltaire Foundation
Western Society for Eighteenth-Century Studies

Editor's Note

I am honored to have been selected as the new editor of *Studies in Eighteenth-Century Culture*, which has held a mystique for me since I first discovered it in graduate school. I was awed at first, no doubt, by its impressive gilded hardcover, but not less by the range and depth of its contents. This impression was only deepened when a member of my UT Austin eighteenth-century studies dissertation group, Scarlet Bowen, placed a superb article on *Pamela* and the language of young female servants in its hallowed pages.

I write here primarily to thank the outgoing editors, David Brewer and Crystal Lake, who deserve all the credit for having assembled this volume. I have merely shepherded their work—and that of the authors of these excellent articles—through the production process. And yet, by tradition, only my name is credited in gold lettering on the cover. David and Crystal have been stellar editors, firmly steering *SECC* forward in the direction charted out by their equally impressive predecessors, Eve Tavor Bannet and Roxann Wheeler. David and Crystal could not have been more helpful and accommodating in our transition.

Although the vast majority of the pieces and clusters published in *SECC* were originally presented at an ASECS-affiliated conference, any work publicly presented by an ASECS member is eligible for consideration. If you are involved with a colloquium, workshop, or other public forum in which remarkable eighteenth-century scholarship is presented, please consider sending submissions or queries to SECC@ASECS.org. It is my ambition to maintain our status as the place to find the most exciting new work in our field, whether authored by graduate students or ASECS eminences.

Letters "à la Sévigné": A Seventeenth-Century Model for the Eighteenth Century

CHLOE SUMMERS EDMONDSON

In 1765, Voltaire informed Étienne Noël Damilaville that "the empress of Russia wrote me a letter *à la Sévigné*."[1] Voltaire's compliment was apt, given that Catherine the Great had been taught to write letters emulating the style of Marie de Rabutin-Chantal, marquise de Sévigné (more commonly, Madame de Sévigné).[2] In his correspondence, Voltaire remarked so frequently on letters written "à la Sévigné" that it became an expected and coveted compliment.[3] He wrote to Frederick II in 1739 that "your style in French has reached such heights of exactitude and elegance, that I imagine you were born in the Versailles of Louis XIV… and that madame de Sévigné was your wet nurse."[4] Similarly, Voltaire wrote to the Countess of Bentinck, "I read your letter to the King; you were named the Sévigné of Germany."[5] But what does it mean to write a letter "à la Sévigné," and how did her letters become the model *par excellence* for eighteenth-century letter writers?

The dominance of the Sévigné model is evident from comments like Voltaire's that appear throughout the correspondence of eighteenth-century individuals.[6] What's more, the scholarly engagement with Sévigné's letters and, more broadly, with eighteenth-century correspondence has been extensive over the last half-century. With respect to Sévigné's letters, the discussion has been strongly shaped by the debate over whether her letters were primarily spontaneous and intimate, as Roger Duchêne claims, or written as a "work of art" with an eye toward literary posterity, as Bernard Bray has posited.[7] These two poles have continued to define the field, even as scholars have added nuance to these positions. While acknowledging the coexistence of *both* of these elements in Sévigné's writing, scholars have tended to come down on the side of Sévigné having invented a new genre of personal letter writing, and to make arguments that account for the singularity of Sévigné's letters to her daughter.

Through a formal analysis of Sévigné's letters, Cécile Lignereux demonstrates how Sévigné forges a mode of authentic communication that intensifies her personal relationship with her daughter through deformalizing epistolary conventions and heightening confidentiality and reciprocity.[8] Bruno Méniel explores the legacy of the aesthetic category of "the natural" in seventeenth-century letter writing, which "neither excludes rules, nor conscious artistic intention," but then suggests that Sévigné assumes a position whereby "that which shocks the conventions suits the communication between her and her daughter."[9] Similarly, Nathalie Freidel takes a socio-literary perspective that seeks to resolve the debate between Duchêne and Bray, highlighting the presence of the worldly and the personal in Sévigné's letters.[10] Nonetheless, Freidel ultimately argues that Sévigné invented and brought to its pinnacle the new genre of the *lettre intime*.[11]

Studies of eighteenth-century correspondence more generally reflect similar debates, foregrounding the rise of personal and sentimental letter writing, and framing the letter as the privileged site of self-expression. Even in studies that highlight the diversity of types of letters in this period, the emphasis tends to fall upon the personal letter, which is likened to the diary.[12] What's more, this turn to a private and sentimental epistolary paradigm is attributed, in Janet Altman's words, to "the publication of Mme de Sévigné's letters [that] ushered in a new kind of writing."[13] According to this view, Sévigné's posthumously published letters marked the dawn of a new regime of letter writing, one that broke with the rigid courtly codes and repression of the self that typified epistolary practices in the seventeenth century.[14] Naturally, as Altman notes, the transformation of epistolary practices from gallant, courtly letters toward more personal and sentimental ones cannot be attributed solely to the publication and influence of Sévigné's letters.[15] Rather, as I will demonstrate, the publication, framing, and reception of Sévigné's letters in the eighteenth century rendered them emblematic of an already burgeoning paradigm of sentimental epistolary writing, because of their perceived authenticity, sentimentality, and freedom of expression.[16] Sévigné's editors, commentators, and critics alike reinforced this understanding of her letters and upheld them as the epistolary model to follow.

As scholars note, Sévigné's intimate letters to her daughter, while constituting the majority of her epistolary corpus that has been preserved, do not represent the breadth of her letter writing. And yet the peculiarity that it should be Sévigné's letters to her daughter that became a model to imitate has not been much investigated. Moreover, as Freidel and Lignereux note, the intimate and free expression contained in these letters was only possible thanks to the "exceptional" nature of their close relationship.[17] If we examine the place of Sévigné's letters in the evolving ideals for letter writing, what comes to the fore is precisely this tension between sentimental and private letter writing, on the one hand, and the pervasive social pressures associated with letter writing, on the other.[18] Freidel has provided significant nuance to how we think about the notions of the public and the private at this time, showing how these spheres were mutating and how Sévigné's letters reflect this transitional moment.[19] Other scholars too have noted the blurred boundaries that characterize eighteenth-century letter writing, with Geneviève Haroche-Bouzinac underscoring the "semi-collective status" of Voltaire's letters.[20] My quarrel is by no means with the personal status accorded to Sévigné's letters to her daughter, which do seem to satisfy the criteria for intimate letters.[21] Instead, what I seek to reflect on are the greater implications of this "exceptional" mother-daughter context becoming the model for eighteenth-century letter writers.[22]

Sévigné's letters in her lifetime, their editorial framing, and the discourse on letter writing in epistolary manuals reveal a tension between an epistolary ideal of authentic self-expression and a social culture that both demanded careful self-presentation and did not guarantee private communication.[23] In this essay, I will highlight examples from Sévigné's letters that reveal the social exigencies of letter writing in her lifetime and juxtapose these with how the posthumous editions of her letters framed them and established the model of a letter "à la Sévigné." Finally, I will examine letter-writing manuals from the seventeenth and eighteenth centuries to contextualize how Sévigné's letters were emblematic of the growing valorization of sentimental and sincere letter writing. Treatises and letter-writing manuals alike perpetuated the Sévigné model and made it normative: they adopted and disseminated the same discourse, advocated writing in a sentimental and singular style, and integrated her letters into their theories and rules for eighteenth-century letter writers.

Nonetheless, the rigid courtly codes of letter writing persisted and collided with the emergence of new epistolary aesthetics and values in these manuals' promotion of Sévigné as the model to imitate. The epistolary ideal upheld in both the editions of Sévigné's letters and in letter-writing manuals would seem to mark a departure from the courtly regime of letter writing in the seventeenth century. Yet letter-writing practices remained very much the same in terms of the social function of the letter, with circulation and publicity continuing to be hallmarks of epistolary culture.[24] While the new epistolary model signaled a different ethos and aesthetic than courtly letters, social concerns and pressures persisted. In this sense, eighteenth-century letter writing was in large part shaped, I argue, by the shadow of Louis XIV's regime of letter writing, in the confrontation of courtly social practices with the emergent values of sentimental and sincere communication. With the Sévigné model of letter writing, what emerges is a need to negotiate the epistolary ideal of authentic, sentimental, and singular self-expression with the very real social pressures of possible publicity, thereby promoting a mode of feigning authenticity in letters in order to accommodate the two opposing social demands.

Sévigné's Letter Writing in Real Life

The tension between the valorization of sentiment and the highly codified nature of social interactions in seventeenth-century court society is evident in Sévigné's own letter writing. After her daughter's marriage and departure from Paris, Sévigné certainly devoted increasing attention and time to corresponding with her daughter, but her letter-writing practices encompassed the full range of correspondence that any eminent individual of her status would write on a regular basis. As Fritz Nies has shown, Sévigné maintained a correspondence network of at least 35 individuals, based on the letters of hers that have been preserved; if we take into account her mention of other letters and correspondents in the surviving letters, this circle can be expanded to over 120 correspondents, four-fifths of whom belonged to the French aristocracy.[25] Sévigné thus wrote to an array of correspondents of varying degrees of intimacy, and her letters bore all the hallmark signs of the courtly epistolary culture in which she lived.

The majority of Sévigné's letters reflect the style and epistolary etiquette that her aristocratic correspondents would expect from her, such as respecting the appropriate length of a letter, giving and receiving compliments, and responding point by point to the contents of letters that she received. Sévigné never fails to satisfy the social customs that dictate that certain letters must be written for specific occasions, such as letters of thanks, letters of condolence, and letters of congratulation for a birth, marriage, or newfound honor or military exploit.[26] The importance to her of this etiquette is clear when she reminds her daughter to write such letters. She suggests in a letter on 20 June 1672 that "I recommend that you write to M. de La Rochefoucauld for the death of his stableman and the injury of M. de Marsillac."[27]

Sévigné's reputation as a model letter writer was not merely enjoyed posthumously; it was a widely held opinion by her contemporaries in French society. Sévigné knew that her letters circulated in society and were read, shared, and complimented in the salons.[28] Catherine Montfort-Howard draws our attention to a letter from Madame de Coulanges to Sévigné, alluding to the circulation of Sévigné's letters and the positive reactions to them: "Your letters are making all the noise they deserve, as you see. It is certain that they are delicious, and you are just like your letters."[29] The sociality of letter writing for Sévigné's contemporaries is evident throughout Sévigné's letters. On numerous occasions Sévigné makes reference to reading a letter from her daughter that was not addressed to her, but rather was addressed to another acquaintance. In the spring of 1671 alone, this happened repeatedly. Sévigné mentions that M. de Coulanges "also showed me a letter that you wrote him, which is very amiable. All your letters please me; I see the ones that I can."[30] In letters on 20 March, 15 April, and 22 April she writes to her daughter complimenting her on her lovely letters to the comte de Guitaut, her brother, and M. de Coulanges, letters that Sévigné clearly saw or heard read aloud while visiting with her friends.[31] On other occasions, Sévigné comments directly on instances in which she shared her daughter's letters in her social circles: for example, "I read [your letter] to M. de La Rochefoucauld; he laughed about it heartily."[32]

She was also aware that letters and one's network of correspondents could have a direct bearing on one's reputation. As Freidel notes, a prime example of this is Sévigne's concern for her own image after the discovery of her correspondence with Nicolas Fouquet, superintendent of finances, during his arrest, investigation, and lengthy trial.[33] As Altman has shown, in the seventeenth century, individuals were increasingly conscious of the impact letters could have on their social standing.[34] Sévigné's letters thus pose a predicament for would-be interpreters as they are characterized by two opposing frameworks. On the one hand, Sévigné was firmly entrenched in a culture of courtly letter writing. And yet, on the other hand, the posthumous publication of her intimate letters to her daughter, the editorial framing of these editions, and much of the recent scholarship have focused on how her letters inaugurated a new genre of private letters that reveal the authentic interior self. Duchêne frames seventeenth-century letters as falling into two categories: letters were either private, spontaneous, sincere outpourings of emotion, or, if they adhered to epistolary conventions, they were written with literary intention and thus no longer *real* letters.[35]

This binary, however, does not take into account the cultural history of letter writing in this period. You do not need to have an eye toward literary posterity for there to nonetheless be certain pressures imposed on you in your letter writing. The act of consciously crafting a letter does not in any way alter its status as a letter. What's more, while some scholars claim that letter writers were unconcerned with the possibility of eventual publication, they do not consider how the widespread practice of circulating letters, as well as concerns over social reputation, may have affected epistolary activity.[36] Nies addresses this to a certain extent through his notion of a "secondary public."[37] His analysis of whether Sévigné took into account the expectations of her public, however, remains within the context of literary aesthetics, as he is concerned primarily with whether expectations concerning style shaped her letter writing, not preoccupations with reputation or social identity.[38]

The centrality of letter writing in social life can be seen, for instance, in how often Sévigné's friends ask whether they are mentioned in Madame de Grignan's letters. In one letter, Sévigné tells her daughter: "And I say: 'No, not yet, but you will be.' For example, mention a bit M. d'Ormesson, and the Mesmes. There is a crowd eager to be in your thoughts."[39] Here, Sévigné emphasizes the way in which letters constituted a part of social etiquette, and the necessity of paying compliments to a wide social circle through letters. On multiple occasions Sévigné instructs her daughter regarding to whom to pay compliments. In another letter, Sévigné insists, "Make a few mentions of certain people in your letters, so that I can tell them so."[40] Just a few days later, she thanks her daughter "for having mentioned Brancas."[41] Sévigné appreciates that her daughter pays compliments in her letters to her social circle, and returns the favor by participating in the same ritual.[42] What's more, she comments on her daughter's epistolary style, simultaneously praising it and prescribing how her daughter ought to compose her letters. For instance, on 18 February 1671, Sévigné writes: "You write extremely well; no one writes better. Never abandon the natural … it makes for a perfect style."[43] Later that year, she gives her daughter some gentle advice: "Do not be afraid to spend too much time on certain points. You are far from this fault; on the contrary, at times you leave us wanting something more."[44]

While Sévigné may feel at liberty to freely express her emotions in her letters to her daughter, she clearly takes pride in and cares about how Madame de Grignan writes her letters and how these letters shape both her daughter's image in society and her own. As Dena Goodman notes, the social reputation of both a mother and a daughter "depended on the daughter's ability to craft a letter that could be read aloud and passed around with pride."[45] Yet, as I will demonstrate, this aspect of Sévigné's letter writing—and epistolary practices more broadly—is obscured by the editorial framing of her letters in the eighteenth century.

The Publication and Reception of Sévigné's Letters in the Eighteenth Century

The first editions of Sévigné's correspondence were published in 1725 and 1726 surreptitiously—without *privilège* and without the permission of her family—in Troyes, Rouen, and La Haye, based upon a manuscript copy that had been given by her granddaughter, Pauline de Simiane, to the comte de Bussy's son, Amé-Nicolas de Bussy. The first official edition was edited by the chevalier Denis-Marius de Perrin in 1734 and consisted of 614 letters, some derived from original autograph letters and some from copies. Following Madame de Simiane's death, Perrin published a second official edition, in 1754, adding new autograph letters to which he had not had access in 1734. These two editions were the only eighteenth-century editions to be edited based on original autograph letters, and they were reprinted throughout the century, with the editorial prefaces from the early volumes included in the subsequent editions. Though Perrin—like other editors of correspondence in the period—took a great many editorial liberties, editing out certain portions of letters and correcting style, grammar, and spelling, the eighteenth-century criticism of Sévigné's letters was overwhelmingly based on the two Perrin editions.[46] Perrin's prefaces were continually reread, commented on, and cited.[47] Perrin's editorial work, therefore, not only framed how the letters were initially presented to the public, but also shaped how her style would be portrayed and interpreted throughout the century.

Already in May 1726, the *Mercure de France* dedicated several pages to the first publication of Sévigné's letters, writing that "the style is simple ... light, natural, & very affectionate; the narrations are lively & short: it is a model, & perhaps what is most perfect in this genre."[48] From the moment of their earliest reception, Sévigné's letters were thus upheld as models of the genre. The description of her style as "simple," "naturel," and "très affectueux" provides a rudimentary idea of how the Sévigné model would be framed for eighteenth-century audiences. As we will see, her commentators throughout the century continued to portray her letters and style according to these core features. Her "style négligé" is consistently emphasized, with Perrin writing in the preface to his 1734 edition that "the only reflections one will find here on the style of madame de Sévigné, I believed I had to borrow from her. ... 'I use only one stroke of the quill, thus my letters are very *négligées*.'"[49] The idea of her letters being written with "one stroke" evokes authenticity and suggests that the letters contain the spontaneous transcriptions of her thoughts and feelings. The 1737 "Avertissement" similarly underscores that her letters are marked by "no affectation, no apparent art ... it is only ever the *beau naturel* which lets itself be seen."[50]

The 1737 "Avertissement" to Sévigné's letters suggests that a key component of the felt naturalness of these letters is the fact that they were private, "written only for Madame de Grignan, & Madame de Sévigné could not have imagined that they would one day be in the hands of everyone."[51] Sévigné's letters are thus models because of the free, spontaneous, and authentic expression of thoughts that results, on the one hand, from the particularly intimate nature of the mother-daughter relationship, and, on the other, from the expectation of one-to-one private communication. Perrin, as scholars have noted, points out the contrast between Sévigné's letters to her daughter and "all those which were not written to this dear daughter."[52] The published editions uniformly characterize her letters as models because they are spontaneous instances of unconstrained expression. The editors consistently praise her "style négligé" and the lack of artfulness in her letters. They attribute this "naturel" to Sévigné's epistolary situation. In other words, the intimate nature of the relationship and the expectation of private communication are framed as conducive to free self-expression. Moreover, it is not just a matter of "natural style," as the 1754 edition underlines, asking, "Is it certain that she would have arrived at this point of perfection that we remark in these Letters, if in writing them, she had not abandoned herself entirely to *her* natural?"[53] The contents of the letters are portrayed as revealing Sévigné's "nature," in the sense of her innate character.

The notion that Sévigné's letters reveal her identity is emphasized in editions across the century. Although Perrin omits certain portions of her letters that he deemed uninteresting to the public, he insists that "I did not dare to cut out any of the sentiments of maternal love … because it is this that constitutes the core of Madame de Sévigné's character."[54] At the time of the letters' initial publication, Sévigné's extreme sentimental attachment to her daughter was considered rather odd, and as scholars have noted, Perrin had to make editorial decisions that would effectively readdress her letters to a new public and anticipate the negative reactions of readers.[55] Yet, as we see in the passage just quoted, already in the 1730s, what was considered unconventional in Sévigné's letters is nonetheless framed as inextricably associated with her identity. This equivocation between the sentimental style, the content of her letters, and the "core of [her] character," is a constant theme in editions of her letters. The "Avertissement" of 1737 even frames these letters as "precious remains of [her] spirit & [her] heart."[56]

In sum, Sévigné's letters were promoted as models of the epistolary genre from their initial publication on, and eighteenth-century editions of Sévigné's letters presented them as sincere, sentimental, and intimate, praising them for the way in which they revealed a singular self. In 1751, the *Mercure de France* described the overall acclaim that Sévigné's letters had garnered:

"Antiquity would have no objections to this illustrious woman, and posterity will place her among the small number of immortal Writers who created the glory of the last century."[57] Even Sévigné's critics admired her letters for "the *esprit*, the natural, the *style négligé* ... the vivacious imagination ... the style of conversation."[58]

The emphasis on "her natural" accords with the chevalier Louis de Jaucourt's definition of *le Naturel* in the *Encyclopédie*: "the temperament, the character, the humor, the inclinations that man has from birth ... that education can cultivate with glory, but which [education] cannot give."[59] The term thus designates one's innate character and sensibilities. Jaucourt contrasts the "good natural" with "artificial humanity reduced to art."[60] He encourages his readers to live "a type of life congruent with the character of one's heart and spirit."[61] There is thus an association established in this definition of "naturel" between one's individual character, emotions, and "esprit," which is illuminating in the context of its repeated use to describe Sévigné's letters. As far back as 1694, *Le Dictionnaire de l'académie française* indicates that "naturel" "signifies also, that which is not disguised, altered, made-up, but rather as Nature made it."[62] Naturel was thus understood similarly to *sincère*, or to how we understand "authentic" today—acting in accordance with one's innate character and inclinations, without artifice.[63] However, le naturel also designated an aesthetic and rhetorical category, which is obscured by the editorial insistence on the link between Sévigné's "natural" style and her close relationship with her daughter. Both "the natural" and "negligence" were aesthetic categories anchored in the tradition of courtly behavior, which emphasized disguising effort in order to *appear* natural.[64]

Imitating Sévigné's Authenticity as a Normative Model in Epistolary Manuals

In order to understand the stakes of Sévigné's letters becoming posthumously integrated into the normative discourse of epistolary manuals, it is critical to situate the rise of an ideal of epistolary authenticity in the letter-writing manuals of the seventeenth and early eighteenth centuries. Before epistolary manuals firmly anchored letter writing in courtly life in the seventeenth century, conduct literature already had a long history of prescribing codes of behavior, etiquette, and self-presentation in the real-life interactions of the aristocracy. From Castiglione's *Cortegiano* (1528) to Gracián's *Oráculo* (1647), conduct literature in early modern Europe theorized how individuals should cultivate practices of "dissimulation" and "artifice" for "social gains."[65] These techniques for court-focused social interactions and self-presentation depended on the courtier's ability to hide the effort and intent involved. As Jorge Arditi puts it, conduct literature in France—most notably Nicolas Faret's *L'honneste-homme ou, L'art de plaire à la court* (1630), an extension of Castiglione's *Cortegiano*—"draws a more rigid picture of the infrastructure of social relations of court societies" and insists that "the would-be courtier should know how to feign; for feigning allows a person to weather the storms and navigate through the dangers of the court."[66]

Unsurprisingly, this ethos is at the core of Faret's *Recueil de lettres nouvelles* despite his repeated calls for frankness (*franchise*) and writing "without affectation."[67] There are thus indications of friction between these two modes of interaction—courtly sociability and the emerging premium placed on sincere letter writing—as early as 1639.[68] As Elizabeth Goldsmith's work highlights, the transition from a courtly "ideology of sociability" to a "new ideal of sincerity" was already underway in the last decades of the seventeenth century.[69] Yet I would argue that this transition is less a gradual replacement of the former by the latter than the promotion of a feigned authenticity in letters in order to accommodate the new ideal of epistolary communication within existing social practices. This particularly comes to the fore in Antoine Furetière's *Essais de lettres familières sur toutes sortes de sujets* (1695), which points to how courtly letter-writing practices were colliding with the valorization of sincerity.[70] Antoine Furetière notes that those who express their emotions poorly do so because "they seek things other than what they have in their hearts," which would seem to gesture toward the new ideology of sincerity and sentimentalism.[71] Yet even as he lauds the natural expression of sentiment as a model for letter writing, Furetière boasts that he "speaks of love as if [he] were really in love," suggesting that the skill to be learned is how to feign strong emotion convincingly.[72]

In a similar vein, early eighteenth-century letter-writing manuals reveal the persistent influence of courtly practices and the tricky ways in which the increasing premium placed on sincere letter writing clashed with the more rigidly codified codes of expression inherited from the seventeenth century. Goldsmith points to Jean Léonor Le Gallois de Grimarest's epistolary manual, written in 1709, as an example of the new regime of sincere and sentimental letter writing because of his statements criticizing earlier manuals, which "have neglected sentiments and they must dominate in a letter."[73] And yet, such statements reveal only a fraction of the epistolary guidelines in Grimarest's treatise. A closer look makes clear that his valorization of sentiment in letters is not so simple, and hardly signals the dawn of a new era in which letters freely expressed the self. Grimarest certainly insists on the importance of sentiment, criticizing seventeenth-century manuals for their "sterility of sentiment" (*TMEL*, 4). Indeed, many of the qualities he values anticipate those for which Sévigné's letters will be praised. For example, Grimarest insists that it is "nature which touches us in a Letter; we want the truth without ornament" (*TMEL*, 90). However, focusing on Grimarest's privileging of sentiment and le naturel in letters ignores the tenuous line between freedom of expression and the codified rules and norms that still characterized epistolary practices in this period.

Grimarest's letter-writing ethos is summed up in his claim that one should write with "the same simplicity and openness of heart" as one would use in person—provided that "the rules of *politesse* are observed" (*TMEL*, 29).[74] He emphasizes that all letter writers must follow "the general rules of *bienséance* that polite society observes exactly, & which are ... dangerous to neglect" (*TMEL*, 112). In particular, his lengthy sections on epistolary ceremonial serve as reminders of the persistence of highly codified social interactions, despite all the rhetoric of sentiment and naturalness. What's more, Grimarest reminds letter writers that "just as we judge the character of a person more severely by his letters, than by his conversation ... it is of consequence to manage one's reputation carefully," which points to the centrality of self-presentation in epistolary practices (*TMEL*, 14). What this example highlights is the extent to which letter-writing practices were still constrained by courtly codes of social interaction and by self-presentation, existing social practices, and concerns regarding the circulation of letters beyond the addressee.

Given the rise of this epistolary ideal of writing in a natural and sentimental manner, it should come as no surprise that literary treatises and letter-writing manuals echoed Perrin's framing of Sévigné's letters as the model to follow and integrated her letters into their theories and guidelines for letter writing.[75] As early as 1735, we find Sévigné's letters held up as models in the Abbé Trublet's *Essais sur divers sujets de littérature et de morale*, a treatise in which Trublet defines le naturel.[76] Trublet particularly points to the genre of letter writing as a key arena of "the natural," underscoring that "the rule of writing naturally, even if a general rule, concerns even more particularly some works than others, for example letters."[77] Trublet writes, "Racine is less natural than Mme de Sévigné, but he is [natural] enough for the genre in which he writes. ... Editing would have taken from Mme de Sévigné's letters what charms us. ... Also, it would be dangerous to touch them and to want to correct their *négligences*."[78] Trublet's emphasis on the "négligences" of Sévigné's letters, their "naturel," and their lack of "*travail*" thus echoes the characterization of her letters by Perrin the previous year.

Even more significant is the integration of Sévigné into letter-writing manuals throughout the eighteenth century. Compared to editions of her letters, which thrust her into debates about her literary merit, letter-writing manuals brought her into the realm of normalizing epistolary practices.[79] While the extent of the impact of these manuals on actual practices is cause for debate, historians, linguists, and literary scholars agree that they did exert normative pressures on their users.[80] The intended public of these manuals was literate and elite, and, as Sybille Grosse has shown, these manuals aimed to prescribe social codes and behaviors as much as language and style.[81] Mastering letter-writing norms was considered indispensable, a kind of mastery that required both linguistic and social prowess.[82] As Goodman demonstrates, eighteenth-century individuals relied on epistolary manuals for models to imitate and principles intended to help them write "just as easily" as they spoke.[83] The inclusion of examples from Sévigné in these manuals is thus especially interesting to consider, and the remainder of this essay will examine Louis Philipon de La Madelaine's *Modèles de lettres sur différents sujets*.[84]

In 1761, Sévigné occupies a central place in Philipon de La Madelaine's epistolary manual, with her letters cited around forty times. Scholars tend to view this manual as a turning point in the genre because it rejected the courtly codification of language in favor of a more sentimental and intimate kind of letter, and it is indeed one of the few manuals to survive the French Revolution.[85] Yet the principles outlined in this manual are remarkably consistent with the epistolary ideals upheld in earlier texts.[86] Like others, Philipon de La Madelaine maintains that letter writing must be natural, simple, and the expression of one's emotions. He insists that "it is in Nature that one must seek the principles of ... the art of writing Letters."[87] He stresses that "when friendship, when confidence, directs the quill," then "it is for the heart alone to dictate" (*MLDS*, 9, 16). He valorizes feelings over thought in the writing of letters, reiterating the trope that dates back to the seventeenth century that women are naturally better letter writers, as they are "better suited to feeling than thinking" (*MLDS*, 37).[88] What's more, the terms he uses to describe the ideal epistolary style reiterate those used by Sévigné's editor and commentators, and perpetuate the same ideal: "the easy [*aisé*] style ... that beautiful Nature, which when imitated constitutes all the merit of Art," "that air of liberty," and "singularity of expression" (*MLDS*, 16–17).

A closer look at Philipon de La Madelaine's manual, however, reveals precisely the tension between the model that is being promoted—writing in a natural, sincere, sentimental way—and the reality of the social conventions surrounding letter writing and the risks of publicity. Even as he is promoting letting the heart dictate one's letters and using one's own singular form of expression, Philipon de La Madelaine dedicates substantial sections to epistolary ceremonial and social conventions, signaling just how much letter-writing practices were still bound up in the rituals and social codes of court society.[89] Indeed, aside from some citations from Voltaire's letters, most of the models included in this edition are letters from the seventeenth-century court. Even in the latter half of the eighteenth century, many of the principal types of letters that elites needed to write were a far cry from the sentimental Sévigné model that was being promoted. A central part of demonstrating that one belonged in elite society was writing the correct letters on the correct occasions in the correct way, full of "formules de politesse."

What's more, while promoting the "natural and easy style," Philipon de La Madelaine emphasizes that "the first preoccupation of Art must be to hide itself," reinforcing that the number one rule of his epistolary ideal is not writing authentically but rather appearing "naturel" and "négligé"—in other words, feigning authenticity (*MLDS*, 18). Most significantly, Philipon de La Madelaine reinforces the social realities of letter-writing practices and the risks of publicity, noting that it has become a common custom to not sign all of one's letters to a frequent correspondent, as "there is less risk, if the Letter gets lost" (*MLDS*, 47). Philipon de La Madelaine also qualifies the notion that the heart must dictate one's letters, warning that "even in the most tender effusions of the heart, prudence must guide your quill. Every day we repent for having said too much; and yet words disappear the moment they are spoken. Writing, on the contrary, gives existence to one's thoughts; & we often have occasion to blush from something that we wrote in a transport of familiarity, in an enthusiasm of friendship or tenderness. A Letter can be intercepted, & used as a weapon against you; even the heart of a friend can change, no matter how attached he seems to you. Mme de Maintenon used to say: We are deceived every day by friends of thirty years; she spoke correctly" (*MLDS*, 54). Philipon de La Madelaine's insistence on "prudence" guiding one's quill, as opposed to one's heart, underscores his overall guidance with respect to letter writing. He ultimately insists that the social realities of letter writing should guide what individuals choose to put in their letters. He emphasizes the materiality of the letter and its potential to cause regret or embarrassment. He even employs the lexicon of weaponry to emphasize how letters can be turned against the letter writer. The tension evident in Philipon de La Madelaine's manual highlights the way in which social pressures and conventions created a media environment that promoted seemingly authentic self-expression.

The Sévigné model certainly signaled a new letter-writing style compared to the courtly regime of seventeenth-century letters, but it also constituted in its own right a new set of letter-writing norms for individuals to follow and imitate. Without doing away with the social practices that governed courtly letter writing, the eighteenth century adopted Sévigné's intimate correspondence with her daughter as a new model for letter writing. The posthumous editorial framing of Sévigné's letters in the eighteenth century as new, sincere, and natural overshadows the seventeenth-century roots of the valorization of sentiment in letters, which rose to prominence within a court context that privileged above all the cultivation of appearances. Moreover, while the personal letter certainly took off in the eighteenth century, letter writing remained firmly entrenched in practices of sociability.

Far from suggesting that Sévigné's letters to her daughter were inauthentic, the purpose of this essay is rather to reflect on the publication, reception, and integration of these letters into normative expectations regarding letter writing, and to highlight the tension between the epistolary ideal of authentic self-expression and the letter-writing practices that were shaped by the court culture of the ancien régime. In conclusion, I turn my attention to the stakes of such a model being promoted for imitation. Some may question why this matters at all, given that collections of letters and epistolary manuals had been serving as models for over a century. What's more, the desirability of writing in a "natural" style or with négligence is well documented in its ethos of creating the appearance of effortlessness. Yet much of the debate about Sévigné's letters, and letters more broadly, has hinged upon the relative value of writing spontaneously or authentically, as opposed to doing so with literary intention, all of which fail to engage with the social aspects of letter writing.

Letter writing was a sociological and mediatic revolution, and correspondence became firmly established as the primary mode of daily communication in this period.[90] Social commerce was conducted by letter in the absence of face-to-face interaction, and those letters were material traces of the process that had a direct bearing on one's image vis-à-vis others and in society. Letters had the power to effect changes in one's material circumstances. Voltaire, for instance, successfully avoided the Bastille on more than one occasion by actively denying more controversial works in his correspondence, knowing that the Black Cabinets would be reading them.[91] In *The Presentation of Self in Everyday Life*, Erving Goffman theorizes how social interaction invites a desire to manage impressions, and warns against mistaking performed character in a given interaction for the "true" self of an individual. Yet, as Erving Goffman demonstrates, these social performances also implicitly rely on a moral contract in which others are meant to accept that you are who you claim to be, and actually possess those attributes.[92] The epistolary moral contract is thus one in which you are assumed to be representing yourself authentically. The notion of "feigning authenticity" aims to capture the practice of presenting oneself in letters in a way that satisfies the ideal of the Sévigné model's sentimental and personal style of letter writing, in a social culture of correspondence that was not wholly defined by private and intimate relationships.

Furthermore, since eighteenth-century letter writers were eminently aware of these social realities, they could leverage the Sévigné model to achieve specific goals, such as writing an ostensibly personal letter with the knowledge, expectation, and hope that it would circulate beyond the addressee. In the winter of 1762, eager to change his reputation and respond to Chrétien Guillaume de Lamoignon de Malesherbes's portrayal of him as being consumed by "black bile," Jean-Jacques Rousseau wrote four letters to Malesherbes, each in a seemingly personal register.[93] In the first letter, he confesses, "It is with an outpouring of my heart that I write to you, and I would not know how to do otherwise."[94] In another, Rousseau writes, "Here I am already at the end of my second sheet of paper. I will need yet another … I am sorry, M: while I enjoy speaking too much of myself, I do not like to speak of myself to everyone."[95] When he refers to these letters in *the Confessions*, he will echo many of the qualities attributed to Sévigné's letters. Rousseau claims that these letters were "written without drafts, quickly, with one stroke of the quill, without even having been reread," and he describes them as transcriptions of "everything that passed through [his] heart."[96] Nevertheless, he notes that Malesherbes showed these letters around Paris, highlighting Rousseau's desire for these allegedly private letters to reach a wider public.[97] Rousseau's championing of the Sévigné model in his letters to Malesherbes underscores the way in which seemingly private letters can still be intentional and strategic instances of self-presentation.

While it is beyond the scope of a single essay to provide a thorough investigation of similar cases of letter writing, Rousseau's letters to Malesherbes give us a snapshot of a letter writer employing the Sévigné model in a context that most certainly was not the close relationship between a mother and her daughter. With respect to letters, the question is how mediation affects first-person writing and shapes the possibilities for an authentic presentation of the self.[98] What is striking about the establishment of the Sévigné model is that it signals a moment in the history of mediated communication when authentic and personal self-expression was valorized as a primary style of communication through a medium and in a social context in which privacy was not guaranteed. This results in an epistolary culture that expected one to make one's interior life "outwardly visible," or, at the very least, provide the illusion of such visibility, which prefigures the practices of personalized expression that we see in today's media systems.[99]

Notes

I would like to thank numerous colleagues for their generous feedback on earlier versions of this essay, including John Bender, Margaret Cohen, Dan Edelstein, Hans Ulrich Gumbrecht, Joshua Landy, and Geoffrey Turnovsky. It has also benefited from the insights of the reviewers, for which I am grateful.

1. Voltaire to Damilaville, 13 November 1765, D12979, in *Correspondence and Related Documents*, ed. Theodore Besterman, *Les Œuvres complètes de Voltaire*, vols. 85–135 (Geneva: Voltaire Foundation, 1966–77). All subsequent letters from the *OCV* are cited with Besterman's document numbers. All translations from French to English in this essay are mine.

2. See Kelsey Rubin-Detlev, *The Epistolary Art of Catherine the Great* (Liverpool: Liverpool University Press, 2019), 36, 89–92.

3. See Catherine Montfort-Howard, *Les fortunes de Madame de Sévigné au XVIIème et au XVIIIème siècles* (Tübingen: G. Narr Verlag, 1982), 56; see also 60n158.

4. Voltaire to Frederick II, 15 April 1739, *OCV* D1978.

5. Voltaire to Charlotte Sophia van Aldenburg, Countess of Bentinck, 1750/51, *OCV* D4325.

6. Montfort-Howard, *Les fortunes de Madame de Sévigné*, 83.

7. Duchêne, *Écrire au temps de Mme de Sévigné: Lettres et texte littéraire* (Paris: Libraire philosophique J. Vrin, 1981), 31; Bray, "Quelques aspects du système épistolaire de Mme de Sévigné," *Revue d'Histoire Littéraire de La France* 69, nos. 3-4 (1969): 494, 505.

8. Lignereux, *À l'origine du savoir-faire épistolaire de Mme de Sévigné: Les Lettres de l'année 1671* (Paris: Presses universitaires de France, 2012), 69–70, 77–78.

9. Bruno Méniel, "Mme de Sévigné et la rhétorique du naturel," *Exercices de rhétorique* 6 (2016): 3, 8.

10. Freidel, *La Conquête de l'intime: Public et privé dans la "Correspondance" de madame de Sévigné* (Paris: Honoré Champion, 2009), 15–16, 25.

11. Freidel, *La Conquête de l'intime*, 25, 179. Nicolas Garroté furthers this notion of Sévigné having created an intimate genre through a close study of her invention of an intimate language that is her own; see his *Poétique de Madame de Sévigné: L'invention d'une langue* (Paris: Presses Universitaires de France, 2023).

12. See Dena Goodman, "Letter Writing and the Emergence of Gendered Subjectivity in Eighteenth-Century France," *Journal of Women's History* 17, no. 2 (2005): 11, and *Becoming a Woman in the Age of Letters* (Ithaca: Cornell University Press, 2009), 2; and Marie-Claire Grassi, *L'art de la lettre au temps de La nouvelle Héloïse et du romantisme* (Genéve: Slatkine, 1994), 17. See also Benoît Melançon, *Diderot épistolier: Contribution à une poétique de la lettre familière au XVIIIe siècle* (Saint-Laurent: Les Editions Fides, 1996), 8.

13. Janet Altman, "The Letter Book as a Literary Institution, 1539–1789: Towards a Cultural History of Published Correspondences in France," *Yale French Studies* 71 (1986): 49, 55.

14. Altman, "The Letter Book as a Literary Institution," 55.
15. Altman, "The Letter Book as a Literary Institution," 57.
16. On the rise of sentimentalism, see William Reddy, *The Navigation of Feeling: A Framework for the History of Emotions* (Cambridge: Cambridge University Press, 2001), chapter 5; see also David J. Denby, *Sentimental Narrative and the Social Order in France, 1760–1820* (Cambridge: Cambridge University Press, 1994).
17. Lignereux, *À l'origine du savoir-faire épistolaire*, 80. See also Freidel, *La Conquête de l'intime*, 178.
18. Freidel, *La Conquête de l'intime*, 162.
19. Freidel, *La Conquête de l'intime*, 15–16.
20. Haroche-Bouzinac, *Voltaire dans ses lettres de jeunesse, 1711–1733: La formation d'un épistolier au XVIIIe siècle* (Paris: Klincksieck, 1992), 18. See also Bernard Bray, who underscores that correspondence in the ancien régime was defined by circulation ("Quelques aspects du système épistolaire," 500).
21. See Freidel, *La Conquête de l'intime*, 153.
22. Lignereux, *À l'origine du savoir-faire épistolaire*, 80.
23. See Altman, "The Letter Book as a Literary Institution," 40; see also Giora Sternberg, "Epistolary Ceremonial: Corresponding Status at the Time of Louis XIV," *Past and Present* 204 (2009): 33–88.
24. See Roger Chartier, Alain Boureau, and Cécile Dauphin, *Correspondence: Models of Letter-Writing from the Middle Ages to the Nineteenth Century* (Cambridge: Polity, 1997), 21; see also Jay Caplan, *Postal Culture in Europe, 1500–1800* (Oxford: Voltaire Foundation, 2016).
25. Nies, *Les Lettres de Madame de Sévigné: Conventions du genre et sociologie des publics*, trans. Michèle Creff (Paris: Honoré Champion, 2001), 54.
26. See Nies, *Les Lettres de Madame de Sévigné*, part 1. For the conventions of condolence letters, see Cécile Lignereux, "Une routine de la civilité épistolaire: L'expression de la condoléance," *Exercices de rhétorique* 6 (2016). https://doi.org/10.4000/rhetorique.437.
27. Sévigné to Madame de Grignan, 20 June 1672, letter no. 284, in *Correspondance*, ed. Roger Duchêne, 3 vols. (Paris: Éditions Gallimard, 1972), 1:538.
28. Nies, *Les Lettres de Madame de Sévigné*, 45.
29. Quoted in Montfort-Howard, *Les fortunes de Madame de Sévigné*, 18.
30. Sévigné to Madame de Grignan, 18 March 1671, letter no. 146, in *Correspondance*, 1:189.
31. Sévigné to Madame de Grignan, 20 March, 15 April, and 22 April 1671, letter nos. 147, 156, and 158, in *Correspondance*, 1:193, 1:222, and 1:231.
32. Sévigné to Madame de Grignan, 1 April 1671, letter no. 150, in *Correspondance*, 1:206.
33. Freidel, *La Conquête de l'intime*, 164.
34. Altman, "The Letter Book as a Literary Institution," 40.
35. Duchêne, *Écrire au temps de Mme de Sévigné*, 31.
36. See English Showalter, "Authorial Self-Consciousness in the Familiar Letter: The Case of Madame de Graffigny," *Yale French Studies* 71 (1986): 120; and Bernard

Bray, "L'Épistolier et son public en France au XVIIe siècle," *Travaux de linguistique et de littérature* 11 (1973): 7–17.

37. Nies, *Les Lettres de Madame de Sévigné*, 39.
38. See Nies, *Les Lettres de Madame de Sévigné*, part 1.
39. Sévigné to Madame de Grignan, 11 March 1671, letter no. 143, in *Correspondance*, 1:182.
40. Sévigné to Madame de Grignan, 18 February 1671, letter no. 136, in *Correspondance*, 1:161.
41. Sévigné to Madame de Grignan, 27 February 1671, letter no. 140, in *Correspondance*, 1:173.
42. See Sévigné to Madame de Grignan, 27 March 1671 and 22 April 1671, letter nos. 149 and 158, in *Correspondance*, 1:203 and 1:232.
43. Sévigné to Madame de Grignan, 18 February 1671, letter no. 136, in *Correspondance*, 1:161.
44. Sévigné to Madame de Grignan, 7 June 1671, letter no. 171, in *Correspondance*, 1:267.
45. Goodman, *Becoming a Woman in the Age of Letters*, 100.
46. See Nathalie Freidel, "Brève histoire des éditions," in Madame de Sévigné, *Lettres choisies*, ed. Nathalie Freidel (Paris: Gallimard, 2016), 524.
47. Montfort-Howard, *Les fortunes de Madame de Sévigné*, 51–52.
48. *Mercure de France*, Avril 1726, 971–72. https://gazetier-universel.gazettes18e.fr/periodique/mercure-de-france-1-1724-1778.
49. Sévigné, *Recueil des lettres de Madame la marquise de Sévigné, à Madame la comtesse de Grignan, sa fille*, 6 vols. (Leiden, 1736), 1:xi–xii. This is a reprint of the 1734 edition.
50. Sévigné, *Recueil des lettres de Madame la marquise de Sévigné à Madame la comtesse de Grignan, sa fille*, nouvelle édition augmentée, 8 vols. (Paris, 1763), 5:xli–xlii. This is a reprint of the 1754 edition.
51. Sévigné, *Recueil des lettres de Madame la marquise de Sévigné* (1763), 5:xli–xlii.
52. Sévigné, *Recueil des lettres de Madame la marquise de Sévigné* (1763), 5:xliv–xlv.
53. Sévigné, *Recueil des lettres de Madame la marquise de Sévigné* (1763), 1:x–xi. Emphasis mine. Méniel echoes this in his analysis of Sévigné's style, arguing that she subverts epistolary conventions and expresses "her natural" ("Mme de Sévigné et la rhétorique du naturel," 9).
54. Sévigné, *Recueil des lettres de Madame la marquise de Sévigné* (1736), 1:x.
55. Montfort-Howard, *Les fortunes de Madame de Sévigné*, 52. See also Altman, "The Letter Book as a Literary Institution"; and Showalter, "Authorial Self-Consciousness."
56. Sévigné, *Recueil des lettres de Madame la marquise de Sévigné* (1763), 5:xxxix–xl.
57. Quoted in Montfort-Howard, *Les fortunes de Madame de Sévigné*, 72.
58. Montfort-Howard, *Les fortunes de Madame de Sévigné*, 56.

59. Jaucourt, "Le Naturel," in *Encyclopédie, ou Dictionnaire Raisonné des Sciences, des Arts et des Métiers*, ed. Denis Diderot and Jean le Rond d'Alembert (Paris, 1751–72), https://artflsrv04.uchicago.edu/philologic4.7/encyclopedie0922/navigate/11/268.

60. Jaucourt, "Naturel," in *Encyclopédie*.

61. Jaucourt, "Naturel," in *Encyclopédie*.

62. "Naturel, Naturelle," in *Le Dictionnaire de l'Académie française* (Paris, 1694), https://artflsrv04.uchicago.edu/philologic4.7/publicdicos/navigate/4/1461.

63. "Sincère" was defined in 1694 in *Le Dictionnaire de l'Académie française* as "Véritable, franc, qui est sans artifice, sans déguisement," https://artflsrv04.uchicago.edu/philologic4.7/publicdicos/navigate/4/6558.

The 1787 *Dictionnaire critique de la langue française* adds "Agir, parler *sincèrement*," https://artflsrv04.uchicago.edu/philologic4.7/publicdicos/navigate/7/2864.

64. See Nies, *Les Lettres de Madame de Sévigné*, 25–91; Bray, "Quelques aspects du système épistolaire," 492. See also Méniel, "Mme de Sévigné et la rhétorique du naturel"; and Bernard Bray, "Le style épistolaire: La leçon de Madame de Sévigné," *Littératures classiques* 28, no. 1 (1996): 197–209.

65. Jacob Soll, *Publishing the Prince: History, Reading, and the Birth of Political Criticism* (Ann Arbor: University of Michigan Press, 2005), 84. On the reception in France of Castiglione's *The Book of the Courtier*, see Peter Burke, *The Fortunes of the "Courtier": The European Reception of Castiglione's "Cortegiano"* (University Park: Pennsylvania State University Press, 1996). On self-presentation through Castiglione's *sprezzatura*, see G. R. F. Ferrari, *The Messages We Send: Social Signals and Storytelling* (Oxford: Oxford University Press, 2017), 113–65.

66. Arditi, *A Genealogy of Manners: Transformations of Social Relations in France and England from the Fourteenth to the Eighteenth Century* (Chicago: University of Chicago Press, 1998), 127, 134.

67. Nicolas Faret, *Recueil de lettres nouvelles: De Messieurs Malherbe, Coulomby, Boisrobert, Molière, Plassac, Brun, Silhon, Godeau, Conac, Breval, Faret, Racan, Balzac, Auvray et autres*, ed. Claude Prudhomme, 2 vols. (Paris, 1639), 1:273, 1:60–65.

68. On court culture and social interaction, see Giora Sternberg, *Status Interaction during the Reign of Louis XIV* (Oxford: Oxford University Press, 2014); Jean-Marie Apostolidès, *Le roi-machine: Spectacle et politique au temps de Louis XIV* (Paris: Editions de Minuit, 1981); Emmanuel Bury, *Littérature et politesse: L'invention de l'honnête homme (1580–1750)* (Paris: Presses universitaires de France, 1996); and Norbert Elias, *La société de cour* (Paris: Calmann-Levy, 1974).

69. Elizabeth C. Goldsmith, *Exclusive Conversations: The Art of Interaction in Seventeenth-Century France* (Philadelphia: University of Pennsylvania Press, 1988), 31–32, 35.

70. For a similar observation, see Pierre Richelet, *Les Plus belles lettres des meilleurs auteurs françois*, ed. Daniel Horthemels (Paris, 1689).

71. Furetière, *Essais de lettres familières sur toutes sortes de sujets: Avec un discours sur l'art épistolaire* (Bruxelles, 1695), 216.

72. Furetière, *Essais de lettres familières*, 216.
73. Grimarest, *Traité sur la manière d'écrire des lettres et sur le cérémonial, avec un discours sur ce qu'on appelle usage dans la langue française, par M. de Grimarest* (Paris, 1735), 6. Subsequent citations will be made parenthetically as *TMEL*.
74. On la politesse in seventeenth- and eighteenth-century France, see Bury, *Littérature et politesse*; and Philippe Raynaud, *La politesse des Lumières: Les lois, les moeurs, les manières* (Paris: Gallimard, 2013).
75. It is also worth underscoring, as Dena Goodman points out, that "women and girls were guided by a steady stream of print editions of women's letters, especially those of Sévigné" (*Becoming a Woman in the Age of Letters*, 148).
76. Grassi, *L'art de la lettre*, 383.
77. Trublet, *Essais sur divers sujets de littérature et de morale* (Paris, 1735), 85.
78. Trublet, *Essais sur divers sujets*, 87.
79. While Montfort-Howard has studied the critical reception of Sévigné's letters by the literary community and how it contributed to building Sévigné's reputation, she does not consider how the Sévigné model impacted actual epistolary practices.
80. See Janet Altman, "Teaching the 'People' to Write: The Formation of a Popular Civic Identity in the French Letter Manual," *Studies in Eighteenth-Century Culture* 22 (1993): 147–80; Sybille Grosse, *Les manuels épistolographiques français entre traditions et normes* (Paris: Honoré Champion, 2017); and Alain Boureau, "The letter-writing norm, a medieval invention," in Chartier, Boureau, and Dauphin, *Correspondence*, 24–58.
81. Grosse, *Les manuels épistolographiques français*, 18–19, 76.
82. Grosse, *Les manuels épistolographiques français*, 76. See also Gérard Ferreyrolles, "L'épistolaire, à la lettre," *Littératures classiques* 71 (2010–11): 21.
83. Goodman, *Becoming a Woman in the Age of Letters*, 136.
84. For another example of an epistolary manual in which Sévigné is featured prominently, see Eléazar de Mauvillon, *Traité général du style avec un traité particulier du style épistolaire* (Amsterdam, 1756).
85. See Goodman, *Becoming a Woman in the Age of Letters*, 135. See also Altman, "The Letter Book as a Literary Institution," 57–58, and "La politique de l'art épistolaire au XVIIIe siècle," in *Art de la lettre, art de la conversation, à l'époque classique en France: Actes du colloque de Wolfenbüttel, octobre 1991*, ed. Bernard A. Bray and Christoph Strosetzki (Paris: Klincksieck, 1995), 140–41.
86. See Grosse, *Les manuels épistolographiques français*, 206, 208.
87. Philipon de la Madelaine, *Modèles de lettres sur différents sujets* (Lyon, 1761), 5. Subsequent citations will be made parenthetically as *MLDS*.
88. See Charles Cotin, "Au Lecteur: Sur les lettres des dames," in *Oeuvres galantes en prose et en vers de monsieur Cotin* (Paris, 1665). See also Goodman, *Becoming a Woman in the Age of Letters*, 139–40.
89. Grosse acknowledges that Philipon de La Madelaine does not entirely break with the courtly system of the ancien régime. Such a break does not occur until the publication of the *Secrétaire des Républicains* in 1793 (*Les manuels épistolographiques français*, 208).

90. See Wolfgang Behringer, "Communications Revolutions: A Historiographical Concept," *German History* 24, no. 3 (2006): 333–74.

91. See Nicholas Cronk, "Voltaire and Authorship," in *The Cambridge Companion to Voltaire*, ed. Nicholas Cronk (Cambridge: Cambridge University Press, 2009), 39.

92. Goffman, *The Presentation of Self in Everyday Life* (New York: Anchor Books, 1959), 13, 35.

93. Malesherbes to Rousseau, 25 December 1761, in *Electronic Enlightenment Scholarly Edition of Correspondence*, ed. Robert McNamee et al., https://www.e-enlightenment.com.

94. Rousseau to *Malesherbes, 4 January 1762*, in *Electronic Enlightenment*.

95. Rousseau to *Malesherbes, 26 January 1762*, in *Electronic Enlightenment*.

96. Rousseau, *Les Confessions*, ed. Michel Launay, 2 vols. (Paris: GF Flammarion, 1968), 2:338.

97. Rousseau, *Les Confessions*, 2:338.

98. Media scholars have underscored the impact of social pressures on mediated self-expression; see danah boyd, "Why Youth (heart) Social Network Sites: The Role of Networked Publics in Teenage Social Life," in *Youth, Identity, and Digital Media*, ed. David Buckingham (Cambridge: MIT Press, 2008), 119–42.

99. See Fred Turner, "Machine Politics: The Rise of the Internet and a New Age of Authoritarianism," *Harper's Magazine*, January 2019, 33; see also Alice Marwick, *Status Update: Celebrity, Publicity, and Branding in the Social Media Age* (New Haven: Yale University Press, 2013); and Michael Serazio, *The Authenticity Industries: Keeping It "Real" in Media, Culture, and Politics* (Stanford: Stanford University Press, 2023).

Emotions, Work, and Form in the Diary of Edmund Harrold, 1712–15

ROBERT STEARN

What can be learned about how non-elite writers understood and navigated their social worlds by investigating the practices, styles, and uses of their writing? To explore this question, this essay examines the manuscript diary of Edmund Harrold, written between 1712 and 1715. Harrold (1678–1721) was a precariously solvent Manchester wigmaker, barber, sometime medical practitioner, bookdealer, and auctioneer. Written in order to keep track of and reform his conduct, especially his drinking, the diary pays close attention to the social pressures influencing Harrold's behavior. Facing both inward and outward, it is characterized by stylistic variety as much as by spiritual anguish: self-recrimination is intermixed with moments of order and contentment; prayers and religious devotions punctuate descriptions of work, reflections on social interactions, and notes on books or sermons. Taking style as "both a linguistic mode of social relation and a social use of a material means of production," and drawing on the historiography of household labor and domestic service, this essay argues that Harrold used his diary to develop a distinctive account of everyday emotional life in and around the social relations of work in the household, while sharing textual practices, cultural resources, and religious preoccupations with many other autobiographers, elite and non-elite.[1]

Harrold's diary has, in the last two decades, been a productive site for investigations into the meanings of work, identity, and masculinity.[2]

Historians of print and religious culture have deepened our understanding of Harrold's reading, the book trades that enabled it, and the forms of sociability that were premised upon it: how Harrold bought, sold, loaned, rented, procured, mended, read, and discussed books in his shop, at the bookseller's, and in the alehouse, with a group of three friends. These exchanges constituted an important part of Harrold's livelihood as well as an extra-familial and extra-parochial religious community.[3] The present essay aims to extend recent investigations of the diary's stylistic qualities, such as K. Tawney Paul's analysis of the vocabulary used by Harrold to conceptualize work and other non-leisure activities, and Michael Smith's attention to the diary's moments of affective intensity, which draw upon the language of the Psalms.[4] Building on these studies, and on Craig Horner's invaluable historical and editorial work on the diary and Harrold's reading materials, this essay uses the issue of style to focus on the practical and processual aspects of Harrold's writing, and investigates how he appropriated and put to use in the analysis and evaluation of his social world ideas, forms, and writing strategies derived from various sources, not all of them textual. In so doing, it draws on recent studies of the generic heterogeneity of early modern and eighteenth-century life writing, which have foregrounded the material practices of autobiography.[5] It is oriented by how studies of non-elite writing have considered the meaning and uses of literacy in the context of individual lives, and, more recently, have incorporated this analysis into investigations of England's changing social structure.[6]

The essay is in two parts. It begins with an examination of how Harrold used shared discursive materials, formal elements, and practices of book use to shape both his writing and his life. Of varied origin, these ways of writing and of using writing were turned by Harrold to the analysis of social relations. The second section then turns to a specific thread in Harrold's writing—his description of his courtship of two female servants, following the death of his second wife—and explores how Harrold's narration of these events and the terms in which he evaluated his relationships with these women reveal his awareness of different styles of work-related emotional acuity. Comparing Harrold's writing about servants with treatments of the same topic by middling and gentry writers, including Sarah Cowper, Dudley Ryder, and Ralph Josselin, I find that Harrold used the techniques outlined in the first section of this essay to articulate a nuanced understanding of everyday emotional life in the context of household labor, presenting it as an arena of tactics and skill. Ultimately, I consider how the account of work and emotion in Harrold's diary might illuminate the meaning of service in early eighteenth-century British culture.

"Lay down the best rules": Writing the Diary

Harrold's diary was written as part of a life characterized by wresting time for "thoughts on b[oo]ks and discourse" from the necessity to "work close al[l] day."[7] When he was not occupied by wigmaking, shaving, or cutting and collecting hair, Harrold read and wrote in his shop, as well as in the rooms he shared with his wife, children, lodger, and servant. He sometimes serially recorded his incremental progress through a book (*Diary*, 35). His reading materials included histories, poetry, and prose fiction, but most were religious works—a set of texts common to both Harrold and elite autobiographers.[8] In October 1712, as he was reading a sermon in John Norris's *Practical Discourses upon Several Divine Subjects* (1707) on "naturall and morall vanity," Harrold remarked: "I see it verified every day by experience" (40).[9] The conclusions that Norris drew from scripture spoke to Harrold's analysis of the world and his sense of his own powers within it.

Harrold used both Anglican and Nonconformist devotional manuals, like the *Practical Discourses*, as a resource in his writing, turning their blueprints for Christian living toward an analysis of social relations. In a long entry for 5 July 1712, Harrold reviewed his last month's conduct:

> I bless God yt I have not been drunken, yet Ive sometimes broken my rules more than I willingly would. Indeed when a man is in company, it has a great influence upon him to stay and yt many times to excess, so yt causes second thoughts and those relentings and wishes yt he had not so done. Thus we do and undo and run on circularly one while pleased anon displeased with ye same thing, and how should it be otherwise. Can we attain to perfection in this imperfect state? No surely, for all ye things on or in ye Earth will not satisfie those sublime souls of ours. Therefore we must seek another object to fix our affections on and yt is God, where ye more we search into his nature and attributes, the more we shall desire to know, because he is the center of our hapyness, temporall and eternall. (15)

Analyzing what he elsewhere called the "snare of society" (28, 81), Harrold's analysis of the vicissitudes of intention and self-recrimination in this entry draws on the broad Protestant emphasis on the cultivation and direction of feeling, which was modeled by Norris and many of the other authors that Harrold read and by sermons that he heard at Manchester's Collegiate Church, including the one on which he reports at length in the diary's first entry.[10] Most saliently, the importance of regulating one's affections by directing them to the correct (heavenly) objects in order to live well was the point of departure for William Sherlock's *A Practical Discourse*

Concerning Death (1689). Harrold borrowed this book on 22 June 1712, began reading it immediately, and had finished it by 1 August at the latest.[11] A further proximate influence on the entry of 5 July 1712 is the practice of meditation. Manuals such as Joseph Hall's *Invisible World* (1651), which Harrold had been reading on 1 July, offered him another model of how to incite and analyze feeling, while interpreting the sensuous world in a way that would reveal the spiritual.[12] Even when "very busie ... in ye world," Harrold was determined to "go" as often as possible "to God, both pub[lic and] private especially by meditation," as its proponents advised (48).[13]

Sermons, devotional manuals, and meditation offered Harrold stylistic resources as well as conceptual ones. The 5 July entry quoted earlier is notable for containing significantly less abbreviation and fewer telegraphic sentences than much of Harrold's daily writing. As Harrold moves from the "I," who is subject to rules, to the "man," who is in company, he shifts into the plural first person in order to describe and exhort, adopting the characteristic style of devotional manuals and printed sermons. Harrold's assured progression from question to answer to rules for living based on the correct ordering of desire has the cadence of an abbreviated version of Sherlock's prose, while its movement from sin to hope recapitulates as commentary the "micro-narrative of grace" characteristic of many introspective passages in the diary.[14] Harrold's qualified self-satisfaction in this moment of retrospection is suggested by his ability to adopt the idiom of these pious books, as he perhaps also did when composing the "diss[ertation] of friendship" that he read to a business associate in June 1714 (104). By thus aligning his own voice with these earnest Christian authorities, Harrold also, through what Hartley calls "style as interpellation," shares in the subject position implied by their discourse.[15]

Elsewhere, stylistic discontinuity is visible in the middle of an entry, indexing how Harrold fit writing around his work and further indicating the deliberateness of his use of other spoken and written genres. On 25 June 1712, Harrold recorded his dissatisfaction with the day: at ten in the morning he had "neglected all dutys," but would "indeavour to fetch it back by 12." These abbreviated phrases are then followed by a meditation on Proverbs 27:17 ("as iron sharpens iron, so doth ye countenance of man to man in conversation"). The tense shift and sudden reduction in the size of the script in the next sentence suggest that it was written after an interruption: "Thus about 11 yn I perform'd duty pub:[lic] [and] pri:[vate]" (12). Harrold's meditation on the cognitive and spiritual value of good conversation was thus vocalized as the "duty" to which he refers in the final sentence (or it at least prepared him for that performance).[16] The modulation of style was crucial to enabling Harrold to redeem wasted time and alter his emotional state.

Between May and July 1715, Harrold copied several chapters from Charles Povey's *Meditations of a Divine Soul* (1703) into his diary. These represent another inflection of his style, this time with a negative emotional charge. Harrold's transcriptions occupy the bulk of the final fifth of his book.[17] Povey's text, modeled on an oral/aural speech situation, is composed of layered voices. Copying the chapter on "the great folly of intemperance in drinking," after undertaking a review of his own life, Harrold added "Instance Self" before transcribing Povey's rendition of a drunkard's lament (*Diary*, 118–19, 133). This speech is set off in both Povey's printed book and Harrold's manuscript by quotation marks (*Harrold*, 69v). Harrold thus identifies himself with a textual example and, in the process of writing, aligns his voice both with Povey's first person and with the notional speech of this drunkard. The sot's complaint that "none of my former pretended Friends can give me ease" echoes Harrold's own earlier observation that "liquorish people" oblige former companions, who are now "low in pocket," to "cramp" themselves and "give place."[18] Harrold added the gloss "sad work" at the foot of the page to conclude Povey's catalog of the drunkard's symptoms (*Harrold*, 70v; *Diary*, 134), referring both to the content and to the act of copying.[19]

As well as compressing and transposing Povey's text, Harrold also augmented it with parenthetical additions and explanations, specifying, for instance, that the greatest comfort of which drunkenness would deprive him was "ye use of my Reason."[20] In contrast to his earlier alignment of his writing self with the plural first person of practical divinity, Harrold here inserted his "I" into Povey's text in the objectified discourse of the drunkard in order to humble himself, and watch himself being humbled, as well as to record his verification by experience of what he had read.[21] He had "too much experienced true" the drunkard's symptoms (119). In this, Harrold's practice echoes that of other readers of pious manuals, such as the Massachusetts educator Joseph Tompson (1640–1732), in whose journal, Matthew Brown argues, writing can be seen as a form of "culminating sincerity" in which transcription serves as a sacral offering or performance.[22] Modulations of voice or style in writing and transcribing were a means of analyzing the social world. Understood as traces of performance, vocal or otherwise, they were also opportunities to enter into new, shared positions of knowing and feeling. They disclose the capacity of writing to produce both affective states and knowledge about the self in its web of social relations.

Harrold's "rules" were a crucial means of guiding his own conduct and another way of producing knowledge about himself through writing and rereading. The diary is punctuated throughout by references to Harrold departing from or returning to these "rules," "resolutions," and "measures."[23]

The practice in which they were most required was Harrold's drinking, which led to ill health, mental distress, and the loss of credit, business, and money.[24] For several months after the death of his second wife, Sarah Boardman, in December 1712, Harrold drank especially heavily; his references to "broken rules" cluster around this time (56). Between January and April 1713, he made a series of resolutions to drink less, prompted by admonitions from acquaintances, sermons he heard or read, and his own reflections.[25] On 1 April 1713, Harrold's four-month-old daughter, Sarah, died. For Harrold, this signaled the need for "an universall reformation": aided by consultation with friends, he would "lay down the best rules and put ym in practice" (67).

Harrold also framed rules in response to being publicly admonished, such as when, on 16 August 1713, the chaplain Radley Ainscough refused to marry Harrold and Ann Horrocks because he was "a madman in drink" (85). Chastened, Harrold wrote out four rules, setting limits on the times, quantity, and locations of his drinking.[26] His rules were formed with an eye to his reputation, as well as his soul: if he could not "keep government up," Harrold knew, he would be "a laughing stock to men" (56, 17). After his brief imprisonment for drunkenness on the occasion of George I's coronation, he was "scoffed and derided and jeered" by "ye mobb" at an auction (110, 112). Harrold might darkly joke about his conduct ("keep't up decorum as usuall in my house" [56]), but his rules were there to enable him to undertake his duty, both publicly and privately, "to God and man," to "God and self," and to "God, neigh[bou]r and self."[27] He also drafted written rules for business associates and prospective romantic partners.[28] His hopes that he would be able to live in accordance with these resolutions are often addressed, in prayer, to a divine interlocutor: rulemaking became a form of dialogue between the writer and God, as well as between the self as a subject and as an object.[29] Harrold's rules—shared with friends, governing himself and his household, and undertaken in view of God and the local public—were a social fact, as well as a topic in his diary entries.

A "rule" was a template for action, projected into the future from the moment it was made. By assessing how closely he had adhered to the way of living laid down by the rule, Harrold could evaluate his progress, develop a sense of his own capacities, and give meaning to his narrative through an animating intention, even if that meaning was one of failure. In July 1712, moved by reading Hall's *Invisible World* to reflect on his own "tryalls," Harrold described his method: "I keep close to my rules in generall, and when I break ym, I put it down, day and date and all to humble my soul with etc" (14, 15). That Harrold reread his diary (and another, now lost, autobiographical work) is suggested not only by his references to doing so, but also by nonverbal features of his book.[30] Like many autobiographers who recorded vows, resolutions, and covenants in their diaries and reread them in order to judge and humble themselves (and following a shared set of published examples), Harrold added *notae* to his book in order to facilitate discontinuous reading and his own—and perhaps others'—later navigation of it.[31] He inscribed the foot of thirty-six of the ninety-two pages of his manuscript with a # sign, highlighting notable events, such as his marriage to Ann Horrocks on 22 August 1713.[32] Harrold often used the beginning or end of the month, and sometimes anniversaries, to review his conduct (often concluding with an "amen").[33] Many of these moments are also marked by a # sign. Enjoining himself to "note on this date always, amen" the four rules that he set down in August 1713, Harrold prospectively engaged his future superintendence (85). However, by the anniversary of this date, Harrold's diary keeping was sparse and he took no note of it.[34]

Harrold also used sound patterning to pick out particular moments—a formal strategy that aligns with his habit of using antithesis to form his concluding sentences and his recourse to the # symbol and other aspects of the mise-en-page. On 31 December 1714, Harrold wrote: "this being the last day of month and last oth year, I declear yt I see poverty apear, and for to ber it, I prepare, o my God" (114). The entry—and the page—ends with Harrold supplicating "blessed Jesus … amen amen amen #" in the hope of support as he vows to reform his conduct in the new year (*Harrold*, 66v; *Diary*, 115). Rhyme was used to identify a more positive turning point on 23 September 1712: "Resolv'd yt drunkeness I will refrain, since it hath got me such a name. … Thro' Gods assistance, Ile make resistance and alwayse flee all such designing company" (34). Other, more imperfect rhymes ("consent," "rent," "event") mark his preparation to move to a new house on 29 September 1714, the final entry for that month (109). In each case, the outcome is referred to God. Quite insistent rhyme and assonance seems to have been used on 26 March 1715 by the "very malancholly" Harrold as a bulwark against despair: "No one sure can self secure or keep it pure from sin. But thou alone triune three one wthin ye Trinity there be, which makes one God in unity" (118).

In other places, sound patterning is employed to sharpen rhetorical figures of augmentation or antithesis: June 1713 was "Begune with cros[s]es and los[s]es but sobriety" (75). Sound patterning of this kind—sometimes making use of words with a common base, such as "temperance" and "intemperance" (119), "assist" and "resist" (103), "use" and "abuse" (17)—abuts Harrold's habit of concluding entries, especially the final entry of the month, with a series of nouns grouped in twos or threes in relations of amplification or antithesis: "this month ended in primeness, grief and sorrow, pain and shame, and loss, and times and seasons has their revolutions and visisitudes";

"frugality and extravigantcy, discord, division and conformity, peace and unity in my family."[35] In two entries of this kind, the concluding rhyme and assonance coincides with the foot of the page and is marked by "amen," the # sign, and perhaps the year: "amen # # 1713"; "amen amen #" (*Diary*, 75, 119; *Harrold*, 40v, 72r). Rhyme separates these moments of summation from the surrounding text and the flow of events that it records.

Harrold was not unusual among seventeenth- and eighteenth-century non-elite autobiographers in using rhyme. Indeed, many wrote far more extensively in verse: as Brodie Waddell notes, Roger Lowe, John Dane, Joseph Bufton, and Joseph Ryder all wrote poetry in their diaries.[36] Harrold's use of sound patterning most resembles Lowe's. Turning to poetry at moments of emotional crisis, Lowe inscribed his present worries into a hopeful providential narrative.[37] Harrold's brief uses of rhyme are less metrically regular than Lowe's pentameter couplets. However, Harrold's more elaborate compositions, such as "Resolv'd yt drunkeness I will refrain," make use of an accentual tetrameter, a form historically linked to oral expression (34).[38] Lowe also transcribed into his diary poetry that was in circulation, both his own poems addressed to specific persons and verse that he was given, from metrical psalms to medical charms.[39] Harrold—acting as a local scribe, as did many non-elite autobiographers—similarly wrote out verses for others and composed his own satirical poetic "episel" regarding a fellow wigmaker, Thomas Genkinson, which attracted "report" (36, 97, 105, 107).[40]

These writing practices, together with Harrold's use of tetrameter, assonance, and end rhyme within his diary entries (formal strategies found nowhere in writings by elite autobiographers, although many of them collected poetry), point to a context of composition that was shaped by orally oriented forms of verse of the sort used for proverbs and practical guidance, as well as by ballads and songs; they suggest a mnemonic or possibly incantatory use for these textual moments, as does Harrold's segue from rhyme into proverbialized scripture ("times and seasons") and his affixing of the year's date to these entries.[41] Harrold's use of the # sign has a similar amplificatory potential: entries concluding the crisis months of April and May 1713 are multiply marked with amen, date, and the # sign.[42] Like Harrold's writing himself into Povey's *Meditations*, but undertaken through materials that would have felt communal, rhymed conclusions mediate the construction of Harrold's self through language made external.

Rulemaking, rhyme, creative transcription, and stylistic modulation were uses of writing that enabled Harrold to interpret the world in order to act in it and which organized and oriented his emotions. These shared discursive materials and formal strategies derived from overlapping social spaces and uses of language: discussion with friends and business associates in the shop and alehouse, hearing sermons during communal worship, and the reading of religious and other sorts of text in print in an array of settings. Harrold's use of them put him in dialogue with interlocutors both mundane and divine. The next section of this essay considers how Harrold marshaled these techniques in his descriptions of work, service, and the family in the context of his courtships. In so doing, it foregrounds the inflection of class in his analysis.

"She [is] a maneger": Service, Courtship, and Everyday Emotions

Like most middling families, Harrold's household was a hierarchically organized economic unit whose various members undertook work both paid and unpaid in order to ensure its survival—a circumstance that was fundamental to Harrold's evaluation of his relationships with prospective romantic partners.[43] Harrold relied on the waged labor of a maidservant for housework and care work, in addition to the housework, care work, home production, and remunerated retail and service work performed by his wife, Sarah, with whom he collaborated in managing matters of joint economic interest.[44] Sarah took in washing at her shop (an occupation that overlapped with the tasks of domestic service, but was of higher status than going to the houses of others to wash). She also sold secondhand clothes and oversaw the room they rented to a lodger.[45] On 11 September 1712, six weeks before Sarah gave birth, she and Harrold reached an agreement that, until the new year, she would "refrain washing cloth[e]s" and he would not drink to excess, which suggests that the physical toll of Sarah's labor and the economic consequences of his alcoholism were similarly matters of joint interest (32).

The labor of his wife and their servant appear in Harrold's diary alongside his own work as the determinants of good living. Harrold's rulemaking (and his diary keeping more generally) can be understood as an element of the non-remunerated, non-leisure, end-oriented activity that was intermixed with his work. In the terms that K. Tawney Paul excavates from Harrold's diary, this intellectual activity was his "employment," as opposed to his "business" (his management-aligned capacity to earn an income through labor and the use of credit, which linked getting a living to ordering a household) or his "work" (the specific tasks he undertook that involved the expenditure of effort).[46] Harrold understood his own spiritual and physical maintenance to depend on this "employment": together with his multi-occupational and managerial labor, and the labor of his wife and their servant, it contributed to a morally and materially adequate "living." It was in this sense that Harrold extolled "ye hapynes of regular living and keeping under ye body in subjection to reason and religion" and "ye masteries" that opposed "irregular living" and would "please w[i]f[e]" (111, 59, 12). Multiple entries define regular, fixed, or settled living as sobriety, brisk business, good reading, and profitable conversation, and understand irregular living to mean drunkenness and other nonsexual appetitive activity that had deleterious effects on his physical and spiritual health, household economy, and family relations.[47] After Sarah's death, Harrold married Ann Horrocks and noted with satisfaction on 25 September 1713 his achievement of a "settled" and "fix'd life," which depended on "housekeeping by servants and wife," as well as good business and the regulation of his own affections by rules and conscious decisions (89). For Harrold, settled living required both a personal and a collective effort; it was predicated not only on what he did individually, but also on what his household did.

Harrold was never himself a servant, although he had served an apprenticeship (a distinct but related state of temporary subjection).[48] However, men and women around him entered and exited servitude in potentially disquieting ways. The trajectory of a friend and "brother" wigmaker, Robert Crossley, is illustrative (87, 92). After becoming reacquainted with Crossley in August 1713, Harrold began a business partnership with him in October, selling him his stock of hair and paying him a wage as his traveling agent. However, the following June, Crossley broke up his shop and, pursued by bailiffs, sent his wife and child to Jersey, before entering into service with a Dr. Lucas of London.[49] Harrold was conscious that he might experience the same "distress" (104). Like many non-elite autobiographers whose fathers had died when they were young, Harrold struggled to maintain the position of his father, a tobacconist and Manchester officeholder, and was acutely conscious of his precarity.[50] Like many middling authors, he worried about his family's downward mobility, especially in the leaner times with which the diary concludes.[51]

Harrold's relative social proximity to servants is reflected in his approach to their instruction, which contrasts with that of elite autobiographers. He was conscious of the religious responsibilities pertaining to "masters of familys" and noted several sermons on the topic.[52] The diary also refers frequently to the performance—or lack thereof—of family religious observance (which he called "duty"), as well as to his own "public" and "private" duties.[53] However, Harrold neither agonized over nor despaired about how godly his maids, Betty Cook and Alice Hardman, were. Nor did he fret about their unruliness, unlike the clergyman Ralph Josselin.[54] Harrold was not emotionally disturbed by his servants or worried about their propensity to lie and steal in the way that gentry writers, such as Sarah Cowper, Mary Rich, and Elizabeth Freke, often were.[55] Instead, Harrold went drinking with servants.[56] Servants, for

Harrold, were objects of both greater indifference and greater intimacy than was the case for elite autobiographers. Indeed, Harrold courted and married women who worked as servants.

In the spring of 1713, following the death of Sarah Boardman the previous December, Harrold wrote about the satisfactions and false steps of his new courtships. These were clearly motivated in part by his need for domestic labor and help looking after his young children, Anna and Esther (the baby, Sarah, was with a wet nurse).[57] The courtships were concurrent with his attempts to employ a housekeeper. In December 1712, Harrold's drinking partner, Thomas Abram, promised Harrold that he would bring Ann Moore from Salford to be his housekeeper; at the time, the servant, Betty Cook, was looking after the house and children alone.[58] Moore arrived by March 1713, by which time Cook had already been replaced by Alice Hardman (hired at the alehouse in January).[59] On 31 August, while paying Hardman's wages, Harrold heard that she and Abram had married. Hardman gave birth to a child in December.[60] The problems of courtship and hiring, marriage and household labor, were intertwined for Harrold and his male associates in ways that differ from the frequently coercive dynamics of sexual relationships between male employers and female servants within their households.[61] As Laura Gowing suggests, the practical possibility of an elevation from the position of servant to that of wife and mistress was, for servants, "part of the realm of economic opportunity."[62]

Harrold's diary is largely silent in terms of his evaluation of Moore, Cook, Hardman, and the other waged women who successively worked in his household.[63] However, the narratives of his courtships disclose a wealth of information on this topic, for he assessed potential partners based on characteristics related to their aptitude as servants.[64] May 1713 found Harrold in a welter of uncertainty, canvassing friends for advice regarding a possible marriage to Ellen Howorth, a widow who seems to have worked as a servant at Chetham's College.[65] Harrold's entry for 25 May displays much of this uncertainty and the strategies he deployed to navigate it:

> I think I must do as [Thomas] Abram servant did [by] go[ing] to God for direction in this matter as he did, and by instances make inferences now, as this night I toul'd her I'd come towards 9. She said she would not be out oth way then. So Ile put this petition in my prayers, that if it be Gods will, we go together. For good things will al[l] conspire thereto. If not, she'l be out oth way, and so I must then be satisfied yt providence hath not determined us together So [to] my mind, Gods will, what he binds, Ile not loose. I did so, found her not out of ye way, but she sent me words of desire to come thither, for all was clear. I

> did so, and stay'd till 12 past, and abundance of conference we had about things. I know she loves better yn else where, but yet reports are fals[e], fortune lowe in cash, but I believe would be good in proofe. Only I must confess, she [is] a maneger, but is manag'd. She wants to be sattisfied. I wo'nt do it yet. I try her patience a little further. (74)

This entry records Harrold creating the conditions in which he could perceive the "direction" of the plans of Providence in order to assess the state of his courtship.[66] He was uncertain whether he should remarry, and he hoped for God's direction, as he had since he had first begun to "think of women again" on 8 March (64). In sentences that were apparently paused twice for action to occur and then restarted with an "I did so," Harrold receives a hopeful sign: Howorth is available, and they spend the evening together.[67] The further hesitations with which the entry concludes reflect Harrold's uncertainty about Howorth (to whose "infirmitys" Harrold had earlier alluded) and her estimation of him (62).

This diary entry brings Harrold's religious concerns to bear on the everyday in another way as well. The "[Thomas] Abram servant" to whom he refers is not only, as Craig Horner's editorial insertion suggests, the servant of Harrold's friend Thomas Abram, who had been mentioned in several previous entries, but also a servant of the biblical Abraham. The manuscript reads: "I must do as Abram Servant did" (*Harrold*, 40r). In Genesis 24, this servant is sent by Abraham to find a wife for his son, Isaac: arriving at a well, he prays for and receives a sign as to which of the women drawing water should be chosen as a wife for Isaac. Abraham's servant was often mentioned as an exemplar in early modern servant handbooks and household guides.[68] Harrold might have come across the story in a sermon or any number of printed texts, including Isaac Ambrose's *Prima, Media, et Ultima*, which he read and sold in early 1712, and Hall's *Invisible World*, which he read in July 1712, in which Abraham's servant is used to demonstrate how events that apparently arise from natural causes "yet are effected by the ministration of Angels."[69]

The affinities between Thomas Abram (closely associated with servants in Harrold's life) and his biblical namesake and the analogy between Rebekah—who serves the servant of Abraham—and Howorth each augment the significance of this moment. While elite autobiographers frequently refer to themselves as servants of God, this does not appear to have prompted them to consider relations between themselves, servants in scripture, and the servants in their households. Instead, domestic servants take on the role of aids to self-reflection, prompting the writer to adopt the position of a servant of God or to identify themselves with a particular scriptural servant. In the process, the real servant whose action occasioned the reflection fades from view. Even the modestly situated clergyman Ralph Josselin, whose immediate family members worked as servants, did not consider it worthwhile to explore his own practical interactions with servants in the light of scriptural examples, but rather used servants as instances of the workings of Providence or as evidence of God's dealings with him.[70] "I meet with trouble in my servants, lord I am a worse servant unto thee," runs a typical reflection.[71] Harrold makes use of the same analogical resources as Josselin and more elite writers, but repurposes them to imagine a dialogue in which a servant is an active party.

What kind of evaluation of that dialogue is involved in Harrold's description of Howorth as a "maneger" who "is manag'd"? He otherwise uses "manageing" and "management" to describe the conduct of business (7, 23). The passage certainly suggests, as Paul notes, that Harrold's courtship decisions were informed by the expectation that his wife's work would contribute to the support of the household.[72] The entry presents Harrold's encounter with Howorth as not only an uncertain situation to be tested against providential ordering, but also as a contest of management that sees Howorth and him each maneuvering to get the better of the other. The primary sense of "management" in the early eighteenth century was governmental or object-oriented conduct involving skill, tact, and dexterity, which—especially when practiced by subordinates—might shade over into cunning, trickery, and plotting.[73] In relation to service specifically, being a manager or "getting the management" referred to servants' ability to turn the tables on their superiors and seize control of the household by exploiting some characteristic weakness of their employer.[74]

Putting the claims about Howorth's and Harrold's "management" in relation to work in the household, then, Harrold's identification of Howorth as a "maneger" points, first, to the stock of social and household knowledge she has accumulated through service.[75] She "is manag'd" in that she was currently subject to others at work. However, the phrase can also be interpreted as a statement about the interpersonal aspects of courtship: Howorth is a manager insofar as "she's sharp, has wit enough, if she be but good humour'd," as Harrold had written on 30 April, in an entry marked with a # sign at the foot of the page (*Harrold*, 37r; *Diary*, 146). Howorth sought, he believed, to test him and draw matters to a sharp conclusion, but Harrold was determined to manage her by deferring any final resolution. Howorth's approach to management is registered by the serially interrupted nature of the entry; Harrold's sense of what it is to manage is suggested by the reflexive patterning in his phrasing (the "maneger ... manag'd"), which, like Harrold's half-rhyme of "instances" and "inferences," isolates the "now" of "this night" and so recalls the rhymes and antitheses that pepper the diary entries considered in the previous section of this essay.

The distinctiveness of Harrold's conception of management in the context of courtship and household labor can be clarified by comparing his writing to two diaries by more elite writers. In December 1711, the widowed Sarah Cowper (1644–1722)—who employed five servants and whose manuscripts are a compendium of data about household government—complained that it was "very Difficult to Mannage" an argument with her maids, due to their "cunning" and unscrupulous use of language.[76] For Cowper, servants' conversational abilities, and their conduct more generally, attested to their moral and cognitive otherness. Minimizing her own power, she presented interactions with servants as a test of skill in handling an erratic and resistant object.[77] Harrold held no such views, but nonetheless understood servant-related qualities in Howorth as a kind of practical knowledge to which he had to respond in kind.

Interactions with servants also played a role in the formation of the law student Dudley Ryder (1691–1756), who used his diary (1715–16) to analyze his acquaintances' conversational styles and to reflect on his inability to be "agreeable to the ladies."[78] The university educated Ryder, son of a dissenting linen draper, was more socially distinguishable from his servants than Harrold. When Ryder's extended family had to amuse themselves on a rainy evening in Berkhamsted, servants provided the entertainment: his "sister dressed up the servants in odd strange dresses and brought them in to divert us. We all laughed heartily" (*Ryder*, 99). Nonetheless, servants were for Ryder, as for Cowper, a proving ground for interpersonal skill. Ryder was careful to maintain a distance from the maidservant employed by his landlady, but described a more familiar interaction with a "shop maid" on 26 September 1715, when accompanying a friend to buy a hat: "I began to jest and rally with her a little and did it better than I think I ever did such a thing before … ; she answered me very handsomely and sometimes wittily" (*Ryder*, 55–57, 91, 107 [quotation]). This entry follows a month of particularly intense complaints about his awkwardness around "strange ladies" (*Ryder*, 70). On the day after the interaction with the shopworker, by contrast, Ryder congratulated himself for having "got more into the way of raillery than ever" (*Ryder*, 109). Servants—like the "very pretty agreeable face" that "seemed to be a servant maid," whom Ryder encountered in a coach—were possible objects for appraisal (*Ryder*, 37). They also provided a low-stakes arena in which to sharpen his wit and try out his studied confidence—a process of self-fashioning that Ryder, like Harrold, undertook in concert with his diary keeping.

How Ryder's self-conception was affected by such conversations can be clarified by comparing the attention that he paid servants to his periodic interactions with sex workers. With the latter, Ryder, who had been initially perturbed by being touched and propositioned, was explicit that his aim was to be able to competently handle a conversation and so bolster his "assurance and confidence" and "boldness" in other spheres of social interaction (*Ryder*, 49, 67, 274). On the occasions when Ryder's interest in an encounter was driven by his own desire, he nonetheless congratulated himself if he was able to talk "tolerably well."[79] For Ryder, interacting with sex workers and servants was a test of his social and discursive mettle that confirmed his masculine self-possession and conversational dexterity: his ability to "manage" and not be managed (*Ryder*, 71). The potential dangers of these encounters were mitigated by his place in a hierarchy of status and employment: whatever else they were, servants and sex workers were not prospective spouses. For Harrold, on the other hand, there was no enabling separation between the categories of "servant" and "potential wife": he recognized that the styles of communication that were developed through navigating household labor were also involved in "words of desire." Nonetheless, Harrold's identification of Howorth as a "maneger" attests to a similar interest as Ryder's in the competent performance of particular genres of conversation, albeit with higher stakes, and suggests that his self-conception was similarly contingent upon that performance.

Despite Harrold's hopeful invocation of Providence, he and Howorth fell out. In his account of his next courtship, the question of service and management reappears, with a different accent and a renewed emphasis on textuality. After discovering that Howorth preferred a rival suitor, Harrold turned to Ann Horrocks, a Nonconformist who also seems to have worked as a domestic servant, or at least lodged with a "m[aste]r," from whom Harrold sought consent to marry.[80] On 19 June 1713, assessing Horrocks's character in terms that again overlap with her success in service, Harrold wrote: "she says Im sharp courtier, and she does not like on't, but I beleive she does. She's very loving and pleasant company, quiet and easie of temper, and gets her love whome ever she lives with" (77). Harrold's relief at now being the "sharp" one is clear, but his description also has occupational resonances: contemporary handbooks for maidservants routinely promised that their readers would be equipped to get or gain the love of the households in which they worked.[81] Harrold knew that Horrocks was "concern'd ... to do well in ye world" (78). On 5 July 1713, he wrote that he would "manage things to my own mind to turn her" (79). Three weeks into this increasingly one-sided campaign of "power and policy," Harrold proclaimed himself (somewhat prematurely) "m[aste]r of affections and power and might in her" (82).

It is notable, since Howorth's "management" had involved putting obstacles in the way of their meeting, that Harrold and Horrocks were able to stay up all night together on several occasions in July, a time that Harrold used to "try her temper" (82).[82] These late-night conversations were "hard tryals about love and conformity, and serviss and trouble, child birth and conveniencyes and inconvenientcies," in Harrold's summary antithesis on 31 July (82–83). The conclusiveness implied in this end-of-the-month entry was premature: after a multiday drunken "ramble," Horrocks annulled their banns on 11 August—"ye reason of it, conformity etc" (83, 84). Meeting on subsequent afternoons following this public break, Harrold and Horrocks continued to discuss the possibilities of her conforming to the Church of England and his remaining sober; they ultimately married on 22 August (83–85, 86).[83] In this later stage of the courtship, Harrold's writing is again punctuated by "did so," as he looked for indications of Providence in whether or not there were barriers to his meeting with Horrocks on a particular day. He found himself no longer the manager (82, 84).

Some concurrent business dealings also left traces in the style and layout of the diary. Their "hard trialls" are marked on 24 July by a # sign in the right-hand margin (*Harrold*, 45v). On its own, this sign would be of limited use as a navigation aid, since it is partially obscured by the curve of the page toward the gutter. However, it is supplemented by two other # marks, at the foot of the page, which appear to be related to significant developments in Harrold's occupational life.[84] On 24 July he also drew up some written "rules" for a projected business partnership with the wigmaker Thomas Genkinson, while the foot of the page records Harrold's prayer that God "turn ye face of my affairs towards settledness, yt I may once more live Xstian like # again #" (*Harrold*, 45v; *Diary*, 82). A few days later, Harrold "lay'd forth" three "propositions" to Horrocks (85). The # sign serves here to mark for review key terms in the string of entries that follow; it links together marriage and business as the determinants of a "settledness" that would, he hoped, be effected with the aid of writing.

Harrold's evaluations of his relationships with Howorth and Horrocks engaged with their moral characters, but also with their actions and their demeanor in both paid and unpaid fields of work. He regarded the latter as different ways of managing the emotional and practical negotiations of marriage. Harrold's use of terms drawn from the world of service indicates the extent to which his assessment hinged upon their practical competencies, but also reveals his awareness of different styles of work-related emotional acuity and a sensitivity to shifts in their relative power. These passages suggest that the emotional content of housework, care work, and household managerial labor (including labor that extended outside the home) were areas of interest for members of the literate non-elite.

For eighteenth-century employers, as Carolyn Steedman has shown, servants were "there to think with, as well as to cook their dinner and buckle their shoes."[85] In writings by aristocratic and gentry writers of the seventeenth and early eighteenth centuries (such as Anne Halkett, Sarah Cowper, and Mary Rich), the lower sort, with their distinctive appearance, forms of labor, and patterns of speech, were as much objects on which to meditate as personnel to be managed.[86] Writing about servants was a way to analyze society and also a way in which employers could sharpen the contours of their own personalities, by enlisting servants as fantasized witnesses to and narrators of their employers' lives—a role that they had played in Izaak Walton's biographies in the seventeenth century and continued to play for Virginia Woolf at the turn of the twentieth century.[87] *The Spectator* encouraged this knowledge and knowingness in essays that were notionally by, as well as about, servants. It was read critically by Cowper, who admired Mr. Spectator's methods of government but thought him too optimistic about the character of servants, and avidly by Dudley Ryder, who considered its delineation of characters a guide to society and a useful topic of conversation.[88] For Cowper, as for Ryder, however, conversational engagement with servants, whether in the exercise of household government or in the enjoyment of raillery, was a test of skill.

Writing during slow moments in the working day, Harrold did not record any reflections on the institution of service. He was too close to service to think it worthwhile or plausible to consider servants as a group about which one might generalize. Nonetheless, Harrold's biblically informed assessment of work and love in the context of service and household labor offers an example of how shared cultural materials can be appropriated and used differently, depending not so much on a writer's social location, as on the nature of their project.[89] Most of the discursive materials and stylistic models that Harrold used to describe his social world and anatomize the pressures influencing his conduct (such as his fashioning of rules or making vows and resolutions) were shared across the culture, as was his aim of self-management. Harrold's use of rhyme, derived from the oral circulation of verse, was open to, though apparently not usable by, elite autobiographers. The modulations of style and creative transcription present in his diary are, to give just one example, in plentiful evidence in Cowper's books, which are composed of a tissue of quotations. Harrold's downward social trajectory and struggles with alcohol addiction put him in a position to use these shared cultural materials in unusual ways. He was able to connect the primarily individual strategies of self-regulation undertaken through his diary to the collective labor necessary to sustain and reproduce himself and his household.

Harrold's unusual approach to the use of examples of servants from the Bible, like his enjoyment of management-related wordplay to describe his prospective spouses, shows him as both a participant in and an antagonist toward a shared culture, using common but differently inflected languages of work and emotions to distinct ends.[90] Harrold, like Ryder and Cowper, was interested in the kind of practical knowledge and tactical nous involved in sustaining a conversation with a woman who might work in his household. However, the inadequacy of this phrasing to describe the nature of Harrold's interest in Howorth or Horrocks indicates just how different the problems of household labor and desire confronting Harrold were compared to those that Ryder and Cowper faced. However, that need not suggest that his version of "management" was wholly sealed off from theirs. Rather, Harrold's writing offers an opportunity to explore how relations between service, work, and the emotions were conceived by a non-elite subject, enmeshed in the same culture as the elite writers whose testimony in print and manuscript still sets the terms for historical understanding of the specifically emotional aspects of labor and household relations, notwithstanding the exciting recent scholarship that has recovered the terms of discrimination, interpretation, and self-understanding that servants used to describe and account for their own experience.[91]

Notes

1. Daniel Hartley, *The Politics of Style: Towards a Marxist Poetics* (Leiden: Brill, 2016), 141.

2. See Hannah Barker, "Soul, Purse and Family: Middling and Lower-Class Masculinity in Eighteenth-Century Manchester," *Social History* 33, no. 1 (2008): 12–35; and K. Tawny Paul, "Accounting for Men's Work: Multiple Employments and Occupational Identities in Early Modern England," *History Workshop Journal* no. 85 (2018): 26–46.

3. See Michael Powell, "Taking Stock: The Diary of Edmund Harrold of Manchester," in *Light on the Book Trade: Essays in Honour of Peter Isaac*, ed. Barry McKay, John Hinks, and Maureen Bell (London: British Library, 2004), 37–49; and Michael Smith, "Print, Friendship and Voluntary Devotional Communities in North West England, c. 1660–1730," in *Communities of Print: Books and Their Readers in Early Modern Europe*, ed. Rosamund Oates and Jessica Purdy (Leiden: Brill, 2022), 136–54.

4. Paul, "Accounting for Men's Work," 30–32; Michael Smith, "Translating Feeling: The Bible, Affections and Protestantism in England, c.1660–c.1750," *Studies in Church History* 53 (2017): 311–23.

5. See Margaret Ezell, "Domestic Papers: Manuscript Culture and Early Modern Women's Life Writing," in *Genre and Women's Life Writing in Early Modern England*, ed. Michelle Dowd and Julie Eckerle (Aldershot: Ashgate, 2007), 33–48; and Adam Smyth, *Autobiography in Early Modern England* (Cambridge: Cambridge University Press, 2010).

6. See James Amelang, *The Flight of Icarus: Artisan Autobiography in Early Modern Europe* (Stanford: Stanford University Press, 1998); Paul, "Accounting for Men's Work"; Margaret Spufford, "First Steps in Literacy: The Reading and Writing Experiences of the Humblest Seventeenth-Century Spiritual Autobiographers," *Social History* 4, no. 3 (1979): 407–35; Brodie Waddell, "'Verses of My Owne Making': Literacy, Work and Social Identity in Early Modern England," *Journal of Social History* 54, no. 1 (2020): 161–84; and Susan Whyman, *The Pen and the People: English Letter Writers, 1660–1800* (Oxford: Oxford University Press, 2009), 75–158.

7. *The Diary of Edmund Harrold, Wigmaker of Manchester, 1712–15*, ed. Craig Horner (Aldershot: Ashgate, 2008), 14, 17. Subsequent citations will be made parenthetically in the main text when I am directly quoting from the diary and in the notes as *Diary* when I am describing or paraphrasing it. I retain Horner's use of square brackets to identify his insertion of missing, illegible, or omitted words.

8. See Horner's introduction in *Diary*, xxiv.

9. Harrold found Norris "very pertinent" to an argument with his wife two weeks later (44), and continued reading over the following days (*Diary*, 45, 47).

10. *Diary*, 1–2, 9, 40, 64. See Andrew Cambers, *Godly Reading: Print, Manuscript and Puritanism in England, 1580–1720* (Cambridge: Cambridge University Press, 2011), 47, 52, 76–80; Alec Ryrie, *Being Protestant in Reformation Britain* (Oxford: Oxford University Press, 2013), 17–95; and Smith, "Translating Feeling." The High Church commitments of the chaplains and fellows at the Collegiate Church aligned with Harrold's own; see Horner, "Introduction," in *Diary*, xxviii.

11. *Diary*, 10, 24. In the same month as he borrowed the Sherlock book, Harrold read similar works by Edward Sparke, Isaac Ambrose, and Ezekial Hopkins (*Diary*, 6, 8–9, 10).

12. *Diary*, 14, 20, 30, 117. See also Marie–Louise Coolahan, "Redeeming Parcels of Time: Aesthetics and Practice of Occasional Meditation," *Seventeenth Century* 22, no. 1 (2007): 124–43.

13. Coolahan, "Redeeming Parcels of Time," 124–28. For instances of Harrold doing so, see *Diary*, 15, 30, 103.

14. Tom Webster, "Writing to Redundancy: Approaches to Spiritual Journals and Early Modern Spirituality," *Historical Journal* 39, no. 1 (1996): 53.

15. Hartley, *Politics of Style*, 91.

16. Several entries record Harrold's thankfulness for good conversation in the narrow sense (see *Diary*, 19, 27, 42, 117).

17. "Edmund Harrold: His Book" (1712–15), Mun.A.2.137, 69r–91r, Chetham's Library, Manchester. Subsequent citations to this manuscript will be made parenthetically and in the notes as *Harrold*. Where it is necessary to refer to both Horner's edition (which does not reproduce Harrold's nonverbal marks) and the

manuscript of the diary, the citations will be separated by a semicolon. Harrold's extracts from Povey are printed in *Harrold*, 120, 133–45.

18. Povey, *Meditations of a Divine Soul: or, the Christian's Guide, Amidst the Various Opinions of a Vain World* (London, 1703), 385; *Diary*, 117.

19. See also *Diary*, 133, 134.

20. *Harrold*, 70v. Horner reads this as "Yn, so of my reason": *Diary*, 134. For creative transcription, see *Harrold*, 71v–72r, 74v, 90v–91r. See also Whyman, *Pen and the People*, 86–87.

21. Harrold described the effect of rereading his own autobiographical writing in these terms; see *Diary*, 3, 15, 35.

22. Brown, "The Thick Style: Steady Sellers, Textual Aesthetics, and Early Modern Devotional Reading," *PMLA* 121, no. 1 (2006): 79.

23. See, for example, *Diary*, 17, 31, 55, 56, 62, 63, 76, 116.

24. *Diary*, 60, 112.

25. *Diary*, 55, 57, 64, 65, 68.

26. *Diary*, 85. These rules elaborate on Harrold's "very good rule" not to drink in the morning, which he had set down on 9 July 1712 (17).

27. See *Diary*, 12, 36, 85, 113, 114, 82, 90.

28. *Diary*, 82, 85.

29. *Diary*, 17, 85. See Margo Todd, "Puritan Self-Fashioning: The Diary of Samuel Ward," *Journal of British Studies* 31, no. 3 (1992): 241; and Webster, "Writing to Redundancy," 48–50.

30. For Harrold rereading, see *Diary*, 3, 14, 31, 118.

31. See Andrew Cambers, "Reading, the Godly, and Self-Writing in England, circa 1580–1720," *Journal of British Studies* 46, no. 4 (2007): 806, 815–18; Ezell, "Domestic Papers," 36–38, 46; Matthew Kadane, *The Watchful Clothier: The Life of an Eighteenth-Century Protestant Capitalist* (New Haven: Yale University Press, 2013), 43–83; Webster, "Writing to Redundancy," 44–48; *The Diary of James Clegg of Chapel en le Frith, 1708–55*, part 1, ed. Vanessa Doe (Matlock: Derbyshire Record Society, 1978), xii, 6, 14, 16, 20–21, 23; and Horner, "Introduction," in *Diary*, xxviii–xxix. For Harrold reading Isaac Ambrose, who advocated daily writing and review, see *Diary*, 7–11. For sermons on the duty of self-examination and on "watchfulness," see *Diary*, 38, 61.

32. *Harrold*, 3v, 11r, 12v, 18r, 22r, 25v, 27r, 32v, 34v, 36r, 37r, 39r, 40v, 43r, 45v, 48r, 51v, 52v, 53v, 55v, 56r, 58r, 61v, 63v, 64r, 64v, 66v, 68r, 72r, 74v, 75v, 78r, 79v, 82v, 83r, 90r. For his marriage, see *Harrold*, 48v; *Diary*, 86.

33. *Diary*, 15, 23–24, 30, 36, 50, 55, 59, 63, 69, 75, 77, 87, 90, 93, 96, 98, 100, 104, 109, 111, 114, 116. For pages ending "amen," see *Harrold*, 15r, 15v, 17r, 18r, 19r, 24v, 28v, 29r, 33v, 35v, 43r, 46r, 47v, 52r, 53v, 55r, 55v, 57v, 59r, 60v, 65v, 68v. For pages ending with a double or triple "amen," see 37r, 39r, 56r, 56v, 57r, 62v, 63r, 66v, 72r.

34. See *Diary*, 106.

35. *Diary*, 75, 89–90. See also *Diary*, 45.

36. Waddell, "'Verses of My Owne Making,'" 166–72.

37. See *The Diary of Roger Lowe of Ashton-in-Makerfield, Lancashire, 1663–74*, ed. William Sachse (New Haven: Yale University Press, 1938), 80, 113, 118–19; Waddell, "'Verses of My Owne Making,'" 172.

38. See Carolyn Steedman, "Poetical Maids and Cooks Who Wrote," *Eighteenth-Century Studies* 39, no. 1 (2005): 18–22; and T. V. F. Brogan, "Ballad Metre," in *The New Princeton Encyclopedia of Poetry and Poetics*, ed. Alex Perringer and T. V. F. Brogan (Princeton: Princeton University Press, 1993), 118–20.

39. *Diary of Roger Lowe*, 33, 35, 17–18, 76, 101–3. Lowe's two verse epitaphs (29–33, 54) may also have been shared.

40. Whyman, *Pen and the People*, 81–82. The poem seems to have been provoked by Genkinson proving "fals[e]," after he and Harrold began a partnership in which Harrold undertook work for Genkinson (*Diary*, 105, 82, 97, 98).

41. Adam Fox, *Oral and Literate Culture in England, 1500–1700* (Oxford: Clarendon Press, 2000), 24–26, 135, 184–86, 206.

42. *Harrold*, 37r, 40v; *Diary*, 69, 75.

43. Jane Whittle, "A Critique of Approaches to 'Domestic Work': Women, Work and the Pre-Industrial Economy," *Past and Present* no. 243 (2019): 35–70.

44. Paul, "Accounting for Men's Work," 26, 39–40; *Diary*, 30, 49. On these categories, see Whittle, "Critique of Approaches to 'Domestic Work.'"

45. Peter Earle, *A City Full of People: Men and Women of London* (London: Methuen, 1994), 126; *Diary*, 49.

46. Paul, "Accounting for Men's Work," 30–32.

47. *Diary*, 12, 17, 55, 59, 75, 77, 81, 96–97, 117. Harrold's understanding of regular and irregular living drew upon scripture: after hearing a sermon on 2 Corinthians 11:19, he interpreted the biblical passage as advice on how to remain "temperate" (*Diary*, 59).

48. Horner, "Introduction," in *Diary*, xviii; Tim Meldrum, *Domestic Service and Gender, 1660–1750: Life and Work in the London Household* (Harlow: Longman, 2000), 132, 155, 161–64.

49. *Diary*, 92–95, 100, 104, 105, 107; Horner, "Introduction," in *Diary*, xxii.

50. Spufford, "First Steps," 420; Horner, "Introduction," in *Diary*, ix–xii, xxvi; *Diary*, 37n7, 92.

51. *Diary*, 109. See Matthew Kadane, "Self-Discipline and the Struggle for the Middle in Eighteenth-Century Britain," in *In Praise of Ordinary People: Early Modern Britain and the Dutch Republic*, ed. Margaret Jacob and Catherine Secretan (Basingstoke: Palgrave Macmillan, 2013), 266–69; Michael Mascuch, "Social Mobility and Middling Self-Identity: The Ethos of British Autobiographers, 1660–1750," *Social History* 20, no. 1 (1995): 45–61; and Whyman, *Pen and the People*, 112–58.

52. *Diary*, 23. See also *Diary*, 16, 29.

53. *Diary*, 21, 18, 11, 12, 43, 45, 89, 93, 100.

54. *The Diary of Ralph Josselin, 1616–1683*, ed. Alan Macfarlane (Oxford: Oxford University Press for the British Academy, 1976), 253, 470, 552, 553, 580; and Alan Macfarlane, *The Family Life of Ralph Josselin, a Seventeenth-Century Clergyman: An Essay in Historical Anthropology* (Cambridge: Cambridge University Press, 1970), 40–44, 49, 54, 93, 132.

55. Sarah, Lady Cowper, "Diary. Volume the First" (1700–1702), DE/P/F29, 10, 16–17, 18, 19–20, and "Diary. Volume the Fifth" (1709–11), DE/P/F33, 318, Hertford Archives and Local Studies (hereafter HALS); *The Remembrances of Elizabeth Freke, 1671–1714*, ed. Raymond Anselment (Cambridge: Cambridge University Press, 2001), 72, 157, 159; *The Occasional Meditations of Mary Rich, Countess of Warwick*, ed. Raymond Anselment (Tempe: Arizona Centre for Medieval and Renaissance Studies, 2009), 83.

56. *Diary*, 75.

57. *Diary*, 50, 58, 60.

58. *Diary*, 53, 55, 57.

59. *Diary*, 58, 66, 75.

60. *Diary*, 87, 97.

61. Meldrum, *Domestic Service and Gender*, 100–127.

62. Gowing, "The Haunting of Susan Lay: Servants and Mistresses in Seventeenth-Century England," *Gender and History* 14, no. 2 (2002): 192. See also Michelle Dowd, *Women's Work in Early Modern English Literature and Culture* (New York: Palgrave Macmillan, 2009), 21–56.

63. Harrold did record giving Cook some of Sarah's "workday" clothes after her death (*Diary*, 52–53).

64. Harrold also assessed Horrocks's "cash" and clothes (*Diary*, 81, 82).

65. *Diary*, 68, 68n5, 74, 75.

66. Alexandra Walsham, *Providence in Early Modern England* (Oxford: Oxford University Press, 1999), 19–20. Harrold was not generally a seeker after signs. However, in July 1712 he recorded the omen of an uncracking pot "in order to observe ye event concerning theirs or our familyes to come" (22).

67. *Diary*, 5, 9, 22, 28, 34, 43, 59, 75, 82, 84, 101, 113. Several other entries in the diary include phrases like "did so," "as so," "done," generally in the context of work, to indicate that a task narrated prospectively in the previous sentence has now been accomplished or that the outcome of an event is now known. On several occasions, although not in this case, abrupt discontinuities in the size and appearance of Harrold's script or in the color of his ink suggest a substantial break in composition. See, for example, the alterations in his hand on 20 June 1712 (*Diary*, 9; *Harrold*, 4r) and in the ink on 28 May 1713 (*Diary*, 75; *Harrold*, 40v). In the entry for 31 August 1712, the tiny script used for Harrold's retrospective summary ("thus ended this month") is clearly discontinuous with the sprawling hand of the earlier part of the entry (*Diary*, 30; *Harrold*, 14v).

68. See, for example, William Gouge, *Of Domesticall Duties: Eight Treatises* (London, 1622), 631.

69. *Diary*, 7n3, 8, 11, 14.

70. *Diary of Ralph Josselin*, 47–48, 67, 432, 435, 514, 529, 599. Josselin's sister served for several months in his household (*Diary of Ralph Josselin*, 15; Macfarlane, *Family Life of Ralph Josselin*, 148). Like Harrold, Josselin supplied the funds to set up at least one daughter in service, either to pay for her board and lodging or to supplement her wages (*Diary of Ralph Josselin*, 77; Macfarlane, *Family Life of Ralph Josselin*, 49).

71. *Diary of Ralph Josselin*, 470. For a similar procedure, see *Occasional Meditations of Mary Rich*, 66.

72. Paul, "Accounting for Men's Work," 39.

73. *Oxford English Dictionary*, s.vv. "management (*n.*)," last modified July 2023, https://doi-1org-10066f06p081f.erf.sbb.spk-berlin.de/10.1093/OED/7522524058 and "manager (*n.*), " last modified July 2023, https://doi-1org-10066f06p081f.erf.sbb.spk-berlin.de/10.1093/OED/7718573462.

74. Delarivier Manley, *The Adventures of Rivella*, ed. Katherine Zelinsky (Peterborough: Broadview, 1999), 80, 89, 102; Nicholas Zinzano, *The Servants Calling* (London, 1725), 43; Daniel Defoe, *Religious Courtship (1722)*, ed. G. A. Starr, in *Religious and Didactic Writings of Daniel Defoe*, ed. W. R. Owens and P. N. Furbank, vol. 4 of 10 (London: Pickering and Chatto, 2006), 233, 234; Defoe, *The Great Law of Subordination Consider'd* (London, 1724), 72–73, 116, 122.

75. See Jane Whittle, "Servants in Rural England c. 1450–1650: Hired Work as a Means of Accumulating Wealth and Skills before Marriage," in *The Marital Economy of Scandinavia and Britain, 1400–1900*, ed. Maria Ågren and Amy Erickson (London: Routledge, 2015), 89–107.

76. Cowper, "Diary. Volume The Sixth" (1711–13), DE/P/F34, 67, HALS.

77. Cowper, "Diary. Volume The Sixth," 6, 184, 208.

78. *The Diary of Dudley Ryder, 1715–1716*, ed. William Matthews (London: Methuen, 1939), 92. Subsequent citations will be made parenthetically and in the notes as *Ryder*.

79. *Ryder*, 71–72. For these encounters, see *Ryder*, 85, 218, 292, 331, 369. Only one diary entry unambiguously records sexual activity with a sex worker (138).

80. *Diary*, 86; Horner, "Introduction," in *Diary*, xiv.

81. See, for example, *The Compleat Servant-Maid; or, The Young Maiden's Tutor* (London, 1677), 1; or [Eliza Haywood], *A Present for a Servant-Maid: or, The Sure Means of gaining Love and Esteem* (London, 1743), title page.

82. *Diary*, 79, 80, 82, 83.

83. Harrold was concerned about the consequences of Nonconformity: he had agonized about the salvation of Sarah Boardman, also a Nonconformist, in her last illness (*Diary*, 52).

84. Harrold uses a # sign in the margin on one other occasion (63v), where it is similarly paired with a # sign at the foot of the page.

85. Steedman, *Labours Lost: Domestic Service and the Making of Modern England* (Cambridge: Cambridge University Press, 2009), 222.

86. See, for example, Anne Halkett, "Ocationall Meditations" (1658/9–60), MS 6490, 21–28, 124–29, and "Occationall Meditations" (1660–63), MS 6491, 71–75, National Library of Scotland, Edinburgh; Sarah Cowper, Diaries (1700–1716), DE/P/F29–F35, HALS; *Meditations of Mary Rich*, 43, 61, 66–68, 73–74, 80, 83, 105, 140, 143, 160–61.

87. See Carolyn Steedman, "Servants and Their Relationship to the Unconscious," *Journal of British Studies* 42, no. 3 (2003): 316–50; Andrea Walkden, "The Servant and the Grave Robber: Walton's 'Lives' in Restoration England," in *Writing Lives: Biography and Textuality, Identity and Representation in Early Modern England*,

ed. Kevin Sharpe and Steven Zwicker (Oxford: Oxford University Press, 2008), 319–36; and Alison Light, *Mrs Woolf and the Servants* (London: Penguin, 2008).

88. Cowper, "Diary. Volume The Sixth," DE/P/F34, 94, 177, 181, HALS, commenting on numbers 294, 500, and 512 (*The Spectator*, ed. Donald Bond, 5 vols. [Oxford: Oxford University Press, 1987], 3:49, 4:273, and 4:317); *Ryder*, 46, 62–63, 70, 111, 117, 120–23, responding to numbers 88, 96, and 292 (*The Spectator*, 1:372–76, 1:405–9, and 2:291–94).

89. See Amelang, *Flight of Icarus*, 240–43; and Roger Chartier, "Reading Matter and 'Popular' Reading: From the Renaissance to the Seventeenth Century," in *A History of Reading in the West*, ed. Guglielmo Cavallo and Roger Chartier, trans. Lydia G. Cochrane (Cambridge: Polity, 1999), 269–83.

90. See Susan Wiseman, "The Maid of Haddon: Event, Text and Women in Derbyshire Literate Culture," *Women's Writing* 26, no. 1 (2019): 71–87.

91. See Paula Humfrey, ed., *The Experience of Domestic Service for Women in Early Modern London* (London: Routledge, 2011); Charmian Mansell, *Female Servants in Early Modern England* (Oxford: Oxford University Press, 2024); Alexandra Shepard, *Accounting for Oneself: Worth, Status, and the Social Order in Early Modern England* (Oxford: Oxford University Press, 2015); Steedman, *Labours Lost*; and Steedman, "Poetical Maids."

"Not for mere children": Charlotte Smith's Feminist Novels for "Young Persons"

JOANI ETSKOVITZ

In 1794, Charlotte Smith set out to invent a new kind of book for "young persons." In a reply to her editor's suggestion that she, a near-destitute mother of twelve, write for children in order to turn a quick profit, Smith pitched "a sort of School book, calculated not for mere children, but for young persons from twelve to sixteen."[1] The preface to her first book of this sort, *Rural Walks* (1795), identifies her daughter's intellectual needs as her inspiration: "in the very little time that the incessant necessity of writing for the support of my family allows me to bestow on the education of a girl between twelve and thirteen, I have found ... that something of this kind was still wanting."[2] Wanting it was. Smith sold two additional books modeled on *Rural Walks*, *Rambles Farther* (1796) and *Minor Morals* (1798), proving her fictional Mrs. Woodfield's assertion that "no person is too young to be taught to think" (*RW*, 10). What kind of thinking does *Rural Walks* teach, and how, formally, does it engage adolescent readers? Smith's books for young persons depict a process of creative learning—of wandering, questioning, and storytelling—that landed her in the middle of a culture war over the roles of wonder and curiosity in girls' education.

Smith's new "kind" of book offers a window on how eighteenth-century experiments with gender and genre shaped ideas about adolescence.[3]

Her female, middle-class "young person" is not today's "young adult," a psychological term that claims to transcend gender categories; nor is she the "hypothetical young reader" or gendered and classed "juvenile" audience that, according to Felicity Hughes and Teresa Michals, eighteenth-century authors invoked in making moral and aesthetic judgements about novels that were read by people of all ages.[4] Smith's "young person" is closer in kind to the female "teens" that Mitzi Myers, Stephanie Hershinow, Katherine Gustafson, and Katherine Kittredge have identified in the works of Maria Edgeworth, Frances Burney, Sarah Trimmer, and Jane Austen. She is at once a curious character, a quixotic reader, and a semi-fictional authorial persona.[5] In these roles, Smith's "young person" has all the "imaginative power implicit in the idea of adolescence" that Patricia Meyer Spacks locates in both the eighteenth and twentieth centuries, but her empowerment was not a consequence of the "real and imagined sexual energy" of Samuel Richardson's Pamela.[6] On the contrary, Smith's "young person" channels the intellectual energy that Spacks identifies in twentieth-century depictions of youth as a "quest, searching, seeking, grasping, testing in an effort to find the proper 'course.'"[7]

Smith's assertion that tweenage and teenage female readers had intellectual needs was a feminist intervention in late eighteenth-century pedagogy and educational literature. By the 1790s, fashionable urban schools were facilitating what Peter Borsay has termed a "compression of the stages of late childhood and adolescence," which trained girls ages seven through sixteen to seek out balls and leisure activities: "marketplaces for the bartering of elite brides."[8] This curriculum taught "female accomplishments," from drawing to dancing, that served as a social receipt for an expensive education and could lead to a transactional marriage, like the one that truncated Smith's adolescence at age fifteen.[9] Smith launched her literary career with a subtle rebellion against this "prodigious stroke of domestic policy to sell me like a Southdown sheep."[10] The same *Elegiac Sonnets* that paid the abusive Mr. Smith's way out of the King's Bench Prison named their author "Charlotte Turner Smith of Bignor Park."[11] As "Turner," Smith imaginatively returned to age twelve, when she left her Kensington school to live with her aunt.[12] A decade after the *Elegiac Sonnets*, this personal history furnished the frame story for *Rural Walks*. To involve both her fictional female adolescents and her readers in the "wandering and adventure" that she learned at Bignor, Smith created a kind of book that I am identifying as an experimental feminist young adult novel.[13]

Rural Walks reimagines Smith's local adventures within a fictional female peer group, expanding adolescence into an empowering time when girls as young as seven, but especially around thirteen, learn to direct their own educations. Elizabeth Dolan has shown how this "crucial moment" relies on what I see as an adventure—a departure from home before marriage to learn from an alternative mother figure—to "inspire the girls to love learning."[14] My reading is indebted to Dolan's, but diverges from her focus on marriage and motherhood, as well as from the more general scholarly preoccupation with Smith's lessons for adult educators rather than young thinkers. Instead, I explore how Smith's new kind of book imagines a form of gendered adolescence "grounded ... in interconnection and nurturance" that Myers describes in Edgeworth's later "growing up fictions for girls."[15] This mode of identification with a peer group away from home is prescient and associated in twentieth-century YA with a rebellious spirit that Spacks and Gustafson think is at odds with eighteenth-century didactic and courtship plots.[16]

The idea that Smith subverted narratives depicting marriage as the immediate end of girlhood dates back to early critiques of her publications, such as Richard Polwhele's *The Unsex'd Females* (1798). This poem positions Smith in her own rebellious peer group: "See Wollstonecraft, whom no decorum checks / Arise, the intrepid champion of her sex; / ... She spoke, and veteran Barbauld caught the strain ... And charming Smith resign'd her power to please, / Poetic feeling, and poetic ease."[17] Smith celebrates Anna Laetitia Barbauld throughout *Rural Walks*, and Smith's contemporaries classed her with the "Cursed Barbauld Crew": Charles Lamb's catchall for women writers who learned from Mary Wollstonecraft via Barbauld. Lamb maligned the Crew not because they wrote educational texts for girls (as did Lamb), but because he agreed with Coleridge that children's stories ought to use marvels, such as "Magicians & Genii," to spark their wonder.[18] Teresa Michals's summary of Lamb's complaint—that the Crew depicted growing up as "a steady increase in reason rather than a traumatic loss of wonder"—draws out his adherence to an Enlightenment opposition between reason and wonder that supposedly separated Wollstonecraft's "rational mothers" from Romantic poets.[19]

Yet, as Polwhele's oddly complimentary critique suggests, Smith's feminism differed from that of her predecessors. As a poet, Smith does not fit neatly into narratives about the Enlightenment opposition between reason and wonder, notwithstanding her association with the Crew. Stuart Curran sees her first prose work, *The Romance of Real Life* (1787), as an interrogation of the "structural roots of the late Enlightenment," and Susan Wolfson has suggested that Smith's books for young people are "junior romances of real life."[20] As I will show, Smith motivated her female readers to resist the dichotomy between wonder and reason, instead teaching a mode of curiosity that served to connect these phenomena.

To understand what "curiosity" and "wonder" meant for Smith, it is worth going back to Wollstonecraft. Smith's stated "purposes of your education" in *Rural Walks* ("to make you reasonable and happy" [*RW*, 15]) echo Wollstonecraft's calls for educators to offer girls "reasonable answer[s]" that "excite their curiosity."[21] Smith took these ideas further, teaching girls how to discover their own answers so that they could surpass the limitations placed on their studies. Barbauld's letter to a young female student exemplifies some of these limitations. Although Barbauld wrote that "every woman should consider herself ... rational," she nonetheless instructed her student, "you cannot investigate."[22] Barbauld also asserted that young women should not attempt to "understand the mysteries" underlying what they memorize or to seek "professional knowledge."[23] Her concerns about what kinds of investigation made a learner "professional" were timely. While "laborious curiosity" was a mark of professionalism for male scientists, popular Bluebeard stories were driving even progressive educators to describe "curious" women in misogynist terms: for example, Maria and Richard Lovell Edgeworth call Bluebeard's wife "a curious, tattling, timid, ridiculous woman."[24] What worried Barbauld and Edgeworth about girls' curiosity was its potential to latch onto subjects that they deemed inappropriate, from men's work to private lives.[25]

Smith crafts a narrative solution to the concerns expressed by Barbauld and the Edgeworths.[26] *Rural Walks*, *Rambles Farther*, and *Minor Morals* simulate conversations among adolescent girls and their mentors that identify which phenomena ought to provoke their curiosity and which they should ignore. Smith understood that, due to restrictions like Barbauld's, girl readers would, on a country walk, encounter natural and social mysteries: phenomena that were novel and initially inexplicable. The trick was getting readers to see the novel features of their natural and social environs as wonderful. Smith suggests that novelty can provoke wonder as effectively as "Magicians & Genii"—but every wonderful phenomenon that she depicts turns out to be explicable, once a wondering adolescent asks a peer or mentor about it.[27] This process brilliantly inverts an eighteenth-century narrative technique, which Stephanie Hershinow identifies, of suspending fictional teens in ignorance because "inexperienced characters require explicit and expansive depictions of social life."[28] In contrast, Smith's teens and tweens describe their own experiences through dialogues that lead from discovery to self-making: a core function of twentieth-century YA literature, according to Spacks.[29] Wonder and curiosity ultimately transform the limits on girls' education into opportunities for Smith's female young people to direct their own educations, as they move through local geographic spaces and navigate the social space between childhood and adulthood.

A Narrative Form for Feminist Curiosity

Smith's preface to *Rural Walks* introduces the book as a composite text: "unit[ing] the interest of the novel book with the instruction of the schoolbook, by throwing the latter into the form of dialogue, mingled with narrative, and by giving some degree of character to the group" (*RW*, 3). For Smith, "interest" isn't a Johnsonian means to the more laudable end of instruction. It is part of what she is teaching. Smith wants her readers to be so interested in their books that they become curious learners, asking questions that carry them beyond memorization, through interpretation, and into knowledge creation that draws upon a variety of genres, from the novel to science writing. What "narrative" form did Smith use to "mingle" these genres and inspire wonder?

In *Letters of a Solitary Wanderer* (1800) Smith offers clues, considering how "narrative" may inspire interest in the subjects prioritized in middle-class boys' education: "young persons, who have no taste for any thing but narrative, may sometimes by the ... Novel, learn what they would never have looked for in books of Geography or Natural History."[30] Smith's Wanderer then issues four pages of "criticism," comparing the kinds of "narrative" in Richardson's novels to the "romance-novel or novel-romance of the present," to Shakespeare's plays, to the "Arabian tale," and to "fable."[31] As this list—and, particularly, the hybrid terms "romance-novel or novel-romance"—suggests, Smith is reflecting on the challenge of creating a composite genre for young persons in the *Letters of a Solitary Wanderer*, which David Lorne Macdonald introduces as "unified, first of all, by a concern with narrative itself."[32] Macdonald compares the Wanderer's epistolary frame "metanarrative" with the "narrative levels" of *Frankenstein*.[33] The core of *Frankenstein* is Safie's story, and the clearest example of a layered narrative that Smith cites in her works for young persons is the "Arabian tale." When Smith considers how the "Arabian tale" ought to be combined or compared with novels, she repeatedly uses the term "collect" to describe how authors fill stories with actions (probable or improbable) and characters (realistic or unrealistic).[34] Writing, according to her Wanderer, is a process of nesting characters and events within a narrative form, or "find[ing] a fable proper to bring them forward."[35]

The Wanderer's meditation on collecting and the "Arabian tale" genre suggests a formal component of Smith's prose writing for young persons. Although Smith's *Letters* don't refer to her previous works by name, she concluded *Minor Morals* two years earlier with a feminist "Arabian tale" about an adolescent girl's escape from slavery to an all-female literary community.[36] And, in both *Rambles Farther* and *Minor Morals*, Smith writes about the *Arabian Nights Entertainments*: a "household title" that, according to Srinivas Aravamudan, inspired "fertile fictional modes, sitting ... between the novel and the fable."[37] James Beattie's chapter "On Fable and Romance," in *Dissertations Moral and Critical* (1783), introduces the *Arabian Nights* as "the only *collection*, that I am acquainted with, of Oriental fables ... which most young people in the country are acquainted with."[38] Perhaps not coincidentally, Smith's Wanderer repeats the examples that Beattie gave of how the *Arabian Nights* shaped books for "young people."[39]

The *Arabian Nights* offered Smith a popular model for female agency in storytelling as well as a narrative form in which to nest the psychological reflections of the novel within feminist instruction. Readers in the 1790s were already enthusiastic, as Ros Ballaster has shown, about "hybrid form[s] ... [of] domestic fiction and the oriental tale" depicting "the formation of modern Enlightenment subjectivity ... characterized as female."[40] *Rural Walks* embeds short stories and lessons within dialogues that are, in turn, situated within a frame narrative that chronicles adolescent girls' intellectual and social development. The lessons in each dialogue range from stories about women's lives to descriptions of marine biology to literary criticism, all of which shift the mindsets of the characters within the frame narrative. There are three main effects of cycling through genres and narrative levels in this way: curiosity, a sense of temporal stasis, and the gradual psychological healing of the characters in the frame narrative. These are akin to "the time-gaining" and "healing" effects of the *Arabian Nights*.[41]

Smith's formal use of the *Arabian Nights* to gain narrative time for female adolescents—both characters and readers—is in the spirit of Scheherazade, as it resists the normative pedagogical practices that were compressing childhood and rushing young girls into marriage. In the *Arabian Nights*, this "time-gaining" effect is the product of Scheherazade's ability to make Schahriar "curious" with her nested stories and the wonders within. She uses her "agency ... of the tongue and of time" to delay her execution and to save younger women from taking her place in marriage.[42] The most curious aspect of Scheherazade's stories is their narrative connection, as Antoine Galland suggests in his preface to the *Arabian Nights Entertainments*: "What can be more ingenious, than to compose such a prodigious Quantity of pleasant Stories, whose Variety is surprising, and whose Connexion is so wonderful?"[43] Similarly, for Smith's readers, curiosity not only comes from encounters with wonderful phenomena on her fictional adolescents' rambles, but also from the experience of figuratively rambling through different genres.[44] *Rural Walks* creates a sense of temporal stasis by layering many stories within a frame narrative that depicts gradual shifts in its female characters' psychologies, making time for adolescent identity development.

Rural Walks Toward Curiosity

In *Rural Walks*, a thirteen-year-old Miss Caroline embodies the psychological dangers of compressing girlhood and adulthood, bringing the "darkness of a December night" and a cold "air of haughty superiority" into her cousins' rural home (*RW*, 6). While Caroline lived in London until her mother's recent death, Elizabeth (thirteen) and Henrietta (eleven) grew up with their mother, Caroline's Aunt Woodfield. Mrs. Woodfield is an older, wiser version of Caroline, whose own "accomplishments" left her only with the "necessity of retiring from the world" at age thirty-five, after her husband died (*RW*, 5). Woodfield immediately spots the tension between Caroline and her daughters and holds out the promise of stories as an incentive to explore their house. As they approach Caroline's bedroom, Woodfield gestures to a shelf and asks after her books, beginning the first of two parallel discussions about books that set the pedagogical agenda of the two volumes of *Rural Walks*. When Caroline replies "sighing" that she has "but very few," she reveals the mindset that Woodfield needs to help her change in volume 1 (*RW*, 7). Caroline cares about the quantity of books that she possesses—how they will look on her shelf—more than the stories they contain, so Woodfield promises to "find ways to increase your collection," positioning herself as a provider of stories, like Scheherazade (*RW*, 7).

This frame narrative, in which a female character enters a bedroom and promises stories to adjust the mindset of a new family member, recalls the *Arabian Nights*. As Caroline approaches the bedroom, Smith describes her mindset in masculine and invasive terms. Woodfield repeatedly observes the "strong resemblance" and "likeness she bore to her father," a military man conquering and colonizing abroad (*RW*, 6). As in the *Arabian Nights*, Dinarzade enters the bedroom with the sultan (Caroline) and Scheherazade (Woodfield). Elizabeth questions both Woodfield and Caroline, prompting their dialogues and bookending their stories with expressions of curiosity. As Ballaster has shown, eighteenth-century characters inspired by Dinarzade often served as "recipient, conduit, and interpreter," reminding the reader that a "third term can deflect, redirect, even block" narrative meaning.[45] Playing Dinarzade, Elizabeth often supports Woodfield in redirecting Caroline's attention.

However, just as Dinarzade's presence reminds the reader of the *Arabian Nights* what is at stake if Scheherazade fails to change the sultan's mind, Elizabeth represents the threat that Caroline poses to Woodfield's community of middle-class women. Elizabeth is susceptible to her cousin's example, and volume 1 of *Rural Walks* plays out the danger that this teenage "third term" may start amplifying Caroline's harmful ideas. Early in her stay,

Caroline's dialogues are occasioned by her longing for balls and suitors, her insults toward her cousins' way of life, and her ignorance of her new social and natural environment. In turn, the short stories embedded within these dialogues often depict the threats that a marriage-minded education posed to middle-class adolescents, with results ranging from embarrassment to familial suffering and death.[46] These stories suggest that if *Rural Walks* cannot change its characters' and readers' perspectives on women's education and marital prospects, the consequences may be lethal—and these are the life-and-death stakes of the *Arabian Nights*.

In response to this danger, Smith maps out a pedagogical trajectory toward adolescent self-regulation that readers without a real Aunt Woodfield could follow. In the early dialogues, Woodfield gives the girls techniques to identify and discourage their longing for wealth and urban leisure so that they can develop a sense of curiosity and initiate later dialogues themselves. When Caroline extols the luxuries of London and imagines her country neighbors as "twaddlers and quizzes," Elizabeth begins thinking in her language, calling her neighbor "a bore" (*RW*, 13, 14).[47] In reply, Woodfield dismisses urban luxuries as boring—"it is not wonderful" that their neighbor does not care about them—and mocks "the absurdity of pretensions to what one cannot reach" (*RW*, 14, 15). Instead of acting like an adult authority and correcting Caroline, Woodfield plays the teasing peer. She has only to mention "*your* pretensions" for Caroline to realize "I *am* to be mortified," which effectively announces the narrative death of her threatening, condescending persona (*RW*, 16). In turn, Smith's reader learns how to redirect harmful attitudes within peer groups, without the assistance of an adult educator or a ban on curiosity.

This strategy transforms Caroline from a threat into a more equal interlocutor, as the reader learns from her question at the start of volume 2. She asks after the books that Woodfield promised on their first night together: "May I ask what the books are?" (*RW*, 57). Since Caroline is no longer thinking about books as objects to be amassed and counted, Woodfield helps her learn how to properly interact with books, which will in turn help her understand what they are. Woodfield recalls the books that she read at two stages of her life— her childhood until age eleven and her subsequent youth—and her memories cast her in the role of a fellow adolescent learning how to read, communicate, and think. Before age eleven, Woodfield read unsupervised, in a house without novels, "delight[ing] in the little narratives ... in the Spectator, Guardian, Tatler, World, Rambler, [and] Adventurer" (*RW*, 57).[48] Woodfield suggests that these periodicals trained her memory, describing how she read them "with such avidity and interest, that I believe I could now repeat every one" (*RW*, 57–58). Memorizing short, composite works prepared Woodfield to interpret longer ones. At age eleven, Woodfield secretly subscribed to a circulating library that provided her with Richardson's *The History of Sir Charles Grandison*. When she was caught in the act of novel reading, her father told her "that the more I read the better he should be pleased. ... He blamed me, however, for doing any thing clandestinely" (*RW*, 58). Consequently, Woodfield developed a social method of reading in which girls select their books, discuss them, and develop a capacious desire to learn from genres beyond the novel.

Woodfield's story anticipates William Godwin's argument in "Of Choice in Reading" (1797). Godwin considers what would happen if a "daughter is prohibited from novel reading" and imagines that "a wall of separation is thus erected between children and adults ... reciprocity is destroyed."[49] A better alternative would be a social space between childhood and adulthood in which girls contribute to their communities, much as the Edgeworths' *Practical Education* recommended: "let their useful curiosity be encouraged; let them make a part of the general society of the family."[50] Godwin explains how "to curiosity, it is particularly incident, to grow and expand itself under difficulties," and suggests that restricting a daughter's reading would reduce her desire to learn to mere reaction.[51] His defense of girls' self-regulated curiosity is an argument that *Rural Walks* makes earlier and in a more activist form: teaching adolescent girl readers to leverage curiosity and choice to develop their memories, friendships, and powers of analysis.

Woodfield's narrative approach of introducing her own adolescent self into the dialogue prompts Caroline to engage with her as an imagined peer and to begin answering her own question as to "what the books are." Caroline playfully builds on Woodfield's interest in Richardson, laughing about Sir Charles's "dull" manners and out-of-date wig (*RW*, 59). While her remarks may sound silly, they are emblematic of a larger problem—Richardson's "tedious" detail—that Smith critiques in her *Letters of a Solitary Wanderer*.[52] When Woodfield teases Caroline that Charles may not have worn a wig, Caroline's response reveals that their dialogues have made her memory as keen as her aunt's, recalling that "Lovelace complains, in one of his letters, that his wig was wet" (*RW*, 59). This is a remarkable attention to detail for a teenager who recently saw books as objects to count, rather than stories to investigate, and Woodfield recognizes Caroline as "minutely well read" and draws her into an interpretive discussion that includes Shakespeare (*RW*, 61). Elizabeth, who is listening, later remembers Woodfield's willingness to serve as an imagined peer in debates about fiction, and she picks up where Caroline leaves off in the third dialogue of *Rambles Farther*, "Wonders." Unlike Caroline, who begins her metafictional dialogue with a conciliatory question, Elizabeth launches "Wonders" by departing from Woodfield's intended lesson. It is through Elizabeth's metafictional intervention that Smith delivers her most direct statement on the place of curiosity, wonder, and the *Arabian Nights* in girls' education.

Rambles Farther, into "Wonders"

"Wonders" takes place at the seaside and begins in a scientific register that Elizabeth expands to include theories about genre and pedagogy. When Woodfield describes a shell as "one of these little convoluted palaces lined with pearl," Elizabeth resists her prompt to consider "the small half-animated creature for whose residence it was fitted."[53] Instead of discussing marine biology, Elizabeth wishes to "write a fairy tale, in which all manner of improbable fancies might be put ... at the bottom of the sea, and describe a palace" (*RF*, 133). She takes her mother's palace metaphor, but instead of using it to embellish a scientific story, she pivots into a fairy tale. Elizabeth's intervention illustrates and then rebuts a contemporaneous argument against young persons' having choice in their reading and opposing the wonderful "little narratives" that Woodfield praises in *Rural Walks* (*RW*, 57). James Beattie, for example, reflects that his similar childhood reading "left no trace in my memory" due to their distracting focus on the "wonderful."[54] Likewise, in *Adelaide and Theodore*, Stéphanie Félicité, comtesse de Genlis, considers children's reading habits until age thirteen and identifies the *Arabian Nights* as a text likely to inhibit their memories, claiming that "struck with the wonderful, they will remember nothing."[55] Smith, on the other hand, identifies wonder as a literary phenomenon that authors should winnow from "improbable fancies" and then plant in scientific texts for young readers.

Elizabeth's interest in "improbable fancies" is productive, launching a conversation on how girls can become authors and naturalists by remembering a variety of genres, identifying their useful components, and remaking them into composite stories. She and Woodfield shift their conversation from natural science to fantastic maritime texts, including the *Tempest*, to "histories," "romances," and "novels," and they identify two deterrents to learning that fantastic stories and histories have in common (*RF*, 133–35). First, fantastic tales and histories often use stock characters to set their plots in motion. Second, the plots of many fantastic tales, novels, romances, and histories are identical and thus equally improbable. Woodfield's example for these arguments reveals her persistent suspicion of Elizabeth's "improbable fancies": the "mischief-working character [who] is supplied by an uncle or guardian ... who, with little more probability than if a griffin or a mer-man was introduced, carries away the luckless beauty" (*RF*, 135). Woodfield's critique draws on an "anti-marvelous aesthetic" that, according to Lorraine Daston and Katherine Park, influenced rational education and natural science in the late eighteenth century. This aesthetic equated "'verisimilitude' in art with 'order' in nature," but paradoxically used readers' "opinions ... as to what was possible or proper," rather than "fact," to measure plausibility.[56]

Elizabeth's reply is Smith's demonstration of what adolescent girl readers have to offer in debates about what is "proper" for their education and ought to be plausible in their lives. She adds a feminist dimension to Woodfield's critique, arguing that "I had rather read fictitious tales, though I know them not to have even a resemblance of the truth, than history, which is nothing in general but a melancholy account of the crimes some wicked men have been guilty of, to destroy other men not less wicked" (*RF*, 135). Elizabeth is frustrated with misogynist narratives that just recount men's violence—truths that are not yet and should not ever be part of her lived experience.[57] Her interest in fairy tales, it turns out, is a search for stories that don't replicate unrelatable patriarchal narratives and so discourage female readers. Elizabeth is trying to imagine a kind of anti-patriarchal narrative that she would find interesting and "proper." To that end, she provokes Woodfield into exploring what fantastic, improbable stories can do that histories and novels can't.

Woodfield also has a feminist goal: to make sure that no narrative distracts young women from gaining the education that her generation lacked. When Elizabeth hints that a lack of probability isn't the problem with patriarchal narratives—"it is not always the most improbable of these sort of histories that amuse the least" (*RF*, 135)—Woodfield responds that this is because of the way in which Elizabeth has been taught to react to them. Elizabeth's ability to calmly analyze stories is a result of progress in girls' education. "You, Elizabeth," Woodfield says, "have been rather taught to see every object around you as it really is, than to be either pleased or frightened by the fables which, when I was in the nursery, were admitted" (*RF*, 135). This education bolsters Elizabeth's authority as a mature interlocutor, and when Woodfield reveals that her nursery maid's frightening tales distracted her from noticing scientific phenomena on rural walks, she temporarily becomes a vulnerable child looking to Elizabeth for direction. Woodfield's memories of these stories are traumatic. They leave her disoriented as she admits, "I know not how, Elizabeth, we have wandered from coral alcoves and arbors of shell-work to legends" (*RF*, 136).

Smith offers the reader a way out of this traumatic episode by prefacing it with a concession from Woodfield regarding improbable stories: "if I could be amused with the book called the Arabian Nights, it would be with those parts of it that are most wild and improbable" (*RF*, 135). Whereas the rest of "Wonders" complicates a series of binaries, of improbable versus probable and fairy tales versus histories, this mention of the *Arabian Nights* introduces degrees of wildness and wonder to the conversation. It is no coincidence that "Wonders" imitates the formal aspects of the *Arabian Nights* that Galland called "so wonderful": the "quantity," "variety," and "connexion" of its stories.[58] "Wonders" contains a wide variety of stories, ranging from fairy tales and criticism to science, religious reflections, economics, history, and geography. Woodfield's distressed puzzlement, "I know not how, Elizabeth, we have wandered," admits that their movement through genres is wild and improbable. This metafictional wandering occasions fear for Woodfield—a significantly different emotion than Elizabeth's curiosity—because Woodfield has forgotten the larger context, or narrative frame, of the stories of her girlhood. "Wonders," like the *Arabian Nights*, nests stories within stories, and Woodfield clarifies that her traumatic childhood experiences were born not out of "our love of the marvelous," but rather from her nurse's tendency to locate the "evils of life" in her immediate environment, without using a fictional frame to foster critical distance (*RF*, 135–36). Woodfield recovers from these memories by returning to her present narrative frame and recounting a maritime tale, thereby reversing her confusing trajectory from "arbors of shell-work to legends."

Smith thus identifies what wonderful tales do better than histories, novels, and romances. They interest young readers enough to memorize associations between their lessons and their settings or narrative frames. This makes wonderful tales a powerful vehicle for lessons on local or fictional rambles. The oddly metafictional way in which Woodfield recovers—refocusing on a layer of wonderful stories between naturalistic observation and childhood memories, moored in her maritime surroundings—shows how Smith is teaching wonder by degrees in *Rambles Farther*. She embeds prompts for stories within the seaside setting of "Wonders," and these prompts lead to fairy tales and science lessons. The prompt for Elizabeth's wonder, which fosters her critical inquiries, is novelty. Woodfield suggests that "in looking over this immense collection of water ... your imagination immediately went forth to the wonders contained in its bosom. This is because you are not accustomed to see it" (*RF*, 136). Although Smith attributes her most controversial ideas about how novelty and wonder can inspire girls' learning to the size of the sea, hinting that Elizabeth is overwhelmed, the cause of Elizabeth's initial curiosity was a metaphor about a tiny shell.

Elizabeth's literary interest in the metaphor of the shell palace may initially seem a distraction from examining the "minute works of nature," but it leads her to model and critique a process of wondering that motivates science lessons well beyond her particular story (*RF*, 132). Rosamond's similar "curiosity" in Edgeworth's "Wonders" (1813) "echoes through the nineteenth century," as Mitzi Myers has shown, suspending the famous Rosamond in a period of "growing up."[59] Smith's "Wonders" offers a metafictional blueprint for this extended adolescent wondering and learning, including strategies that real-life Elizabeths could use to create hybrid narratives to replace old histories. One strategy is to borrow wondrous images, metaphors, and expressions of curiosity from fantastic tales like the *Arabian Nights* and then set them in environments that girls can wander through to identify local encouragements of learning. Another strategy is to foster metaphoric wandering by adapting the layered structure of the *Arabian Nights*: connecting a variety of genres within a frame narrative, thus guiding the reader's mind to wander and wonder.

Minor Morals by and for Adolescent Feminists

Elizabeth's interest in using wonder to create a new kind of "proper" story for adolescent girls, empowering them to oppose the psychological threats of patriarchal narratives, motivates Smith's final work of prose for young persons. While the frame narrative of *Rural Walks* imagines a virtually all-female community in which Caroline initially represents a masculine threat, *Minor Morals* shows how adolescent girls were not safe intellectually (or physically) on rural walks. On an "An Evening Ramble in the Forest," Smith's adolescent girls overcome the psychological harm of disempowering stories. As a reward, they meet a young woman straight out of a feminist "Arabian tale" and learn about her story of outsmarting and escaping her enslaver. This liberating trajectory continues in the frame narrative, as the women engineer their lives to spend time away from their husbands and brothers, choosing instead to form a community of girl authors.

Smith's "Ramble" sends Sophia (age twelve) and her cousin Mary (nine) into the woods with a Charlotte who, like her author, carries them from one genre to another and ultimately to a female community (*MM*, 294). Charlotte guides Mary and Sophia from their study of plant "specimens" into gothic fiction (*MM*, 294). Her quixotic play, "fancying ourselves like the wandering Lady in Comus," forces the girls to confront their fears of threatening men in literature and life (*MM*, 295). Although Charlotte insists "there is no danger here," she does not yet understand that stories like *Comus* pose a psychological danger, evident in their power to interrupt Sophia and Mary's learning with fears of kidnapping (*MM*, 295). Charlotte learns her lesson when the girls realize they are lost. They become a gaggle of Catherine Morlands, experiencing "mute amazement not unmingled with dread" (*MM*, 296) when a Stranger appears and brings *Comus* to life, offering to "direct you to another house" (*MM*, 299). Charlotte, although "alarmed," tells Sophia and Mary that "we can do nothing now but trust ourselves," and as though in answer to this readiness to rely on female community, a woman steps out of the cottage, shattering the gothic atmosphere (*MM*, 299). She offers information that the Stranger, her son, should have given sooner: their family name (Airsley) and their connection to Charlotte's family. More importantly, she introduces them to her other son and his wife, Zulmine, whose story of escaping slavery guides the girls into a new genre.

Zulmine's narrative contrasts women's communal work toward liberation with men's ineffective attempts to manage them. The male characters conform to national stereotypes and the gender roles of gothic novels: a Turkish husband who purchases child wives, "French privateers" who kidnap women, two British naval officers who want to rescue them, and a "cunning Italian" who helps for a price (*MM*, 302–5). Airsley risks flattening Zulmine into these national and gendered stereotypes, asking if Charlotte has "national dislikes," but Charlotte resists, insisting that "I should like extremely to hear an account" of Zulmine's story (*MM*, 301). Although Airsley narrates this account, only the female characters in Zulmine's narrative defy stereotypes, form friendships, and save themselves.[60] In the narrative, after Zulmine is kidnapped and purchased, she meets Zelmahide, the wife of her enslaver. Zelmahide "fears for the loss of her liberty, or even her life" should she ever lose her violent husband's favor (*MM*, 302). This mindset initially sets her at odds with Zulmine, whom Zelmahide worries will become "so formidable a competitor" for her husband's "heart" (*MM*, 302). However, once Zelmahide perceives her supposed rival's terror, she "venture[s]... with considerable art" to see if she can help Zulmine escape (*MM*, 302). Further, she asks for "the consent of Zulmine" in arranging her flight, thereby putting Zulmine in charge of her own future (*MM*, 303).

This transformation, from would-be competitors to consensual collaborators, puts Zelmahide and Zulmine in the positions of Scheherazade and Dinarzade: resisting a violent husband by exchanging questions and information. As in the *Nights*, this partnership keeps one woman alive and the other unmarried due to their joint daring and cleverness. For much of the story, Zelmahide works on her plan to liberate Zulmine in the absence of the Englishmen, who waste narrative time regretting their inability to free Zulmine on their own. Meanwhile, Zulmine's collaboration with Zelmahide transforms Zulmine into a character with emotions, rather than a threat in Zelmahide's eyes. She becomes Zelmahide's "trembling friend, now no longer her dreaded rival" (*MM*, 303). Zulmine only manages to escape because Zelmahide dresses her as a boy and directs the Englishmen to flee moments before shots are fired at them.

Ultimately, Zulmine and Zelmahide's story offers an alternative to the male characters' fixed, national senses of honor and their inability to act without women's consent and leadership. Their narrative inspires a literary-critical conversation involving the *Arabian Nights* and a sonnet that Charlotte wrote. This discussion inspires the girls to expand their "studious circle," in which Zulmine finally gets to narrate her own stories (*MM*, 306). Charlotte, Sophia, and Mary are "delighted to hear from her accounts of the people and the places she had seen, so unlike what they had been accustomed to" (*MM*, 306). Although Smith does not relay these stories, they break down cultural boundaries among the girls, teaching them "that sense and goodness may be the product of every part of the world" (*MM*, 306). When a character out of the *Arabian Nights* steps into a "Ramble in the Forest," she inspires adolescent girls to explore what counts as a good story and who can tell one.

Giving Stories to Girls and Understanding Their Origins

Smith's *Minor Morals* leaves the reader with a group of young women developing the kind of new stories that Elizabeth wants to create in *Rambles Farther*. Both books imagine ways of delaying the threats that came with adulthood. In Smith's experience, these dangers included marriage to predatory men, or being "'sold <u>a legal prostitute</u> in my early youth' to a 'monster.'"[61] Smith's metafictional efforts to teach adolescent girls curiosity are her response to the poverty, homelessness, and spousal abuse that she both personally endured and witnessed among other women. When Smith was working on the *Rural Walks* series, her daughter Augusta was ill, and she was trying to fund her travel to the seaside to recover.[62] Augusta would die at age twenty, when Smith was writing *Rambles Farther*, and "Wonders" unfolds in the environment that was supposed to heal her.[63] Smith imagined another kind of healing in this dialogue: a therapeutic change in the mindset of young women. If Smith could make her readers curious learners, perhaps they would not rush toward marriage as their only option for survival.

Smith was aware that most adolescent girls wouldn't have a Bignor Park, an Aunt Woodfield, or a private library to support their education. While writing *Rural Walks*, Smith herself lacked this stability. Soon after, she wrote a letter identifying her books as her one source of emotional and financial security, lamenting an approaching sale of "the last property I have or can trust to for future subsistence—my books."[64] This context reveals the primary task for Smith as a feminist author and educator. Before teaching girls how to respond intellectually to their reading, she had to give them as many stories as possible. Perhaps the most impressive feat of Smith's works for young persons is their capacious quoting, paraphrasing, and excerpting from a wide variety of genres: all to offer readers a layered library to provoke their curiosity without creating a disjointed narrative. Any adolescent reader lucky enough to purchase one of Smith's books or to live near a circulating library where one was available would receive a starter pack for interdisciplinary learning.

Today, any scholarly reader who engages with Smith's new "kind" of book for "young persons" will have another kind of starter pack. Smith offers a beginning for syllabi and studies investigating the global feminist history of the YA novels that continue to inspire our students' curiosity about literature and culture. Historians and literary theorists of eighteenth-century fiction ought to be curious about literature for adolescent girls for the same reasons that Smith was. Feminist YA novels continue to influence our students and the literary marketplace, giving tweens and teens narratives with which to think critically about their gender identities and their rights. As scholars, we cannot hope to identify early examples of these fictions and understand what they taught young readers without tracing their global roots—especially when it comes to texts that ironically present themselves as local stories, such as Smith's.[65] If we are to grasp how subversive adolescent girls' curiosity and self-guided learning were to Western cultural norms, then we must ask how they found narrative forms through fictions from the East.

Notes

1. Smith to Thomas Cadell, 11 June 1794, in *The Collected Letters of Charlotte Smith*, ed. Judith Phillips Stanton (Bloomington: Indiana University Press, 2003), 127. For Smith's finances, see Susan J. Wolfson, "Charlotte Smith: 'To Live Only to Write & Write Only to Live,'" *Huntington Library Quarterly* 70, no. 4 (2007): 634; and Loraine Fletcher, *Charlotte Smith: A Critical Biography* (Basingstoke: Macmillan, 1998), 235.

2. "*Rural Walks*" in Charlotte Smith, *The Works of Charlotte Smith*, ed. Stuart Curran, vol. 12, *Rural Walks, Rambles Farther, Minor Morals, A Narrative of the Loss of Catherine*, ed. Elizabeth A. Dolan (London: Pickering & Chatto, 2007) iv. Subsequent citations to *Rural Walks* will be made parenthetically as *RW*. Subsequent references to this set will be abbreviated as *Works*.

3. My dissertation identifies and historicizes the feminist adventure novel, an Anglo-American genre that grew from *The Thousand and One Nights* and empowered female readers to negotiate their identities, rights, and educations between childhood and adulthood. While feminist adventure novels were not exclusively about or for

teenagers, I combine reception studies with a history of prescient ideas surrounding adolescence from the eighteenth through early twentieth centuries to argue that this genre is a primary root of young adult (YA) fiction. I am scheduled to defend in Spring 2025 at Harvard University under the direction of Deidre Lynch. I have also published an article drawn from the first chapter: "Sarah Fielding's Feminist Literary Pedagogy, in Which Nasty Women Become Novel Writers," *ELH* 90 no. 1 (2023) 29-54.

4. See Hughes, "Children's Literature: Theory and Practice," *ELH* 45, no. 3 (1978): 542–43; and Michals, *Books for Children, Books for Adults: Age and the Novel from Defoe to James* (Cambridge: Cambridge University Press, 2014), 4, 9–10.

5. Myers identifies Edgeworth's fiction "tailored for a teen audience" as "historical young adult literature" that encourages quixotic reading ("Quixotes, Orphans, and Subjectivity: Maria Edgeworth's Georgian Heroinism and the (En) Gendering of Young Adult Fiction," *The Lion and the Unicorn* 13, no. 1 [1989]: 21–22). Hershinow notes that Burney presented herself as a "teen writer" (*Born Yesterday: Inexperience and the Early Realist Novel* [Baltimore: Johns Hopkins University Press, 2019], 115); Gustafson calls attention to Sarah Trimmer's 1802 assertion that "all young gentlemen and ladies [are] Children, till they are fourteen, and young persons till they are at least twenty-one" ("Assimilation and Indeterminacy: *Moral Tales for Young People*, *Belinda*, and Edgeworth's Destabilizing Fictions of Maturity," *Eighteenth-Century Fiction* 29, no. 4 [2017]: 639). Kittredge elaborates that Trimmer's books for "labouring-class teenage girls" are "literary forbears" of YA ("'For the Benefit of Young Women Going into Service': Late Eighteenth-Century Proto-Young Adult Novels for Labouring-Class Girls," *Women's Writing* 23, no. 1 [2016]: 107–8).

6. Spacks, *The Adolescent Idea: Myths of Youth and the Adult Imagination* (New York: Basic Books, 1981), 7. Spacks regards puberty as the beginning of adolescence (6).

7. Spacks, *Adolescent Idea*, 265.

8. Borsay, "Childhood, Adolescents and Fashionable Urban Society in Eighteenth-Century England," in *Fashioning Childhood in the Eighteenth Century: Age and Identity*, ed. Anja Müller (Aldershot: Ashgate, 2006), 59.

9. Borsay, "Childhood, Adolescents and Fashionable Urban Society, " 56–57.

10. Smith to the Earl of Egremont, 4 February 1803, in *Collected Letters*, 522.

11. See Jacqueline M. Labbe and Elizabeth A. Dolan, "Introduction," in *Placing Charlotte Smith*, ed. Jacqueline M. Labbe and Elizabeth A. Dolan (Bethlehem: Lehigh University Press, 2021), 9.

12. Labbe and Dolan, "Introduction," 6.

13. See Claire Knowles, "'Far from My Native Fields Removed': Gentility, Displacement, and the Idea of Home in the Life and Poetry of Charlotte Smith," in *Placing Charlotte Smith*, 50.

Smith created the market for this kind of literature. Her 1795 title page names "Children" as her audience, even though her preface identifies "girls of twelve or thirteen," "young persons," and readers "emerging from childhood." By the fourth edition of *Rural Walks* (1800), the new subtitle, "intended for the use of young persons," coincided with Smith's criticism in *Letters of a Solitary Wanderer* (1800) on experimental writing for "young persons." See Elizabeth A. Dolan, "Introduction," in Smith, *Works,* Vol. 12, vii; and Labbe and Dolan, "Introduction," *Placing Charlotte Smith,* 12.

14. Dolan, "Collaborative Motherhood: Maternal Teachers and Dying Mothers in Charlotte Smith's Children's Books," *Women's Writing* 16, no. 1 (2009): 10.

15. Myers, "Quixotes, Orphans, and Subjectivity," 25.

16. Spacks, *Adolescent Idea*, 236; Gustafson, "Assimilation and Indeterminacy," 639.

17. Polwhele, Richard, and Thomas James Mathias. *The Unsex'd Females: A Poem, Addressed to the Author of The Pursuits of Literature.* Vol. no. 38293. Early American Imprints. (New-York: Re-printed by Wm. Cobbett, 1800), 16, 19, 21. See also Stuart Curran, "Charlotte Smith, Mary Wollstonecraft, and the Romance of Real Life," in *The History of British Women's Writing, 1750–1830*, ed. Jacqueline M. Labbe (London: Palgrave Macmillan, 2010), 200; and Judith Pascoe, "'Unsex'd Females': Barbauld, Robinson, and Smith," in *The Cambridge Companion to English Literature, 1740–1830* (Cambridge: Cambridge University Press, 2004), 210–12.

18. See Norma Clarke, "'The Cursed Barbauld Crew': Women Writers and Writing for Children in the Late Eighteenth Century," in *Opening the Nursery Door: Reading, Writing and Childhood, 1600–1900,* ed. Mary Hilton, Morag Styles, and Victor Watson (London: Routledge, 1997), 91–92.

19. Michals, *Books for Children, Books for Adults*, 105; Wollstonecraft, "A Vindication of the Rights of Woman," in *A Vindication of the Rights of Men; A Vindication of the Rights of Woman; An Historical and Moral View of the French Revolution*, ed. Janet Todd (Oxford: Oxford University Press, 1999), 71.

20. Curran, "Charlotte Smith, Mary Wollstonecraft,," 196; Wolfson, "Charlotte Smith," 643, 650.

21. Wollstonecraft, *Thoughts on the Education of Daughters* (Bristol: Thoemmes, 1995), 18.

22. Barbauld, *Selected Poetry and Prose*, ed. William McCarthy and Elizabeth Kraft (Peterborough: Broadview Press, 2002), 475, 480.

23. Barbauld, *Selected Poetry and Prose*, 476.

24. Lorraine Daston and Katharine Park, *Wonders and the Order of Nature, 1150–1750* (New York: Zone Books, 1998), 328, 355, 343; Edgeworth and Edgeworth, *Practical Education* (London, 1798), 613.

25. The Edgeworths distinguish between "curiosity ... excited to accurate and laborious researches" and "the idle curiosity of others." This juxtaposition of "laborious curiosity" with "meddling curiosity" dates to the *Encyclopédie* (Edgeworth and Edgeworth, *Practical Education*, vi–vii; Daston and Park, *Wonders and the Order of Nature*, 328).

26. Although *Rural Walks* predates *Practical Education* and departs from Barbauld's ideas, Mary Hilton identifies *Practical Education* as "configur[ing] an experimental and holistic method of 'discovery' in education," and Michals credits Barbauld and Edgeworth with creating "age-leveled series of books" (Hilton, *Women*

and the Shaping of the Nation's Young: Education and Public Doctrine in Britain, 1750–1850 [Aldershot: Ashgate, 2007], 121; Michals, Books for Children, Books for Adults, 105–10).

27. This path from noticing novelties, through wonder, to studious curiosity was one that Francis Bacon and René Descartes taught: "novelty, rarity, variety, strangeness, and ignorance of causes" provoked wonder; "wonder caught the attention; curiosity riveted it" (Daston and Park, Wonders and the Order of Nature, 311, 314, 331). Sarah Tindal Kareem shows how novelists "solicit[ed] wonder ... adopting techniques used by seventeenth-century scientists" (Eighteenth-Century Fiction and the Reinvention of Wonder [Oxford: University Press, 2014], 3).

28. Hershinow, Born Yesterday, 3.

29. Kittredge identifies a similar mode of female "self-fashioning" in nineteenth-century novel characters' direct speech (Spacks, Adolescent Idea, 4; Kittredge, "'For the Benefit of Young Women Going into Service,'" 110).

30. Smith, Letters of a Solitary Wanderer (Poole: Woodstock Books, 1995), vi–vii.

31. Smith, Letters of a Solitary Wanderer, 26.

32. Macdonald, "Introduction," Smith, Works vol. 11, The Letters of a Solitary Wanderer, ed. Macdonald (London: Pickering & Chatto, 2007), viii.

33. Macdonald, "Introduction," xiv.

34. "It undoubtedly seems easier to collect surprising events, which, in connecting, setting probability aside, neither time, action, or place ... need be adhered to ... than to collect, as Richardson does, a set of characters acting and speaking so exactly as such people so circumstanced would act and speak in real life" (Smith, Letters of a Solitary Wanderer, 24–25).

35. Smith, Letters of a Solitary Wanderer, 25. The term "fable," which appears one sentence before "Arabian tale," was a flexible genre category. In A Natural History of Birds (1807), Smith adapts Bidpai's, La Fontaine's, and Aesop's fables, and according to Ballaster, Johnson's definition of "fable"—"'a feigned story intended to enforce some moral'"—informed feminist experiments with the Nights and the novel (Fables of the East: Selected Tales, 1662–1785 [Oxford: Oxford University Press, 2005], 2). See too Jacqueline M. Labbe, "'The Absurdity of Animals Having the Passions and the Faculties of Man': Charlotte Smith's Fables (1807)," European Romantic Review 19, no. 2 (2008): 157–62.

36. Dolan calls this "an adventure story with an Arabian Nights flair" ("Introduction," xvii).

37. Aravamudan, Enlightenment Orientalism: Resisting the Rise of the Novel (Chicago: University of Chicago Press, 2012), 12, 29. Alf Layla wa-Layla became Antoine Galland's Les Mille et Une Nuits (1704–17), which went viral in England as the Arabian Nights Entertainments (see Robert L. Mack, "Cultivating the Garden: Antoine Galland's Arabian Nights in the Traditions of English Literature," in The Arabian Nights in Historical Context: Between East and West, ed. Saree Makdisi and Felicity Nussbaum [Oxford: Oxford University Press, 2008], 54–55).

38. Beattie, Dissertations Moral and Critical: On Memory and Imagination. On Dreaming. The Theory of Language. On Fable and Romance. On the Attachments of Kindred. Illustrations on Sublimity (London, 1783), 509–10 (emphasis mine).

39. They both held up "necromancers" and "Genii" as examples of characters from the *Arabian Knights Entertainments* (and the "Arabian tale" more generally) to compare to Richardson's characters (Beattie, *Dissertations Moral and Critical*, 511; Smith, *Letters of a Solitary Wanderer*, 25).

40. Ballaster, "Narrative Transmigrations: The Oriental Tale and the Novel in Eighteenth-Century Britain," in *A Companion to the Eighteenth-Century English Novel and Culture*, ed. Paula R. Backscheider and Catherine Ingrassia (Oxford: Blackwell, 2005), 86.

41. See Fedwa Malti-Douglas, *Woman's Body, Woman's Word: Gender and Discourse in Arabo-Islamic Writing* (Princeton: Princeton University Press, 2019), 11.

42. Ballaster, "Narrative Transmigrations," 78.

43. Quoted in Ballaster, *Fables of the East*, 18.

44. See Dolan on Smith's "impressive experiments in form": "the collection of tales for children and the natural history handbook," "the gothic, the sentimental, the Bildungsroman, the fairy tale, the adventure story, and the exotic tale" ("Introduction," *Works*, Vol 12., xvi).

45. Ballaster, "Playing the Second String: The Role of Dinarzade in Eighteenth-Century English Fiction," in *The Arabian Nights in Historical Context*, ed. Makdisi and Nussbaum, 98, 90.

46. For an overview, see Dolan, "Introduction," xviii.

47. Gustafson reads Woodfield as aiming to discourage teasing, like Dorothy Kilner's village teacher, but I think she is embracing the playfully antagonistic energy of Sarah Fielding's Jenny Peace or Jane Collier's *The Art of Ingeniously Tormenting*. I read Woodfield as a woman who uses teasing as a means of arriving at the "social benevolence" that Gustafson and I agree is her goal ("Coming of Age in the Eighteenth-Century Novel" [PhD diss., University of Pennsylvania, 2012], 132–34). Smith does identify Fielding's *Little Female Academy* as a model in *Minor Morals*: see Smith, "*Minor Morals*" in *Works* vol. 12, 217–18. Subsequent citations will be made parenthetically as *MM*.

48. Beattie identifies in these publications "many fables in the eastern manner" (*Dissertations Moral and Critical*, 511). Aravamudan confirms that they featured "extracts from the *Nights*" (*Enlightenment Orientalism*, 69).

49. William Godwin, "Of Choice in Reading," in *The Enquirer. Reflections on Education, Manners, and Literature. In a Series of Essays.* (Philadelphia, 1797), 103–4.

50. Edgeworth and Edgeworth, *Practical Education*, 587.

51. Godwin, "Of Choice in Reading," 105.

52. Smith contrasts Richardson's outdated details with the evergreen "Arabian tale" (*Letters of a Solitary Wanderer*, 25).

53. Smith, "*Rambles Farther*" in *Works* vol. 12, 132–33. Subsequent citations will be made parenthetically as *RF*.

54. Beattie, *Dissertations Moral and Critical*, 510–11.

55. Stéphanie-Félicité de Genlis, *Adelaide and Theodore, or, Letters on education (1783)* in *Chawton House library series. Women's novels*, ed. Gillian Dow, no. 2 (London: Pickering & Chatto, 2007), 32.

56. Daston and Park, *Wonders and the Order of Nature*, 358.

57. Elizabeth could mean "men" as in "humans," but her examples of "mischief-working" characters and their opponents in "histories" are all men. Women only appear in these texts as objects stolen by men, according to Elizabeth, which is why she is speaking out against these narratives.

58. Quoted in Ballaster, *Fables of the East*, 18.

59. For example, Myers asserts that Rosamond's attitude in "Wonders" influences Louisa May Alcott ("Reading Rosamond Reading: Maria Edgeworth's 'Wee-Wee Stories' Interrogate the Canon," in *Infant Tongues: The Voice of the Child in Literature*, ed. Elizabeth Goodenough, Mark A. Heberle, and Naomi B. Sokoloff [Detroit: Wayne State University Press, 1994], 61–62).

60. Smith may have had Airsley narrate Zulmine's story in order to avoid giving adolescent readers a detailed an account of the harem where Zulmine was imprisoned, and which she presumably would have described.

61. Wolfson, "Charlotte Smith," 640–41. Emphasis is Smith's.

62. Fletcher, *Charlotte Smith*, 235–37.

63. Fletcher, *Charlotte Smith*, 239.

64. Smith to the Earl of Egremont, 4 February 1803, in *Collected Letters*, 522.

65. Here, as in my dissertation, I am responding to Aravamudan's call to investigate "the impact of collections of fiction such as *The Arabian Nights* ... on global literature and culture." Smith's work and other early, overlooked YA novels span the genre dichotomies that Aravamudan critiques: "Novels Make Readers ... love home / keep company with fellow citizens ... reason like adults," whereas "Oriental Tales Make Readers ... love travel / keep company with strangers ... imagine like children" (*Enlightenment Orientalism*, 19–20).

Richard Coeur de Lion: Fighting Queens, Gothic Politics, and Heterosexual Pleasure on the English Stage

ROBERT W. JONES

From the mid-eighteenth century onward, it was possible for an idea of the medieval past to play a constitutive role in a variety of political discourses and cultural practices. Broadly Gothic themes, locations, and plots, including idealizations of the chivalric past, were sought by writers who wished to cater to a new taste for the old. Many of these investments might reasonably be described as possessing a broad political affiliation. The commitment was rarely explicitly party political, but the Gothic, whether in fiction, on stage, or elsewhere, was most often associated with patriotic or loyalist positions, especially during the final decades of the century.[1] To images of castles, damsels, knights, and other Gothic business it was possible to add affecting images of kings and queens that justified the role of modern monarchs. Thomas Warton is a fine example of such Gothic politicking. He took his position as poet laureate seriously, penning works in praise of the king and appearing to deploy the distant past to justify the present and to shape the future. Warton's verses to George III commend his resolution in war, his kindness in peace, and, in a nice turn of phrase, his prominence as a "patron king." Warton was equally interested in kings as warrior figures, "in azure steel array'd." He praised Richard I, often styled Coeur de Lion, directly in "The Crusade." His "Ode for the New Year" for 1786 continued this thought by comparing George III to Richard I, while Warton took on the role of Richard's "favourite minstrel," Blondel de Nestle, thereby placing himself at his sovereign's side.[2] These were bold moves. Richard I was not an embodiment of modern kingship, but rather a feudal monarch used to holding sway and a swaggering conqueror. Several writers, including Robert Burns and John Wolcott (Peter Pindar), found Warton's framing of George III as a warrior king worthy of complaint.[3] Nigel Leask has described how Burns deplored Warton's verse, before offering up his own complex reflections on the place of kings.[4] Not all respondents to Warton were so thoughtful. Richard Tickell and Joseph Richardson (who were members of a group of satirists, the Esto Perpetua Club, supported by the Foxite Whigs) mocked Warton in their *Probationary Odes for the Laureateship*. They deplored his clumsy installation of kingly authority on crusading terms. Nor were they inclined to indulge Warton's cosplay elevation of George III into an exemplary monarch.[5]

This tussle over the meanings of the past is characteristic of the 1780s. The decade has often been seen as preoccupied, in both cultural and political terms, with the lengthy process by which a nation defeated in North America reached what Linda Colley terms its "apotheosis, finding a new direction under George III."[6] The period has recently been reconsidered by Daniel O'Quinn, who has characterized it as gripped by a "post-American condition," a cultural moment dominated by a near-feverish attention, especially in the theater, to the task of finding an imaginable and bearable future at once compatible with the aspirations of the middling sort and with a recalibrated sense of the nation's moral purpose. The performance of gender, both onstage and off, O'Quinn argues, embodied a realm of affect, with leading players acting as avatars of deeper cultural longings.[7] O'Quinn's valuable work recovers the fractious particularity of the 1780s, revealing it as a decade of difficult and troubling peace. As Britons were to discover, war is never over, even if you want it to be. The experience was varied; if some prospered, others did not. For the most culturally prominent opposition group, the Foxites, this was distinctly the case. For much of the decade they were out of power and unlikely, it seemed, ever to return. They had triumphed early in April 1780 with John Dunning's successful motion that "the influence of the Crown has increased, is increasing, and ought to be diminished."[8] Since that high point, they had been beaten and bowed. Briefly in government in 1783, in coalition with Lord North, they lost office when George III (partly motivated by a dislike of their leader, Charles James Fox) instructed a Lord of the Bedchamber to alert the House of Lords to his inevitable displeasure should it pass Fox's India Bill, a clumsy attempt to restrain the worst excesses of the East India Company. The Lords duly complied.[9] Ignominiously ejected, although still supported by newspapers like the *Morning Chronicle* and the *Morning Herald*, the Foxites retreated into pleasure: denied government, they enjoyed themselves enormously, while still maintaining their opposition to presumptive, kingly power. In clear and present contrast stood William Pitt, George III's newly favored prime minister, austere and seemingly abstemious, loyal, and very much in charge.[10] Such an evident opposition of habits, preferences, opinions, and affiliations constituted its own deeply personal biopolitics of personal performance, which in turn created an atmosphere in which all forms of culture became mediated as political claims, even when they were not couched explicitly in the language of party.

It was into this contested political and cultural environment that both licensed theaters, Covent Garden and Drury Lane, launched productions of the French comic opera *Richard Coeur de Lion* during the autumn of 1786. Both productions were lavish, with specially commissioned sets, musical arrangements, and fine costumes that made them expensive to stage. Star performers were recruited to play opposite one another. The promise of competing productions generated much interest in the press, as it was surely designed to do.[11] Such direct competition was unusual, even within the fiercely competitive duopoly created by the Licensing Act of 1737, although rival Shakespeare productions sometimes battled for their share of the theatrical public. But on this occasion, both theaters sought prestige, political alignment, and revenue by pursuing expensive, musically rich, and spectacular productions of *Richard Coeur de Lion*, a work not previously staged in Britain. Entertainments like *Richard Coeur de Lion* in which actors sang, rather than the professional singers employed for oratorios, were a high point of any theatrical season. Such productions, another being James Cobb and Stephen Storace's *The Haunted Tower* (1789), have been understudied and their several purposes (securing each theaters' finances, promoting celebrity, and providing spectacle) sidelined by scholars in favor of apparently more serious dramas, yet they were instrumental in keeping both houses afloat. Musical entertainments and comic operas could also play key roles in the political orientation of each theater. Never simply facile diversions, musical entertainments operated within what has been termed the "continuous political argument" of the repertoire.[12] Their success relied in part on the deployment of celebrity performers in astonishing roles, which enabled deep parasocial connections with the audience and so ensured that such entertainments were part of the "domiciliary" turn that Gillian Russell argues defined late Georgian culture, as public spaces became increasingly privatized.[13] This essay, by returning our attention to a moment of theatrical competition, hopes to encourage further interest in a form of drama that held a vital place in the repertoire at both Covent Garden and Drury Lane. In the case of Drury Lane's production of *Richard Coeur de Lion*, we also get a cleverly staged form of resistance to the growing influence of the Crown via a proffered identification with sexualized celebrity power. To fully grasp this deeply Foxite accomplishment, we need first to be clear about the kinds of resources—textual, technical, and otherwise—on which both theaters could draw.

Rival Richards: The *Comédie-Italienne*, Covent Garden, and Drury Lane

Richard Coeur de Lion first appeared as an *opera comique* by Michel-Jean Sedaine and André Ernest Modeste Grêtry in Paris two years before its first production in London. The opera staged Blondel's fabled quest for King Richard I, imprisoned in Austria after he had been waylaid returning from the Crusades. It opens with Blondel arriving at the house of Sir Williams and his daughter Laurette. Sir Williams (a Welsh squire living in an Austrian village) reveals that there is a mysterious prisoner held at a nearby castle. Soon after, Laurette confesses that she is in love with Florestan, the castle's governor. Sensing that his search might be nearing its end, but not knowing how to proceed, Blondel sings, "O Richard, ô mon Roi" ("Oh Richard, Oh my King").[14] His song laments the loss of his monarch and expresses his anguished loyalty: "L'universe t'abandonne; / Sur la terre, il n'est que moi / Qui s'interesse à ta personne" ("The universe has abandoned you / On earth there is no one but me / Who is interested in you") (8). Countess Marguerite, who is also searching for King Richard, enters soon afterward and extends her assistance. Blondel goes to the castle alone, and there sings of his burning ardor ("une fièvre brûlante"), to which the king replies in song (25). This is the great moment of the opera: a unity of voices, but also one between subject and monarch. Their singing attracts Florestan's attention, and his soldiers seize Blondel. Blondel secures his release by offering to broker a meeting between Florestan and Laurette. Having returned to the village, Blondel reports he has seen the king and a plan for his rescue is commenced. During the final act, the countess's soldiers storm the castle and free their king. The victorious soldiers sing, "Ah! quel bonheur, quel plus beau jour / C'est un Roi qui vous doit un si beau jour" ("What happiness, what a beautiful day / It is a king who owes you such a beautiful day") (44). This triumphant scene brings together fighting knights, reunited lovers, and much patriotic singing. Despite a theatrical *levèe en masse*, it is Blondel's discovery of Richard that is the work's central drama: the subject saving his king through the devoted performance of his art. Countess Marguerite, by contrast, is little more than a cipher, a convenient means of supplying the necessary troops. Scholars have largely agreed that Sedaine and Grêtry's *Richard Coeur de Lion* enacts its creators' royalist aspirations, which, like Warton's verse, were articulated through a recreation of the Angevin monarchy as Gothic spectacle.[15]

The multiple Gothic elements offered by the French *Richard Coeur de Lion*—falling battlements, fighting knights, and bardic minstrelsy—were suited to the fashionable tastes of late eighteenth-century London, but there were aspects of the opera that were far less palatable. English audiences often decried French or Italian dramas as supercilious or unduly ornate. Nor was kingship understood in Britain as it was in France. For Drury Lane, which was owned by the Foxite Whig politician Richard Brinsley Sheridan, the opera was distinctly awkward. Idealizing the Revolution of 1688–89, the Whigs cherished the role of Parliament and even, under certain restrictions, that of the people. The Norman yoke had been thrown off for good, they believed, and the people (that is, "independent" men) ought to govern under a crown properly restricted; as Sheridan expressed it in *Pizarro* some years later: "The throne WE honour is the PEOPLE'S CHOICE."[16] From this perspective, Blondel's passionate loyalty could easily appear too credulous or as the actions of a mere favorite (and the Foxites had had enough of those by 1786). Such reservations did not trouble Covent Garden, for whom *Richard Coeur de Lion* provided a welcome chance to stage a rousing historical spectacular. Although Covent Garden eschewed the musical challenge posed by Grêtry's score, introducing simpler English ballad tunes instead (mostly by William Shields), its staging spared no expense, reflecting the ebullience of Thomas Harris's management of that theater. Nor was Harris, as has been claimed for Sheridan, making his theater a "supplementary site" for Whig politicking. His politics were quite different.[17] Creating the script needed by Covent Garden, Leonard Macnally expanded Sedaine's pastoral subplot by adding bawdy scenes between servants and rustics, notably a surprisingly long scene in which the hunting of rabbits is treated comically.[18] Referring to a well-known source of bawdy jokes, the *General Advertiser* thought that it obvious that the "Covent-Garden translator has called Joe Miller to his assistance."[19] While supposedly regrettable, the change in tone was not unexpected. When the *Morning Post* anticipated the rival productions, it predicted that "the *humours* of [the] pieces" would be "widely different," a view that the published play texts, as well as the reviews of the performance, fully support.[20] Macnally's text is bawdy, even vulgar, and the whole enterprise is much rougher and more immediately comic than anything that the French opera had contained.

There was more to Covent Garden's *Richard Coeur de Lion* than mere bawdy, though. It retained the fundamental chivalric quest of the *opera comique* and its resolution via Blondel's loyal craft. Macnally's script is arguably most remarkable for its emphatic patriotism. Blondel's patriotism is central to the project, as it was for Sedaine and Grétry. In Macnally's translation, Blondel sings: "RICHARD, my liege, my gallant king, / The universe abandon thee. ... A British minstrel hopes to prove, / His loyalty and love, / Nor seeks reward but from above. ... Richard, my friend, my patriot king, / Blondel remains / To break thy chains" (8). Kings are right and deserve their subjects' loyalty. The idealization "of a "patriot king" had first appeared in Viscount Bolingbroke's *Letters on the Spirit of Patriotism* in 1738, becoming a mainstay of the opponents to Robert Walpole's ministry. The phrase was then claimed by George III and his supporters after 1760, making Macnally's deployment of it a political gesture.[21] To make such loyalism still more unmistakable, a chorus of knights sing, "Soldiers strike home! / Britons ne'er flee; / Glory's our cause / Richard we'll free (53).[22] The opposition-supporting *Morning Chronicle* duly denounced such "violent professions of loyalty" and "elaborate encomiums on our free constitution" as wholly inappropriate to the offered entertainment.[23] Small wonder then that George III, dressed nattily in a "velvet blue suit" (the queen wore a "silk pompadour gown"), soon attended Covent Garden to enjoy the performance.[24] Macnally and Covent Garden had also been quick, holding their premiere on 16 October, with their rivals at Drury Lane lagging more than a week behind to open on 24 October.[25] While the delay put Drury Lane at a commercial disadvantage, it had assets that would enable their eventual triumph. It is upon those efforts and developments that I will now focus, keeping in mind the political agenda that had been set by the Covent Garden production and the different theatrical and political habitus that would frame a production of *Richard Coeur de Lion* at Drury Lane.

Richard Coeur de Lion: Translated, Revised, and Repurposed

Drury Lane benefited from Thomas Linley's greater talents as their director of music. His skills meant they retained much more of Grétry's musical score, which was something the *Morning Post* appreciated in advance.[26] An additional factor in Drury Lane's success was their scenographer, Thomas Greenwood, who was responsible for the construction of the magnificent castle required for the final act. Perhaps most importantly of all, they could draw on the services of John Burgoyne as their translator and dramaturge. He had already proved adept at writing for the stage, both before and after his disastrous role in the American War. Burgoyne's pedigree as a sentimental dramatist no doubt helped alert the *Morning Post* that the "*humours*" of the rival versions would be distinct. There would be no bawdy at Drury Lane. Drury Lane's cast, which included John Philip Kemble and Dorothy Jordan, then in her second season at the theater, was superb. Although Covent Garden employed Elizabeth Billington, Margaret Martyr, and George Inchbald, they lacked the celebrity draw of their counterparts at Drury Lane. James Boaden's remembrance of the Drury Lane production stresses the importance of the acting talent that Drury Lane was able to deploy:

> The vast popularity of Sedaine's *Richard Coeur de Lion*, in Paris, graced or rather *informed* by the divine music of Grêtry, set both our theatres to work to prepare it for the English stage. [Burgoyne] with great happiness, introduced Richard's Queen, in the situation of Blondel, and Mrs Jordan accepted the part of Matilda; while the majestic figure of Kemble was seen by the audience taking his melancholy exercise in the prison of Leopold, Duke of Austria. ... Perhaps no production ever had more effect than the Richard of Drury Lane; and so fascinating was its *ensemble*, that no alteration made afterwards, in the cast was felt otherwise than as an injury; and more voice or more science in the principals only told the opera intruders that there was a truth and a grace beyond *their* reach, and that if you did not touch the *heart*, you did nothing.[27]

Boaden emphasizes the opera's multifaceted production, while underlining the emotional impact of the performance, especially its passionate appeal to the heart. He is probably thinking of the moment when Kemble's King Richard sings to his queen and, later, when they are reunited after the storming of the castle. These scenes, discussed below, united music and terrific visual spectacle. With no expense spared, *Richard Coeur de Lion* was the triumph of Drury Lane's season. Brought forward as an afterpiece, initially paired with *The Winter's Tale*, it was performed a total of thirty-eight times in its first season, a rarely matched achievement. Revenues, crucially, were consistently high.[28] Newspaper reviewers were more equivocal. Some lamented the opera's French origins, while others questioned individual performances; but overall, the production was very well received. Such commercial and popular success was the result of much effort on the part of Drury Lane, not least in the provision of costumes and scenes, as reviewers were more than happy to acknowledge.[29]

To bring the French opera so successfully to the English stage, Burgoyne and the Drury Lane company had responded to the many challenges posed by Sedaine's *Richard Coeur de Lion* and did so in several mutually supporting ways. These require careful consideration. According to Linda Hutcheon, all translations entail many acts of reframing and recalibration. As a text moves from one language to another, it is made to fit an entire new context and often serves a new purpose. This repurposing—or, as she calls it, "indigenization"—reflects conscious choices undertaken for traceable ends; this is a valuable insight for what happened at Drury Lane to the text Burgoyne prepared and the way in which it was performed.[30] Burgoyne, we should not forget, was part of the Whig writers group that had burlesqued Warton. Just as importantly, he was working for Sheridan's Drury Lane, and like Sheridan was an opposition member of parliament and not well-liked by George III. He had therefore political and personal reasons for changing *Richard Coeur de Lion*, and a context in which to do that. His work on the text of Sedaine's *Richard Coeur de Lion* is best characterized combining both a clear gothicisation and a careful avoidance of the political commitments he had inherited from the French version. While he kept most of the existing text, translating Sedaine's words rather than replacing them (as Macnally had done), Burgoyne overwrote much of their political resonance with sentiment and forms of heterosexual identification, the confident ebullience of which was entirely and deliberately congruent with the social and cultural maneuvers of the Foxite Whigs.[31] More specifically, Burgoyne repositioned Sedaine's opera to lie within the gendered conventions of Gothic romance, which frequently suggested, to the dismay of critics like Bishop Hurd, that women could take on important roles and intervene in the action as fighting queens, plucky fugitives, or cunning nuns.[32] As a result of this shift in emphasis and focus, Burgoyne's text differed considerably from the rousing patriotism that appeared on stage at Covent Garden and in Sedaine's originally-scripted royalism. Drury Lane's *Richard Coeur de in Lion* was a Gothic questionably heteronormative drama, well suited to Foxite ends and proclivities, as well as to wider theatrical tastes, to which we will turn shortly. Gender, as a point of both identification and difference, became crucial, as did the operations of genre and repertoire as subsystems for meaning production.

Burgoyne subtitled his work *An Historical Romance*, abandoning the generic designation of comic opera preferred by Sedaine and Macnally. The shift made women (and interest in them) more critical to the drama. Sedaine and Grêtry had scarcely used their Marguerite; save for one emotive song, it was all Blondel.[33] Macnally followed suit, though he granted her, to some mockery, the name of Richard's actual queen, Berengaria. Burgoyne called her Matilda instead, a more English name.[34] He transformed the part as well. The advertisement to the playbook explains that "*In adapting the following scenes to the English stage, no adventitious matter has been introduced: some liberty, however, has been taken in effecting the principal incidence of the piece: the discovery of* Richard's *confinement being now given to* Matilda *in place of* Blondel; *as well to increase the interest of the situation, as to avoid the less affecting interposition of the heroine in the latter part of the drama.—The elegant author of this Romance will pardon a freedom which has been taken with no other view than that of giving the best assistance of our stage to his admired composition.*"[35] The swipes at Macnally's "adventitious" additions aside, Burgoyne recalibrates genre and its meanings carefully. Owning the "liberty" he has taken by replacing ever-loyal Blondel with lovelorn Matilda, he insists that the change has been made to *"increase the interest of the situation."* Commenting on this passage in its review of the published text, the *European Magazine* pronounced that the "alteration ... does great credit to the taste and judgment of the person who made it, since it gives the whole piece and its business a natural, and more powerful interest."[36]

Several theatrical and political purposes were served by the substitution of Matilda for Blondel, not least because it gave a much greater part to Jordan, creating a still more 'powerful interest' in that role. As Chelsea Philips has argued, Jordan's personal and theatrical predicaments, whether real or merely imagined, were a key part of her growing celebrity, and would always influence how the play was understood in performance. Newspaper reviews generally singled out Jordan, as if she were the dramatic focus above all else.[37] The significance of Jordan's presence on stage and the recalibration of her part was understood as hugely important, even before the Drury Lane version opened. On the day before the premiere, the *Morning Chronicle* reflected on the likely change to the tone of the repertoire at Drury Lane, hitherto dominated by tragedies which gave full vent to Sarah Siddons's terrific performances of "exemplary filial piety." If the reports received from the greenroom were correct, the paper predicted, *Richard Coeur de Lion* "cannot fail of having an extraordinary run; if so, we must probably for a little time bid adieu to the *Queen of Tears*," because Jordan, who had been all "ease and veracity" in a recent production of *Twelfth Night*, would soon hold sway.[38] The creation of a larger part for Richard's consort changed the narrative significantly, placing its focus firmly on a woman searching for her lover. A woman on her own in a foreign land did indeed heighten the *"interest of the situation,"* especially because Jordan was young, beautiful, and talented. Her introduction changed *Richard Coeur de Lion*, intensifying its focus on the predicament of women, and directing focus away from the loyal pieties of Siddons's tragic muse and toward an easier, more politically ductile performance, one imaginable as consistent with Foxite Whiggery and, just as importantly, bourgeois self-projection.[39]

With modern celebrity animating the Gothic, Burgoyne's text was never the last word. Once in production and live on stage, further remodelling and realigning *Richard Coeur de Lion* was achieved by the precise performance of roles that Burgoyne had reimagined, or even created afresh which he placed within a newly "indigenized" Whig-Gothic setting, itself resting on pre-existing celebrity identification. While such identifications might have enabled forms of lurid gratification, the roles taken by the actresses were performed and coded within what Terry Eagleton famously termed the 'femininization of discourse', enabling the production to present its remediation as moralized pleasure.[40] Burgoyne's achievement is best described as an example of sentimental Gothic in which on-stage chivalry is celebrated and framed by the medieval discourses present within the action and dialogue. Crucial ideological labor occurs as sentimental Gothic consequently enables a stylized mode of performance in which women or values associated with women are conspicuously displayed, but which also offers a viewing position that catered to a latent chivalric impulse within the contemporary moment. The commercialized and leisured audiences described by Russell and O'Quinn enjoyed the chivalric display of sentimental Gothic as a form of pastiche, but also as a call to better actions, as part of a wider cultural renovation. Vital to this appeal was the presence of actresses, who, as Felicity Nussbaum has explained, inhabited a telling duality. When they performed on stage they appeared both in their assigned dramatic role and as known actors with a well-recorded life off stage, enjoying considerable celebrity in each guise. The complex work undertaken by the Drury Lane *Richard Coeur de Lion* ensured that these opportunities were knotted together with a political imperative that was Foxite in its broad aspiration to establish a mutually beneficial relation between the monarch and the actions of the people. Yet this lofty public ambition had to be reconciled with more extravagant forms of attraction to women (often figured as a certain susceptibility to beauty and to sexual impulses otherwise denied in Georgian society), alongside horse racing, gambling, and theatrical nights out. Staunchly both heterosocial and heterosexual, Foxites were rarely keen to separate public and private with any degree of care. Overspill was often the defining feature of their behavior, as heterosexual dalliance came to characterize elite cultural forms.

The Medieval Past as Sexual and Sentimental Spectacle

Amidst Burgoyne's many other adjustments, the casting of Jordan had a double capacity: she provided a locus for romance and the performance of femininity, but she also altered the ways in which the politics of the plot were articulated. Her lovelorn femininity becomes the opera's keynote, supported by what had previously been Blondel's much-repeated theme ("Une fièvre brûlante"), which gained fresh power from its new, now female—but cross-dressed—performer. At the end of her life, Jordan told Helen Maria Williams that she had appreciated the role of Matilda, as it gave her an opportunity to attempt a more plaintive demeanor. The role, she said, "savoured of the pathetic." Fiona Ritchie is skeptical on this point, suspecting the correcting force of anxious retrospective.[41] But it might be useful to think how the performance of a certain quality of plaintiveness on Jordan's part, combined with the appearance of sexual availability (the attribute that Ritchie suspects Jordan was seeking to deny), served to enhance the ideological work of Burgoyne's refashioning of the opera. This potential would have been evident from the start. When Jordan first appeared on stage she was disguised—and so cross-dressed—as a blind minstrel with a bandeau over her eyes, who was being led by Antonio, a male role taken by professional singer Maria Theresa Romanzini, a talented mezzo-soprano. Consequently, it is Matilda, not Blondel, who first sings of her love for the king:

>Oh, Richard! Oh, my love
>By the faithless world forgot;
>I alone in exile rove,
>To lament thy hapless lot. (8)

Fidelity and infidelity are the central themes of the aria: Matilda's love is contrasted with the faithlessness of friends and the irregularities of fortune. She sings of her "One faithful heart, / From tenderest truth, / Tho' hopeless, will never depart" (6). Love is privileged above all else, such that Matilda seems the artless victim of her own chaste desire, while Richard is elegantly passive, an object of female admiration.

Sedaine's version is different in both its purpose and meaning: Blondel sings of Richard's abandonment with the love of a subject, making his declaration of loyalty the expression of a political passion—a desire to serve his king, whom he regards as exemplary. Similarly, Macnally had his Blondel sing: "Richard, my liege, my gallant King."[42] When Matilda sings of her love for Richard, it rewrites the political implications of Sedaine's text, replacing loyalty with love. A woman singing about her lover, even if he is also her king, is different than a servant singing about his master, who doubles as his king. There was also a difference of voices. Jordan's talents as a singer were notable, not least for her plaintive evocativeness. Her voice would have avoided the sonorous power that characterized the Blondel songs when they had been sung in Paris by Jean-Baptiste Guignard, a renowned tenor. What Jordan offered instead was precisely the capacity to provide an audience with opportunities to savor the "pathetic" that saw her cast as Cora in Richard Brinsley Sheridan's hugely successful sentimental-cum-anticolonial *Pizarro* in 1799.[43]

However, Burgoyne not only invented Matilda, he also changed Richard, softening his character and making him more dependent on the efforts of others. The effect of this was to recast a monarch who, according to David Hume, "passionately loved glory," was "haughty, and cruel" and, consequently, "oppressive, and somewhat arbitrary"; in other words, Richard was a brutal Norman king.[44] Burgoyne's Richard is quite different. He is not a tyrant, but a lonely captive. Where Drury Lane's production coincided with Hume's preoccupations, however, was in its deployment of affect and encouragement of a felt proximity to historical figures, a key feature, as Mark Salber Philips has noted, in eighteenth-century sentimental historiography.[45] With this in mind, it is important to reflect upon what Richard signifies in this more emotive scenario, not least because his recalibration is a fundamental part of the sentimental Gothic that the opera becomes. While Burgoyne's action focuses on the efforts of a woman, Richard remains important as the object of her quest, but he is essentially passive, awaiting rescue. His subdued appearance is apparent at the beginning of act 2 when he is seen for the first time. Alone on the castle's battlements, he is taking what Boaden calls his "melancholy exercise" with the castle's governor in close attendance. When Florestan departs, the king soliloquizes in a speech unique to Burgoyne's text:

> Oh heart! Burst not!—Oh God!—oh misery! Is this to be my lot forever! In the vigour of my days, circled with conquering laurels, the Christians shield! The scourge of haughty Palestine? Am I doom'd, Am I doom'd by a vile traitor's craft, to wear my life away in ignominious bondage! O that the efforts of my fierce despair could reach the ears of my brave distant soldiers! How would it fire their hearts to learn that their king!—their leader! but Richard is forgot, deserted by his people—by the world!—O my glory!—O ye records of my valour! O memory of my victories! What do you avail? (*he looks on a picture*)—Image of her I love!—come—O! calm, console my heart—soothe for a moment the keen sorrows that destroy me! (24)

This speech is little more than a succession of exclamations. No argument, or even much sense, is advanced. Richard simply runs through a gamut of emotions: rage, jealousy, hope, recrimination, despair. The imprisoned king makes successive appeals: to the soldiers who are enjoined to rescue him, and rebuked for not having done so; to his own self-esteem, which succumbs to his mounting sense that his "glory," "valour," and "victories" amount to little and are "forgot"; and finally to Matilda, for whom he longs, but cannot see, except in "*a picture.*" The feeling portion of the audience, to whom sentimental Gothic was directed, could see his doubts and fears and might offer their own sympathetic response, but without necessarily subordinating or sacrificing their independence to do so. As a performer, Kemble became renowned for his ability to convey strong, contrasting emotions, and the part was doubtless created with this specialty of Kemble's in mind. The scene would certainly have required his gift for "brooding inaction" to work, as Richard seems almost entirely static, fixed in a "vast tableaux."[46]

Kemble's role as Richard exemplifies the eighteenth-century investment in the performed legibility of the speaking body, with the speaker's authority deriving from the physical sincerity of his expressed feelings.[47] Such an effect might seem to be threatened by the dissonance of Richard's emotions, which, even in a comic opera, appear scarcely compatible with the demands of medieval kingship. It is not Gothic in that way, but rather sentimental. A king of England has been recreated as a sentimental spectacle, available to be seen in his lonely isolation, his masculinity and majesty troubled but not completely undercut. Despite his captive stasis, Richard is emotionally dynamic; he becomes, at least in part, like other captive figures familiar from sentimental literature, such as Laurence Sterne's *A Sentimental Journey*.[48] The portrayal of the crusader king as a man of impassioned but imprisoned sentiment is apparent when it is compared with the scenes that Burgoyne took directly from Sedaine. For example, Richard's abject speech upon his losses appears in stark contrast to the ways in which Sir Owen (replacing Sedaine's Sir Williams) had remembered him at the close of the previous act. Sir Owen's song (sung by Blondel in Sedaine's opera) relishes Richard's exertions against "Sultan Saladin": "Coeur de Lion loves the wars, / Richard's joy is blows and scars" (21). This is Richard as a hypermasculine warrior king, not the moping captive seen on the battlements of Florestan's castle. Sir Owen, a devotee of the bottle, stresses Richard's independent, vigorous masculinity. Race plays a decisive role in this realignment as well, because Saladin, by contrast, is at once servile and tyrannical:

> Let the Sultan Saladin,
> Play the rake in Palestine,
> While he claims his subjects duty,
> He is himself a slave to beauty,
> Wearing baser chains than they. (21)

Although Sir Owen's boozy lines veer toward a cruder point, what is primarily articulated here is an alignment of toxic masculinity with unpalatable kingship. Saladin's race and gender appear deviant because he lacks the power to win loyalty through anything other than force; he can only ever be a "rake in Palestine," neither free himself, nor able to do anything beyond subjugating others. His susceptibility to women is not an admirable form of heterosociability, but rather a specifically gendered failing.

The importance of sexual propriety, and, consequently, sexual expression, is confirmed when Matilda, still disguised as a blind minstrel, sings beneath the castle's battlements, and Richard answers. The only visual record of the production reveals that this scene was dominated by a massive castle that fills the stage (see Figure 1). What is striking is how diminished the actors look and how large the distances between them appear. This is most likely an attempt to capture the visual coup de theatre created by the set, rather than an accurate depiction of its actual dimensions; but it does indicate just how important the act of singing across a void would have been. The engraving reveals, in conjunction with the music and the words, an intention to create a scene of tremendous scale and emotional poignancy, rather than regal display. This occurs most obviously when, having found each other, Richard and Matilda burst into song. First, she recollects "his earliest love in happy days—of love for her, who now uncertain of his fate—yet shares his misery." She then sings a fond lament: "One night in sickness lying, / A prey to grief and pain." Richard immediately recognizes who is singing and exclaims, "O God, that voice!" (26). Encouraged, Matilda continues: "When aid of man was vain." When she stops to listen, Richard is, according to Burgoyne's stage direction, gripped by "*the extremes of surprize, hope, and joy*," but nonetheless sings in reply:

> The gentle tears soft falling
> Of her who I adore,
> My tender hopes recalling,
> Did life and love restore.

On hearing him, Matilda "*appears greatly agitated; she even appears almost fainting.*" However, she is still able to reply in song:

> A mighty king doth languish,
> Within a prison's gloom;
> Ah! Could I share his doom.
> Ah! could I soothe his anguish. (27)

There is not much here to mark out Richard as haughty or cruel. The moment of their reunion hinges upon their performance of agitation, this time shared. Their communion is complete when they sing in parallel:

RICHARD	MATILDA
The gentle tears soft falling	My gentle tears fast falling,
Of her so long ador'd,	For him so long ador'd,
My tender hopes recalling,	His tender hopes recalling,
Have love and life restor'd.	Have love and life restor'd. (27)

![Engraving: Mr Kemble and Mrs Jordan in the Characters of Richard & Matilda, in Richard Cœur de Lion. Act II Scene 1.]

Figure 1. *Mr. Kemble and Mrs. Jordan in the Characters of Richard & Matilda in Richard Coeur de Lion*, 1787. Engraving, 6½ x 4⅜ inches. Call no. ART File B957.2 no. 1. Image 21286. Courtesy of the Folger Shakespeare Library (Artwork in the Public Domain; Photograph provided by Folger Imaging Department.)

This is a gorgeous outpouring of sentimental love. Although a gendered distinction between the two is maintained by their selection of different pronouns, Richard is deeply affected. He is not free and independent. But neither is he rakish. It was doubtless this somewhat unmanly effusiveness that prompted Horace Walpole to complain to Lady Ossory that "turning the ferocious Richard into a tender husband is intolerable"—a remarkably stern judgment, given that Walpole had previously told her that Burgoyne had "written the best modern comedy" because of his grasp of high life and the correct tone required to represent it dramatically.[49]

The reunited lovers barely finish singing before Matilda is captured by Florestan's guards and Richard is returned to his cell. Matilda secures her own release, as Blondel does in the earlier versions of the scene, by tempting Florestan with her knowledge of Laurette and the village feast planned for the following evening. The exchange establishes a moment in which male susceptibility to women is set up in opposition to a sense of masculine duty. In this exchange, acceptable masculinity resides somewhere between heterosexual interest and manly resolve. Simple abstinence would be countergeneric and against the expectations and wishes of the audience. Love must conquer all. This is a form of male sexuality which although it is deeply fixated on its chosen object, differs sharply from that of the rakish Saladin, who is incapable of permanent longing, much less attachment. The power of Richard's willingness (and that of the audience as well) to succumb to the attractions of Matilda-Jordan is evident in a letter from Mary Tickell to her sister, Elizabeth Sheridan, that recounts her experience of seeing the scene performed: "The Audience were all ears & eyes, they c:d not bear the smallest interruption to their attention—[during] the prison Scene between Mrs Jordan & Kemble, I believe you might have heard a Pin drop in the Upper Gallery—but when the Guards seiz'd Matilda & Kemble was oblig'd by the Governor to retire ... the whole of the Situation struck so forcibly on the minds of the audience, that it was like an electric Shock—and they gave such repeated Applause & Bravo's that it was quite charming[.] I never saw an audience applaud so properly, and with such genuine feeling in my Life."[50] Only days earlier, Tickell had been suspicious of Jordan's performance, believing that she attracted too much attention to herself.[51] By her later account, the audience delighted in the poignant dynamic between queen and king, Jordan and Kemble, who were being torn asunder by both grand historical circumstances and the petty officiousness of the castle's guards. Sentimental Gothic's focus on the predicament (and ingenuity) of a woman at once active and engagingly vulnerable produces a great deal of theatrical affect. Gothic history becomes romance. Royalist politics are overwritten by modern chivalric pleasure.

With much of its ideological work complete, the final act of *Richard Coeur de Lion* is concerned with preparations for King Richard's rescue. In quick succession, Matilda reveals her true identity to Blondel, just as the seneschal sent by her father arrives with a retinue of knights. They immediately return to the castle, which is stormed by the knights and Sir Owen's peasants. The stage direction is long. Several phases of a battle are described, the castle's walls collapse, and Sir Owen and Blondel join Richard in routing the remaining guards. Matilda enters only as the fight concludes, but she nonetheless dominates the scene visually. By the time she strides the battlements, Jordan had made a costume change, trading her minstrel's breaches for a dress of white satin, seemingly to very good effect.[52] "God Save the King" was then sung to celebrate (with no apparent concern regarding its anachronism). Once released, Richard speaks to his liberators, and to the audience, and confirms Matilda's crucial role:

> Oh love! Oh gratitude! you impede and not inspire my efforts to express the fond transports which swell here—Neglected by my subjects, forsaken by the thankless world.— When sorrow had beat down my heart's defence—courageous hope! But oh!—Matilda! What can I say to thee, my soul's beloved! My deliverance! My reward! (*Embraces her.*) (*To* Sir Owen, &c.) I have more thanks to pay. My heart feels all it owes. And when to my native England I return, so may I prosper in my subjects love, as I cherish in the memory of my sufferings here—a lesson to improve my reign—compassion should be a monarch's nature—I have learn'd what 'tis to need it—the poorest peasant in my land, when misery presses, in his *King* shall find a friend." (50-1)

Richard is choked with emotion and chastened too, humbled by his release. In his gratitude to a woman, he might even seem unmanned. He is certainly overcome: "My heart feels all it owes." The fullness of his heart seems to prompt his promise to return to England a better man and a better king. From now on, he will be a protector of the poor, newly aware of the necessity of compassion because of his own past need for it. This happy consummation reanimates the most liberal version of Richard's return (the good king reclaiming his throne after a period of tyranny), one that is often central to the Robin Hood legend. This is a Whig fantasy of kingship (a king restored by "the PEOPLE'S CHOICE"), drawn from an utterly different moral and political universe than Hume's grim monarch.

Love's Redemption

Richard Coeur de Lion did not end with the redemption of the king—not quite. That "not quite" is important because the addition of some further material prevents the apotheosis of Richard from having the final word. Instead, the subplot gets the last flourish, when Matilda brings Florestan and Laurette together. As she does so, Matilda commends her husband's erstwhile gaoler for his "honour" and "justice," emphasizing his masculine duty only as it is subsumed within romance. Watched by the remaining cast, all three sing:

> Oh! Blest event!—Oh! glorious hour!
> Liberty and love we sing;
> Oh! may they with resistless power,
> Protect the blessings which they bring! (50–51)

So it all ends with "Liberty and love," rather than the rescue of the king. Consummation is ultimately more important than restoration. Indeed, despite the obvious temptation that these lines provide, there is no need to rhyme "sing" with "king," unless you really want to. More important is what "love and liberty" will "bring" to all: a better future. Subtle and not so subtle politicking came together with exuberant performance in the Drury Lane version of *Richard Coeur de Lion* in order to make a political intervention. Where Macnally's version is grossly and clumsily patriotic, Burgoyne's text is more nuanced. It mediates the past, muses on kingship, and considers the relations between subjects and their monarch. Love is the theme which modulates the political.

Earlier that year, the Foxites had expressed a similar preference for sexuality and reform, when they had crowded together at Drury Lane, and later in Lord Derby's townhouse, to applaud Burgoyne's comedy of the *bon ton*: *The Heiress*, starring Elizabeth Farren.[53] Farren, Derby's partner (though only later his wife and countess), played Lady Emily, who was forced to wait for her worth to be recognized. Only belatedly does her lover, Clifford, realize, after his own wealth has been restored, that he loves and must marry her. But first, Clifford and Lady Emily must recognize the value of the middle-class figures of the play, whose kindness, propriety, and good sense has underwritten their return to fortune.[54] The acceptance of Farren-as-Emily as a legitimate bride is simultaneously a social and a parasocial phenomenon, with middle-class audience members and elites each taking something from it based on their identification or acquaintance with the leading player. The conclusion of the plot marks a return to propriety (and wealth) that could tantalizingly prefigure the return of the Foxites to office, if only they would change their ways. Burgoyne anchored his appeal to his friends (Fox, Tickell, and Sheridan all attended Derby's afterparty) on moments of restoration encapsulated in a love plot that was at once wish fulfillment, a prediction of the future, and a promise to reform.

These connections, at once personal and national, were equally vital to the production and success of *Richard Coeur de Lion* because it was on these heterosocial and heterosexual terms that it became possible to imagine the romance of the Gothic past, and hence the contemporary future, in ways that could respond to the loss of the North American colonies and yet resist apparent tyranny. Men needed to reform, as did kings, and the process was to be guided by a woman, just as Matilda had led Richard. The crafty favorite is here pushed into the background. To remake the royalist *Richard Coeur de Lion* in this way required a conscious decision to disregard the generic and ideological weight associated with loyalist Gothic. James Watt defines the form as having an admonitory function, a tendency to rebuke the present, which was in part a legacy of the lost war for America. A common complaint was the present's lack of martial resolution, as compared to the valor of the ancient past. Warton's odes adopt a position much like this. Watt identifies patterns of setting and scenery in loyalist Gothic: castles feature prominently, but rarely supernatural events; the scenario is English and medieval; the action is, above all, serious and high-minded. It is also masculinist in nature, still harping on military glory and past triumphs. To this degree, loyalist Gothic frequently sets itself in opposition to the "feminised space of romance production."[55] Burgoyne chose, as he adapted *Richard Coeur de Lion*, to offer a different kind of gender politics and, in so doing, to make a different sort of political intervention. His *Richard Coeur de Lion* employs merely the scenery of loyalism. Masculinity is, insofar as Richard embodies it, passive, even lovelorn. Its martial exploits are in the past, while its sexual ones are in the present or even the future. Women, cross-dressed or expensively turned out (they are both, of course), act as the true agents of most of the action. Normative, heterosexual masculinity is objectified and reduced to mere spectatorship. There is loyalty to the monarch and it might even be said to be celebrated, but only in relation to liberty. Such liberty gets a distinctly Foxite spin, too, as befits its appearance at a site of commercialized, as well as elite, leisure. Specifically, liberty thrives most when a monarch is chastened politically but not sexually.

This is a distinctly Foxite form of politics, which makes it possible to imagine Drury Lane as a Foxite theater that, having commissioned work from a known Foxite politician (Burgoyne was the MP for Preston), had appropriated and translated a French royalist comic opera for their own ends. If they stopped short of what Hutcheon would regard as full "indigenization," they certainly at least made the story English again. By changing its meanings and its emphases, they remade *Richard Coeur de Lion* in their own image, with sexual pleasure and sentimental identification replacing homosocial fealty. Moreover, it was good to look at—Jordan especially. Even so, it's not quite correct to claim that Drury Lane's version of *Richard Coeur de Lion* was an avowedly partisan drama. At the very least, it was not consistently so (Kemble's role and performance would be an obvious sticking point). Ultimately, Drury's Lane's *Richard Coeur de Lion* is Foxite mostly on account of what they chose not to do. Yet it remains valuable to think about how the play might have appeared (or simply felt) Whiggish or how it might have worked on a Whig theatergoer who was worried about kings and tyrants, but also keen for luxuriant pleasure and a good night out. Such ardent yet convivial affiliations need to be seen as a set of cultural assumptions, styles, and habits. The Foxites were sociable and distinctively heterosocial in many respects, although they enjoyed the masculine pleasures of gambling at their clubs. They were correspondingly homophobic as a result, mocking William Pitt for his apparent aversion to "the fair."[56] Fashionable women were figures around whom events were organized or parties held. Susceptibility to women, to their beauty, charm, and talents, whether truly felt or merely performed, was central to the Foxite self-image and determined how Foxites behaved in the quasi-public world of routs, assemblies, and theaters. Toying with the possibility of forsaking these pleasures, the Drury Lane *Richard Coeur de Lion* imagined a future that did not rely on either ultra-loyalism or monarchical benevolence, but rather one that enjoined the monarch to act for the people. It was the Foxites, figured as Matilda or Lady Emily, who would lead this rescue of the nation. It is perhaps possible to imagine this alignment most readily on an evening such as 20 November 1786, when Burgoyne chose for his benefit a pairing of Sheridan's *The School for Scandal* with *Richard Coeur de Lion*. Then, with Farren as Lady Teazle and Jordan as Matilda, the house was full and the ticket receipts were pleasingly high.[57]

Notes

This essay was first delivered at the Congress of the International Society for Eighteenth-Century Studies in Rome in July 2023. I benefited on that occasion from the intelligent and perceptive questioning of the panel. Since then, I have been admirably guided by David Brewer, George Boulukos, and the two anonymous readers for *Studies in Eighteenth-Century Culture*, whose care and insight have improved this essay considerably. I would also like to thank Dafydd Moore for sticking with me on the long march from the train station to the conference venue when, in 38°C heat, we came to realize that not all roads lead to the University of Rome.

1. See Paula Backscheider, *Spectacular Politics: Theatrical Power and Mass Culture in Early Modern England* (Baltimore: Johns Hopkins University Press, 1993); James Watt, *Contesting the Gothic: Fiction, Genre, and Cultural Conflict, 1764–1832* (Cambridge: Cambridge University Press, 1999); and Fiona Price, "Ancient Liberties? Rewriting the Historical Novel: Thomas Leland, Horace Walpole and Clare Reeve," *Journal for Eighteenth-Century Studies* 34, no. 1 (2011): 19–38.

2. Warton, *The Poetical Works of the Late Thomas Warton* (Oxford: Oxford University Press, 1802), 87, 38–40, 104–7, 108–15.

3. Burns, *Poems Chiefly in the Scottish Dialect* (Kilmarnock, 1786), 113–18; and Peter Pindar, *Ode upon Ode; or, a Peep at St James's; or New Year's Day; or What You Will* (London, 1787).

4. Leask, *Robert Burns and Pastoral: Poetry and Improvement in Late Eighteenth-Century Scotland* (Oxford: Oxford University Press, 2010), 137–43.

5. [Tickell and Richardson], *Probationary Odes for the Laureateship with a Preliminary Discourse by Sir John Hawkins* (London, 1785). See also Leslie Mitchell, *The Whig World: 1760–1837* (London: Hambledon Continuum, 2005), 23, 55.

6. Colley, "The Apotheosis of George III: Loyalty, Royalty and the British Nation, 1760–1820," *Past and Present* no. 102 (1984): 94–129.

7. O'Quinn, *Corrosive Solace: Affect, Biopolitics, and the Realignment of the Repertoire, 1780–1800* (Philadelphia: University of Pennsylvania Press, 2022), 185.

8. *Parliamentary History of England from the Earliest Period to the Year 1803*, 36 vols. (London: Bagshaw, 1806–20), 21:340–68.

9. See John Cannon, *The Fox-North Coalition: Crisis of the Constitution, 1782–4* (London: Cambridge University Press, 1969), 124–28, 133. See also L. G. Mitchell, *Charles James Fox and the Disintegration of the Whig Party* (Oxford: Oxford University Press, 1971).

10. See Cannon, *Fox-North Coalition*, 228–31; Mitchell, *Whig World*, 135–37.

11. See *Morning Post*, 13 October 1786; and *Public Advertiser*, 16 October 1786.

12. Daniel O'Quinn, *Entertaining Crisis in the Atlantic Imperium, 1770–1790* (Baltimore: Johns Hopkins University Press, 2011), 16.

13. Russell, *Women, Sociability and Theatre in Georgian London* (Cambridge: Cambridge University Press, 2007), 9–11. See also Joseph Roach, *It* (Ann Arbor: University of Michigan Press, 2007).

14. Sedaine, Richard, *Coeur de Lion: Comédie en Trois Acts en Prose et en Vers mis en Musique* (Paris: Brunet, 1786), 8. Further references given parenthetically. Translations mine.

15. See David Charlton, *Grétry and the Growth of Opéra-Comique* (Cambridge: Cambridge University Press, 1986), 231–32, 240–48; Laura Mason, *Singing the French Revolution: Popular Culture and Politics, 1787–1799* (Ithaca: Cornell University Press, 1996), 46–48, 52–54, 56–60; and Mark Ledbury, *Sedaine, Greuze and the Boundaries of Genre* (Oxford: Voltaire Foundation, 2000), 283–84, 288–89. See also David Charlton and Mark Ledbury, eds., *Michel-Jean Sedaine (1719–1797): Theatre, Opera and Art* (Aldershot: Ashgate, 2000).

16. Sheridan, *Dramatic Works of Richard Brinsley Sheridan*, ed. Cecil Price, 2 vols. (Oxford: Clarendon Press, 1973), 2:669. See also Mitchell, *Whig World*, 138–44; and Matthew McCormack, *The Independent Man: Citizenship and Gender Politics in Georgian England* (Manchester: Manchester University Press, 2005), 56–79.

17. See David Francis Taylor, *Theatres of Opposition: Empire, Revolution, and Richard Brinsley Sheridan* (Oxford: Oxford University Press, 2012), *103–8, 111–13;* and Warren Oakley, *Thomas "Jupiter" Harris: Spinning Dark Intrigue at Covent Garden Theatre, 1767–1820* (Manchester: Manchester University Press, 2018).

18. Macnally and Sedaine, *Richard Coeur de Lion. A Comic Opera, as Performed at the Theatre Royal Covent Garden. Taken from a French Comedy of the Same Name, Written by Monsieur Sedaine* (London: Cadell, 1786). Citations given parenthetically in text.

19. *General Advertiser*, 20 October 1786.

20. *Morning Post*, 13 October 1786. See also *General Evening Post*, 17 October 1786; *Morning Chronicle*, 17 October 1786; and *Morning Post*, 17 October 1786.

21. See Simon Varey, "Hanover, Stuart, and the Patriot King," *British Journal for Eighteenth-Century Studies* 6, no. 2 (1983): 163–72; David Armitage, "A Patriot for Whom: Afterlives of Bolingbroke's Patriot King," *Journal of British Studies* 36, no. 4 (1997): 397–418; and Juriaan M. van Santvoort, "Chivalrous Models of Patriot Kingship: Gilbert West, Lord Lyttelton and the Idea of a Patriot King," *History of European Ideas* 44, no. 1 (2018): 14–34.

22. On Macnally's somewhat scandalous career, see Warren L. Oakley, *A Culture of Mimicry: Laurence Sterne, His Readers and the Art of Bodysnatching* (London: MHRA, 2010), 53–76.

23. *Morning Chronicle*, 17 October 1786.

24. *General Advertiser*, 20 October 1786.

25. Charles Beecher Hogan, ed., *The London Stage, 1660–1800: A Calendar of Plays, Entertainments and Afterpieces, Together with Casts, Box Receipts and Contemporary Comment: Compiled from the Playbills, Newspapers and Theatrical Diaries of the Period. Part 5, 1776–1800*, 3 vols. (Carbondale: Southern Illinois University Press, 1968), 2:927–29.

26. *Morning Post*, 14 October 1786.

27. Boaden, *Life of Mrs Jordan,* 2 vols. (London, 1831), 1:96–97.

28. Hogan, *London Stage*, 2:929–35.

29. See *General Advertiser*, 25 October 1786; *Morning Chronicle*, 25 October 1786; and *Public Advertiser*, 25 October 1786.

30. Hutcheon, *A Theory of Adaptation* (London: Routledge, 2006), 141–53. I am grateful to Anna Paluchowska-Messing, my co-panelist at the 2023 ISECS, for drawing my attention to Hutcheon's valuable book.

31. See Mitchell, *Whig World*, 39–42, 45–48, 50–53.

32. See Harriet Guest, "The Wanton Muse: Politics and Gender in Gothic Theory after 1760," in *Beyond Romanticism: New Approaches to Texts and Contexts*, ed. Stephen Copley and John Whale (London: Routledge, 1992), 118–39.

33. Sedaine, *Richard Coeur de Lion*, 35–36.

34. See *Morning Post*, 20 October 1786; and *General Advertiser*, 21 October 1786.

35. Burgoyne, *Richard Coeur de Lion: An Historical Romance* (London, 1786), "Advertisement." Subsequent references to this text will be made parenthetically.

36. *European Magazine*, 10 October 1786, 298.

37. Phillips, *Carrying All Before Her: Celebrity Pregnancy and the London Stage, 1689–1800* (Newark: University of Delaware Press, 2022), 161–206; *Morning Chronicle*, 26 October 1786; and *Morning Post*, 28 October 1786. It is worth noting that Jordan had not yet become the reputed mistress of the Duke of Clarence, so her connections to royalty were entirely theatrical, see Claire Tomalin, *Mrs Jordan's Profession: The Story of a Great Actress and a Future King* (Harmondsworth: Penguin, 1995), 113–14.

38. *Morning Chronicle*, 23 October 1786.

39. See O'Quinn, *Corrosive Solace*, 152–58.

40. Eagleton, *The Rape of Clarissa: Writing, Sexuality and Class Struggle in Samuel Richardson* (Oxford: Basil Blackwell, 1982), 13.

41. Richie, *Women and Shakespeare in the Eighteenth Century* (Cambridge: Cambridge University Press, 2014), 129–30. See also Helen E. M. Brookes, *Actresses, Gender, and the Eighteenth-Century Stage: Playing Women* (New York: Palgrave Macmillan, 2014), 93–116.

42. Macnally, *Richard Coeur de Lion*, 8.

43. See Selena Couture and Alexander Dick, introduction to Sheridan, *Pizarro: A Tragedy in Five Acts*, ed. Selena Couture and Alexander Dick (Peterborough: Broadview Press, 2017), 38–40.

44. Hume, *The History of England from the Invasion of Julius Caesar to the Revolution of 1688*, 6 vols. (London, 1762), 1:353–54.

45. Phillips, *Society and Sentiment: Genres of Historical Writing in Britain, 1740–1820* (Princeton: Princeton University Press, 2000), 60–78.

46. See Robin Simon, *Shakespeare, Hogarth and Garrick: Plays, Painting and Performance* (London: Paul Holberton Publishing, 2023), 87; and O'Quinn, *Corrosive Solace*, 187. See also Joseph W. Donohue, *Dramatic Character in the English Romantic Age* (Princeton: Princeton University Press, 1970).

47. See Boaden, *Life of Mrs Jordan*, 97. See also Paul Goring, *The Rhetoric of Sensibility in Eighteenth-Century Culture* (Cambridge: Cambridge University Press, 2005).

48. See Markman Ellis, *The Politics of Sensibility: Race, Gender and Commerce in the Sentimental Novel* (Cambridge: Cambridge University Press, 1996), 71–79.

49. Walpole to Ossory, 15 December 1786 and 14 June 1787, in *Correspondence of Horace Walpole*, ed. W. S. Lewis et al., 48 vols. (New Haven: Yale University Press, 1937–83), vol. 33: 546, 563–64.

50. Tickell to Sheridan, 25 October 1786, Folger MSS Y.d.35, fols. 281–82, Folger Shakespeare Library. Emphasis original.

51. Tickell to Sheridan, 23 October 1786, Folger MSS Y.d.35, fol. 277.

52. Tickell to Sheridan, 18 October 1786, Folger MSS Y.d.35, fol. 273.

53. Tickell to Sheridan, 14–15 January 1786, Folger MSS Y.d.35, fol. 239.

54. Burgoyne, *The Heiress, A Comedy* (London, 1786). This play was first performed on 14 January 1786 and frequently produced into the 1786–87 season.

55. Watt, *Contesting the Gothic*, 42–44, 58, 68.

56. See [Richard Tickell, George Ellis, French Laurence, and Joseph Richardson], *Political Miscellanies: Part the First* (London, 1787), 21–22.

57. On 30 November 1786 Drury Lane paired *The Heiress* with *Richard Coeur de Lion*.

"Queer Periodical Temporality": Spinsterhood in the Eighteenth-Century English Periodical

FAUVE VANDENBERGHE

The rise of newspapers and periodicals in the late seventeenth and early eighteenth centuries brought about a change in how and, importantly, *when* audiences consumed literary texts. Periodicals and other serially published texts internalized clock time. As Stuart Sherman and Benedict Anderson have famously argued, their (by definition) *periodic* and punctual publication cycles cultivated a national readership of the newly emerging middling sort, who could read the same essays and news at more or less the same time.[1] Periodicals not only regulated the news cycle and public opinion, but also influenced domestic and more normatively feminized temporalities and values, often finding themselves in the "fluid zone between public sociability and private domesticity."[2] As feminist scholars have shown, periodical literature does not always easily conform to the highly gendered Habermasian divide between public and private spheres. From women's fashion trends to marital advice, periodical literature has always been intensely concerned with women's interests.[3] While women certainly had agency in the literary marketplace, periodicals have nonetheless often been credited as important vehicles for enforcing and consolidating rigid gender norms and heteronormative structures over the course of the eighteenth century.[4] Kathryn Shevelow and Shawn Lisa Maurer, for example, have shown how periodical literature produced and regulated increasingly narrow models of sentimental, domestic, and familial femininity and masculinity.[5] Periodicals were integral to cultivating a distinctly British, homogenous reading public with shared and gendered genteel and domestic values.

Despite their incessant promotion of sentimental, middling-sort values, most periodical personas—or "eidolons"—were conspicuously unmarried. Both *The Spectator*'s (1711–12) titular Mr. Spectator and *The Tatler*'s (1709–11) Isaac Bickerstaff, for example, are fashioned as coffeehouse wits and gentlemanly bachelors. Female eidolons (regardless of whether they were created by male or female writers) were similarly often defined by their singledom, and so relegated to the realm of spinsterhood. *The Female Tatler*'s (1709–10) Mrs. Crackenthorpe, *The Drury-Lane Journal*'s (1752) Roxana Termagant, Christopher Smart's Mary Midnight in *The Midwife* (1750–53), and Frances Brooke's Mary Singleton in *The Old Maid* (1755–56) are all decidedly unmarried spinsters portrayed with varying degrees of flattery and seriousness. This perhaps uncomfortable relationship between married private life and public authorship arises precisely because periodicals oscillate between different spheres and audiences. According to Manushag Powell, periodical writers' indebtedness to their readers supplanted a successful marriage: "marriage and authorship are opposing and mutually exclusive institutions."[6] While periodicals promoted marriage and the sentimental family as laudable ideals, marriage was foreclosed for eidolons—especially female eidolons, who received greater public scrutiny.

In this essay, I will examine this vexed relationship between periodicals and the gradual normalization of marriage and heteronormativity. How do we reconcile this consistent policing and producing of the idealized heterosexual family with eidolons who manifestly resist such easy categorization? The answer lies, I suggest, in the complex temporal affordances of periodicals. I argue that attention to the ways in which periodicals operate in and over time allows us to put some pressure on the genre's supposedly central role in establishing and reinforcing heterosexual ideologies. It is in the ephemeral and continually shifting nature of the periodical that, I propose, the stable reinforcement of heteronormativity can be resisted. While the periodicity and regularity of the periodical contributed to the creation of a sturdy national reading public, its fragmentariness, ephemerality, and open-endedness necessitated gaps and ruptures, which, in turn, created a space free from such hegemonizing ideologies.

In pursuing these questions, I will be developing a methodological framework in order to tease out the intimate overlaps between periodical and queer or nonnormative temporalities. In what follows, I study two female eidolons with arguably nonnormative gender identities: Isaac Bickerstaff's half-sister Jenny in *The Tatler* and Mary Singleton in *The Old Maid*. The canonical status and long-lasting legacy of *The Tatler* make it particularly ripe for revisiting the ways in which marriage and gender were conceptualized during the inception of periodical literature and how that influenced later periodicals. The exceptionally positive portrayal of spinsterhood in *The Old Maid* and its keen self-awareness of the periodical tradition make it a useful counterexample to further explore the centrality of marriage in periodical literature.

I propose that the periodical's temporal form punctuates and undermines the narrative development of the figure of the spinster author, frustrating movements toward marital and moral closure. In many ways, the gaps and spaces between the individual issues of periodicals parallel the social gaps created by the nonnormative spinster. Both of the eidolons I will be examining are introduced as opinionated and unmarried, and are wrestling to a greater or lesser extent with the pressures of marriage that the periodical's sentimental undercurrents necessitate. But both periodicals also seem to undercut their own normative ideologies. *The Old Maid*'s early end never actually allowed the embedded marriage plot to resolve. While Jenny is eventually married off in *The Tatler*, contemporary short-lived spin-offs of the paper envision an alternative life trajectory for her that does not include marriage. Ultimately, I argue that the periodical's ephemerality and fragmentariness offer glimpses of queer possibilities that lie outside of the heteronormative rubric that periodicals otherwise work to naturalize and promote. In studying these two eighteenth-century periodicals within their material and gendered contexts, I hope to offer a theoretical and methodological spur for how we might begin to think about what I term "queer periodical temporality."

Queer and Periodical Temporalities

In recent years, temporality has become a favored topic in eighteenth-century studies. Scholars have taken a keen interest in how time was construed, debated, and—perhaps most pressingly—*experienced* during this period.[7] That scholars of the eighteenth century show a particular interest in temporality makes perfect sense, since the period's various scientific and technological revolutions resulted in vastly altered experiences of time. However, despite the importance of the eighteenth century to the ways in which time and temporality were understood scientifically, experientially, and socially, what we might call eighteenth-century "periodical time" has remained largely untheorized since Stuart Sherman's landmark study, *Telling Time: Clocks, Diaries, and English Diurnal Form* (1996). This relative silence is in stark contrast with scholars of nineteenth-century periodical culture. Under the influence of Margaret Beetham's psychoanalytic conceptualization of "open" (feminine, disruptive) and "closed" (masculine, dominant) time, nineteenth-century periodicals have been understood as formally dependent upon time.[8] Beetham elucidates the periodical's ambiguous relation to time: it claims to be of the moment, but simultaneously points back to past issues and forward to the uncertain future of upcoming issues.[9] Its very periodicity and cyclicity—or "periodical-ness," as Mark Turner calls it—is essential to what defines the periodical as a form of print.[10] While periodicals have a built-in sense of constancy and regularity (by virtue of being published daily, weekly, or monthly), their seriality also presupposes waiting, interruptions, and what Turner calls "indeterminate gaps in media time."[11] He contends that "in these breaks in the narratives of periodicals and in the lapses in time—over a day, over a week, over a month—is where meaning resides. That pause is when the interaction and communication occurs, and that period of waiting and reading is the link between the past and the future."[12]

What I argue here is that scholarship on periodical time has much in common with what queer theorists have termed "queer time" or "queer temporalities": both insist on indeterminate gaps and futures and the synchronicity of many different temporalities. While Beetham positions the periodical's openness and disruptiveness within a psychoanalytic feminist framework, I explore the queer dimensions of these temporal affordances. Jack Halberstam broadly defines queer time as an alternative relation to time that "develop[s], at least in part, in opposition to the institutions of family, heterosexuality, and reproduction."[13] Building on Halberstam's work, Elizabeth Freeman introduces the idea of "chronobiopolitics," defining it as the collective cultural impetus that favors schedules, rhythms, and types of temporal experiences that seem natural to privileged heteronormative structures (such as marriage, reproduction, and the accumulation of wealth).[14] Queer temporalities, on the other hand, are "visible in the forms of interruption" and "points of resistance to this temporal order."[15] Relatedly, José Esteban Muñoz has coined the concept of "queer futurity," arguing that "queerness is essentially about the rejection of a here and now and an insistence on potentiality or concrete possibility for another world."[16]

Queer futurity, then, is an alternative way of envisioning the future (and the ways in which kinship and communities operate in those futures) that develops along queer timelines. It directly resists the strictures of what Lee Edelman has termed "reproductive futurism," the temporal constructions that "perpetuate as reality a fantasy frame intended to secure the survival of the social in the Imaginary form of the Child."[17] In this cultural logic, queerness is figured as a negative, "future-negating" force. While these theorists are writing about the twentieth century, their work nonetheless offers some useful points of departure for understanding the ways in which eighteenth-century literature employs (interruptions and ruptures of) time and narrative to communicate alternative, queer, and nonreproductive social behavior.[18]

My theorization of queer periodical time is also indebted to work in queer narratology. Robyn Warhol writes that "the centrality of narrative in shaping heteronormativity and with it queer subjectivity has been acknowledged by virtually every major queer theorist," and pays particular attention to narrative temporality and teleology as intrinsically heterocentric.[19] Writing about seriality and the domestic marriage plot, for example, Warhol argues that "due to its structurally mandated impulse to defer ending indefinitely, serialized domestic fiction has always tended to undermine the heterocentric marriage plot by unravelling instances of closure that turn out to be only provisional."[20] In the context of eighteenth-century studies, such scholars as Paula Backscheider, Susan Lanser, Catherine Ingrassia, and Alice Tweedy McGrath have called attention to how literary forms that in one way or another resist easy narrative closure—picaresque stories, patchwork narratives, certain amatory fictions, or, as I argue here, periodicals—offer ample potential for finding queer stories, in part because they foreclose the familiar teleology of the heterosexual marriage plot that characterized proto-sentimental fiction.[21] While I am indebted to queer narratology in my insistence on gaps and ruptures, my approach here is not explicitly narratological. Rather, I am interested in how periodical print media and their relationship to temporality influence, create, and possibly undermine heterocentric gender ideologies lodged in periodical discourse. In the sections that follow, I offer some ways in which we might approach texts within this queer periodical-temporal framework. I consider concrete markers of the periodical's unique temporal affordances—its thematic and narrative heterogeneity, the casual reading habits to which it was subject, its illegitimate spin-offs—within the gendered politics of the form.

Jenny Distaff's Marriage in *The Tatler* (1709–11)

I turn first to Jenny Distaff, Isaac Bickerstaff's half-sister in *The Tatler* and arguably the first discursively female eidolon in a British periodical. She first appears early in *The Tatler*'s run, in issue number 10. She reappears five more times, in numbers 35 through 38, and then, almost a year later, in number 247. In some ways, she fulfills the same role as Bickerstaff in creating and maintaining a national reading public. She upholds the regularity of the publication, with her brother "having a sudden occasion to go out of town, order[ing] [her] to take upon [herself] the despatch of the next advices from home."[22] She is also in charge of keeping *The Tatler*'s readership updated on national and international news: each issue ends with letters containing Continental news from St. James Coffee-House. At the same time, as Iona Italia writes, Jenny allows "the paper" to "claim to speak for and to women more directly."[23] Indeed, Bickerstaff's sprightly younger sister announces that she will mostly discuss women's issues: "It is so natural for women to talk of themselves, that it is to be hoped all my own sex, at least, will pardon me, that I could fall into no other discourse" (1:96). In the subsequent essays attributed to her, she writes wittily about marriage, satirizes comic male types, and describes her romantic life in amatory terms.

As the first discursively female eidolon, Jenny has a complicated relationship with marriage and family. She disappears as an essayist for over a year after issue number 38, but we learn more about her narrative arc from her brother's essays. He reforms—or "browbeats," to borrow Powell's words—his witty and lively sister into marriage.[24] He would "get her an agreeable man for her husband," one who can manage her "sluttish" behavior of "consulting her glass and her toilet for an hour and a half after her private devotion, sit[ting] with her nose full of snuff, and a man's nightcap on her head, reading plays and romances" (2:215, 2:218). Despite her own reservations regarding marriage, and her explicit resistance to it, she is nevertheless married off to the aptly named Tranquilus in issue number 79. In the wake of that event, Jenny is almost wholly reduced to her status as a wife, notwithstanding the many squabbles she has with her husband or even her living alone in London for a while. In the issues that follow her marriage, we learn how she came to Bickerstaff "with a very matron-like air," "enter[ed] the room with a decent and matron-like behaviour," and "appear[ed]" as the "true figure of conjugal affection" in her "looks and gestures" (2:303, 2:441, 3:460).

When Jenny returns as a contributor in number 247, she resumes her biting wit, but is nonetheless more deferential than she had been in her earlier essays. She responds to a (presumably fictional) letter from Disconsolat Almeira, which, since it concerns "the cause of [her] sex," her brother "bid [her] answer" it (4:374). Almeira is turning to *The Tatler* for marital advice. Her lover "had promised that he would marry [her], but [she] find[s] all he said nothing; for when the question was put to him, he wouldn't" (4:374). Jenny's advice evinces her trademark scathing wit: modern men are "false swains," "perjured lovers," and "nauseous rogues that pretend to deceive [women]." However, Jenny lays the blame for that on women. If a "woman is treated as a mistress, and not a wife," it is her own fault: "We have contributed to our own deceit. The truth is, we do not conduct ourselves as we are courted, but as we are inclined" (4:377, 4:378). Although Jenny's essay takes an ambiguous stance toward marriage, it ultimately condemns the unbridled passions and naïveté of women for their faulty marriages.

I am not interested in reclaiming Jenny Distaff as a proto-feminist heroine. Her conservative narrative is symptomatic of the middling-sort values so often promoted in *The Tatler*. Rather, I hope to use Jenny's arc to think through the ways in which the fleetingness of early periodical culture and the accompanying happenstance nature of periodical reading habits helped crystallize gender norms. Particularly important for understanding how periodicals were consumed in the early decades of the century is the sheer ephemerality and transitoriness of the market for them. As Christina Lupton writes, "circulating in coffeehouses, conspicuous on drawing room tables, or even recycled as tobacco papers, the unbound *The Spectator* was itself implicated in the full spectrum of the paper economy. ... It too was liable to casual, 'accidental reading' (and also to being thrown away as rubbish)."[25] It seems safe to assume that issues of *The Tatler*, like those of other periodical publications, were rarely read in their entirety, in the intended order, or even with much knowledge about their internal continuity. Indeed, there is a roughly three-month gap (thirty issues) between Jenny's penultimate essay and her reappearance in Bickerstaff's marital scheme. Despite her neatly arranged narrative trajectory from buoyant protégée to stately matron, Jenny's marital teleology is broken up by the cadence of the publication cycle. It is precisely in "indeterminate gaps" like these that alternative "meaning resides."[26] Jenny was a fleeting character within an already ephemeral form: for some, Jenny might only have been Bickerstaff's matronly sister referenced in passing in later issues, while for others, the early Jenny—the satiric coquette who rages about marriage and "ten millions of things more against men"—might have been the only Jenny with whom they were familiar (1:299).[27]

That some read Jenny primarily as the latter—a sprightly, unmarried critic—is evidenced by the publication of *The Whisperer* (1709), a short-lived periodical that ran for twenty-two issues (though only two are extant) and that appropriated the character of Jenny Distaff. One symptom of the transient periodical marketplace is the sheer number of such short-lived periodicals that were launched in conversation and association with more established publications such as *The Tatler*. It was a relatively common trope for early periodical essayists to invent relative-eidolons or for entirely separate publications to appear with a supposed familial link to more established periodicals such as *The Tatler*. As Tedra Osell writes, this "indicat[ed] their generic affiliations in an era when 'family' was often seen as the 'natural' manifestation of 'the social.'"[28] According to Bickerstaff, such periodical newcomers were "numberless Vermin that feed upon this Paper, and find their Sustenance out of it: I mean, the small Wits and Scribblers that every Day turn a Penny by nibbling at my Lucubrations" (4:257).

The Whisperer was one of those "numberless Vermin that [fed] upon" *The Tatler*, and Jenny served as its principal eidolon. She decidedly ignores and rejects marriage and so escapes *The Tatler*'s rigid temporality. In issue number 1, she complains that her brother "design'd [her] a Husband, chosen altogether by his own Notions of the Convenient and the Happy." Instead, she "thought fit to avoid the Match, by Giving him the Slip, and Setting up for [herself]."[29] She writes: "My Brother must be allow'd to know Tempers and Constitutions as well as any Man breathing; and yet he thought it possible to persuade me, who had a Taste of innocent Liberty, and bright Conversation, to be shut up with Mr. Scrape-all."[30] The *Whisperer*'s Jenny resolutely opts for public intellectual life with its "bright Conversation," a life seemingly incompatible with the marriage envisioned by her brother. She models her periodical on *The Tatler*, blending astute social criticism with commentary on public affairs. In the first issue, she promises that she will avoid "Panegyrick" and endeavor to "set ill Action in their proper Light and exercise the necessary Scourge on urgent Occasions."[31] As a true member of the "Family of the *Staffs*," she is "a Friend to Innocence; a Foe to Vice."[32] Indeed, in issue number 3 (the only other one extant), Jenny adopts Bickerstaff's persona as a gently satiric coffeehouse wit. As she is "tasting some Tea, at Mr. Cocoa's," she ridicules its visitors, from a pedantic writer to a well-off lady having an extramarital affair.[33]

The Whisperer serves as an example of the ways in which eighteenth-century casual and unregulated reading practices gave way to readerly interpretations that took creative license to invent new meanings in *The Tatler*'s temporal gaps. *The Whisperer* queers Jenny: she disavows marriage, existing resolutely in opposition to heteronormative social demands. While for *The Tatler*'s Bickerstaff, Jenny's marital and domestic fate is fixed, this supposedly illegitimate spin-off freed her from marriage and envisioned an alternative life for her as a satiric periodicalist in the coffeehouses. While *The Whisperer*'s Jenny Distaff was the first periodical spinster of her kind, she was certainly not the last. As we will see in the next section on Frances Brooke's *The Old Maid*, the representation in periodicals of (consciously) unmarried women became increasingly entangled with the sentimental family unit as the century progressed.

Mary Singleton's Spinsterhood in *The Old Maid* (1755–56)

Domestic womanhood and motherhood became increasingly important in the period after *The Tatler* was published. In the mid-eighteenth century, fears of population decline were rampant and reproduction was the key way for women to prove their social worth.[34] The old spinster, a figure of derision and disdain, was often satirically portrayed as physically deformed, sexually frustrated, and financially precarious. Older single women were heavily criticized precisely because they failed or refused to marry. Frances Brooke functioned as *The Old Maid*'s sole editor and principal contributor, writing under the guise of "Mary Singleton, Spinster." While adopting an eidolon was common for eighteenth-century periodicals, Brooke's choice of an old maid was, given this social context, relatively unconventional. Indeed, her decision has been explained by scholars such as Iona Italia, Elizabeth Larsen, and Manushag Powell as an attempt to reframe the old maid as a figure of moral authority and integrity, rather than the butt of innumerable jokes.[35]

I am similarly interested in Brooke's use of the emerging language of novelistic sensibility in her periodical essays. By looking at sensibility's relationship to heteronormativity, we can see how the periodical's serial, ephemeral, and open-ended nature disrupts the underlying heterosexual logic of the sentimental marriage plot. Ultimately, this creates a space for what we might call "queer spinsterhood." This is not to automatically equate all forms of eighteenth-century spinsterhood with queerness, but rather to understand women's conscious choice of singledom as inherently resistant to heteronormative structures and their accompanying notions of reproductive futurism. Literary representations of spinsters, such as Brooke's Singleton, are fertile ground for finding voices that are structurally outside of the bounds of heteronormative sentiment.[36]

I am particularly interested in Singleton's unmarried and child-free status in relation to the sentimental framing device employed by *The Old Maid* because of the role that sentimentalism and sensibility have played in formalizing future-oriented ideologies predicated upon reproduction. The marriage plot and the domestic family gained increasing importance during the mid-eighteenth century due to the emerging dominance of sentimentalism. Scholars of sentimentalism have emphasized the close intertwining of sex and sentiment, showing how heterosexual relationships became increasingly sentimentalized and subsequently naturalized over the course of the century.[37] For example, Paul Kelleher has argued that sentimental literature presented "heterosexual desire as the source and at times the very prerequisite for moral virtue and ethical sociability."[38] With its narrative progression toward marriage and domestic kinship, the eighteenth-century novel thus eagerly participated in the gradual normalization and naturalization of heteronormativity.

Though, as an old maid, Singleton falls squarely outside of the logic of the marriage plot, *The Old Maid* nonetheless engages with this emerging aesthetic of sentimentality. In the first issue, Brooke's eidolon cleverly maps her life onto a recognizable sentimental narrative: born into a wealthy family, Singleton falls in love with a man from a lower social class against the wishes of her father. However, this stereotypical setup immediately falls flat: they simply fall out of love and break off their engagement. While Singleton is said to be still receiving many romantic offers, she resolves to remain single. She is painfully aware of the criticism that unmarried older women like her receive, writing that old maids are "the most useless and insignificant of all God's creatures": a truly "future-negating" force.[39] Despite this, Singleton hopes to be of service to the community through her instructive writing. Within the first few pages of the periodical, Brooke thus introduces and immediately subverts the marriage plot. Like Jenny in *The Whisperer*, Singleton decides to fulfill her duty to society through writing, instead of marriage.

However, the first issue does not entirely escape the heterosexual logic of "reproductive futurism" inherent to sentimental and marital temporalities. Singleton introduces two more characters: her niece Julia and Julia's friend Rosara. Here, *The Old Maid* anticipates Sherman's and Anderson's idea that the periodical reading public stands in for the nation. Singleton takes up "[her] duty to [her] country," as she describes it, by raising and educating her niece Julia, whose mother died in childbirth (7). While the first issue portrays an ambiguous view of womanhood and heteronormativity, Singleton nonetheless tries to legitimize herself by modeling herself as a domestic mother figure whose purpose it is to ensure that her niece, too, enters into marriage in order to both figuratively and literally reproduce the nation. Singleton configures this frame narrative about Julia and Rosara in sentimental and novelistic terms throughout the rest of the periodical. Singleton describes Julia, for example, as having an "inexpressible sweetness in her countenance," a mind that "is the feat of every grace and every virtue," and "as so gentle that [Singleton] can make her tremble by a look of anger" (9–10). Much like Jenny in *The Tatler*, Julia and Rosara are portrayed as virtuous, sensible heroines, well on their way to marriage under the guidance and support of a relative.

The Old Maid's ephemeral and thematically fragmentary nature, however, forecloses the predictable finality that marriage plots usually offer. Such fragmentation and miscellaneity was typical for periodicals. Singleton, for instance, proudly describes her publication as "a ragout" that consists of "various kinds of mental provision," "without considering how the different tastes may mix and agree" (118). Julia and Rosara feature regularly in the periodical, but such narrative moments are often nothing more than a pretense to discuss other more topical, philosophical, or political matters. In issue 17, for example, Singleton takes the two young women to the theater, which leads into a long piece of theatrical criticism about a recent performance of *King Lear*, just as issue 20 provides an account of a tea table with Mr. Belville, Julia's love interest, that quickly turns into a reflection concerning French politics and history. Blending history, political commentary, and theater criticism with a sentimental framing device, *The Old Maid* is both thematically and narratively fragmentary.

Because of this fragmentation, Brooke is also able to put Julia's and Rosara's seemingly traditional sentimental narrative in dialogue with Singleton's reflections on spinsterhood and marriage, offering the women in her periodical other viable and respectable options. For example, Singleton opens issue 21 with an anecdote in which she refuses to allow a meeting between Rosara and her love interest. Rather than resolving this issue, Singleton ruptures Julia's and Rosara's sentimental narratives and quickly moves on to other matters. Singleton recounts a nocturnal vision in which she was commanded to choose between the goddesses of Marriage and Celibacy. She was initially led to the temple of Marriage, which was "embosomed in a shade of myrtles and oranges; the linnets in pairs warbled in the branches, the doves cooed to their mates, the flowers exhaled unspeakable odours" (178). The path to the temple of Marriage was easy and open, which made Singleton's "heart dance with pleasure": the god of Marriage "was gay and florid; his air inspired joy and festivity. ... Love, Honor, Respect and Wealth, stood on each side of him" (178). However, at the last possible moment, Singleton noticed how she "saw behind the throne Care with wrinkled brow and haggard eyes; Discord crowned with scorpions; Jealousy stung by Furies; and Slavery bearing a yoke and loaded with chains" (179).

Appalled by the reality of marriage, Singleton decides to make her way to the temple of Celibacy, which is "composed of evergreens, which cast a gloomy and melancholy shade, the way was rough and thorny, ... the solemn silence cast a damp upon [her] heart which almost tempted [her] to return to the deity [she] had just rejected" (180). When she meets the other goddess, Singleton notices that "her countenance was severe, her complexion pale and unanimated ... Chastity and Pride supported her train; before her stood Neglect, Contempt and Derision, but as her port was majestic and haughty, she overlooked them and kept her eyes fixed upon a very beautiful personage at her hand, who, from her easy composed mien, [Singleton] rightly guessed to be *Tranquility*" (180). Though the rejection of marriage initially seems appalling, Singleton quickly warms up to the goddess. She writes: "Her whole form seemed more pleasing as I advanced, and I was already inclining to enlist under her banners, when, waving her hand, a youth approached, lovely as the blush of spring; his air was noble and disengaged. ... I discovered him to be *Liberty*. I gave him my hand in transport of pleasure, and he with a smile of approbation delivered me to *Peace* and *Contentment*, the constant companions of his steps; commanding them to lead me to the temple of Happiness" (181). Convinced by the promise of liberty, peace, happiness, and contentment, Singleton rejects the shackles of marriage and instead chooses spinsterhood. Singleton's vision is a complex representation of spinsterhood: it at once illustrates the courage and strength of women choosing singledom, while also pointing to the social derision they will encounter.

Brooke puts this reluctant celebration of spinsterhood in dialogue with the sentimental courtship narratives of Rosara and Julia. She also importantly challenges the affect that is usually associated with the rejection of heterosexual marriage. As both Edelman and Halberstam have argued, in conventional heteronormative logic, queer affect is regularly characterized negatively as disappointment, failure, or disillusionment.[40] *The Old Maid* similarly portrays Singleton's choice of spinsterhood as bleak, cold, and unattractive, but then immediately destabilizes that valuation by showing that it has brought Singleton the ultimate peace and contentment. In doing so, Brooke subverts the joyous transcendence and virtuous contentment typically associated with the sentimental marriage plot.

The ephemeral and open-ended nature of the periodical also interrupts and undermines Julia's and Rosara's marital teleology. *The Old Maid* immediately makes clear that it does not aim to present a particularly coherent or long-lasting narrative. In the first issue, Singleton proclaims: "Amidst the present glut of essay papers, it may seem an odd attempt in a woman to think of adding to the number; but as most of them, like summer insects, just make their appearance and are gone; I see no reason why I may not buz amongst them a little, though it is possible I may join the short-liv'd generation and this day month be as much forgot as if I had never existed" (1). Likening herself to a "summer insect" that might "buz" among a "short-liv'd generation" and then die, Brooke makes no claims to canonicity. Her journal's ephemeral existence means that Julia's and Rosara's stories never actually progress toward their logical conclusion of marriage. *The Old Maid*'s readers do not learn the fates of these two young women. In the final issue, number 37, Singleton announces that she plans to take a break to "stretch [her] wings" and "rest [her] pen a little," in part because she is "tired of the confinement of writing every week." She leaves open the option of returning: "If we do meet again, why, we shall smile: if not, why then this parting was well made" (304). Rather than offering a comfortable marital closure, the *The Old Maid*'s abrupt ending leaves Julia's and Rosara's stories hanging.

The Tatler and *The Old Maid* are texts written at two distinct moments during the development of the periodical. They also have vastly different gender politics. Whereas *The Tatler* forces Jenny Distaff into marriage, *The*

Old Maid seems—at least to some extent—to embrace queerness. Both, too, have different relations to ephemerality and temporality. *The Old Maid* embraces its existence as a short-lived "summer insect," while *The Tatler* positions itself against such "Vermin" and hopes instead to attain traditional and long-lasting literary value. Notwithstanding these bids for canonicity, *The Tatler* took on a rich alternative and unregulated life of its own in the literary marketplace of the 1710s. Despite these differences, it is worth putting these two texts in conversation with each other. These periodicals and their receptions offer rich examples of how the transient nature of periodical print culture creates temporal gaps, ruptures, and opportunities for readers to make the text their own. It was those gaps that could facilitate nonnormative and queer readings of periodical texts that fall squarely outside of the hegemonic gender ideologies that this era's periodical culture seemed to promote.

That periodicals operate along complex timelines and life cycles—ones that are simultaneously uncompromising and disruptive—is not a new assertion. Scholars in nineteenth-century periodical studies, especially, have long been concerned with the unique temporal affordances of this "most time-oriented of print forms."[41] The periodical developed as a cultural product amid vast technological, political, social, and cultural changes. These changes were heavily classed, gendered, and racialized, which, in turn, shaped periodical time. Beetham, for instance, considers the gendered nature of periodical time from a psychoanalytic feminist perspective, in which periodicals operate within a complex interplay between "feminine" (or open and disruptive) and "masculine" (or closed and dominant) time.[42] What I hope to have shown in this essay, however, is that it is fruitful to put such feminist considerations of periodical time in conversation with more recent theoretical work on queer temporalities. In my reading of two eighteenth-century periodicals—*The Tatler* and *The Old Maid*—I have worked toward developing a theoretical model of what we might tentatively term queer periodical temporality. Such an approach considers periodical time—with its heterogeneity and indeterminate, idiosyncratic temporal trajectories—as rife with queer potential.

Notes

I would like to thank Nicole Aljoe, Victoria Barnett-Woods, and Misty Krueger for their detailed comments and suggestions regarding this essay.

1. Sherman, *Telling Time: Clocks, Diaries, and English Diurnal Form, 1660–1785* (Chicago: University of Chicago Press, 1996); Anderson, *Imagined Communities: Reflections on the Origin and Spread of Nationalism* (London: Verso, 2006).

2. Markman Ellis, "Sociability and Polite Improvement in Addison's Periodicals," in *Joseph Addison: Tercentenary Essays*, ed. Paul Davis (Oxford: Oxford University Press, 2021), 142–63.

3. For how *The Spectator* and *The Tatler* regulate gender norms, see Erin Mackie, *Market à la Mode: Fashion, Commodity, and Gender in "The Tatler" and "The Spectator"* (Baltimore: Johns Hopkins University Press, 1997).

4. For a landmark study on women's active involvement in periodical culture as writers, readers, contributors, editors, and subjects, see Manushag N. Powell and Jennie Batchelor, eds., *Women's Periodicals and Print Culture in Britain, 1690–1820s: The Long Eighteenth Century* (Edinburgh: Edinburgh University Press, 2018).

5. Shevelow, *Women and Print Culture: The Construction of Femininity in the Early Periodical* (New York: Routledge, 1989); Maurer, *Proposing Men: Dialectics of Gender and Class in the Eighteenth-Century English Periodical* (Stanford: Stanford University Press, 1998).

6. Powell, *Performing Authorship in Eighteenth-Century English Periodicals* (Lewisburg: Bucknell University Press, 2012), 137.

7. See, for example, Christina Lupton, *Reading and the Making of Time in the Eighteenth Century* (Baltimore: John Hopkins University Press, 2018); Jesse Molesworth, "Introduction: The Temporal Turn in Eighteenth-Century Studies," *The Eighteenth Century* 60, no. 2 (2019): 129–38; and Amit S. Yahav, *Feeling Time: Duration, the Novel, and Eighteenth-Century Sensibility* (Philadelphia: University of Pennsylvania Press, 2018).

8. Beetham, "Open and Closed: The Periodical as a Publishing Genre," *Victorian Periodicals Review* 22, no. 3 (1989): 98.

9. See Beetham, "Time: Periodicals and the Time of the Now," *Victorian Periodicals Review* 48, no. 3 (2015): 324.

10. See Turner, "Periodical Time in the Nineteenth Century," *Media History* 8, no. 2 (2002): 183–96.

11. Turner, "Periodical Time," 194.

12. Turner, "Periodical Time," 194.

13. Halberstam, *In a Queer Time and Place: Transgender Bodies, Subcultural Lives* (New York: New York University Press, 2005), 1.

14. Freeman, *Time Binds: Queer Temporalities, Queer Histories* (Durham: Duke University Press, 2010), 4.

15. Freeman, *Time Binds*, xxii.

16. Muñoz, *Cruising Utopia: The Then and There of Queer Futurity*, 10th anniversary edition (New York: New York University Press, 2019), 1.

17. Edelman, *No Future: Queer Theory and the Death Drive* (Durham: Duke University Press, 2004).

18. For the utility of queer time as a concept in eighteenth-century studies, see Emma Katherine Atwood, "Fashionably Late: Queer Temporality and the Restoration Fop," *Comparative Drama* 47, no. 1 (2013): 85–111; Ziona Kocher, "Squaring the Triangle: Queer Futures in Centlivre's *The Wonder*," *Humanities* 10, no. 1 (2021) https://doi.org/10.3390/h10010053; and Michael Nicholson, "Fugitive Pieces: Walpole, Byron, and Queer Time," *The Eighteenth Century* 60, no. 2 (2019): 139–62.

19. See Robyn R. Warhol and Susan Lanser, eds., *Narrative Theory Unbound: Queer and Feminist Interventions* (Columbus: The Ohio State University Press, 2015).

20. Warhol, "Making 'Gay' and 'Lesbian' into Household Words: How Serial Form Works in Armistead Maupin's 'Tales of the City,'" *Contemporary Literature* 40, no. 3 (1999): 382.

21. See Backscheider, *Elizabeth Singer Rowe and the Development of the English Novel* (Baltimore: Johns Hopkins University Press, 2013); Lanser, "Sapphic Picaresque, Sexual Difference and the Challenges of Homo-Adventuring," *Textual Practice* 15, no. 2 (2001): 251–68; Ingrassia, "'Queering' Eliza Haywood," *Journal for Early Modern Cultural Studies* 14, no. 4 (2014): 9–24; and McGrath, "Unaccountable Form: Queer Failure and Jane Barker's Patchwork Method," *The Eighteenth Century* 60, no. 4 (2019): 353–73.

22. Richard Steele, *The Tatler*, 4 vols. (Cambridge: Cambridge University Press, 2015), 1:91. Subsequent citations will be made parenthetically.

23. Italia, *The Rise of Literary Journalism in the Eighteenth Century: Anxious Employment* (London: Routledge, 2005), 43.

24. Powell, *Performing Authorship*, 139.

25. Lupton, *Reading and the Making of Time*, 35.

26. Turner, "Periodical Time," 194.

27. It is also important to acknowledge that, by the mid-eighteenth century, collected volumes of *The Tatler* were a standard part of domestic libraries, which changes the ways in which these periodicals were consumed. It is primarily in the early circulation of the unbound half-sheets that discontinuities like the ones I am investigating were a pervasive possibility.

28. Osell, "Tatling Women in the Public Sphere: Rhetorical Femininity and the English Essay Periodical," *Eighteenth-Century Studies* 38, no. 2 (2005): 286.

29. *The Whisperer*, no. 1, facsimile in *Contemporaries of the Tatler and Spectator*, ed. Richmond P. Bond (Los Angeles: William Andrews Clark Memorial Library, 1954), 27.

30. *The Whisperer*, no. 1, 27.
31. *The Whisperer*, no. 1, 27.
32. *The Whisperer*, no. 1, 27.
33. *The Whisperer*, no. 3 (18 October 1709). Single-sheet publication.

34. See Cindy McCreery, "Lustful Widows and Old Maids in Late Eighteenth-Century English Caricatures," in *Lewd and Notorious: Female Transgression in the Eighteenth Century*, ed. Katharine Kittredge (Ann Arbor: University of Michigan Press, 2003), 112–32.

35. See Italia, *Rise of Literary Journalism*; Elizabeth Larsen, "A Text of Identity: Frances Brooke and the Rhetoric of the Aging Spinster," *Journal of Aging and Identity* 4, no. 4 (1999): 255–68; and Powell, *Performing Authorship*.

36. Singleton is far from the only eighteenth-century example of such a "queer spinster." Some well-known novelistic examples would be the women in Sarah Scott's *Millenium Hall* (1762), whom Jason Farr thinks represent "queer ... viable alternatives to heterosexual union" (*Novel Bodies: Disability and Sexuality in Eighteenth-Century British Literature* [Newark: Rutgers University Press, 2019], 72).

37. See, for example, Nancy Armstrong, *Desire and Domestic Fiction: A Political History of the Novel* (Oxford: Oxford University Press, 1987); G. J. Barker-Benfield, *The Culture of Sensibility: Sex and Society in Eighteenth-Century Britain* (Chicago: University of Chicago Press, 1992); Ana de Freitas Boe and Abby Coykendall, eds., *Heteronormativity in Eighteenth-Century Literature and Culture* (London: Routledge, 2016); and Claudia L. Johnson, *Equivocal Beings: Politics, Gender, and Sentimentality in the 1790s—Wollstonecraft, Radcliffe, Burney, Austen* (Chicago: University of Chicago Press, 2009).

38. Kelleher, *Making Love: Sentiment and Sexuality in Eighteenth-Century British Literature* (Lewisburg: Bucknell University Press, 2015), 7.

39. Brooke, *The Old Maid* (London, 1756), 2. Subsequent citations will be made parenthetically.

40. See Halberstam, *The Queer Art of Failure* (Durham: Duke University Press, 2011), 88.

41. Beetham, "Time," 325.

42. Beetham, "Open and Closed," 98.

Close Encounters and Stranger Things: Angelica Kauffman's First Years in London

WENDY WASSYNG ROWORTH

Angelica Kauffman (1741–1807) was one of the most successful and well-known artists in the second half of the eighteenth century. She was celebrated internationally as a portrait painter and her literary and historical subjects were widely reproduced as prints and on furniture, textiles, fans, ceilings, porcelain, and embroidery during her lifetime and well into the twentieth century. In 1810, just three years after her death, Giovanni De Rossi published the first biography of Kauffman, and since the early nineteenth century, other biographies, exhibitions, scholarship, and collections of documents—including Waltraud Maierhofer's outstanding edition of Kauffman's extensive correspondence—have expanded our knowledge of this prolific artist and her career.[1] Yet more of Kauffman's captivating story can still be revealed—or questions raised—when lost artworks of hers or archival materials associated with her come to light.

The years between Kauffman's arrival in London in June 1766 and her appointment as a Founding Member of the Royal Academy of Arts in December 1768 were a pivotal time in her career. As a female artist, she attracted attention, and her Continental training in both portraiture and history painting made her popular in fashionable society, as well as a valuable addition to the London art establishment. Two Kauffman paintings from

1766–67—one rediscovered and one previously unknown—add to what is known about her private and work life in London as a foreigner making her way among family and friends in an international community of artists, printmakers, publishers, architects, surgeons, a poet, and an apothecary. Even before she arrived in England, Kauffman had become something of a celebrity, if not a curiosity, among British tourists and residents in Italy in the early 1760s, when she was traveling with her father, Johann Joseph Kauffmann, to study art in churches and private collections. Her sketchbook from this period includes informal portrait drawings of the cicerone James Byres; the Anglo-Americans Benjamin West, John Morgan, and Samuel Powel; and the English artist Nathaniel Dance, who painted her portrait in Rome in 1764 (see Figure 1).[2] He portrayed Kauffman as a demure young woman, fashionably dressed in a lace-trimmed gown and fur. She holds her portfolio and a *porte-crayon*, a drawing tool with black chalk at one end and white chalk at the other. Dance and Kauffman were expected to marry, but by the time they arrived in London two years later the engagement had ended.[3]

The same year, in Naples, Kauffman painted portraits of Cecil Brownlow, the 9th Earl of Exeter (1725–95), and of David Garrick (see Figure 2). The latter was one of the first pictures she exhibited in London in 1765. The animated informality of her portrayal of Garrick brought her to the attention of the London art world even before she moved there the following year.[4] Lord Exeter acquired the Garrick portrait and Nathaniel Dance's portrait of Kauffman, and he continued to be one of her most enthusiastic and supportive patrons in England.[5]

The English travelers whom Kauffman met in Venice in 1765 encouraged her to go to London, where, she was assured, she would find eager patrons who would appreciate her talent and pay more than she could earn in Italy.[6] Among those tourists was Samuel Sharp (1709–78), who was described by Georg Heinrich von Berenhorst (1733–1814) as "a surgeon from Bath travelling the world with three female offspring, as ugly as the others were pretty."[7] When Sharp returned to England in 1766, he published his travel journal, *Letters from Italy describing the customs and manners of that Country*, which became notorious for his disparaging views of Italian culture and customs.[8] However, despite Sharp's disapproval of Italian manners, it's not likely he would have agreed that Kauffman should relocate to London. In his opinion, the English painters he met in Rome, who would have included Nathaniel Dance and Gavin Hamilton, were doing well and should stay there. In London, he feared, "they will quit their works of genius, and be totally absorbed in portrait-painting, the stumbling-block on which all painters fall." Moreover, he asserted that "while they live humbly and soberly in Rome, in London it is dissipation and extravagance."[9]

Figure 1. Nathaniel Dance, *Angelica Kauffman*, Rome, 1764. Oil on canvas, 83 x 69 cm. Courtesy of the Burghley House Collection.

As an ambitious and talented painter, Kauffman took the advice of others and resolved to pursue her career in London. Lady Bridget Wentworth (1714–74), wife of the British Resident in Venice, John Murray (c. 1712–75), was preparing to return to England in 1765 and offered to accompany Kauffman on the journey.[10] Joseph Kauffmann consented to the arrangement and made plans to join his daughter in England after he took care of some business at home.

Figure 2. Angelica Kauffman, *David Garrick*, Naples, 1764. Oil on canvas, 83.8 x 69.2 cm. Courtesy of the Burghley House Collection.

When Kauffman arrived in London on 22 June 1766, she stayed with Lady Wentworth on Charles Street, Berkeley Square, while she visited artists' studios and became acquainted with the London art world. In a letter to her father on 12 July she described Joshua Reynolds as "the first," a very good painter with a "pennello volante" ("flying brush") that created a wonderful chiaroscuro effect.[11]

After several weeks, she was eager to set up her own studio and moved into lodgings at 27 Suffolk Street, Pall Mall, with the family of Robert Boyne Home (c. 1713–86), a British army surgeon. She arranged one of her four rooms as a painting studio and another as a space in which to display her finished work, as was the custom in London. On 1 September 1766, Kauffman wrote to one of Sharp's daughters, Miss Anne Sharp, in Bath, describing her "recent removeal and my having begun some Portraits which take up my time a good deal." She asked after the family's health, informed Anne Sharp that Lady Wentworth was well, and referred to a miniature painting: "a triffle not worth your mentioning, but if it gives Miss Anne pleasure I am happy I had the honour to paint it."[12]

On 10 October 1766, Kauffman wrote to her father to tell him how well she was doing in London. She reported that Lord Exeter and Countess Spencer, whom they had met in Italy, were very kind and that the earl had introduced her to Joshua Reynolds, whose portrait she was painting. She explained that London was expensive, although she hoped to find an affordable house in a neighborhood in which she could receive fashionable clients, and she urged her father to delay his journey until spring to avoid the cold, damp weather.[13]

In the same letter, Kauffman described her living arrangement with the Homes, who were so welcoming that the two daughters treated her as their sister. The elder, Anne Home (1742–1821), had been engaged to marry John Hunter (1728–93) since 1764, the same year that she published her first poem in the *Edinburgh Review*.[14] Hunter had served with Anne's father as an army surgeon and taught anatomy in London. His elder brother, the surgeon and anatomist William Hunter (1718–83), was physician to Queen Charlotte and, after 1768, Professor of Anatomy for the Royal Academy of Arts.

A painting by Kauffman of a mournful figure with a funerary urn has been identified as possibly a portrait of "Mrs. John Hunter" (see Figure 3).[15] However, it's unlikely that the picture was intended to be a portrait. The woman's idealized classical profile resembles a drawing of the head of a Roman statue in Kauffman's Italian sketchbook.[16] Nonetheless, the painting was a creative collaboration between Kauffman and Home, whose verses are inscribed below the urn in the lower-right corner of the painting. The words are faint but legible:

> In Memory of General Stanwix's Daughter who was lost in her
> passage from Ireland:
> On the dark Bosom of the faithless Main
> Where stormy Winds and howling Tempests reign
> Far from her Native Fields and Friendly Skies
> In Death's cold arms Fidelia lies.
> Ah! Spare to tell (for she is now no more)
> What Virtue, Beauty, Sweetness, charm'd before

Figure 3. Angelica Kauffman, *The Mournful Muse* (Anne Hunter?), 1766. Oil on canvas, 76.2 x 64 cm. Private collection.

> Here let the Pensive Muse in Silence Mourn
> Where Memory to her name has rais'd the sacred Urn.

This painting served as the model for Kauffman's 1767 etching with Home's verses that commemorated the drowning of General John Stanwix's (1690–1766) daughter on 29 October 1766 (see Figure 4). This sentimental print was produced soon after news of the tragedy was reported in London.

Figure 4. Angelica Kauffman, *The Mournful Muse*, 1767. Etching, 19.1 x 15.6 cm. Courtesy of the Yale Center for British Art, Paul Mellon Collection.

According to press reports, a packet boat carrying the Stanwix family began to leak soon after it left port in Ireland on its way to Wales. Sailors launched another boat to save the passengers, but the general, his wife, his daughter, another relative, and their four servants refused to leave the packet boat, and all were presumed to have drowned. The news articles did not name the daughter, who was from the general's first marriage, although several months later *The Gentleman's Magazine* characterized her as "an aimable and accomplished daughter, the joy of his heart, the delight of his old age."[17]

Home's poem memorialized Stanwix's daughter as Fidelia, although her real name was Susanna. Caroline Grigson has noted that there is a poem in Anne Home Hunter's papers with the title: "An inscription on an Urn to the Memory of Miss Susanna Stenwix unfortunately lost on the Irish seas in 1767."[18] This manuscript and the verses inscribed on Kauffman's painting confirm Home's authorship, her collaboration with Kauffman, and the subject of the verses' identity as Susanna Stanwix (1740–66).

In Kauffman's etching the word "friendship" was substituted for "Memory" in the final line of verse: "Where friendship to her name has rais'd the sacred Urn." Whether the etching was commissioned by an unnamed friend, as the verse implies, is unknown, though Anne Home may have known Susanna Stanwix. Hannah Lyons has suggested that Kauffman's etching, which did not circulate on the print market, may have been intended to be shared privately among Stanwix's friends to commemorate their loss.[19] However, it was also a way to demonstrate her artistry and skill. As Kauffman and her work became increasingly popular in London, she made the most of the opportunity to republish this image as an engraving by Francesco Bartolozzi entitled *Muse* in 1772 and a stipple print by William Wynne Ryland in 1774 (see Figure 5). The 1767 etching was also reproduced as another etching by John Boydell in 1781.

Kauffman's painting of the mournful woman must have meant a great deal to Anne Home Hunter. She kept it all her life, and while it may not have been a conventional portrait, it was nonetheless a reminder of her friend and early collaborator. The picture was displayed in John and Anne Hunter's house, and when Anne died, after a long career as a poet and lyricist, was inherited by John and William Hunter's nephew, Matthew Baillie.[20]

During the months in which Kauffman resided with the Home family, she gave painting lessons to Anne's younger brother, fourteen-year-old Robert Home (1752–1834), who aspired to a career as a professional artist. His portrait of John Hunter was likely one of his earlier efforts, as the anatomy of the anatomist appears somewhat awkward (see Figure 6). Home portrayed Hunter engaged in his work. The small monkey skull beside his inkwell on the desk was most likely the one that is now in the Hunterian collection of

Figure 5. William Wynne Ryland, *In Memory of General Stanwix's Daughter*, 1774. Stipple engraving after Angelica Kauffman. Courtesy of the Wellcome Collection.

the Royal College of Surgeons.[21] In the left background a nearly obscured statue of Artemis of Ephesus, the many breasted goddess of nature and fertility, stands in for the subject of his studies.

In 1769, Robert Home entered the school of the Royal Academy, and beginning in 1773, with Kauffman's encouragement, he spent five years

Figure 6. Robert Home, *Portrait of John Hunter*, c. 1770. Oil on canvas, 48 x 36 cm. Courtesy of the Royal College of Surgeons of England.

studying art in Rome. In 1790 he left Britain to pursue a career in India, where he painted portraits and landscapes, accompanied Lord Cornwallis in the Third Mysore War, and later served as Historical and Portrait Painter at the court of Oude at Lucknow.[22]

By the spring of 1767, Kauffman was earning enough to lease a house at 16 Golden Square in Soho. Her father arrived early that summer to join her, accompanied by her cousin, twelve-year-old Rosa Florini (1755–1812), who came from Morbegno in the Valtellina, where Kauffman and her father lived before their travels in Italy. Rosa resided with them in Golden Square until 1775, when she married Italian architect Joseph (Giuseppe) Bonomi (1739–1808), who had moved to London from Rome in 1767 to work as a draftsman for the architects Robert and James Adam.

Bonomi and Rosa Florini were married on 13 July 1775 in the chapel of the Imperial Embassy, which was one of the few places in London where Catholic marriages could be performed after the Clandestine Marriage Act of 1753 mandated that only weddings performed in the Church of England were legal and binding. The marriage registry lists five witnesses: the bride's uncle, Joseph Kauffmann; Joseph Zucchi from Venice; Joseph Angelini from Rome; the bride's cousin, Angelica Kauffman; and Margarita Sharp.[23] Venetian printmaker Joseph (Giuseppe) Carlo Zucchi (1721–1805) moved to London in 1766 with his brother, painter Antonio Zucchi (1726–95), and both became lifelong friends with Joseph Kauffmann and his daughter. Joseph (Giuseppe) Angelini (1735–1811) was an Italian sculptor who lived for a time in London. Margarita Sharp is not easy to identify, but she would have been another friend and possibly one of Samuel Sharp's daughters.

Joseph Bonomi and Antonio Zucchi were also friends of the French physician and political theorist—and future revolutionary leader—Jean-Paul Marat (1743–93), who moved to London in 1765. According to Joseph Farington (1747–1821), the three friends met at Old Slaughter's coffeehouse in St. Martin's Lane, a favorite place for artists and foreigners in London. Farington describes them as close: "Marat came" to Zucchi's house "in a most familiar manner, a knife and fork being laid for him every day." Marat suggested classical subjects for Zucchi's paintings and borrowed money from him; "Zucchi at that time courted Angelica Kauffman" and "frequently took Marat with him in the evenings when he went to visit her."[24] Another future revolutionary, the French journalist Jacques Pierre Brissot de Warville (1754–93), also noted Marat's association with Kauffman in London, although Brissot's words—"liaisons avec la célèbre Kauffmann"—have been mischaracterized to imply a sexual relationship.[25] This was certainly not true, especially in light of Marat's friendship with Antonio Zucchi and his respect for Kauffman.

As a woman in a male-dominated profession, Kauffman was a likely subject for rumors about her love life and alleged affairs, though she did become entangled in a real scandal during her first year in London. She married a man who claimed to be a Swedish nobleman until he was revealed as an imposter, a bigamist, and an extortionist. Kauffman's disastrous marriage was the subject of gossip at the time and is discussed in her biographies, although there are still some open questions to be answered and intriguing connections to be made.[26]

Giovanni Gherardo De Rossi provided the most detailed account of Kauffman's marriage. He was Kauffman's friend and supporter in the art community in Rome after 1782, when she was a well-established and celebrated artist. His source of information regarding her youth and years in London was an unpublished biography by her old friend and brother-in-law, Giuseppe Carlo Zucchi.[27] Zucchi wrote his biography in 1788 in collaboration with its subject, so it is not surprising that he omitted mention of her humiliating first marriage. De Rossi, however, writing after Kauffman's death, decided he could tell the full story of how she fell victim to an unscrupulous scoundrel. His dramatic fourteen-page account of the marriage and its aftermath was based on Joseph Kauffmann's notes and other family papers, although it reads more like a work of fiction, with its vivid account of threats, tears, and anguish. Whether De Rossi thought this would help to dispel any doubts regarding Kauffman's innocence in the affair or just wanted to tell a good story is unclear. In any case, there is evidence to corroborate the tale he tells.[28]

According to De Rossi, the imposter presented himself in London as a Swedish nobleman, Count Friedrich von Horn, and charmed his way into society. He may have been the real Count von Horn's valet, or, more likely, his illegitimate son, but he was certainly a persuasive rogue. He arrived in London just as Kauffman was enjoying her early success (and her newfound freedom away from her protective father), and she proved to be easy prey for the handsome and charismatic nobleman. He appeared to be modest and kind, professed to be Catholic, and promised that he would share his fortune with her and her good father, to whom he wished to become an obedient son. The villain told her that he expected to receive great riches soon, and when the funds arrived he would ask her to marry him. However, he cautioned, it was necessary to keep his intentions a secret, so that his family would not intervene and keep them apart. Angelica was reluctant to marry without her father's knowledge or consent, but she promised that if what he said was true, she would give him her hand. She trusted in his sincerity and believed that her father would be pleased with her good fortune.

After a while, the so-called Count von Horn appeared to Kauffman in great distress. He explained that his enemies at the Swedish court had denounced him as a traitor and he would soon be arrested. His only hope was the protection of the British royal family, who were fond of Angelica and would not allow her husband to be taken. Fearing for his life, Kauffman agreed to an immediate marriage against her better judgment.

De Rossi wrote that the marriage was performed by a priest in a Catholic chapel without proof of baptism, banns, or witnesses.[29] A hasty and clandestine marriage would have precluded the proper reading of banns or witnesses, and, in fact, there is no record of their marriage in the Imperial Embassy registry in 1766 or 1767 or any other year. De Rossi stated that Kauffman and the so-called count did not live together as man and wife, presumably to keep the union secret, and he added a note asserting that, due to an old wound, "von Horn" was incapable of "becoming physically married," which proved that his actions were motivated by self-interest.[30] Kauffman's reputation as an innocent virgin could be presumed to be intact.

De Rossi reported that, after three weeks of secrecy, "von Horn" sent a Catholic priest to inform Joseph Kauffmann of his daughter's marriage.[31] He was shocked and dismayed and would have been especially upset that his daughter had acted so rashly, just as her career in London was going so well. He confronted Angelica, who tried to defend her behavior, although she realized her mistake when "von Horn" began to insist on his right, as her husband, to her fortune. This had been his aim all along, and Kauffman, an inexperienced foreigner on her own in London, was easily fooled. The villain threatened to carry her off to the Continent against her will if he did not receive the money he demanded. Both father and daughter were frightened and distressed.

Joseph Kauffmann began to make inquiries, and as news of the marriage came out, the so-called Count von Horn's identity, deceptions, and previous history of fraud in Hamburg, The Hague, and other cities were soon revealed. To make matters worse, the scoundrel had abandoned a wife in Germany, and she was willing to testify against him. The imposter was arrested as a bigamist and a con man, but in spite of his cruelty and her humiliation, Kauffman did not wish to see him imprisoned or hanged. She agreed to give him 300 guineas of her hard-earned money—notably less than the 500 he had originally demanded—if he would sign a deed of separation and leave England. He signed the agreement on 10 February 1768 in the name of Christian Brandt, which may well have been his real name, if he was the real Count Friedrich von Horn's illegitimate son by his maid, Christina Brandt.[32]

Another puzzling piece of the story is the record of a second marriage ceremony joining Angelica Kauffman and the so-called von Horn on 20 November 1767, nine months after the unrecorded Catholic wedding and almost three months before the separation agreement. This marriage was performed by George Baddelley, a curate at St. James's Church, Piccadilly, under the authority of a license from the bishop of London. The two witnesses were Kauffman's friends from Suffolk Street: Anne Home and her father, Robert Home.[33] The bride and groom signed the parish register as "Maria Angelica Kauffman" and "Frederic de Horn."[34] This marriage in the Church of England may have been performed to establish a record of a legal union for the sake of her reputation and her father's peace of mind.

After these mortifying revelations, Kauffman refused several legitimate offers of marriage and focused on her career. She must have been reluctant to give up her independence or her growing income: she remained single until 1776, when, at her father's urging, she agreed to marry their old friend, Antonio Zucchi. Her marriage to "von Horn" may have been a sham, but, as a devout Catholic, Kauffman would not remarry without a papal annulment. Giuseppe Carlo Zucchi wrote on the couple's behalf to find out whether an annulment was possible. The annulment granted in June 1778 confirmed that Kauffman's first marriage had been performed in the San Jacopo chapel of the Imperial Embassy on 11 February 1767.[35] They learned later that Christian Brandt, or whoever he was, had died in 1780. Kauffman married Zucchi on 14 July 1781, just before they left London to return to Italy.

There is still more that can be added to this strange story. Some years ago, I came across a reference to a collection of documents related to Angelica Kauffman among the papers of Granville Sharp (1735–1813), the noted scholar and abolitionist.[36] These documents were bundled together inside a paper with the name "Excell FM Graff von Horn" inscribed on top, beside a wax seal. A note added in a second hand detailed the contents: "Enclosed in this paper cover / 20 pieces of paper / and a blue silk case / with 2 commissions / London." The documents include testimonials to military service, certificates of membership in German academies, letters, and accounts, most dated 1762–63, along with some crude drawings that resemble Hebrew letters and several symbols and numbers. The papers appear to have been the property of the real Graf (Count) Friedrich von Horn. A card among the papers provides additional information (see Figure 7):

> The Contents of 2 Packets
> of Papers addressed to Count Horn
> for which I paid 4 Guineas in 1769
> These packets I opened near 17 years
> afterwards in the presence of Sir William Dolben,
> his Sister, & 3 of my own sisters & my brother
> Will[m] 2 May 1786
>
> The above is the
> Hand writing of }   Angelica Kaufman
> Granville Sharp
> C Sharp

The witnesses mentioned were the abolitionist Sir William Dolben (1727–1814); Dolben's sister; Sharp's older brother, William (1729–1810); and Sharp's three sisters: Judith (1733–1809), Frances (1738–99), and Elizabeth (1733–1810). The "<u>C Sharp</u>" who authenticated Granville's signature was

Angelica Kauffman's First Years in London / 123

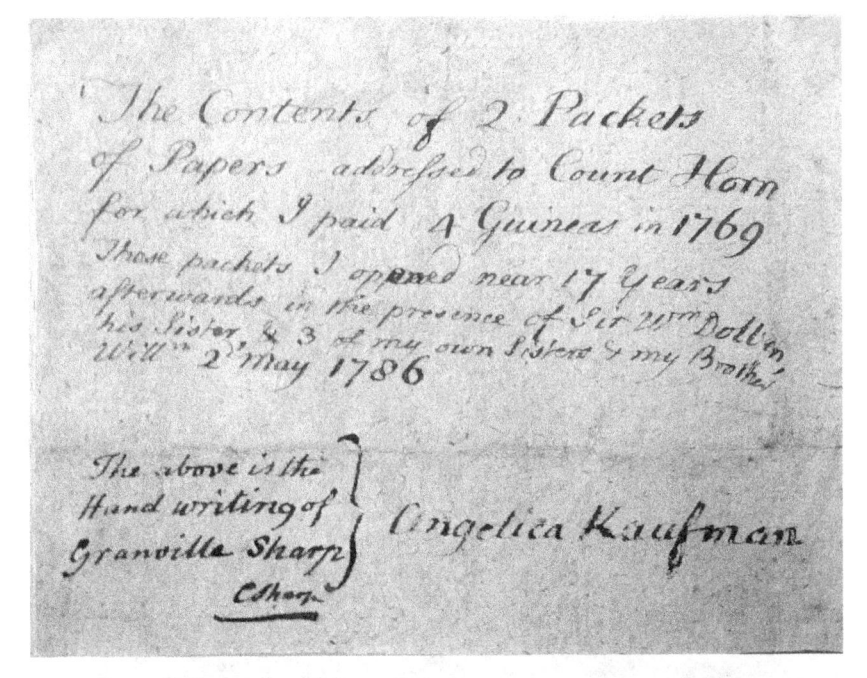

Figure 7. Card accompanying papers related to (probably the real) Count von Horn, purchased by Granville Sharp. Gloucestershire Archives, D3549/13/5/10.

most likely the daughter of Granville's brother James, Catherine ("Kitty") Sharp (1770–1843), who would go on to preserve the family papers.[37]

The close-knit and talented members of the Sharp family were portrayed by Johann Zoffany in 1780 performing together at one of the musical concerts they staged on their barge on the Thames River between 1775 and 1783 (see Figure 8).[38] Granville Sharp is seated in the center between his sister Elizabeth at the harpsichord and his young niece Kitty. His older brother, William, who served as surgeon to George III, stands at the apex of the family pyramid before the banner.

Why and how did Granville Sharp acquire the von Horn papers, and what was Sharp's connection with Angelica Kauffman? There is no direct evidence to connect Kauffman to Granville Sharp, though it's possible that she knew his brother William through her connections with the royal household. Two documents in the packets provide partial answers, while raising other questions.

One of them is a four-page letter in German that the imposter von Horn sent to Kauffman from Venice on 29 September 1769, nearly two years

Figure 8. Johann Zoffany, *The Sharp Family*, 1779–81. Oil on canvas, 115.6 x 125.7 cm. On loan to the National Gallery, London, © Lloyd-Baker Estate.

after their separation agreement. He continued to claim to be the genuine nobleman, signing the letter: "Frederic graf von Horn." It is filled with indignant complaints and angry threats. "Von Horn" accused Kauffman of slander, blamed her for ruining his reputation, and demanded the 300 guineas that she had promised, which he did not apparently receive before he left England. He demanded that she send his papers (presumably, the documents in the two packets), which he needed to travel to Russia where he could secure a position. The scoundrel warned that a bookseller in Germany had a manuscript that "von Horn" had written about Kauffman and her father and his own exoneration, and that it was to be published in English, Italian, and German with the title *Die unglückseligen Früchte der schlechten Erziehung oder das Leben der Kunstmalerin A.K.* (The unfortunate fruits of bad upbringing or the life of the paintress A.K.).[39] He threatened that she would soon see advertisements for it in the *London Evening Post* and other newspapers, and "if you will read your life's story, you will be reminded that [even] the biggest secrets, which often deserve to be publicly punished, are often discovered by miraculous means and revealed to the horror of the world."[40] He boasted that the book would bring him three times the money that she had refused him, which would allow him to obtain permission to remarry. He was leaving right away for Trieste, Innsbruck, and Augsburg, where he would await his future destiny in peace and quiet. After these complaints, threats, and an appeal to Kauffman's tender heart, "von Horn" warned that it was up to her whether her misconduct would be revealed: "I have asked Mr. Granville Sharp to send my papers to me. Up unto now, it depends on you if you will become known to the world. However, once the press has been filled in, you will be too late and, truly, you will rue it."[41] He added that he hoped Kauffman would not deny Sharp three or four guineas for the papers; otherwise she would regret it forever.

This letter establishes a connection with Sharp, although it leaves many questions unanswered and raises still others. Did Sharp give or lend three or four guineas to "von Horn" or someone else who had possession of the papers—perhaps the legal authorities who arrested him? When and why did "von Horn" ask Sharp to send the documents? Sharp was a sympathetic and generous man; why would he assist such a dishonorable character? Did Kauffman pay the "three or four Guineas" as the letter writer requested? If "von Horn" had asked Sharp to send him the papers, why did Sharp hold onto them for seventeen years? By 1786, when the packets were opened, the imposter was dead and Kauffman was no longer in England.

The second document related to Kauffman in the von Horn papers is an undated letter in French signed "F C D H," which presumably stands for "Frederic le Comte de Horn": "Do not doubt any longer Madam, yes I love you! You are right to believe me too wise to assume a false tenderness: I love you only because You deserve to be, and I only await your answer to prove to you on the clearest evidence, that it will only be in the final moment of my life that I will [cease?] to be. All yours."[42] This passionate assertion of his undying love may have been the villain's attempt to persuade Kauffman to marry without her father's consent, although it's more likely that it was an anxious appeal after his real intentions and identity had been questioned. To add to the mystery, the envelope in which this letter had been enclosed was addressed to "Madame Angelica Kaufman / chez M. Brandenbourg / apodicair, ap di Pal Mal / London / St. James" (see Figure 9).[43] Who was this apothecary Brandenbourg, and why would the imposter send a letter to Kauffman at his address? Did her devious lover employ a go-between in order to ensure that Kauffman received his letter without interference from her father or her friends the Home family?

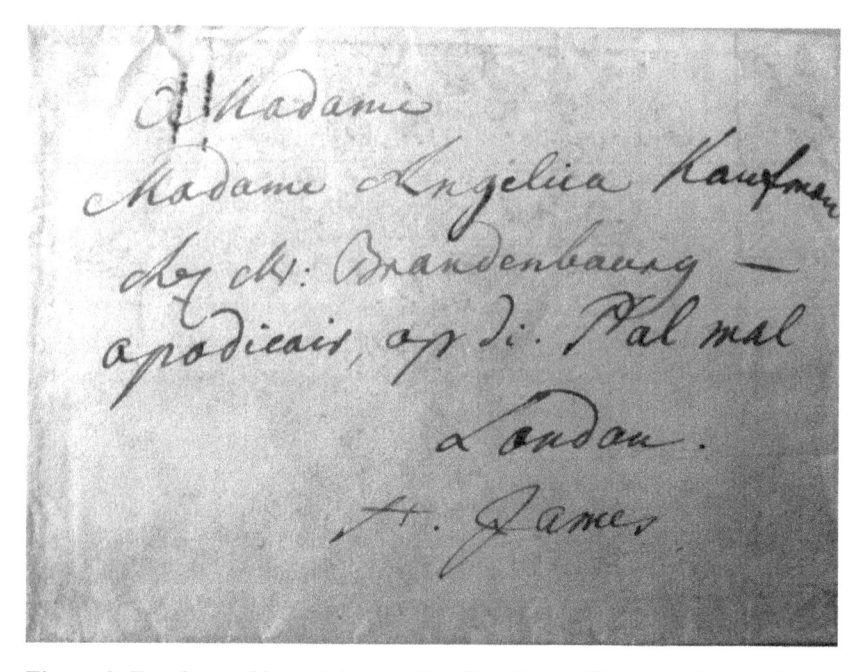

Figure 9. Envelope addressed to Angelica Kauffman. Gloucestershire Archives, D3549/13/5/10.

A previously unpublished painting by Kauffman may provide at least a partial answer (see Figure 10). It is one of a pair of half-length portraits of a man and a woman who are identified by labels on the back of the frames as Augustus Hermann Brandenburg and his wife, painted by Angelica Kauffman at St. James's around 1767.[44] He is posed as a learned gentleman holding his place in a book. His black-and-white jacket with lace-trimmed collar was a seventeenth-century costume popular in English portraits at that time. It is almost identical to Kauffman's 1767 portrait of the Irish politician and judge George Robert Hellen (1725–93) (see Figure 11), which was also commissioned as part of a pair with a portrait of Hellen's wife, Dorothea Daniel Hellen (d. 1806).[45] The nearly identical sizes, poses, and clothing support 1767 as the year in which the Brandenburg portraits were painted, which would make them contemporaries of the Count von Horn affair.

Augustus Hermann Brandenburg, also known as Brande, was one of several members of the Brande family of apothecaries from Hanover who were active in London during the second half of the eighteenth century. He served as court apothecary to George II from 1752 until September 1761, when he became apothecary to Queen Charlotte.[46] Brandenburg/Brande

Figure 10. Angelica Kauffman, *Augustus Hermann Brandenburg or Brande*, 1767. Oil on canvas, 76.8 x 64.1 cm. Private collection.

would have known Kauffman through her connection to Queen Charlotte and other members of the royal family, as well as being a fellow member of the German immigrant community in London. The imposter von Horn may have directed his letter to Kauffman at the apothecary's address during the time when she was working on the Brandenburg portraits in order to conceal their relationship and to make sure that the letter was not intercepted. This is

Figure 11. Angelica Kauffman, *Portrait of George Robert Helen*, 1767. Oil on canvas, 76 x 63 cm. National Gallery of Ireland, Dublin, NGI. 887. Photo © National Gallery of Ireland.

all speculation, but as Frances Gerard wrote in 1892: "The whole business is involved in a strange mystery, out of which it is difficult to grasp any tangible facts beyond that of the false marriage."[47]

What may be most remarkable about Kauffman's first years in London is that in spite of her position as a woman, her status as a foreigner, and a humiliating scandal, she managed to achieve critical and financial success. In December 1768, just ten months after the marriage separation agreement was signed, Kauffman was one of the thirty-four founding members of the Royal Academy of Arts. She benefited from the support and encouragement of her loyal friends, family, and influential patrons in London, but her success was primarily due to her own talent, hard work, and persistence.

Notes

1. De Rossi, *Vita di Angelica Kauffmann, pittori* (Florence, 1810); Kauffman, *"Mit traümte vor ein paar Nächten, ich hätte Briefe von Ihnen empfangen:" Gesammelte Briefe in den Originalsprachen*, ed. Waltraud Maierhofer (Lengwil am Bodensee: Libelle Verlag, 2001). The latter will be cited hereafter as Maierhofer.

2. See Peter Walch, "An Early Neoclassical Sketchbook by Angelica Kauffman," *Burlington Magazine* 119, no. 887 (1977): 98–111; and my "Americans on the Grand Tour and Angelica Kauffman in Rome," in *American Latium: American Artists and Travelers in and around Rome in the Age of the Grand Tour*, ed. Christopher M. S. Johns, Tommaso Manfredi, and Karin Wolfe (Rome: Accademia Nazionale di San Luca, Rome, 2023), 185–93.

3. The Burghley House Collection PIC 180. Kauffman's portfolio in the painting is inscribed: "Angelica Kauffman, painted at Rome 1764 by N. Dance."

4. The Burghley House Collection PIC 176. The picture is signed on the reverse: "Angelica Kauffman pinxt Ano 1764 at Naples." A label on the reverse is inscribed: "David Garrick Esqre painted at Naples 1764 by Angelica Kauffman." The painting was exhibited at the Free Society of Artists, Covent Garden. The printed catalog for the exhibition describes it as: "Mrs Angelica Kauffman, at Rome # 217. Portrait of a Gentleman—This Gentleman is David Garrick; of whom this Portrait would be a very good Likeness, if it was not larger than the Life."

5. Kauffman's portrait of Exeter is now in the Burghley House Collection as PIC 781. It is signed and dated: "Angelica Kauffmann fecit at aua Napolina/Ao 1764."

6. De Rossi, *Vita di Angelica Kauffmann*, 23–24.

7. Berenhorst and Friedrich Wilhelm von Erdmannsdorf, *Un Grand Tour: Deux journaux d'un même voyage en Italie, France et Angleterre (1765–1768)* Champion, Paris, 2014, quoted in W. G. Day, François Colson, and Amélie Junqua, *Sterne in Italy*, https://www.laurencesternetrust.org.uk/sterne/a-sentimental-journey/essay-on-sterne-in-italy-by-w-g-day.

8. Sharp, *Letters from Italy describing the custom and manners of that Country in the years 1765 and 1766. To which is annexed an admonition to gentlemen who pass the Alps in their tour through Italy* (London, 1766).

9. Sharp, *Letters from Italy*, 216–17.

10. De Rossi, *Vita di Angelica Kauffmann*, 23–24. Bridget Wentworth was the daughter of Sir Ralph Milbanke, 4th Baronet of Halnaby. Her first husband, Butler Cavendish Wentworth, the 2nd Baronet Wentworth (1709–41), died young. Her second husband, John Murray, was appointed British ambassador to the Ottoman Empire on 15 November 1765.

11. Maierhofer, 14.

12. Maierhofer, 15.

13. Maierhofer, 16–18. Kauffman's portrait of Reynolds is at Saltram Park, Devon (now part of the National Trust).

14. See Caroline Grigson, *The Life and Poems of Anne Hunter, Haydn's Tuneful Muse* (Liverpool: Liverpool University Press, 2009), 7, 11. The two did not marry until 1771.

15. This picture, now in a private collection, was described by Lady Victoria Manners and G. C. Williamson as possibly a portrait of "Mrs. John Hunter," then in possession of the art dealer A. Tooth & Sons, London. Manners and Williamson illustrated the portrait and noted that "it is suggested that Mrs. John Hunter, whose name is attached to the picture, may have posed for the figure" (*Angelica Kauffmann, R.A., Her Life and Her Works* [New York: Bretano's, 1924], 211–212; illustration opposite page 20).

16. Victoria and Albert Museum, London, E345-48-1927, no. 136, chalk, 285 x 219 mm. See Walch, "An Early Neoclassical Sketchbook." Kauffman used the same drawing as the model for a classical bust on a pedestal in her portrait of Theresa Parker in 1775 (private collection).

17. *The London Magazine* 36, November 1766, 598; *The Gentleman's Magazine* 36, December 1766, 599; *The Gentleman's Magazine* 37, April 1767, 165.

18. Grigson, *Life and Poems of Anne Hunter*, 26, 91.

19. Lyons, "'Exercising the ART as a TRADE': Professional Women Printmakers in England, c. 1750–c. 1850" (PhD diss., Birkbeck, University of London, 2022), 59.

20. See Will J. Hyett, "Some Collections of Paintings in Pittsburgh," *Art and Archeology* 14, nos. 5–6 (1922): 327–28, which describes the picture as "an important painting of Mrs. Hunter by Angelica Kauffmann," which was then in the collection of J. D. Laughlin.

21. Home, *John Hunter*, Royal College of Surgeons, London, RCSSC/P 120; the monkey skull is in the Hunterian collection, RCSHC/DP 203.

22. See Walter G. Strickland, *A Dictionary of Irish Artists*, 2 vols. (Dublin: Maunsel, 1913), 1:500–8; and E. B. Day, *Without Permit*, unpublished typescript biography of Robert Home from 1791 to his death, written c. 1920 (British Library, MSS Eur Photo Eur331).

23. *Protocollum Matrimoniorum Capella Imperialis ab anno Domini 1765 inchoatum*, Westminster Diocesan Archives, London: "testes fuere Josephus Kauffman avunculo sposa, Josephus Zucchi Venetecum, Josephus Angelini Romanus, Angelica Kauffman cognata sposa, Margarita Sharp."

24. Farington, *The Farington Diary*, ed. James Grieg, 8 vols. (London: Hutchinson, 1923–28), 1:8, 1:23–24.

25. Brissot de Warville, *Mémoires (1754–1793)*, ed. Cl. Perroud, 2 vols. (Paris: A. Picard, 1911), 1:196. See too Clifford D. Conner, *Jean-Paul Marat: Tribune of the French Revolution* (London, Pluto Press, 2012), 3, 13.

26. See J. T. Smith, *Nollekens and His Times*, 2 vols. (London, 1828), 1:84; and my "Angelica in Love: Gossip, Rumor, Romance, and Scandal," in *Angelica Kauffman, A Woman of Immense Talent*, ed. Tobias G. Natter (Ostfilden: Hatje Cantz, 2007), 42–51.

27. Helmut Swozilek, ed. and trans., *Memorie istoriche di Maria Angelica Kauffmann Zucchi riguardanti l'arte della pittura da lei professata scritte da G.C.Z. (Giuseppe Carlo Zucchi) Venezia MDCCLXXXVIII* (Bregenz: Vorarlberger Landesmuseum, 1999).

28. De Rossi, *Vita di Angelica Kauffmann*, 33–47. See also Peter Leisching, "Von böser und guter Ehe/Die beiden Heiraten der Angelika Kauffmann," in *Vorarlberger Landesmuseumverein Jahrbuch* (Bregenz: Vorarlberger Landesmuseum, 1991), 373–78.

29. De Rossi, *Vita di Angelica Kauffmann*, 36.

30. "Parmi strano, che quest'uomo, che macchinò tanto per ottenere in isposa Angelica, fosse per circostanze di ferite ricevute incapace di divenirle fisicamente marito. Pure egli stesso a molti suoi conoscenti lo avea svelato, e ciò maggiormente conferma, che un solo spirito d'interesse lo inducesse a cosi nera trama": De Rossi, *Vita di Angelica Kauffmann*, 46n.

31. De Rossi, *Vita di Angelica Kauffmann*, 37.

32. De Rossi, *Vita di Angelica Kauffmann*, 43–46. For more on the von Horn affair, see my "Angelica in Love."

33. Westminster City Archives, St. James's, Piccadilly, Marriage Register 1754–74, no. 344, 20 November 1767. See too Walter Shaw Sparrow, "Angelica Kauffman's Amazing Marriage," *The Connoisseur* 92 (1933): 242–48.

34. Her full name was Maria Anna Angelika Caterina Kauffmann, which she shortened and Anglicized to Angelica Kauffman. Their signatures match the handwriting on other documents known to be written by them.

35. "Einleitung der Ungültigkeitserklärung dieser am 13. Februar 1767 geschlossenen Ehe in der Kapelle der deutschen Gesandschaft in Rom erfolgte erst 1778": documents issued by a tripartite commission of Catholic theologians, one dated 6–20 March 1778 and the other 23 June 1778, now in a private collection, quoted in Claudia Helbok, *Miss Angel, Angelika Kauffmann—Eine Biographie* (Vienna: Brüder Rosenbaum, 1968), 261n13.

36. Sharp's papers are with those of the Lloyd-Baker family of Hardwick Hall in the Gloucestershire Archives, D3549/13/5/10.

37. William Dolben had three older sisters: Elizabeth (1721–1810), Frances (1724–97), and Anne (1725–1820). On Catherine "Kitty" Sharp, see Hester Grant, *The Good Sharps: The Eighteenth-Century Family That Changed Britain* (London: Vintage, 2021), 292–94.

38. Zoffany, *The Sharp Family*, 1779–81, oil on canvas, 115.6 x 125.7 cm, on loan to the National Gallery, London, © Lloyd-Baker Estate. See Brian Crosby, "Private Concerts on Land and Water: The Musical Activities of the Sharp Family,

c. 1750–*c*. 1790," *Royal Musical Association Research Chronicle* 34, no. 1 (2001): 7–10.

39. I am grateful to Professor Walter von Reinhart, University of Rhode Island, for assistance translating "von Horn"'s letter, cited below. For more on the von Horn affair see Wendy Wassyng Roworth, "Angelica in Love: Gossip, Rumor, Romance, and Scandal," in *Angelica Kauffman: A Woman of Immense Talent,* ed. Tobias Natter, exh. cat., Vorarlberger Landesmuseum, Bregenz (Ostfildern, Hatje Cantz Verlag), 2007, 42-50.

40. In the original: "Aber Wenn Sie ihren Lebenslauf lesen, so errinen Sie dass die allergrössten Geheimnisse welches öfters verdienen öffentlich abgestraft zu werden, durch wunderbare Mittel ent deckt und der Welt zum Schrecken offen zu werden."

41. In the original: "Ich habe Herr Granville Sharp ersucht mir meine Schriften zu senden. Noch jetzo längst es von Ihnen ab der Welt bekannt zu werden. Allein wenn einmal die Presse angefüllt ist, so kommen Sie zu spät und warhaftig Sie werden es beräunen."

42. In the original: "N'en douté plus Madame, oui je vous aime! Vous avez raison de me croire trop sage, pour me supposer une tendresse criminelle: je ne vous aime, que parceque Vous — merritté de l'etre, e je n'attant que votre répons, pour vous prover sur l'évidence la plus manifeste, que ce ne serra quand dernier moment de ma vie que je çe serais [cessera?] d'etre / Tout a Vous."

43. Gloucestershire Archives, D3549/13/5/10.

44. Private collection. Both paintings are oil on canvas, 76.8 x 64.1 cm unframed.

45. National Gallery of Ireland, Dublin, NGI 887, 1767, oil on canvas, 76 x 63 cm.

46. See Leslie G. Matthews, "London's Immigrant Apothecaries, 1600–1800," *Medical History* 18 (1974): 262, 269–70; Jennifer Gordon Lloyd Burnby, "A Study of the English Apothecary from 1660–1760" (PhD diss., University of London, 1979), 322; and *Household of Queen Charlotte, 1761–1818*, compiled by J. C. Sainty and R. O. Bucholz, https://tinyurl.com/QCharlotteHousehold

47. Gerard, *Angelica Kauffmann: A Biography* (London, 1892), 97.

Un homme à l'antique: The Visual Vocabulary of Antiquity in Men's Fashion and Democratic Uniforms in Revolutionary France

BRONTË HEBDON

On 1 November 1791, the Italian fashion periodical *Giornale delle nuove mode di Francia e d'Inghilterra* published a fashion plate of a young man in a brown *dégagé* tailcoat with blue breeches, a top hat on his head and a cockade tucked in its band. Describing the plate, the editors paid particular attention to the figure's right hand, which held a long wooden club. They noted that "for some time now, the young men in France have been transformed into many versions of *Hercules*, and it is a pleasant thing for their weak arms to drag a heavy, rough club, which, until now, has only served to frighten young children." The editors then predicted that soon the winds of political change in France would require those same young men to "throw their sticks in the fire."[1] At the date of publication, however, the *Giornale delle nuove mode* was describing a period before wooden clubs became a tool of the *jeunes gens* and their successors, the *Incroyables*, a subcultural group that used them to express their "executive power."[2] Instead, the club connected to the older visual tradition of Hercules, whose strength, divine parentage, club, and lion skin made him a paragon of male prowess in classical antiquity. Antoine de Baecque and Lynn Hunt have noted that in the 1790s, Hercules became a symbol of French republicanism and the force that would be required for the new brotherhood of citizens to vanquish the evils of the monarchical system.[3] Yet Hercules was only one of many classical referents that were deployed in late eighteenth-century French culture. Indeed, as early as the later seventeenth century, the Greco-Roman world became a counterpoint to the perceived decadence of French decorative arts, theater, and even fashion. In 1747, Étienne La Font de Saint-Yenne's *Réflexions sur quelques causes de l'état present de la peinture en France* advocated for the antique as an antidote to that decadence, with the subsequent writings of the comte de Caylus, Johann Joachim Winckelmann, and Denis Diderot further developing a neoclassical aesthetic.[4]

After 1789, the antique continued to be an important point of reference, but the political situation of the 1790s created friction between the idealism of neoclassical aesthetics and the realities of contemporary experience. Ewa Lajer-Burcharth described this period as a crisis of masculinity, noting that even as the Revolution became more moderate after 1794, individual men struggled to retain their subjectivity.[5] This crisis is visible in the history painting of the period, in which the heroic male bodies of the 1780s came to be replaced by youthful, ephebic bodies in the 1790s, a change that Abigail Solomon-Godeau attributes to artists feeling "compelled to imagine the entire spectrum of desirable human qualities, from battlefield heroics to eroticized corporeal beauty, as male."[6] Another means through which this crisis of masculinity was experienced and negotiated in the increasingly masculine public sphere of revolutionary Paris was male fashion. What Daniel Roche described as the "culture of appearances" in the Revolution required sartorial political expression, which I define in two distinct directions.[7] First, male garments needed to reveal more of the body. The clothed silhouette of the 1790s tightened, evolving toward what Elizabeth Amann has called the "art of the cut" and away from an emphasis on materials and ornamentation that characterized men's dress under the ancien régime; Aileen Ribeiro, however, notes that this shift was more of an acceleration of trends from the 1780s than a revolutionary break with the past.[8] Second, the male silhouette—both body and garments together—needed to be socially legible, which the successive governments of the National Convention, the Directory, and the Consulate interpreted as a need for uniformity. Indeed, they went so far as to create systems of male national uniforms, either for all citizens or for those in government positions. Alexander Maxwell describes the development of these uniforms as the creation of a sartorial nationalism to assuage fears about vestimentary malfeasance and class mixing amid the chaos of the revolutionary years.[9]

Similar renegotiations occurred in female dress through the 1780s and 1790s, many of which drew upon the antique.[10] Garments like the *robe à la grecque* proliferated in Paris in the 1790s as an alternative to the artifice of ancien-régime female dress. Yet despite the neoclassical emphasis in women's fashion, and in the visual arts more generally, the influence of the antique on the male silhouette in this period remains underexamined. This essay will explore how antiquity—here broadly defined as Greco-Roman art, culture, and clothing, as interpreted by theorists like Winckelmann and André Lens and artists like Jacques-Louis David—influenced the sartorial development of men's dress and subjectivity in the 1790s. In particular, I will consider how this influence manifests in the shape and articulation of the idealized male body, the desire to return male dress to antique norms of drapery, and the use of antique-style ornamentation to articulate social hierarchies.

The Body

At the Salon of 1787, Jacques-Louis David and Pierre Peyron submitted competing cabinet paintings of the death of Socrates (see Figures 1 and 2).[11] Each relied on both ancient sources, like Plato's *Phaedo*, and modern ones, like Diderot's "De la poésie dramatique," to structure their compositions. In their respective paintings, Socrates sits elevated on a bed, gesturing upward toward heaven with one arm while the other hovers ominously over the cup of hemlock that will take his life. One leg extends outward, an open manacle on the floor below.[12] The similarities in content between the two paintings prompted Louis-François Lefébure to rely on their differences of form when writing his review: "Mr. Peyron's presents a somber site, a quiet sage, moved spectators, a weak drawing, a brush becoming sluggish. It has the advantage of order, and effect, in that it contains a beautiful episode; but that of Mr. David wins through a beautiful thought. We see Socrates there, occupied with both his speech and the cup. His prevails through the beautiful total thought which positions each character in its place, and which gives each figure an appropriate expression. Mr. Peyron's picture is the work of a profound philosopher, and Mr. David's picture is the work of a great reasoner."[13] The major difference Lefébure identifies between the two paintings is Peyron's weaker drawing (a lack of adequate contour), which diminishes the unity of his composition and leaves each figure isolated from the others. Such unity is what David's painting excels at communicating. His use of contour, when combined with gesture and expression, becomes the unifying presence in his artwork and creates the totality that Lefébure calls David's "beautiful thought."

Figure 1. Jacques-Louis David, *The Death of Socrates*, 1787. Oil on canvas, 129.5 x 196 cm. Courtesy of the Metropolitan Museum of Art, New York.

Figure 2. Jean-François Pierre Peyron, *The Death of Socrates*, 1787. Oil on canvas, 98 x 133.5 cm. Courtesy of the Statens Museum for Kunst, Copenhagen.

However, there is one critical element of the paintings, the presentation of Socrates's body, in which the two rivals affirm one another's approach. The physiognomic details of their faces—open mouth, broad and wrinkled forehead, forked beard—align with the typological descriptions of Socrates in texts like Plato's *Symposion* and with the surviving Roman busts of the philosopher, which were based on Lysippos's bronze original from the fourth century BCE.[14] Yet David and Peyron both position Socrates's head on a much younger body with defined musculature and soft, fleshy skin that reveals the veinous and skeletal material underneath. The resulting composite forms are jarring. In Peyron's painting, Socrates's muscles bulge beneath his lilac tunic; in David's, in which a single swath of cloth drapes over Socrates's body, the head and body are so disparate that they seem to operate on separate referential planes.

It is unsurprising that David and Peyron were both occupied with questions of bodily form. Writers like Johann Joachim Winckelmann had been posing such questions to artists for decades in publications like *Reflections on the Imitation of Greek Works in Painting and Sculpture* (1755) and *The History of the Art of Antiquity* (1764). Winckelmann's texts contributed to a robust public discourse on the merits of the antique, with debates on the virtues of the ancients versus the moderns and archaeological discoveries in Herculaneum and Pompeii bringing the classical world into greater public consciousness.[15]

Peyron's and David's paintings give Socrates a muscled, idealized male body. In so doing, they demonstrate how neoclassical artists were propagating the renewed pedagogical emphasis by the Académie on contour and the male form, and reinforcing Winckelmann's particular reading of the supremacy of Greek art. With its idealized form and harmony, Winckelmann's descriptions of surviving artworks from classical antiquity, such as the Apollo Belvedere, which he identified as "the highest ideal of art among the works of antiquity that have escaped its destruction," were formed in relation to the *beau idéal* of a perfect body unmediated by any physical or cultural singularity. This harmony of proportion and form in the male body and the political freedom of Greek men were identified by Winckelmann as the "principal cause[s] of the preeminence of Greek art."[16] The frequency with which Winckelmann was posthumously quoted—the phrase "noble simplicity and quiet grandeur" was often invoked—signifies the continuing influence of his principles.[17] And yet Winckelmann's aesthetics could not survive the rupture of the French Revolution, what Antoine de Baecque calls the "intrusion of history," without evolving—in part because his persistent championing of the Greek over the Roman failed to account for the profound intermingling of Greco-Roman culture.[18]

Baecque and Alex Potts both understand David to be a less than enthusiastic adherent to Winckelmann's aesthetics.[19] In David's most celebrated works like the *Oath of the Horatii* or the *Death of Socrates*, beautiful male forms are often interrupted by the narrative strength of his scenes. Brutus's menacing stare, Socrates's gesticulating limbs, or Horatius's open mouth all stand in defiance of Winckelmann's insistence on the need for a closed singularity of form. David's composition of Socrates's body is also revealing. The forked beard identifies the Greek philosopher, but the wrinkles on his forehead follow the veristic pattern developed in the Roman Republic as a symbol of age and wisdom. Socrates's head, therefore, contains elements of both Greek and Roman cultural ideals, which Caroline Vout identifies as a much more accurate rendering of the Greco-Roman world. Although Winckelmann insisted on the separation of Greek and Roman cultural production as two separate histories, Vout points to Plutarch, who noted that at least since Marcellus's capture of Syracuse in 212 BCE, Roman culture had absorbed and mediated Greek art for its own purposes. This, she claims, often meant creatively reworking Greek works, rather than copying them outright.[20] Winckelman and David, however, in accord with the common understanding at the time, did not recognize the cultural hybridity of the Greco-Roman world, which helps explain why Winckelmann could insist that Rome and its art were subordinate to Greece and Greek art without realizing that many of the works he valorized, like the Apollo Belvedere, were Roman copies, rather than Greek originals.

Similarly, David unknowingly conflates the Greek and the Roman in Socrates's body. In addition to the veristic, Roman portrayal of Socrates's head, his idealized body bears a stark resemblance to one of Winckelmann's favorite artworks: the Belvedere Torso. In the Vatican collection since the mid-sixteenth century, the Belvedere Torso depicts Ajax seated on an animal hide, although Winckelmann thought the torso was that of Hercules.[21] David would probably have encountered the Belvedere Torso during his stay in Rome from 1775 to 1780, when he was known to wander the city with chalk and sketchbook in hand, drawing memorable artworks and scenes.[22] Like the Belvedere Torso, Socrates's body is bare chested with a swoop of drapery folded over his middle, which highlights the slight compression of his oblique muscles as he leans to one side (in the case of the painting, toward the cup of hemlock). The positioning of his legs, splayed across the bed, approximates the trajectory of the torso's legs, which extend beyond their broken edges at an acute angle. Socrates's body thus becomes a composite form in which both Greek and Roman sensibilities and aesthetics are present. Like a Roman portrait bust placed on top of a Greek nude, David renders Socrates's body as both real and ideal, Roman and Greek, and so demonstrates one of the ways in which eighteenth-century audiences interpreted the Greco-Roman world.

David's Socrates was not alone. Caroline Vout and Alice Christ both note that many republican-era Roman statues put a portrait-like Roman head onto an idealized, or even Hellenized, male body.[23] This was because Roman conceptions of masculinity were less tied to bodily proportion and aesthetics than to the civic participation of the man in question, in which the body functioned as an iconographic indicator of character and other traits, like virtue and educational status. As such, the male body seen in Roman sculpture acted as a system of signs, often veiled by the various draping styles of the Roman toga, that communicated the political and social requirements of Roman citizenship, not unlike the male body in postrevolutionary France. An idealized body was therefore only one of many aspects of a sculpture, along with its presentation of clothing and its quality of execution.

David paints Socrates's body according to this logic, with its compositional force encoded within the body's positioning and references to antiquity. As a history painting, David's *Death of Socrates* is also supposed to encourage moral reflection and so elevate its audience. Yet once the Revolution was underway, using an idealized male body as an artistic, cultural, or political symbol required significant modification. In previous centuries, it was the body of the king that carried the rhetorical weight of French nationalism and its attending attributes of civic virtue, morality, and duty.[24] Such was the case when the Estates General was convened in May 1789 for the first time in 175 years: the dress and decoration of Louis XVI's body, lavishly adorned and surrounded by an assembly of men dressed according to their station, visualized what Jürgen Habermas called the "representative publicity" of French political life.[25] After Louis XVI's execution, however, the rhetorical and semantic power of the king's body was split across the many individual bodies of French citizens, with citizenship increasingly coded as active, young, and male, which emphasized the male form and its physical presence in spaces of debate.[26] Throughout the 1790s, men embraced visible indicators of citizenship like cockades, cravats, culottes, and collars, all connected to the ever-changing political atmosphere of revolutionary Paris.[27] These sartorial signals became necessary emblems of individual belief and collective identity because they broadcast a man's civic virtue. As Alex Potts notes, the aesthetic idealism of Winckelmann's *beau idéal* was diminished in the face of these new requirements of sartorial citizenship.[28] The combination of the Greek and Roman body, which we have seen in Winckelmann's texts and in paintings like David's *Death of Socrates*, eventually required the two to be separated into a signifying body and an aesthetic body.

In the late eighteenth century, both Greek and Roman bodies were found in French art and culture. Adaptations of Roman histories for the French stage, such as new productions of Pierre Corneille's *Horace* in 1782 and Voltaire's *Brutus* in 1790, helped the French public correlate Roman political and cultural history with the male body. Students in the Paris *collèges* read Roman authors like Virgil and Tacitus.[29] Some of David's most famous paintings used narratives from Roman history to explore questions of ethics and morality, employing the bodies and expressions of the figures depicted to communicate their virtuous qualities. A new translation of Winckelmann's *History of the Art of Antiquity* by H. J. Jansen, published between 1790 and 1794, renewed attention to idealized Greek male bodies. Yet, as the 1790s progressed, revolutionaries read Winckelmann with an eye attuned to the application of his aesthetics to the present moment. If ideal beauty was made possible through the freedom enjoyed by the ancient Greeks, and if French society now enjoyed a similar freedom after 1789, could the French male body be idealized in a similar way and thereby elevate French art to a status equivalent to that of the Greeks? Like the cultural hybridity seen in republican-era Roman statues or the Greco-Roman composite body seen in David's Socrates, could the French male body exemplify both Winckelmann's Greek *beau idéal* and the rhetorical power of the Roman body? Publications like Athanase Détournelle's *Journal de la société populaire et républicaine des arts* (1794) suggested a solution: clothing. Clothing could structure and idealize the male body, while also signifying the appropriate principles of the Revolution.[30]

Drapery

Combining an idealized body with some type of clothing was no easy task, as Jean-Germain Drouais lamented in a letter to David, his teacher, on 4 July 1787. Drouais was struggling to figure out how to clothe the figure in his *académie* submission, *Philoctetes on the Island of Lemnos*. Of particular concern was the draped material he wished to place around Philoctetes's midsection. He told David that "I'm going to *redress* the model; it doesn't quite work yet. I don't know if this will improve anything."[31] Drouais's struggle to dress Philoctetes was a struggle to drape him in an expressive way. Linguistically, there was no distinction in French between "to dress" and "to drape" (both are *a draper*); for Drouais and other eighteenth-century artists, however, "to dress" a figure and "to drape" a figure implied quite different stylistic idioms: the tailored garments of contemporary fashion or the draped swaths of fabric that approximated classical antiquity.[32] Anne Hollander described this second option as "rhetorical drapery"—drapery that ennobled the body through its associations with the classical past.[33] This ennobling quality took on additional importance after the Revolution, as more men used garments and accessories to express their new political and social identities.

Clothing has always been an idiom through which bodies signify identity, but the constant evolution of fashion in the eighteenth century made art theorists like Caylus, Winckelmann, and Joshua Reynolds claim that in art, the drapery of the ancients was preferable to contemporary dress. The dress of ancient Greece and Rome were similar but not identical; they were distinct styles that developed in conversation with the social and political changes of Greco-Roman history. They were also symbolic indicators of status, gender, and social roles. Yet many assumed that antique garments existed outside the mutability of fashion. Some texts like Caylus's *Receuil d'antiquités égyptiennes, étrusques, grecques et romaines* (1752) described historic garments as if they were unchanging. Other texts, like André Lens's *Le Costume ou essai sur les habillements et les usages de plusiers peuple de l'antiquité* (1776) or Jacques Grasset de Saint-Sauveur's *L'Antique Rome* (1796), used artwork to describe various garments in their histories.[34] While many artists relied on these texts in order to claim historical accuracy, the reality was that few scholars or theorists understood the complexity of antique dress. For example, in *Le Costume,* Lens described the toga as a "garment unique to the Roman empire," but did not chart its development or the shifts it underwent in the transition from the Republic to the Empire, a change that Melissa Rothfus defines as critical to the expression of the garment.[35] Rothfus notes that the toga as depicted on republican-era Roman statues functioned as a symbol of Roman identity through its uniform presentation. The arrangement of the folds could also signify important cultural values in the wearer, like dignity and virtue, just as deviations from that norm—a longer or shorter fold of fabric under the right arm, for example—could communicate a Hellenistic education or social mobility.[36] There existed in neoclassical art throughout the 1780s a similar desire to communicate the virtues of antiquity through draped clothing.

So, in March 1794, when the Société populaire et républicaine des arts, echoing appeals from the National Convention, published a call to design a national uniform for citizens and a civil uniform for government officials, the draped garments of the Greco-Roman world were the obvious choice. The sculptor Jean-Joseph Espercieux asked the Société, "Will this costume be taken from those already known among the Greeks, Etruscans, or Romans? Will we adopt the tunic or the toga?"[37] Joseph Lavallée similarly exclaimed, "that of the Romans, for example, was so noble! The body, so natural under a conservative drapery, was the envelope and the image of a free soul covered under the mantle of the law."[38] Other respondents to the Société's call, such as its president, Pierre-Théodore Bienaimé, and the writer Claude-François Xavier Mercier, invoked Winckelmann by calling for "beautiful simplicity" and "beautiful forms" within male dress.[39] In approximating antique dress,

Bienaimé said the uniform needed to cover the body "without harming the development of the limbs, without hindering their movements, without degrading their beautiful forms," while also "mark[ing] the character of the subject."[40] The Société and the National Convention hoped that reforming male dress in order to express greater virtue, especially through the idiom of antiquity, would encourage the desired ideals of civic participation and freedom that were necessary after the Revolution.[41]

The successful design for an antique-styled uniform came from Jacques-Louis David. On 14 May 1794, he submitted to the Committee for Public Safety his "views and suggestions on the means of improving national costume and of rendering it more appropriate to republican morals and to the character of the revolution."[42] His uniform for a *représentant du peuple* included a short, tan tunic with a standing collar, a tricolor sash wrapped around the waist, and a toque with sheaves of wheat placed over the ear (see Figure 3). The most striking element was a flowing blue cloak tied across the right shoulder and accessorized with a red Brandenburg clasp embroidered with the words "*PEUPLE FRANÇAIS / ÉGALITÉ / LIBERTÉ.*" The way the cloak fell across the figure's body, obscuring it behind a scrim of heavy fabric, imitated the draped appearance of Greco-Roman garments, especially the fabric on the left side, which was folded up and over the left arm. Despite the antiquarianism advocated by Caylus and Lens, the fact that David approximated antique dress, rather than directly imitating an antique garment, was not problematic, nor should it be surprising. Louis Visconti explained in *La clef du cabinet des souverains* that "the ancient artists treated with great freedom the draperies of purely historical figures and knew how to make the costumes of their time picturesque by dint of removing parts of them."[43] If even antique artists had treated drapery in this way, then so too could eighteenth-century artists.

David's design also followed Winckelmann's conviction that the specific garments worn by the Greeks and Romans were less important than the shapes made by the falling fabric. Cut either in a circle, semicircle, or square, the fabric's shape created the beauty of the draped folds against the body, which in turn determined its affect.[44] Yet the particular details of garments like the toga, the chiton, or the paludamentum could undermine the most critical component of drapery: its ahistorical ability to signify. In revolutionary France, as the male body became a metonymic marker of French nationalism, its clothing took on an urgent role in facilitating that identity. David's uniform attempted just such a formulation by simultaneously revealing and concealing the male body beneath its cloak. Hollander has proposed that there was a dialectical relationship between the human body and its clothing: generational bodily ideals and clothing evolved in tandem and were often

Un homme à l'antique / 143

Figure 3. Jacques-Louis David, *Le représentant du people, projet de costume*, 1794. Drawing, 33 x 21 cm. Courtesy of the Musée Carnavalet, Paris.

subject to the same cultural forces, which, in the case of the late eighteenth century, involved appeals to the ennobling power of classical antiquity.[45] As such, the presence of a particular style of clothing could influence the articulation of the body underneath in terms of its form, its movement, and its semantics. Such was the case in David's designs, in which the appropriation of an antique-draped garment signaled a refashioning of the eighteenth-century male body to make it more akin to the Roman body.

None of David's designs were ever fully adopted. The political contingencies of Thermidor, as well as the prohibitive cost of the uniforms, rendered his designs unrealistic. Male fashion had also found a better way to express the antique idiom: not through loose drapery, but rather through a tighter overall silhouette. According to Pierre Bienaimé, the standard aristocratic *habit à la française* of the eighteenth century, made of silk and covered with brightly colored embroidery, did "not lend itself sufficiently to the various operations of civil and military life" because it had been shaped by the culture and tastes of the French court.[46] The second half of the eighteenth century saw a shift away from this courtly influence. What would eventually become dandyism in the early nineteenth century looked like a preference for fit and tailoring in the 1780s. In *The Psychology of Clothes*, John C. Flügel describes these changes as the "great masculine renunciation," in which French men slowly rejected the ostentation of courtly fashion, opting instead for a style of dress associated with the English countryside, where healthy physical activity, participation in public discourse, and fraternal camaraderie were encouraged through the adoption of monochromatic color schemes, riding boots, and frock coats.[47] Once the domain of traditional markers of social value like status and wealth, the *habit à la française* slowly altered the masculine silhouette toward one resembling Winckelmann's *beau idéal*. Over the last two decades of the eighteenth century, suiting reproportioned the male body by elongating the leg and tightening around the torso, thereby revealing more of the body's contour. Thus, even as public figures like Bienaimé and Visconti advocated for greater looseness in male dress, or even the adoption of antique-styled garments, the average Frenchman's clothing actually tightened to his body throughout the eighteenth century.

Pierre de La Mésangère, editor of *Le Journal des dames et des modes*, depicts this developing male silhouette in a fashion plate from 1799 (see Figure 4). The figure wears a brown *habit dégagé* over a white waistcoat and shirt. His upper body is encased in this tailored fabric, which La Mésangère describes as "thinner than it has ever been," and which is layered and darted to fit tautly across his chest. The emphasis in the plate, however, is on the pale yellow pantaloons, which, La Mésangère notes, were "always tight" and tucked into Greco-Roman-inspired mid-calf boots that he calls "buskins."[48]

Un homme à l'antique / 145

Figure 4. Plate from *Le Journal des dames et des modes*, 1799. Engraving, 11 x 17 cm. Courtesy of the Morgan Library and Museum. PML 5687-5707. Purchased by Pierpont Morgan by 1906.

Pantaloons originated in Hungarian hussar uniforms but became part of men's civilian dress in the 1790s. They extended beyond the knee to the calf or ankle and tightened around the leg, achieving a slim fit by being made of a specially prepared leather called chamois or a light-colored wool cut on the bias.[49] Penelope Bryde notes that the buff color of the pantaloons approximated the color of Western European skin, and that therefore, given their tight proportions, they appear to mimic a nude statue.[50]

David's uniforms seem to incorporate these new bodily proportions. Alongside the loose, draped cloak across the figure's shoulders, the tunic conformed to the lines of the body, a sash accentuating the waist. Some of David's uniform designs even include pantaloons, which Madeleine Delpierre called the "narrow sheath which conceals nothing of their forms."[51] Combining the modern and the antique in this way both concealed and revealed the male body, which, in turn, made men like Visconti turn again to the antique to note how "the ancient costume was naturally combined with the nudity of certain parts, a nudity to which the sculptors could still give some arbitrary latitude without harming the costume."[52] If such a combination of clothing and the revealed body was indeed natural, then this tighter silhouette worked much better at communicating the ideals of the new French Republic than David's original designs had done.

By 1800, more and more Parisian men engaged with politics in part through dress, clothing their lower bodies in tight-fitting pantaloons instead of the loose breeches dominant for most of the eighteenth century, and thereby revealing more of their silhouettes and emphasizing the rhetorical nature of clothing and the relationship between the body and its covering. In the plate from *Le Journal des dames et des modes*, for example, the contours of the man's legs and torso revealed his political and social standing much as a badge or cockade would, which is perhaps why men like Maximilien Robespierre insisted that true patriots could recognize political virtue in their fellow men without the need for external symbols like the cockade.[53] The implication in Robespierre's assertion is that the male body could be manipulated to say different things depending on the way in which it was clothed. The tighter silhouette of the late eighteenth century, for example, spoke to the need for representative publicity to a greater degree than had David's uniforms, which concealed most of the male body behind swaths of antique-inspired woolens. The body needed to remain visible in some way if it was to signify, which is how Winckelmann understood the relationship between drapery and sculpture, and why Drouais struggled to properly render *Philoctetes*. A problem remained, however, in maintaining the legibility of clothing amid the constant threat of misappropriation. Within this late eighteenth-century culture of appearances, and especially as the egalitarianism of the Revolution began to fade, what guarantee was there that bodies were clothed appropriately for their class, gender, or political stance? Some type of hierarchical organization was needed to order all these signifying bodies.

Ornamentation

As the Revolution turned into the Terror, all guarantees of vestimentary legibility were called into question, and dressing according to one's political beliefs became a fraught practice, full of both semantic and corporeal danger. Countless individual lives were reduced to markers of identity like those of Jacobin, priest, or aristocrat, while others embraced the fracturing of public trust by adopting subcultural modes of dressing like that of the *jeunes gens* and the *sans culottes*. In the midst of this confusion, Robespierre delivered a speech to the Convention in which he argued for the continued importance of legible virtue: "To what end are we striving? The peaceful enjoyment of liberty and equality. ... What then is the fundamental principle of democratic or popular government, that is to say the essential underpinning which sustains it and makes it work? It is *virtue*. ... The first rule of your political conduct must be to relate all you do to maintaining equality and developing virtue."[54]

Maintaining equality certainly included how one dressed, but after Robespierre's fall from power in July 1794, the Thermidorian leader François-Antoine Boissy d'Anglas spoke of a profound shift in conceptions of equality and virtue: "Civil equality in fact, is all that a reasonable man can claim. Absolute equality is a chimera; for it to exist there would have to be absolute equality in intelligence, virtue, physical strength, education and fortune for all men."[55] Boissy d'Anglas's comments demonstrate how the visual rhetoric of male dress was again shifting in reaction to political events, this time out of concern that immaterial values like equality or virtue could not possibly be expressed within all male bodies. Dressing for equality, let alone becoming equal, was increasingly out of reach. Boissy d'Anglas's position was reflected in the new constitution that went into effect in August 1795, which redefined equality of participation in the public sphere, stipulating who could and could not serve in public office, as well as who qualified for the title of *citoyen*. In 1791, citizenship had been extended to all men over the age of twenty-five capable of paying a tax equivalent to three days' wages, but the constitution of 1795 refined the category in order to restrict it to wealthy adult men.[56] The egalitarianism of the National Convention was superseded by the need for political and economic stability, and virtue, it seemed, was no longer the primary qualification for good governance, nor was its articulation in dress reliable.

All this coincided with the cultural shifts of the Directory, which were described by Aileen Ribeiro as a "release of pent-up emotion" following Robespierre's death, exemplified in the "wildest extravagance in dress in reaction against the Jacobin republic of virtue."[57] Within this charged and somewhat cynical atmosphere, in which citizenship was redefined and political power redistributed among the ruling few, the use of rhetorical drapery and the representative publicity of the male body were no longer desirable. Madeline Delpierre noted that the Directory "ultimately preferred external marks of authority for those who exercised power to absolute equality of clothing among all citizens."[58] On 14 September 1795, in preparation for the transition of power to the Directory, Henri Grégoire outlined a new sumptuary plan that would order male bodies according to this new logic of external marks, one that collapsed men's social and political positions into one. His proposal clothed sixteen of the highest public officials in uniforms with an emphasis on ornamented borders and color to create distinctions between political offices. Such ornamentation would become the key indicator of a man's rank. To support his ideas, Grégoire referenced the practices of antiquity:

> By adopting a costume for the keepers of public authority, you enter into the custom of almost all ancient and modern peoples. Although a distinctive decoration can sometimes fuel an individual's pride and ambition, the ancients did not believe that this inconvenience could ever outweigh the advantage of subjecting the law to the respect ... which is due to it, by personifying it, so to speak. ... In Athens, if someone had behaved disrespectfully towards a magistrate, especially when he had his myrtle crown, which was the symbol of his dignity, he would have been punished with a strong fine and deprived of citizenship rights. We remember this character of the Roman, who, at the sight of the fasces, dismounted to honor the consul. ... Experience proves that the use of uniforms assigned to public officials is one of those social institutions of which the moral character of people is composed: it is, therefore, wise to include this measure in political calculations. ... The language of signs has an eloquence of its own. Distinctive costumes are part of this idiom; they awaken ideas and feelings analogous to their object, especially when they seize the imagination with their brilliance. ... The costume of a public official says to citizens: here is a man of the law. He must be surrounded by all the physical and moral means capable of ensuring its execution.[59]

By drawing a connection between ancient symbols, like the myrtle crown, and the modern uniforms that he wished to create, Grégoire argued for the value of recognizable public imagery as a means of settling political instability. He hoped that such ornamented uniforms would set those in power apart from the masses, thereby visualizing the new hierarchy that became the Directory government and so alleviating the anxieties of a society in upheaval. When Grégoire's plan was accepted, Jacques Grasset de Saint-Sauveur illustrated his designs and included uniforms for the Directors and Ministers, Secretaries and Messengers of State, Representatives of the People, the Council of the Ancients, and the Council of Five Hundred among others.[60] Like David's uniform for a *représentant du peuple*, Grégoire's uniforms reach for the "dignity in the costumes of the Greeks, in those of the Romans" by revealing and obscuring the body.[61] The Directors had two uniforms: a formal one for special events and a *costume ordinaire* for everyday work. The formal uniform of a Director was a blue tunic and red mantle lined with white and embroidered in gold, with a belted scarf and white pantaloons. The *costume ordinaire* included what Grégoire called a *habit-manteau*: a red open mantle with wide lapels and sleeves, a long white vest with a blue belt fringed in gold, and white silk pantaloons (see Figure 5).

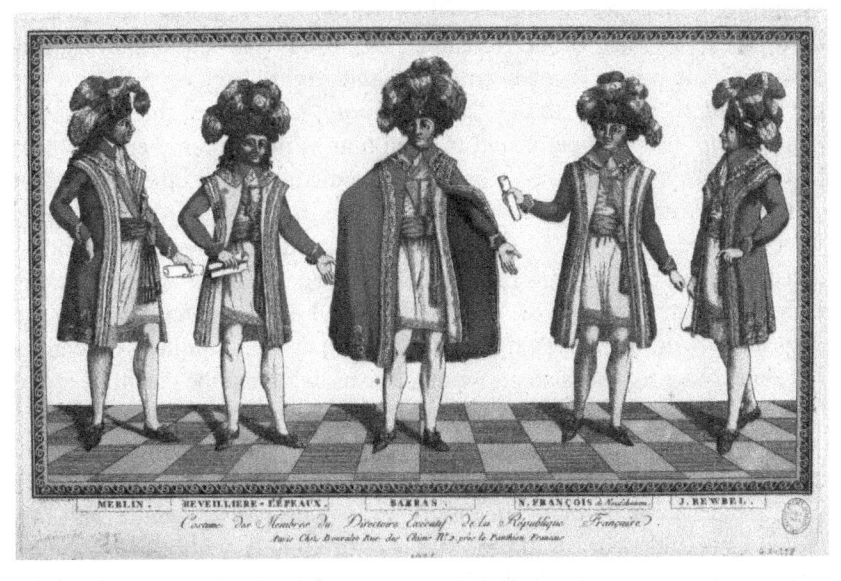

Figure 5. Henri Grégoire's design for the *costume ordinaire* of Directors. From *Costume des membres du Directoire exécutif de la République française*, c. 1796. Engraving, 25 x 39 cm. Courtesy of the Musée Carnavalet, Paris.

Other officials wore variations on this uniform, with ministers wearing the same silhouette in black and red, secretaries in all black, and department administrators in blue and black (see Figure 6). Each role was differentiated from the others by color and with ornament. A Director's *costume ordinaire* included large bands of gold embroidery along the hemlines of the vest and *habit-manteau*, while the minister's *habit-manteau* was ornamented with less extensive patterns of red and black vegetal motifs. The decorative detailing was at its simplest with the lowest-ranking officials, such as department administrators, whose uniforms featured a simple red border along the hemline and cuffs of their *habit-manteau*. Not all roles were included in Grégoire's design hierarchy. For example, the Council of Five Hundred and the Council of the Elders were both outfitted in much longer vests and cloaks that were even more explicitly antique in design, although even they retained a decorative border.

Indeed, the placement of decorative details along the borders of Grégoire's uniforms was itself a reference to antiquity. Greco-Roman textiles were often decorated with bands of color along the edges, but such decorations had different meanings in the classical world. In Greece, clothing was ornamented for religious and civic purposes, although more often to mark events than to designate social roles.[62] Clothing in Rome, however, was a public-facing, material manifestation of a man's social capital and was therefore often used to communicate an individual's position. For example, the toga, as the standard garment of the Roman citizen, used color and ornamentation to specify the wearer's social role. The gold embroidery on the border of the *toga picta*, worn with the *tunica palmata*, represented the *ornamenta triumphalia* of the emperor and marked him as the supreme embodiment of virtue in imperial Rome.[63] Simpler *clavi* distinguished other prominent officials, like senators and equites. First taken from Etruscan culture, clavi were strips of woven or embroidered color that extended over the shoulders and down the front and back of a tunic. The broader stripes worn by senators were called the *latus clavus*, while equites had the narrower stripes of the *angustus clavus*. But these stripes were far from the only signifiers of identity in Rome. Material was also important, as was color and the cleanliness and type of the garment.[64]

Lens's *Le Costume* demonstrates what eighteenth-century men would have known (and not known) about how the Romans used ornament to signify rank. In *Le Costume*, he describes the *latus clavus* and the *angustus clavus* as "braid[s] or band[s] of purple," different in width.[65] But he was unsure what they would look like on a garment, since so few sculptural examples had been found. He did note, however, that garments and certain details could set some men apart from others, as was the case with the *toga*

Un homme à l'antique / 151

Figure 6. Alexis Chataignier, *Costume de minister du Directoire*, c. 1795–99. Engraving, 35 x 22 cm. Courtesy of the Musée Carnavalet, Paris.

praetexta, a style of toga worn by the very young and by magistrates that was ornamented with purple bands on the borders.[66] It should be noted that Grasset de Saint-Sauveur mentions the *latus clavus* in his own book of costume history, *L'Antique Rome*, although, like Lens, he admits to some confusion as to its specifics; he was certain, however, that the bands of color had a "width proportionate to the dignity of the wearer."[67] While the size and articulation of the ornament in Grégoire's designs show a similar organizing principle as was employed in ancient Rome (the higher the rank, the more complex the design), neither he nor Grasset de Saint-Sauveur provide much direction on which patterns or motifs correspond to each position. Of the uniforms for the Council of Elders, Grégoire notes only that the clothing was "ornamented in colored embroidery"; of the Directors' uniforms, he writes that they were "richly embroidered in gold on the outside and on the lapels."[68] Such sparse detail prompted a lack of consistency between the illustrations of the proposed uniforms. For the Directors' uniforms, for example, Grasset de Saint-Sauveur's designs record a type of meandering vegetal arabesque, while those illustrated by Alexis Chataignier use a more abstracted motif. This variety of expression in the surviving engravings suggests a desire similar to that expressed by the drapery in David's uniforms from 1794: a wish to approximate, rather than outright copy, the antique, and so to allow the body and its uniform to present a contemporary social and political identity, rather than only signify something from the Greco-Roman world. But like David's uniforms, fully adopting Grégoire's proved a difficult task, and by 1797, the greatest sartorial symbol of the Directory was not his proposed system, but rather the tricolor scarf worn by the many thousands of civil servants throughout France.[69]

When the *Giornale delle nuove mode di Francia e d'Inghilterra* published its Hercules plate in 1791, the worst years of the Revolution still lay in the future. Before the execution of Louis XVI, the traumas of the Terror, and the collective struggles of each successive French government, the figure of Hercules had appeared indestructible, or, at the very least, strong enough to represent the French public as the ground shifted beneath them. But, as Ewa Lajer-Burcharth has noted, the crisis of masculinity created by the Revolution eventually rejected Hercules as an emblem of masculinity: "The body as the Republic wanted it, as a signifier of social unity and coherence—men as brothers united in fraternal embrace; women as noble mothers caring for their children—is juxtaposed with the body the Republic feared, the body fragmented by the revolutionary process or the body as the agent of fragmentation—the headless men, the castrative women."[70] The ruling men of the French Revolution attempted to create that social unity and coherence by turning to the antique. Male bodies had been remade to engage with the aesthetics of the *beau ideal* throughout the 1780s, but Winckelmann's Greek-styled body was superseded in the 1790s by a body that more clearly signified not just correct aesthetics, but also adherence to the correct codes of moral and civic behavior. As such, the male body became more visible within the public sphere as an active agent, and the masculine silhouette tightened in response. Garments like pantaloons helped French men negotiate the public sphere in a period in which sartorial symbols proliferated and political affiliation was often ambiguous.

The failure of Jacques-Louis David's uniforms in 1794 demonstrates how difficult the revolutionary sartorial environment had become. In their attempt to return eighteenth-century male dress to the aesthetics of the Greco-Roman world, in which loose drapery communicated the honor, virtue, and duty required in a republic (and valorized by revolutionary officials), David's designs ended up concealing too much of the body. A similar aesthetic prevailed in Grégoire's uniforms for the Directory, but the political contingencies of post-Thermidorian France required a different organizing principle. Indeed, the steps taken by the Directory government to enforce a hierarchical system of uniforms distinguished by color and ornamentation revealed just how fragmented the body politic could be—or, indeed, needed to be to stabilize individual identities in the face of profound political change. As such, the visual vocabulary of antiquity could no longer precisely describe or adapt to the political contingencies of the moment, despite the many attempts made throughout the 1790s to draw upon the sartorial traditions of the antique. The proportions of the male body may have shifted to conform to the Winckelmannian *beau ideal*, with elongated legs and square shoulders, but the Directory years proved that an egalitarian view of the male body, homogenous in its expression and united in its nationalist identity, was unrealistic when faced with the practical needs of day-to-day governance. What these attempts at incorporating the antique into men's dress proved, however, was the need for social legibility and the understanding that even the smallest details—a shirt cuff protruding from a coat sleeve, or the tightness of one's pantaloons—could align a man with various social groups and positions. This level of micro-signification (which nonetheless avoided overt symbolism) would become a key part of the sartorial theology of dandyism and so help dominate the rules of menswear throughout the nineteenth century.

Notes

1. *Giornale delle nuove mode di Francia e d'Inghilterra* (1 November 1791), plate 344. Unless otherwise indicated, all translations in this essay are mine.
2. See Elizabeth Amann, *Dandyism in the Age of Revolution* (Chicago: University of Chicago Press, 2015), 96.
3. Baecque, *The Body Politic: Corporeal Metaphor in Revolutionary France, 1770–1800*, trans. Charlotte Mandell (Stanford: Stanford University Press, 1997), 311; Hunt, *Politics, Culture and Class in the French Revolution* (Berkeley: University of California Press, 1984), 94–116.
4. Jean Locquin, *La Peinture d'histoire en France de 1747 à 1785; étude sur l'évolution des idées artistiques dans la second moitié du XVIIIe siècle* (Paris: H. Laurens, 1912).
5. Lajer-Burcharth, *Necklines: The Art of Jacques-Louis David after the Terror* (New Haven: Yale University Press, 1999), 8–70.
6. Solomon-Godeau, "The Other Side of *Vertu*: Alternative Masculinities in the Crucible of Revolution," *Art Journal* 56, no. 2 (1997): 55. See too Thomas Crow, *Emulation: Making Artists in Revolutionary France* (New Haven: Yale University Press, 1995), 2.
7. Roche, *The Culture of Clothing: Dress and Fashion in the "Ancien Régime,"* trans. Jean Birrell (Cambridge: Cambridge University Press, 1996), 501.
8. Amann, *Dandyism*, 1; Ribeiro, *The Art of Dress: Fashion in England and France, 1750–1820* (New Haven: Yale University Press, 1995), 49.
9. Maxwell, *Patriots against Fashion: Clothing and Nationalism in Europe's Age of Revolutions* (Basingstoke: Palgrave Macmillan, 2014), 9, 127.
10. See Amelia Rauser, *The Age of Undress: Art, Fashion, and the Classical Ideal in the 1790s* (New Haven: Yale University Press, 2020); Claire Cage, "The Sartorial Self, Neo-Classical Fashion and Gender Identity in France, 1797–1804," *Eighteenth-Century Studies* 42, no. 2 (2009): 192–215; and Susan L. Siegfried, "Fashion and the Reinvention of Court Costume in Portrayals of Josephine de Beauharnais (1794–1809)," *Apparence(s)* 6 (2015): https://doi.org/10.4000/apparences.1329.
11. Guillaume Faroult, Christophe Leribault, and Guilhem Scherf, eds., *Antiquity Revived: Neoclassical Art in the Eighteenth Century, exh. cat., Louvre Éditions (Museum of Fine Arts, Houston; Louvre, Paris: Gallimard, 2011)*, 174. Peyron exhibited an oil sketch of the *Death of Socrates* at the Salon of 1787 and then submitted the fully finished work two years later in 1789.
12. See Perrin Stein, "Building a Reputation," in *Jacques-Louis David: Radical Draftsman*, ed. Perrin Stein (New York: Metropolitan Museum of Art, 2022), 147.
13. Lefébure, *Vérités agréables ou le salon vu en beau, par l'auteur du coup de patte* (Paris, 1789), 15–16.
14. See, for example, this second-century CE portrait head at the Museum of Fine Arts in Boston: https://collections.mfa.org/objects/151123.
15. See Faroult, *Antiquity Revived*, 20–21, 48.

16. Winckelmann, *The History of the Art of Antiquity*, trans. Henry Francis Mallgrave (Los Angeles: Getty Research Institute, 2006), 333. See too Alex Potts, "Beautiful Bodies and Dying Heroes: Images of Ideal Manhood in the French Revolution," *History Workshop* no. 30 (1990): 6.

17. Winckelmann, *Reflections on the Painting and Sculpture of the Greeks with Instructions for the Connoisseur and an Essay on Grace in Works of Art*, trans. Henry Fuseli (London, 1765), 30.

18. Baecque, *Body Politic*, 186. See too Caroline Vout, *Classical Art: A Life History from Antiquity to the Present* (Princeton: Princeton University Press, 2018), 43.

19. Baecque, *Body Politic*, 185; Potts, "Beautiful Bodies," 2.

20. Vout, *Classical Art*, 54.

21. Winckelmann, "Description of the Torso in the Belvedere in Rome," in *Johann Joachim Winckelmann on Art, Architecture, and Archaeology*, trans. David Carter (Woodbridge: Boydell & Brewer, 2013), 143–48.

22. See Perrin Stein, "Early Training," in *Jacques-Louis David*, 70.

23. Vout, *Exposed: The Greek and Roman Body* (London: Profile Books, 2022); Christ, "The Masculine Ideal of 'The Race That Wears the Toga,'" *Art Journal* 56, no. 2 (1997): 24.

24. See Ernst H. Kantorowicz, *The King's Two Bodies: A Study in Medieval Political Theology* (Princeton: Princeton University Press, 1957), 12.

25. Habermas, *The Structural Transformation of the Public Sphere: An Inquiry into a Category of Bourgeois Society*, trans. Thomas Burger (Cambridge: MIT Press, 1989), 8.

26. See William Rogers Brubaker, "The French Revolution and the Invention of Citizenship," *French Politics and Society* 7, no. 3 (1989): 36–46.

27. See Richard Wrigley, *The Politics of Appearances: Representations of Dress in Revolutionary France* (Oxford: Berg, 2002), 97–134.

28. Potts, "Beautiful Bodies," 6–8.

29. See L. D. Ettlinger, "Jacques-Louis David and Roman Virtue," *Journal of the Royal Society of Arts* 115, no. 5126 (1967): 106.

30. Athanase Détournelle, *Journal de La Société républicaine des arts, séante au Louvre, salle du Laocoon* (Paris, 1794). See also Potts, "Beautiful Bodies," 8.

31. Mark Ledbury, "Unpublished Letters to Jacques-Louis David from His Pupils in Italy," *Burlington Magazine* 142, no. 1166 (2000): 296, 300.

32. See *Le Dictionnaire de l'Académie française*, 4th ed. (Paris, 1762), s.v. "draper": "En termes de peinture & de sculpture, on dit, draper une figure, pour dire, habiller une figure, représenter les habillements. Le talent de bien draper est très-rare."

33. Hollander, *Seeing through Clothes* (Berkeley: University of California Press, 1993), 58.

34. Lens, *Le Costume ou essai sur les habillements et les usages de plusieurs peuples de l'antiquité prouvé par les monuments* (Liege, 1776); Grasset de Saint-Sauveur, *L'Antique Rome, ou description historique et pittoresque, de tout ce qui concerne le peuple romain, dans ces costumes civiles, militaires et religieux, dans ses moeurs publiques et privées, depuis Romulus jusqu'à Auguste* (Paris, 1796).

35. Lens, *Le Costume*, 261.

36. Rothfus, "The Gens Togata: Changing Styles and Changing Identities," *American Journal of Philology* 131, no. 3 (2010): 426, 432–33.

37. Henri Lapauze, ed., *Procès-verbaux de la Commune générale des arts de peinture, sculpture, architecture et gravure de la Société populaire et républicaine des arts* (Paris: J. E. Bulloz, 1903), 266.

38. Lavallée, *Voyage dans le départemens de France* (Paris, 1792), 5.

39. Bienaimé, *Considérations sur les avantages de changer le costume français, par la société populaire et républicaine des arts* (Paris, 1793), 2; Mercier, *Comment m'habillerais-je? Réflexions politiques et philosophiques sur l'habillement français, et sur la nécessité d'un costume nationale* (Paris, 1793), 11.

40. Bienaimé, *Considérations*, 2.

41. See Wendy Parkins, "Introduction: (Ad)Dressing Citizens," in *Fashioning the Body Politic: Dress, Gender, Citizenship*, ed. Wendy Parkins (Oxford: Berg, 2002), 3–6.

42. Archives nationales, France, AF66 no. 15, quoted in Jennifer Harris, "The Red Cap of Liberty: A Study of Dress Worn by French Revolutionary Partisans, 1789–94," *Eighteenth-Century Studies* 14, no. 3 (1981): 299. David initially submitted his designs to the Société on 25 April 1794; see Maxwell, *Patriots against Fashion*, 104.

43. Visconti, *La clef du cabinet des souverains*, 27 May 1804, 5. See too Madeleine Delpierre, "À propos d'un manteau de représentant du peuple de 1798 récemment offert au musée du costume," *Bulletin du Musée Carnavalet* 7 (1972): 17. Antique-styled drapery appeared in the other uniforms that David submitted including designs for a municipal officer, a legislator, a judge, a soldier, and a French citizen.

44. Winckelmann, *History of the Art of Antiquity*, 223.

45. Hollander, *Seeing through Clothes*, 5.

46. Bienaimé, *Considérations*, 2.

47. Flügel, *The Psychology of Clothes* (New York: International Universities Press, 1930), 111.

48. *Le Journal des dames et des modes*, 3 February 1799, 421.

49. See "1800–1809," Fashion History Timeline, last updated 18 August 2020, https://fashionhistory.fitnyc.edu/1800-1809/.

50. Byrde, *Nineteenth Century Fashion* (London: Batsford, 1992), 90; *Le Dictionnaire de l'Académie française*, 6th ed. (Paris, 1835), "couleur d'un jaune très-clair." Cf. Anne Hollander's claim that "to convey the image of unadorned masculine perfection, [tailors] had to remodel the nude male wholly out of cloth, to create an abstract statue of the naked hero carved according to the tailor's rules" (*Sex and Suits: The Evolution of Modern Dress* [London: Bloomsbury Academic, 2020], 64); and Karen Harvey, "Men of Parts: Masculine Embodiment and the Male Leg in Eighteenth-Century England," *Journal of British Studies* 54, no. 4 (2015): 810–11. Harvey describes pantaloons as "skin pulled tight against muscles."

51. Delpierre, "À propos d'un manteau," 17.

52. Visconti, *La clef du cabinet*, 27 May, 1804, 6.

53. Wrigley, *Politics of Appearances*, 235.
54. Robespierre, *Textes Choisis*, ed. Jean Poperen, 3 vols. (Paris: Éditions sociales, 1956), 3:112–115.
55. Boissy d'Anglas, "Discours préliminaire au projet de constitution pour la république française, prononcé par Boissy d'Anglas, au nom de la commission des onze, dans la séance du 5 Messidor, an 3," in *The French Revolution*, ed. P. H. Beik (London: Macmillan, 1970), 317–18.
56. See Maxwell, *Patriots against Fashion*, 128–29.
57. Ribeiro, *The Art of Dress*, 91.
58. Delpierre, "À propos d'un manteau," 16.
59. Grégoire, *Rapport et project de décret préséntés au nom du comité d'instruction publique, sur les costumes des législateurs et des autres fonctionnaires publics* (Paris, 1795), 2–4.
60. Grasset de Saint-Sauveur, *Costumes des représentans du peuple: membres des deux conseils, du Directoire exécutif, des ministres, des tribunaux, des messagers d'état, huissiers et autres fonctionnaires publics, etc. dont les dessins originaux ont été confiés ... au citoyen Grasset Saint-Sauveur* (Paris, 1796), 6.
61. See Maxwell, *Patriots against Fashion*, 108–9; Grasset de Saint-Sauveur, *Costumes des représentans du peuple*, 6.
62. See Herbert Norris, *Ancient European Costume and Fashion* (Mineola: Dover, 1999), 105.
63. Norris, *Ancient European Costume*, 93.
64. See Karen E. Stears, "Dress and Textiles," in *The Edinburgh Companion to Ancient Greece and Rome*, ed. Edward Bispham (Edinburgh: Edinburgh University Press, 2010), 229.
65. Lens, *Le Costume*, 270–75.
66. See Liza Cleland, Glenys Davies, and Lloyd Llewellyn-Jones, *Greek and Roman Dress from A to Z* (London: Routledge, 2007), 190–200.
67. Grasset de Saint-Sauveur, *L'Antique Rome*, 122.
68. Grégoire, *Rapport et project*, 7.
69. See Dominique Waquet, "Costumes et vêtements sous le Directoire: Signes politiques ou effets de mode?," *Cahiers d'histoire. Revue d'histoire critique* 129 (2015): 13.
70. Lajer-Burcharth, *Necklines*, 8–20.

Styling Equiano: Accumulation and Conversion in the *Interesting Narrative*

YAN CHE

Just before his central act of self-purchase, Olaudah Equiano makes another purchase. He recounts that "in this expectation I laid out above eight pounds of my money for a suit of superfine clothes to dance with at my freedom, which I hoped was then at hand."[1] Eight pounds is a large outlay compared to the "forty pounds sterling" that his manumission cost (92). Juxtaposed against the frugality and care with which he accumulates his money for his manumission—he "commences merchant" with "very small capital to begin with; for one single half bit, which is equal to three pence in England, made up my whole stock"—this suit is an extraordinary expense for an extraordinary occasion (86). The magnitude of this purchase suggests that the suit is an essential constituent of Equiano's freedom, reinforced by how he proudly wears it in celebration after his manumission: "In short, the fair as well as black people immediately styled me by a new appellation, to me the most desirable in the world, which was Freeman, and at the dances I gave my Georgia superfine blue clothes made no indifferent appearance, as I thought" (106). Although the "new appellation" of "Freeman" is given an understandable prominence in the sentence, that the clothes make "no indifferent appearance" suggests that the purchase of the suit should complicate our reading of the exchanges that together comprise Equiano's self-purchase.

In this essay, I read his *The Interesting Narrative of the Life of Olaudah Equiano, or Gustavus Vassa, the African, Written by Himself* (1789) as grappling with the implications of an account of manumission predicated upon accumulation, whether of money (the requisite forty pounds); formal signifiers, such as the manumission document and the "superfine" blue suit; or social signifiers, such as the name of "Freeman." On one hand, I show that the *Interesting Narrative* is built upon a logic of capital accumulation that reads each discrete exchange as an act of social recognition that validates Equiano's equality. On the other hand, the accumulation of many individual acts of recognition does not successfully produce social freedom for Equiano. What I term the "paradox of accumulation" reflects the incommensurability of these accounts. I conclude by suggesting that Equiano's account of his conversion to Methodism offers a possible way out of this paradox. Although his conversion narrative animates tropes common to the genre in an accumulative way that parallels the progress of his economic narrative, I argue that Equiano turns to a Pauline system of salvation by grace to simultaneously account for incommensurate systems of value without necessarily resolving their contradictions.

My account of accumulation and its limitations builds upon the work of scholars who have tended to read the limitations of economic exchange for Equiano as problems within racial capitalism as such. Many such readings of the *Interesting Narrative* draw from the foundational arguments made by Houston Baker, who elegantly posits that "only the acquisition of property will enable him to alter his designated status *as property*. He, thus, formulates a plan of freedom constrained by the mercantile boundaries of a Caribbean situation."[2] Baker's formulation is weighed down by a sense of resignation—even pessimism—as Equiano is limited by the conditions of exchange itself that formally exclude him from social and legal equality on account of his race. Building on this sense of constraint, Elizabeth Jane Wall Hinds more explicitly shows that Equiano "may have worked to earn individual 'freedom,' but the work itself placed him squarely within the dehumanizing ideology of capitalism's driving slave market"—suggesting again the inescapability of racial capitalism.[3] Other approaches, even those that are less cynical regarding Equiano's own faith in the emancipatory possibilities of the marketplace, nevertheless concede some of the same limitations. For example, Ross J. Pudaloff argues that "despite his own enslavement, Equiano celebrates commerce and exchange because they make the self a product of exchange. He gains his freedom by purchasing himself and implies that the exchange of money for self can lead to a new and better identity."[4] Pudaloff's sense that exchange and self-purchase "can" produce a new identity tacitly acknowledges that other enslaved writers were not so successful in their attempts at self-fashioning through market exchange.

Moreover, Pudaloff's framework invites us to examine the problem at the margin: in other words, at what point of exchange does Equiano actually become free? Lynn Festa posits that "to buy himself back, Equiano must be a subject already, but only manumission can make him into the subject able to execute the contract he has already performed in order to become that subject. The paradox of the manumission certificate—that one must be a man or woman to become one—is also the paradox of the autobiographical text, which calls into being the writing subject who must exist for there to be a text."[5] In Festa's reading, the manumission is ancillary to the more essential problem of whether Equiano's subjectivity meaningfully "exists" within the conditions of slavery. By contrast, Pudaloff contends that "engaging in trade is the first and essential step in gaining both literal and figurative freedom. Trade encodes Equiano as an agent in a process that necessarily makes each party to a transaction equal by virtue of freely engaging in the transaction."[6] Here, market maketh man, as Pudaloff's assumption of free exchange does not require global conditions of freedom so long as no coercion takes place between the two parties engaged in a transaction. This equality is buttressed by how exchange implies equal valuation, such as it would under a Marxian account of equal exchange values at the moment of exchange. John Bugg's figuration of Equiano's manumission as the exchange of "a guinea for a guinea"—a one-to-one exchange of a gold coin for a West African—elegantly evokes a deep symbolic equality at the moment of exchange as well.[7]

These arguments suggest that the key precondition to market exchange is the possibility of equal participation in the economic marketplace itself. Here, I draw from Axel Honneth's articulation of the conditions of exchange, in which intersubjective recognition is foundational to questions of "who counts as a participant and what can be legitimately treated as an economic good," and so the market adjudicates the division between subject and commodity.[8] For Honneth, the market mechanism "must be able to be understood as a form of cooperation in order to count as understandable and legitimate in the eyes of the participants. … Expressed in terms of recognition, this means that economic actors must have recognized each other as members of a cooperative community before they can grant each other the right to maximize individual utility."[9] My analysis of Equiano's *Interesting Narrative* takes up Honneth's precondition by examining its implied causal mechanism, in which recognition must precede exchange. If this logical relationship holds, then established exchange relations could serve as a posteriori proof that intersubjective recognition has been achieved. But left unclear in this formulation is a question of scale, of how many exchanges and of what kind are necessary to constitute recognition in a "cooperative community." As I will show, this question of scale becomes central to understanding how and where accumulation fails to produce social freedom for Equiano.

I posit that Honneth's understanding of market exchange as legitimated by recognition is homologous to the valences of "style" that Equiano elaborates. Take, for example, Equiano's new name of "Freeman." Equiano transforms "Freeman" from a signifier of his manumission to a mark of distinction through a process in which collective recognition is required to legitimate his newfound freedom. Two forms of value are at play. First, when Equiano explains that "I was named *Olaudah*, which, in our language, signifies vicissitude or fortune; also, one favoured, and having a loud voice and well spoken," the implication is that these meanings are conjoined in his name, his "loud voice" being both signifier and signified of his "favoured" status (27). Likewise, Equiano's joint use of the names "Olaudah Equiano" and "Gustavus Vassa," both of which appear in the full title of the *Interesting Narrative*, establishes his distinctive status. It appears that Equiano took special pride in being named after the sixteenth-century Protestant king of Sweden, electing to use that name for all of his formal correspondence and as his legal identity, despite its being a name given to him while he was enslaved. A royal "style" further reinforces Equiano's autobiographical claim to royal descent, as he recounts that his father was "styled Embrenche; a term, as I remember, importing the highest distinction, and signifying in our language a *mark* of grandeur" (20). When Equiano later guides his trading vessel to port after the death of Captain Farmer, he proudly recounts that "I now obtained a new appellation, and was called Captain. This elated me not a little, and it was quite flattering to my vanity to be thus styled by as high a title as any free man in this place possessed" (111). Therefore, like "Olaudah," "Freeman" signifies a claim to intrinsic value.

Simultaneously, Equiano's placing of himself as the grammatical object, someone to be "styled" or "called," shows that community recognition is a process meaningfully distinct from these claims to intrinsic value. "Styled" is an evocative pun given the especially close relationship between Equiano's suit and his new name and identity: it suggests that Equiano's identity is a function both of his efforts at self-fashioning and a context of social recognition, as the "style" of the suit as self-fashioning runs into the "style" of the name "Freeman" as other-fashioning. "Freeman" is not a name that Equiano can give himself, but instead what "the fair as well as black people immediately styled me," and so it requires the recognition of both "the fair as well as black people" to achieve this effect.

As the communal bestowing of a name befitting Equiano's claims to distinction, being "styled" represents what he envisions as the end stage of a process of market accumulation. Style is a summation, replicating in miniature the accumulation of individual acts of recognition into some sense of collective recognition. Readers of Equiano have used the collective as a way of understanding Equiano's concluding economic vision: for example, Andrew Kopec articulates a sense of Equiano's economic vision as leading to a "reciprocal commercial relationship between both Africa and the slave-buying nations," as well as, more generally, its participation in a plan of "global commerce."[10] More recently, Hannah Wakefield has adapted the same reasoning to describe Equiano's religious vision of a "global, expanding, just Christian church."[11] In these readings of the *Interesting Narrative*, Equiano imagines a radical earthly telos in which abolition entirely transforms the global economic system that Equiano had experienced his entire life. I would add that to achieve a global transformation of the kind that Kopec and Wakefield describe, Equiano leans upon an accumulative process in which he attempts to replicate how he was initially styled "Freeman" in Montserrat.

Reading style as the result of an accumulation of sentiments allows us to attend more closely to how market exchange might be enabled by intersubjective recognition. For Equiano, this operation happens semantically, as he combines the economic and affective valences of "interest" to produce the *Interesting Narrative*. In Samuel Johnson's *Dictionary of the English Language*, "interest" includes a wide range of meanings, especially: "1. Concern; advantage; good"; "2. Influence over others"; and "3. Share; part in any thing; participation: as, this is a matter in which we have *interest*."[12] The combination of "advantage," "influence," and "participation" describes the mutuality implicit in exchange relationships, and the condition of mutual benefit emphasizes interest as *inter esse*—quite literally, what is between two beings.[13] Therefore, interest allows Equiano to figure recognition through discrete instances of exchange. He expresses a preference for trading with Quakers in Philadelphia during his process of accumulating capital to purchase his manumission, because "they always appeared to be a very honest discreet sort of people, and never attempted to impose on me; I therefore liked them, and ever after chose to deal with them in preference to any others" (102). Equiano's favorable view of the Quakers is due not only to their abstract commitments to abolitionist principles, but also to a specific kind of treatment he received while engaged in mutual exchange. He comes to know these Quakers by their works, as he describes them three times before he "was informed they were called Quakers" (102). First, he is purchased from Capt. Doran by Robert King, "a quaker " and "the best master" to be found (73); then he observes that their "benevolence" in Philadelphia has kept "many [freemen] of the sable race" (90) from being captured into slavery; and, finally, as they "never attempted to impose on" him, he "sold [his] goods chiefly" to them (102). The juxtaposition of Philadelphia Quakers with the "infernal invaders of human rights"—Equiano's epithet for those who captured and sold Joseph Clipson into slavery despite his manumission papers—establishes Equiano's embrace of the terms of a liberal understanding of rights against which slavery operates (90).

Equiano's preference for Quakers resonates throughout the *Interesting Narrative* because "imposition" is Equiano's chosen term specifically for infringements of the rights of free Black people. Most commonly, impositions are infringements of property rights. For example, Equiano reads the experience of a "poor creole Negro" (82) who has his fish seized as a type for "such impositions" that he would subsequently personally experience: "that even this poor man and I should some time after suffer together in the same manner" (82). Equiano's concern for property rights is understandable, given the way that property ownership legitimates his freedom from enslavement. Although we cannot know if it was the same suit of "superfine clothes" that Equiano purchased to celebrate his manumission, the frontispiece to the *Interesting Narrative* shows Equiano in a stylish suit, fashionably inhabiting the role of an English gentleman and thereby announcing his status as a "Freeman" to a far broader audience than those of his first dances. But in importing a liberal account of property rights he also imports the limitations of a rights-based framework. Echoing Locke, who concedes that "where there is no judge on earth, the appeal lies to God in heaven," Equiano cries out to God for justice when he and his fisherman friend are robbed of their oranges and limes on Santa Cruz in the process of attempting to "turn merchant": "I was more than once obliged to look up to God on high ... in the agony of distress and indignation, [and] wished that the ire of God in his forked lightning might transfix these cruel oppressors among the dead" (87).[14]

Nevertheless, a Lockean conception of property rights allows Equiano to broaden the meaning of "imposition" to include the infringement of other rights as well. This includes infringements on the right to free movement: Equiano discovers, after his manumission, that to travel in the West Indies "I should advertise myself, and give notice of my going off the island. ... This degrading necessity, which every black freeman is under, of advertising himself like a slave, when he leaves an island, and which I thought a gross imposition upon any freeman" (123). It also includes infringements upon the right to marriage, as when Equiano describes "a very curious imposition on human nature": "a white man wanted to marry in the church a free black woman that had land and slaves in Montserrat: but the clergyman told him it was against the law of the place to marry a white and a black in the church" (88). In each case, an imposition is, as Equiano argues, the treatment of a "black freeman" as though he were "a slave": the restriction of property, movement, and marriage comprises a systematic summation of the specific powers exerted by slaveowners. Imposition, therefore, connotes a colonial spatiality of one space or subject being forcefully occupied by another. That the word "impose" only becomes a favored term in the *Interesting Narrative* after Equiano "commences merchant" suggests that it operates along the same axis as interest: freedom, for Equiano, is proven individually at moments of exchange.

By conceiving of "interest" and "imposition" as opposite experiences, Equiano reveals his reliance upon an accumulative logic to structure his narrative project. This is because throughout the *Interesting Narrative*, Equiano attempts to move from individual to global recognition of his freedom and personhood through the sheer force of quantity. In his concluding arguments, Equiano asks us to compare two countably infinite quantities in the new global economy of consumption to imagine an Africa on equal commercial footing with Britain: "It cost the Aborigines of Britain little or nothing in clothing, &c. The difference between their forefathers and the present generation, in point of consumption, is literally infinite. The supposition is most obvious. It will be equally immense in Africa—The same cause, viz. civilization, will ever have the same effect" (177). Even accounts of Equiano's freedom that understand his transformation more qualitatively nevertheless rely upon Equiano's accumulative impulse.

As his reasoning goes, if each exchange is a moment of recognition, then surely they would culminate in a greater recognition once they were summed up. Shrewdly mathematical, Equiano's account of capital accumulation takes up the power of exponential growth to rapidly effect this transformative exchange:

> At one of our trips to St. Eustatia, a Dutch island, I bought a glass tumbler with my half bit, and when I came to Montserrat I sold it for a bit, or sixpence. Luckily we made several successive trips to St. Eustatia (which was a general mart for the West Indies, about twenty leagues from Montserrat); and in our next, finding my tumbler so profitable, with this one bit I bought two tumblers more; and when I came back I sold them for two bits, equal to a shilling sterling. When we went again I bought with these two bits four more of these glasses, which I sold for four bits on our return to Montserrat; and in our next voyage to St. Eustatia I bought two glasses with one bit, and with the other three I bought a jug of Geneva, nearly about three pints in measure. When we came to Montserrat I sold the gin for eight bits, and the tumblers for two, so that my capital now amounted in all to a dollar, well husbanded and acquired in the space of a month or six weeks, when I blessed the Lord that I was so rich. (86)

Equiano's initial profit margin in glass tumblers is an astonishing 100 percent. But as his capital accumulates, he makes increasingly profitable investments. Once he accumulates enough capital, he undertakes an even more profitable trade in the "jug of Geneva," which profits him five bits on an investment of three bits—an even more substantial margin of 167 percent. Eventually, Equiano makes "three hundred per cent" on "four barrels of pork I brought from Charles Town" (92). Animated by a vision of further growth, he expresses his delight when King purchases a new ship, "the largest" of a "choice of three ... for, from his having a large vessel, I had more room, and could carry a larger quantity of goods with me" (101). King's surprise when Equiano presents him with the requisite forty pounds is as much a reaction to the imminent reality of Equiano's manumission as it is to the means by which Equiano effected it: as Equiano recounts, King replied that "I got money much faster than he did; and said he would not have made me the promise he did if he had thought I should have got money so soon" (104).

Equiano's progress in accumulating capital is enabled by his substantial appetite for risk, as he stakes "my whole stock" in each trade (86). Ironically, by risking the entirety of his property, his property and his freedom become literally conjoined, as he depends upon the successful accumulation of each trip's profits to total the requisite forty pounds. This also explains the existential terms with which Equiano reacts after he is robbed of his fruits on Santa Cruz: "Thus, in the very minute of gaining more by three times than I ever did by any venture in my life before, was I deprived of every farthing I was worth" (87). Equiano's enterprising risk tolerance therefore prefigures Equiano's final self-purchase, as it means that each instance of exchange exposes the preconditions of recognition that establish Equiano's personhood.

Given its seeming effectiveness in attaining his manumission, it makes sense that Equiano relies upon a similar strategy of accumulation with the paratexts accompanying the *Interesting Narrative*. Whereas the first edition of 1789 opened with a table of contents, Equiano moves forward the prefatory paratexts in subsequent editions, beginning with the address "To the Lords Spiritual and Temporal, and the Commons of the Parliament of Great Britain." Equiano thus shows his understanding that the production of interest in the *Interesting Narrative* lies beyond the narrative itself. By the 1793 seventh edition, Equiano was including a notice "To the Reader" responding to accusations made in 1792 that he was in fact born in "the Danish island of Santa Cruz, in the West Indies," rather than on the West African coast. Equiano responds to the attack by arguing that "it is only needful for me to appeal to those numerous and respectable persons of character who knew me when I first arrived in England."[15] Equiano also takes pains to update his list of subscribers in each subsequent edition, so that by the eighth edition, published in Norwich in 1794, the subscriber list totaled 861.[16]

Despite the popular success of Equiano's *Interesting Narrative*, a key problem remains, as the very accumulation of letters of reference and subscribers ironically attests to the inadequacy of this form of accumulation. This is the paradox of accumulation at work once again: the letters are acts of private or personal recognition that are being used to secure a social recognition that would obviate the need for such letters. The problem partly results from a generic mismatch: these references were not sent to individuals hostile to Equiano's cause or that of abolition; one cannot imagine they would be very effective if they had been. There is also the problem of marginal transformation. It is true that Equiano's subscriber list included a prominent cast of abolitionists as well as leading figures in high society.[17] However, it would be implausible to think that the addition or subtraction of any individual subscriber, no matter how prominent, would meaningfully alter the total effect of the subscriber lists. A gap therefore emerges between the mechanism of Equiano's accumulation of subscribers and his desired aim: although forty pounds might purchase his manumission, subscribers cannot be accumulated in the same way as money, nor does their marginal accumulation lead to any defined transformation.

One such letter, dated 19 June 1794—well into Equiano's publishing tour—exemplifies these problems:

> The Bearer of this (Mr. Gustavus Vassa) is a native of Africa was carried into slavery at an early period of Life has passed through scenes most distressing and interesting is truly intelligent was recommended to me by my friend Mr. Buck of Bury who has long known him as a person of great moral worth and in the judgment of charity as a genuine disciple of our common Lord.
> ... I shall consider it as a favor if you will give him such assistance as you think proper in promoting the sale of his publication in doing which you will at the same time render assistance to a worthy man whose sufferings and services (in my judgment) give him some claim on the patronage of the community.[18]

John Mead Ray, the author of this letter, presents himself as the end link in a chain of endless deferrals of personal acquaintance, from "Mr. Buck of Bury who has long known him" to Equiano's intended list of would-be friends. That this letter is not personally addressed to any individual recipient further reinforces the diffusive nature of the chain of character references. In both form and function, Ray's letter closely resembles a bill of exchange, whose value is attested in signatures by both its issuer and its payee, as well as a potentially limitless number of endorsers of the bill as it changed hands.[19] For the bill of exchange, each attestation of value, in the form of a signed endorsement, takes place at the moment of exchange, such that the value of the bill is constantly reaffirmed through the iterative process of exchange itself: the more endorsers, the more certain the bearer can be of the bill's value. But this process of legitimation is only necessary because the bill of exchange does not function like modern fiat currency, whose value is guaranteed by the state, and thus bears a social value independent from the ability to conduct individual transactions with it.[20] The bill of exchange, and other eighteenth-century forms of nonmetallic currency such as bank paper, specifically required external validation because their form did not suggest any intrinsic value.[21]

The parallel logic of the bill of exchange likewise determines Equiano's credit. Even though his credit is constituted by the accumulation of endorsements, each endorsement also ironically attests to his need for such endorsements. This inverse relationship between form and function is established by the very manumission document that seemingly records Equiano's freedom. Even as he reproduces the exact terms of his manumission, Equiano prefaces its appearance in the *Interesting Narrative* with the observation that "the form of my manumission has something peculiar in it, and expresses the absolute power and dominion one man claims over his fellow" (106). The manumission document represents this "absolute power and domination" through its proliferation of near synonyms, enumerating all the ways in which enslavement destroys the agency of the enslaved: "Gustavus Vassa, shall and may become free, have manumitted, emancipated, enfranchised, and set free, and by these presents do manumit, emancipate, enfranchise, and set free, the aforesaid negro man-slave, named Gustavus Vassa, for ever, hereby giving, granting, and releasing unto him, the said Gustavus Vassa, all right, title, dominion, sovereignty, and property, which, as lord and master over the aforesaid Gustavus Vassa, I had, or now I have, or by any means whatsoever I may or can hereafter possibly have over him the aforesaid negro, for ever" (106). In announcing the terms of Equiano's freedom, the manumission document in fact inscribes, in detail, all the ways in which his freedom had been annihilated.

Compounding the problem is the formulaic structure of these letters: Ray's letter is more elaborate than, but not fundamentally different from, either Robert King's letter of 1767 or Dr. Charles Irving's letter of 1776, both included in the *Interesting Narrative*. Here is King's letter: "The bearer hereof, Gustavus Vassa, was my slave for upwards of three years, during which he has always behaved himself well, and discharged his duty with honesty and assiduity" (123). Irving's letter uses similar language: "The bearer, Gustavus Vassa, has served me several years with strict honesty, sobriety, and fidelity. I can, therefore, with justice recommend him for these qualifications; and indeed in every respect I consider him as an excellent servant. I do hereby certify that he always behaved well, and that he is perfectly trust-worthy" (159). As with Ray's letter, each letter reduces Equiano's character to three facts: name, form of acquaintance, and some generally positive qualities. Consequently, these letters obey the same logic as the manumission in inscribing both the exact ways in which Equiano cannot serve as his own witness and his enslaved status more generally. Equiano must supply 861 subscribers and innumerable references throughout his life, when a white man's narrative requires no such external support.

Even Equiano's experience of "style" as accumulation reveals this kind of doubleness. His "Georgia superfine blue clothes" display both the intrinsic value of their wearer as someone far removed from enslavement—a signal reinforced by the high price of "eight pounds"—and his participation, via that same conspicuous consumption, in a social idiom that reads the suit as belonging to a man who could be styled "Freeman."[22] The suit, made of superfine cotton dyed with indigo (both plants grown and produced in Georgia by slave labor), distinguishes its wearer through its stark contrast with the bleak economic conditions of its production. At the same time, those conditions show that Equiano's distinction is dependent upon the slave trade itself, as the suit is both the product of slave labor and purchased with profits derived from the slave trade. When Equiano "commences merchant," he travels and trades throughout the Caribbean by taking advantage of the investments and risks in which his enslaver was already engaged. This includes his adding slaves to "a live cargo, as we call a cargo of slaves" (102). Equiano's adoption of the idiom of enslavers—"as we call a cargo of slaves"—betrays the extent to which his own freedom is built upon both his ability to reduce other enslaved people to "cargo" and to reduce their labor to a product.

This counter-logic driving Equiano's accumulation reproduces the legal oppression of free Black people as well as the material conditions of slavery. The *Interesting Narrative* abounds in cases where freemen are kidnapped into slavery or otherwise abused. Equiano witnesses the case of a free Black carpenter "who, for asking a gentleman that he worked for for the money he had earned, was put into gaol; and afterwards this oppressed man was sent from Georgia, with false accusations, of an intention to set the gentleman's house on fire, and run away with his slaves" (108). There is also the earlier case of Joseph Clipson, who, though he was "always free, and no one had ever claimed him as their property," nonetheless "was taken forcibly out of our vessel" and "carried away" (90) without an opportunity to plead his case before the law. Conversely, in Georgia, when Equiano is accosted along with his friend Mosa, he discovers that because Mosa, "as the man of the house was not free, and had his master to protect him, they did not take the same liberty with him they did with me" (120).

The *Interesting Narrative* attempts to overwrite this counter-logic through the force of plot. As autobiography, the *Interesting Narrative* promises its readers an ending appropriate to the image of gentility portrayed in the frontispiece. Equiano is not alone in producing this kind of retrospective account of accumulation, as the logic of accumulation is integral to how narratives of transformation are told, especially in the abolitionist context. For example, accumulation—as an intellectual and spiritual, rather than material, process—was quickly apotheosized in Thomas Clarkson's *History of the Rise, Progress, and Accomplishment of the Abolition of the African Slave Trade* (1808). In telling the story of this "rise, progress, and accomplishment," Clarkson understands history as the combined result of over a century of intellectual labor. As a grand summary of the opening ten chapters—which begin with "those who favoured the cause of the injured Africans" in 1516 and continue to the formation of the Committee for the Abolition of the Slave Trade in 1787—Clarkson includes a foldout map of many streams joining together. This visualizes the contributions made by different individuals and organizations to the abolitionist cause as "so many springs or rivulets, which assisted in making and swelling the torrent which swept away the Slave Trade" (see Figure 1).[23] Each spring or rivulet is labeled with the name of an individual "forerunner," and the map is divided into two general areas: "the different streams which formed a junction at X, were instrumental in producing the abolition of the Slave Trade in England, in the month of March, 1807, so those, whose effects are found united at Y, contributed to produce the same event in America, in the same month of the same year."[24]

Clarkson's and Equiano's narratives share a reliance on the logic of exponential growth. Superimposed on Clarkson's river map are four horizontal lines unevenly spaced apart; strikingly, Clarkson uses these lines as an approximation of a logarithmic time scale on the vertical axis: "the parallel lines G, H, I, K, represent different periods of time, showing when the forerunners and coadjutors lived. The space between G and H includes the space of fifty years, in which we find but few labourers in this cause. That between H and I includes the same portion of time, in which we find them considerably increased, or nearly doubled. That between I and K represents the next thirty-seven years; but here we find their increase

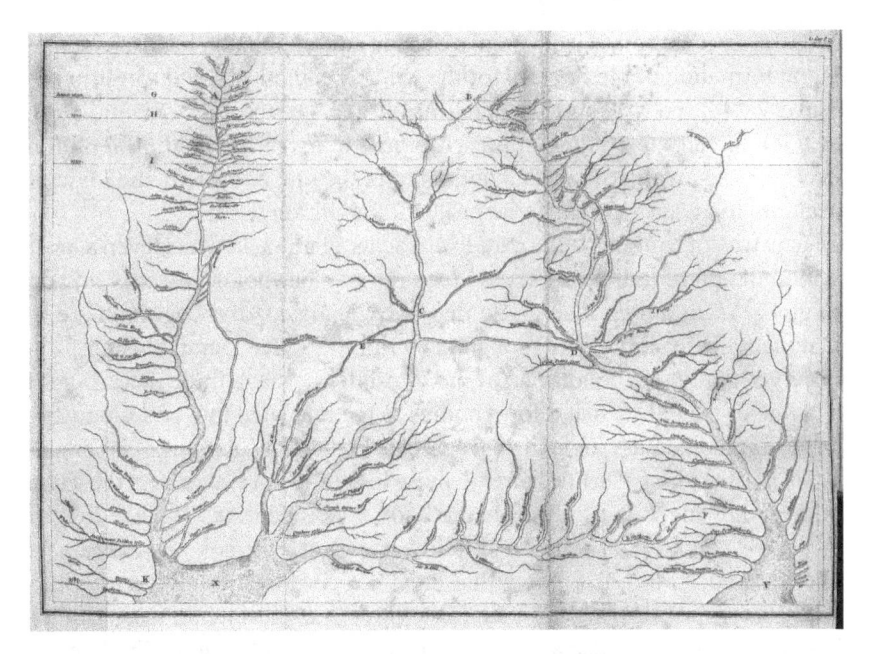

Figure 1. The map in Thomas Clarkson's *The History of the Rise, Progress, and Accomplishment of the Abolition of the African Slave-Trade by the British Parliament*, 1808. Courtesy of the Beinecke Rare Book and Manuscript Library, Yale University.

beyond all expectation, for we find four times more labourers in this short term, than in the whole of the preceding century."[25] Just as the growth rate of Equiano's capital increases the more he trades, so too does the rate of growth of support for abolition over time, until finally the abolition of the slave trade is accomplished. The drama of the river map is also heightened by the relative equality Clarkson assigns the individual tributaries, representing them as largely independent of one another (with the notable exception of the Quakers, who bridge the transatlantic divide). The rivers increase in width as time passes to accommodate the increasing flow of tributaries. Accumulation thus visualized also becomes naturalized: the flow of many smaller rivers into a greater one carries the inevitability of a physical law. The rivers flow down on the page, so that the eye is naturally drawn to the increasing width of the rivers as tributaries join. The mouths of the rivers are also exaggerated in width, with the result that these centuries of accumulation vastly surpass the sum of the individual tributaries: here again is the mathematical property of compound interest at work, of exponential rather than linear accumulation. But the triumphal tale that Clarkson tells is necessarily incomplete: he would, a decade and a half later, be instrumental in the formation of the Society for the Mitigation and Gradual Abolition of Slavery. "Mitigation" and "Gradual Abolition" are terms of accumulation as well, already in contradiction with the totality of the goal of abolition itself. Consequently, it seems that no matter the rate of growth, the logic of accumulation can only carry the project of abolition so far.

One way of explaining the paradox of accumulation, in which even a large accumulation of individual acts of recognition does not necessarily add up to global recognition, is to argue that individual acts of recognition are in fact incommensurable with global recognition. Emilee Durand insightfully observes that in the conditions of the transatlantic slave trade there is both a "logic of capital ... that allows bodies to be translated into commodities" and a complementary logic that "fragments its subjects in terms of labor and in terms of the body."[26] For Durand, these logics do not even affect the same bodies: the "logic that fragments the body to compensate it for the loss of its parts ... applies to [Equiano's] fellow sailors and the colonial officers he encountered," while the "logic that creates a corporeal totality ... applies to enslaved peoples."[27] More literally, however, the incommensurability between these logics also arises from the fact that a collection of body parts does not comprise a body. Because these logics depend on mutually exclusive systems of accounting, the base units are fundamentally incommensurate. This problem can be generalized to the problem of market exchange as well: these "fragmenting" and "corporealizing" logics of capital describe a distinction between the discrete transactions of exchange that individually recognize Equiano and the social recognition necessary for Equiano to become entirely free.[28] Just as one cannot accumulate enough body parts to make whole the loss of a body, one cannot accumulate enough individual acts of recognition to truly constitute social recognition. There is no marginal unit of recognition that can be gained to effect Equiano's desired transformation.

Nevertheless, Equiano continues to rely on an accumulative structure as he moves from economic self-purchase to the rhetorical affordances of accumulation in the *Interesting Narrative*. While Andrew Kopec argues that "Equiano survives the experience and secures his freedom by internalizing and reproducing British protocols of commercial and consumer behavior," Equiano also internalizes and reproduces the protocols of British traditions of novelistic or narrative writing, and especially, in the case of his conversion narrative, evangelical writing.[29] Phyllis Mack's study of conversion narratives in the eighteenth century uncovers many common tropes that Equiano also activates, including vivid dreams, "a true experience of divine grace ... [in which] the singer or reader is called to 'behold' the suffering of Christ and visually follow him to the cross," escape from an "atmosphere of emotional violence ... that they felt powerless to avoid," and a sense of "the writer's deep-rooted loneliness ... as a theological principle [and] as a description of his actual life experience."[30] Readers of the *Interesting Narrative* will be familiar with its many scenes that reproduce these tropes, including Equiano's vision of Christ and his dreams of a shipwreck akin to that of Saint Paul.[31] Equiano's use of these elements exemplifies his keen awareness of the idioms that facilitate affective exchange in his desired audiences, much as he had previously mastered the idioms of economic exchange. Therefore, Equiano's deployment of Methodist literary conventions participates in a system of exchange undergirded by reciprocal recognition as well.

The power of "style" renders Equiano's *Interesting Narrative* as recognizable to his readers in England in 1789 as his superfine blue suit would have been to that first audience in Montserrat twenty-three years prior. Especially important to my argument is Mack's description of how writers in Methodist communities all managed to dream in similar, spiritually resonant ways: as Mack argues, "the Methodist practice of sharing their dreams with others led people to dream in certain ways, so that we can speak of specific images and genres of dreaming."[32] Mack's study of dream narratives shows how even accounts of the subconscious participated in a circulation of common tropes in a spiritual community; this circulation in turn legitimizes the community members who participate in it. Read in this way, the literary accumulation of the *Interesting Narrative* as a summation of incidents that comprise his life, each individually intelligible as tropes, echoes the process of monetary accumulation that Equiano expects will lead to his manumission.[33] To this point, Keith Sandiford argues that "the act of converting experience into narrative allows Equiano to invest his past activities with their proper spiritualized value and so to magnetize potentially the whole audience of Methodist and Calvinist Evangelicals."[34] If so, Equiano's affective relationships with his readers function similarly to his economic relationships with them; both are sites of intersubjective recognition.[35] Thus, Sandiford's observation that Equiano describes his capital accumulation in "similarly minute detail" as his conversion experience captures not only a stylistic feature of Equiano's narrative, but also an essential link between its economic and religious narratives.[36]

What differentiates the product of affective accumulation from the product of capital accumulation is that Methodist conversion posits a total transformation, whereas capital accumulation through market exchange, as I have shown, cannot. Just as I have read style for its implicit representation of the affective results of exchange, here I read conversion as a potent ontological revision that can bridge incommensurate value systems. In economic terms, currency conversion is a transformation not of real value, but of one set of nominal values into another—that is, currency conversion is a matter of changing the denominations one is using to represent some unchanging underlying value. But different currencies in the Atlantic world were complicated by vastly different understandings of value between various European and African cultures and economic systems, such that what held real value for some Europeans may not have held real value for some Africans, and vice versa. The forty pounds exchanged for Equiano's manumission is remote from his sale in the West African town of Tinmah, where "their money consisted of little white shells, the size of the finger nail. I was sold here for one hundred and seventy-two of them by a merchant who lived and brought me there" (36). Because each currency is the product of a different cultural system, conversion is not simply a matter of changing denominations. Rather, Equiano's ethnography of Tinmah emphasizes that it is "their money" that is in use, in contrast to how, in his native Essaka, "money is of little use; however we have some small pieces of coin, if I may call them such" (24). Money, of course, also comes to structure his Caribbean life.

Navigating these incommensurate systems of value was a practical economic matter, a basic accounting skill to manage the divergent currencies of the Atlantic world and their fluctuations; success also implied mastery of the cultural exchanges that undergirded and facilitated the economic transactions.[37] Equiano aligns his learning "a smattering of arithmetic as far as the rule of three" with several other practical skills, recounting that "I knew something of seamanship, and could dress and shave hair pretty well; and I could refine wines ... and ... I could write, and understood arithmetic tolerably well" (67, 74). These skills form the justification for Equiano's not being treated "as a common slave" when he is purchased by King (74). Indeed, this episode leads to Equiano being "styled ... the black Christian" by his shipmates, even though at that point he "did not comprehend" the Bible (68, 67). This striking conjunction brings together several themes that have animated my discussion thus far, as the acquisition of skills—the accumulation of human capital—once again culminates in a "style" being accorded to Equiano. In particular, there is a subtle but poignant moment here as Equiano recounts the deep personal recognition granted to him in this situation: when Equiano recounts his acquisition of writing and arithmetic, he also remembers one "Daniel Queen" who "was like a father to me; and some even used to call me after his name" (68).[38] The accumulation of human capital could not have occurred without the recognition granted to Equiano through this semblance of familial love.[39]

Currency conversion is therefore constituted by an intersubjective recognition like that which undergirds exchange—it is, in ideal form, a translation across value systems rather than a transformation of any intrinsic value. This translation renders intrinsic value legible. Conversion, in these terms, coheres with John Wesley's preference for a Pauline theology of grace; as Misty Anderson has argued, Pauline conversion emphasized a process of spiritual rebirth, in which the old self is entirely destroyed and then instantly and entirely regenerated.[40] Furthermore, Equiano's reliance upon Pauline conversion formally rejects gradually accumulative accounts of transformation as well. Anderson shows that John Wesley embraced "the Pauline model of the instantaneous conversion," especially the "'justifi[cation] by grace through faith' and the 'warming of the heart' that overwhelms the economic metaphor of redemption."[41] Equiano invokes the power of instantaneous change shortly after his manumission, when "the fair as well as black people immediately styled me by a new appellation." Here, the immediacy of conversion bypasses the need for any kind of gradual accumulation of recognition, even the monumental work of transforming one bit into two bits and so on, eventually into an entire commerce between Britain and Africa.

Instead of accumulation, Equiano's poem "Miscellaneous Verses; or, Reflections on the State of my mind during my first Convictions; of the Necessity of believing the Truth, and experiencing the inestimable Benefits of Christianity" seizes upon the capacity of grace to effect unequal exchanges as a means of overcoming the incommensurate logics of equal exchange. The title of Equiano's poem, with its concluding emphasis on the "inestimable Benefits of Christianity," attests to the impossibility of earning such benefits through equal exchange. Crucially, the moment of conversion is described as the sudden divine revelation of an act of grace:

> Yet here, 'midst blackest clouds confin'd,
> A beam from Christ, the day-star, shin'd;
> Surely, thought I, if Jesus please
> He can at once sign my release. (149)

By casting Jesus as a divine revision of Robert King, who "signs" Equiano's "release," Equiano suggests that one act of divine recognition suffices where innumerable acts of human recognition cannot. Likewise, the "blackest clouds" represent the magnitude of Equiano's conversion, in contrast to the bright "day-star" of Christ; but they also suggest Equiano's release from being "confin'd" with other enslaved Black people as the result of a special act of recognition. This divine recognition may prefigure the universal recognition of an imagined eschatology, but here it also describes Equiano's exceptional experience of manumission. Therefore, the complex rhetorical substitution of Jesus for Robert King reproduces the way in which actual manumission requires an active act of recognition.

The conditions of possibility for this substitution are already latent in the manumission episode. When Equiano approaches King, he is initially resistant because, as I discussed above, he is shocked by Equiano's rapid accumulation of capital. But his shock also reflects an awareness of the disparity between Equiano's commodity price and a fuller account of the value of his productive capacity: as Captain Farmer reminds King, "I know Gustavus has earned you more than an hundred a-year" (104).[42] In honoring the manumission price of forty pounds, Robert King would be taking a massive financial loss. Equiano points to other cases in which slaveowners were cognizant of this loss: "I have known many slaves whose masters would not take a thousand pounds current for them" (77). Although Equiano's annuity price cannot reflect his full value as a free person, especially any value beyond that of his productive labor, it nevertheless gestures toward a worth far exceeding forty pounds and thus more closely approaching that full value.

Therefore, what persuades King to sell Equiano his freedom at the commodity rather than the annuity price must be an implicit recognition that Equiano is no longer bound by his commodity price, which makes the price of forty pounds commensurate to Equiano's true value. This is especially the case if we read the underlying transaction as the exchange of forty pounds for the potential of earning over "a thousand pounds current," two disparate accounts of value brought into equality at the moment of exchange. Therefore, by redeeming his freedom for his commodity price, Equiano reverses the process of commodification that began with his first enslavement—if he had redeemed himself for his full annuity price, he would not be truly free since Robert King will still have appropriated the full worth of Equiano's future labor. In practical terms, having to earn that "thousand pounds current" in order to purchase his freedom would plainly show that Equiano is not free. It is in fact the incommensurability undergirding this particular exchange that liberates Equiano: like the implication of Bugg's "guinea for a guinea," only an unequal exchange can effect what no number of equal exchanges can.

Casting Jesus in the role of King therefore draws our attention to how a theology of salvation by grace is one that rejects the possibilities of equal exchange. In reading Equiano's experience of conversion, Lynn Festa argues that "whereas the redemption of manumission involves the exchange of money for man, Christian redemption involves Christ's sacrifice: he accepts Equiano's sin and in exchange gives the gift of grace."[43] What I admire about Festa's framing is her sense that Equiano receives the "gift of grace" in exchange for his sin; this, too, is a catachresis, to use Festa's term for where "the substitution of figural for literal meaning—exchange itself—breaks down."[44] Festa's description therefore captures some of Equiano's own theological discomfort with justification by faith. He describes his own post-conversion experience as "but one text which puzzled me, or that the devil endeavoured to buffet me with, viz. Rom. xi. 6" (146).[45] John Wesley's *Notes on the New Testament* likewise reflects his puzzlement on the complex logic of this verse: "there is something so absolutely inconsistent between the being justified by grace, and the being justified by works, that, if you suppose either, you of necessity exclude the other. For what is given to works is the payment of a debt; whereas grace implies an unmerited favour. So that the same benefit cannot, in the very nature of things, be derived from both."[46] In Wesley's account, grace excludes salvation by exchange because of its connotations of equal recompense, which he likens to "debt"; debt would require some sense of justification through works. By contrast, in an Atlantic world so determined by logics of exchange, such that even Equiano's self-purchase is but the culminating exchange in a long process of intermediate exchanges, Equiano's turn to grace offers to resolve the implicit contradictions of that process of self-purchase without overthrowing them.

Notes

I am grateful to Princeton University and the Hyde Fellowship for providing research travel funding for this project. I deeply appreciate the patient and supportive feedback I have received from many readers throughout this process, especially from my dissertation advisor Susan Wolfson, Lynn Festa, John Plotz, Rebekah Mitsein, and my friend Kirby Haugland.

1. Equiano, *The Interesting Narrative of the Life of Olaudah Equiano, or Gustavus Vassa, the African, Written by Himself*, ed. Werner Sollors (New York: W. W. Norton, 2001), 103. Subsequent citations will be made parenthetically.

2. Baker, *Blues, Ideology, and Afro-American Literature: A Vernacular Theory* (Chicago: University of Chicago Press, 1984), 35.

3. Hinds, "The Spirit of Trade: Olaudah Equiano's Conversion, Legalism, and the Merchant's Life," *African American Review* 32, no. 4 (1998): 636.

4. Pudaloff, "No Change without Purchase: Olaudah Equiano and the Economics of Self and Market," *Early American Literature* 40, no. 3 (2005): 501.

5. Festa, *Sentimental Figures of Empire in Eighteenth-Century Britain and France* (Baltimore: Johns Hopkins University Press, 2006), 143.

6. Pudaloff, "No Change without Purchase," 513.

7. Bugg, "Equiano's Trifles," *ELH* 80, no. 4 (2013): 1045.

8. See Gaël Curty, "Capitalism, Critique and Social Freedom: An Interview with Axel Honneth on *Freedom's Right*," *Critical Sociology* 46, nos. 7–8 (2020): 1340.

9. Honneth, *Freedom's Right: The Social Foundations of Democratic Life*, trans. Joseph Ganahl (New York: Columbia University Press, 2014), 191–92.

10. Kopec, "Collective Commerce and the Problem of Autobiography in Olaudah Equiano's *Narrative*," *The Eighteenth Century* 54, no. 4 (2013): 471–72.

11. Wakefield, "Olaudah Equiano's Ecclesial World," *Early American Literature* 55, no. 3 (2020): 652.

12. Johnson, *A Dictionary of the English Language* (1773), eds. Beth Rapp Young, Jack Lynch, William Dorner, Amy Larner Giroux, Carmen Faye Mathes, and Abigail Moreshead, s.v. "interest, n.s.," accessed February 13, 2024, https://johnsonsdictionaryonline.com/1773/interest_ns. See too Jacob Sider Jost, *Interest and Connection in the Eighteenth Century: Hervey, Johnson, Smith, Equiano* (Charlottesville: University of Virginia Press, 2020), 101.

13. *Oxford English Dictionary*, s.v. "interest," *n*.

14. Locke, *"Two Treatises of Government" and "A Letter Concerning Toleration,"* ed. Ian Shapiro (New Haven: Yale University Press, 2003), 109.

15. Equiano, *The Interesting Narrative of the Life of Olaudah Equiano, or Gustavus Vassa, the African. Written by Himself.*, 7th ed. enlarged (London, 1793), iv.

16. James Green, "The Publishing History of Olaudah Equiano's *Interesting Narrative*," *Slavery and Abolition* 16, no. 3 (1995): 364–65. For a more detailed account of Equiano's self-promotion campaign, see John Bugg, "The Other Interesting Narrative: Olaudah Equiano's Public Book Tour," *PMLA* 121, no. 5 (2006): 1424–42.

17. Green, "Publishing History," 364.

18. MS 132/B/B3, Ginn and Co: records of Cambridgeshire manors, Cambridgeshire Archives, Ely, Cambridgeshire.

19. See Mary Poovey, *Genres of the Credit Economy: Mediating Value in Eighteenth- and Nineteenth-Century Britain* (Chicago: University of Chicago Press, 2008), 36–40; and Christine Desan, *Making Money: Coin, Currency and the Coming of Capitalism* (Oxford: Oxford University Press, 2014), 394–95.

20. Desan, *Making Money*, 32–33.

21. For example, Edmund Burke, in his *Reflections on the Revolution in France*, inveighed against revolutionary *assignats* because they were merely paper, as opposed to paper representing and convertible into real cash deposits. See Rebecca Spang, *Stuff and Money in the Time of the French Revolution* (Cambridge: Harvard University Press, 2015), 9.

22. See Phillip Sykas, "Textiles," in *A Cultural History of Dress and Fashion in the Age of Empire*, ed. Denise Amy Baxter (New York: Bloomsbury, 2017), 10.

23. Clarkson, *The History of the Rise, Progress, and Accomplishment of the Abolition of the African Slave-Trade by the British Parliament* (London, 1808), 32, 259.

24. Clarkson, *History*, 260.

25. Clarkson, *History*, 261.

26. Durand, "'Commencing Merchant': Forms of Feeling and Logics of Capital in Olaudah Equiano's *The Interesting Narrative of the Life of Olaudah Equiano (1789),*" in *Edges of Transatlantic Commerce in the Long Eighteenth Century*, ed. Seohyon Jung and Leah M. Thomas (New York: Routledge, 2021), 52–53.

27. Durand, "'Commencing Merchant,'" 49. Though I find Durand's account of the two logics illuminating, there is a historical problem with her neat dichotomy in that forms of compensation existed for both slaveowners (for nonfatal injuries done to enslaved people) and the survivors of white sailors lost at sea, especially their widows.

28. Durand, "'Commencing Merchant,'" 48.

29. Kopec, "Collective Commerce," 469. More recently, Satit Leelathawornchai has shown an abiding complementarity between Equiano's seemingly utilitarian arguments for mutual economic benefit and his sentimental appeals for the humanity of his fellow Africans; see his "How Utility Pleases: Sentiment and Utility in *The Interesting Narrative of the Life of Olaudah Equiano*," *Eighteenth-Century Studies* 55, no. 1 (2021): 45–63.

30. Mack, *Heart Religion in the British Enlightenment* (Cambridge: Cambridge University Press, 2008), 232, 51, 61, 75.

31. See Wakefield, "Olaudah Equiano's Ecclesial World," 669–74, for the connection between Equiano's shipwreck and Paul's, and how Equiano imagines himself as inhabiting a Pauline evangelical role more broadly in his campaign for abolition.

32. Mack, *Heart Religion*, 231–32.

33. Durand, "'Commencing Merchant,'" 57–60.

34. Sandiford, *Measuring the Moment: Strategies of Protest in Eighteenth-Century Afro-English Writing* (Selinsgrove: Susquehanna University Press, 1988), 132–33.

35. Michael Genovese likens the circulation of eighteenth-century periodicals to the circulation of money; both systems "guaranteed 'validity'" through the process of community circulation itself. Equiano's affective and economic relationships to his readers are analogous. See Genovese, *The Problem of Profit: Finance and Feeling in Eighteenth-Century British Literature* (Charlottesville: University of Virginia Press, 2019), 102–3.

36. Sandiford, *Measuring the Moment*, 133.

37. In examining the benefits of Equiano's numeracy and proficiency in calculation, Tom Wickman argues that Equiano "exposes readers to the complexity of commercial life in the Atlantic world in order to show how challenging it can be to figure out questions of justice and fairness" ("Arithmetic and Afro-Atlantic Pastoral Protest: The Place of (In)numeracy in Gronniosaw and Equiano," *Atlantic Studies* 8, no. 2 [2011]: 193). Similarly, Caitlin Rosenthal reads Equiano's acquisition of numeracy as his leveraging of a "technology of commensuration" ("Numbers for the Innumerate: Everyday Arithmetic and Atlantic Capitalism," *Technology and Culture* 58, no. 2 [2017]: 535). For both Wickman and Rosenthal, the practical skill of calculating by the rule of three represents a means of participating in, and making sense of, an economic system that otherwise formally excludes the enslaved.

38. It is also worth noting the close relationship between Equiano's acquisition of literacy and the recognition that grants him. My analysis here draws from Henry Louis Gates Jr.'s influential account that locates Equiano's self-fashioning in autobiography, as it is "through the act of writing alone, [that] Equiano announces and preserves his newly found status as a subject" (*The Signifying Monkey: A Theory of African-American Literary Criticism* [Oxford: Oxford University Press, 1988], 171). Although Gates consistently and exclusively uses the term "exchange" to refer to scenes of conversation, rather than market transactions, this usage suggests that conversation requires the same kind of recognition that undergirds economic forms of exchange.

39. The almost simultaneous failure of this quasi-familial relationship—in the immediately following paragraph, Equiano is sold to Captain Doran, who seizes his property and accuses him of "talk[ing] too much English"—demonstrates the precarity of imperfect recognition as well, in a way that foreshadows the "impositions" I discussed earlier (68).

40. See Mack, *Heart Religion*, 57; and Anderson, *Imagining Methodism in Eighteenth-Century Britain: Enthusiasm, Belief, and the Borders of the Self* (Baltimore: Johns Hopkins University Press, 2012), 4–5.

41. Anderson, *Imagining Methodism*, 58, 55.

42. The income that Equiano could have generated amounts to vastly more than forty pounds. Assuming the standard 5 percent interest and that Equiano's life expectancy in the West Indies is what he calculates to be "but sixteen years!," and subtracting the four years in which he had already been enslaved, such an annuity would be worth slightly more than £1,600, or forty times Equiano's par value of forty pounds (79).

43. Festa, *Sentimental Figures*, 147.

44. Festa, *Sentimental Figures*, 130.

45. "And if by grace, then is it no more of works: otherwise grace is no more grace. But if it be of works, then is it no more grace: otherwise work is no more work" (Rom. 11:6).

46. Wesley, *Explanatory Notes upon the New Testament*, new ed. (London, 1813), 45.

Bartering Knowledge, Imposing Silence: Indigenous Guanche Presence in Thomas Sprat's *History of the Royal Society of London*

ALLISON Y. GIBEILY

On September 3, sometime around 1655, an English physician set out from the town of Güímar, a small settlement near the northeastern coast of the island of Tenerife. Led by a group of Indigenous Guanche guides, he planned to visit their people's burial caves and the mummified bodies within. As he explains in his report, which is embedded in Thomas Sprat's *History of the Royal Society of London* as "A Relation of the Pico Teneriffe," the physician had lived for several years on the island—one of the three largest islands in the archipelago now known as the Canary Islands. He had by this point established enough of a relationship with the "antient Inhabitants," whom he refers to elsewhere as "the old Cuanchios," to gain access to their most sacred of spaces.[1] This relationship was based in part on his having "done several Eleemosinary Cures amongst them ... which indeared him to them exceedingly." In return for the lifesaving knowledge that the Englishman offered to this community free of charge, the Guanches repaid him with an act that he explicitly recognized as "a favour they seldome or never permit to any."[2]

The Guanches' mode of compensation here is not required, nor is it exacted through the sort of manipulation or force one might expect from colonial actors. Sprat neither obfuscates nor revises the place of the physician in this lopsided power relation. Indeed, as the physician notes, "it is death for any Stranger to visit these Caves or Bodies" without the blessing of their keepers. Rather, the Guanches' decision to grant the English explorer access to this space amounts to a rare "favour"—a word that suggests a complex, tactical, and socially embedded system of knowledge bartering controlled not by the all-seeing empiricist writing his travelogue, but rather by the Indigenous people about whom he writes. Thus, even as the physician goes on to give a more familiarly ethnographic account of what he observes once inside the caves ("about three or four hundred" perfectly preserved bodies sewn up in goat skins with "incomparable exactness and evenness of the seams"), his observations lose some of their totalizing pull when understood as part of a conditional exchange of knowledge.[3] While seemingly freestanding and empirically available, the physician's account is as much a reflection of the Guanches' goodwill and tact as it is the product of his own observations.

Despite its brevity, this episode poses a challenge to the *History*'s goals, which included not only explaining the overarching mission of the Royal Society, founded seven years before, but also reframing scientific inquiry as something universally accessible and necessary for social and political progress.[4] If, as Sprat had noted earlier in his volume, natural philosophers ought to "have their eyes in all parts, and to receive information from every quarter of the earth" and to "have a constant universall intelligence" of that which they seek to describe, how can they possibly do so when such intelligence is not passively "received" but rather negotiated for or granted as a "a favor… seldome or never permit[ted] to any?"[5] If "the Genius of *Experimenting*" occurs "not onely by the hands of Learned and profess'd Philosophers," but also "in the Shops of *Mechanicks*; from the Voyages of *Merchants*; from the Ploughs of *Husbandmen*; from the Sports, the Fishponds, the Parks, and Gardens of *Gentlemen*," what happens when the very merchants embarking on and writing about those voyages—such as the "considerable Merchants and Men worthy of Credit" named on the title page of the "Relation"—meet with resistance from Native populations?[6] How does Indigenous opposition or indifference affect the kind of empiricism at the heart of Sprat's *History*, at the heart of European Enlightenment thinking more generally, and at the heart of its resultant textual archives—the form in which we now most often encounter colonized subjects from the long eighteenth century?

This essay attempts to answer these and other questions by looking at key moments in the "Relation of the Pico Teneriffe" when Guanches barter with, withhold, or otherwise obfuscate their expert local knowledge when interacting with European visitors. While one could certainly read the "Relation" as a typical example of colonial travel writing, in which a European observer writes about an Indigenous population in explicit, objectifying, or even violent terms, often erasing or misrepresenting parts of their culture, I would instead like to demonstrate how such erasure or misrepresentation does not happen purely at the hands of colonial writers. It also results from the actions *and inactions* of Indigenous people themselves, insofar as they appear in colonial documents. Further, we can see this quiet control over the flow of information—these moments of Indigenously imposed ambiguity—borne out in the "Relation" in both its form, including its grammar and typography, and its content.

In highlighting these moments of limited knowledge and archival absence, I do not intend to merely demonstrate how Sprat's *History*, and by extension Enlightenment empiricism more generally, fail to fulfill their many lofty promises. Rather, I aim to show how Guanche ways of knowing and communicating constructively disrupt Enlightenment epistemologies, offering in their place alternative modes for reading and making sense of the abundance of empirical and ethnographic writing published in the long eighteenth century. Joining an ever-growing chorus of voices that ask what we might do with colonial archives other than take them as historical fact or read them "against their archival grain," my treatment of the "Relation" aims to uncover a third, less certain outcome for the analysis and close reading on which our discipline relies.[7] After all, according to Siraj Ahmed, such methodologies are themselves a colonial inheritance.[8] This essay moves away from framing the Canary Islands in terms of their significance to the Spanish imperial project or the European Enlightenment, although I will start by briefly historicizing the region in these two contexts. My goal is instead to reevaluate the ways in which the "Relation" imagines these islands (which contemporary Amazigh people consider part of their Native Tamazgha homelands), using methods from Indigenous and Black studies, disciplines in which scholars have long questioned the authority of colonial archives and demonstrated the many ways that colonized people infiltrated and repurposed them to their own benefit.[9] Taking a cue from Jenny Sharpe's call for us to look for "a positive value of silence, fragment, and loss," I will analyze the strategic ways in which the Guanches imposed archival gaps, confounding the European settlers who relied upon their knowledge.[10] Such archival gaps and the unknowing they foster hold liberatory potential. They help blaze a path toward productive illegibility and question the primacy of, and demand for, universally accessible meaning.

The first textual documentation of the Canaries in the European archive can be traced to Pliny the Elder, whose *Natural History* (79 CE) posits a possible geography of the islands off the northwestern coast of Africa, then thought to be the western extremity of the world.[11] Throughout antiquity and early modernity, the islands occupied a curious place between myth and reality. For early European rulers and explorers, they were best known as the "Fortunate Islands," and, as the moniker suggests, served as both a backdrop on which to project fabled stories from the past and as a stimulus for imagining expansive colonial futures. Whether they were presumed to be the remains of the sunken city of Atlantis or the famous disappearing island of Saint Brendan, the Canary Islands gripped the European imaginary and refused definitive categorization.[12]

The islands were also geographically essential to early modern conquest. Situated strategically between Europe and the Americas, and benefiting from natural wind patterns that made for easier sailing, the Canaries were a critical stopping point in maritime routes, where ships restocked on water and other supplies before continuing west.[13] On one hand, as Judit Gutiérrez de Armas puts it, by the fourteenth century the Canaries were "places of reception, transformation and export of intercultural models and practices."[14] On the other hand, this early interculturalism would pave the way for the conversion, capture, enslavement, and, in many cases, forcible removal of Indigenous Guanches at the hands of European colonizers in the fifteenth and sixteenth centuries.[15]

While various empires had influenced the Canary Islands since antiquity, Spanish colonization in the fifteenth century ultimately took the strongest and most lasting hold over the islands, which remain under Spanish rule today. After the 1479 Treaty of Alcaçovas formalized Spanish control of the Canaries under the Crown of Castile, Spanish forces would go on to conquer the three largest islands of Gran Canaria, La Palma, and finally, in 1497, Tenerife, despite organized uprisings by the islands' different Indigenous populations.[16] Throughout these early years and into the eighteenth century, Spanish imperial ambition was spurred on in large part by Catholic Crusades, the ideology and writings of which, Eyda Merediz explains, "seemed to fluctuate between two poles: a proposal for violent conquests on the one hand, and the pursuit of peaceful missions on the other."[17] The islands' Indigenous inhabitants appear in Spanish colonial writings in a similarly polarized fashion: in some cases, particularly in church documents justifying invasion, they are primitive pagans in need of conversion; in other documents, they are highly civilized, respected stewards of the land.[18]

Spanish playwrights, poets, and historiographers in the sixteenth and seventeenth centuries also took inspiration from the Canary Islands, particularly the Guanches of Tenerife, as they imagined idealized models of intercultural exchange and sought out discreet modes of critique against their own governments.[19] Yet even such idealized interest in Indigenous populations, Edward Said would remind us, also enabled settler-colonial structures by repeatedly replacing real people and places with European imaginings of them.[20] In even more practical terms, the material reality for Indigenous Canarians under Spanish rule was—and continues to be—one of perseverance in the face of dispossession. In one example, when the Spanish Crown divided up Canarian lands to be distributed to settlers in 1501, of the 922 allocations made, only 19 went to Guanches, whose population was estimated to be anywhere between 15,000 and 60,000.[21] In another account provided by records from the bishopric of the Canaries, by 1504 a mere 1,200 Guanche families remained in the entire archipelago.[22]

As colonial interests turned more toward the so-called New World of the Americas, the Canary Islands' commercial significance faded. Its mythical aura, however, remained. A newly energized but nonetheless extractive wave of curious scientific explorers, including the anonymous informants behind the 1667 "Relation," traveled to the Canaries and produced what Mary Louise Pratt would call works of "anti-conquest"—that is, empirical travel writing in which naturalists presented their descriptions as apolitical observations made in the name of scientific advancement, occluding the fact that such ordering, and often depopulating, of the land was itself a byproduct of and contributor to European colonial hegemony.[23] The structure of travel writing from this era also reinforced this ethos, often appearing "episodic and miscellaneous rather than ordered and predictable," lending it a sense of organic serendipity.[24] The generic bricolage in Sprat's *History* functions similarly: the three-part work includes a dedicatory poem celebrating the mission of the Royal Society; a proposal for making wine out of sugarcane; a series of questions and answers between a member of the Royal Society and an administrator of the East India Company in Jakarta; various descriptions of the members' individual experiments; and, of course, the "Relation," as if to demonstrate through its own variety the indiscriminate possibilities for scientific inquiry. Moreover, the Royal Society was one of the most powerful engines behind such exploration and writing, often commissioning explorers and merchants to gather information during their journeys and giving them questionnaires to guide their observations.[25] So critical were these informants that, as Steven Shapin puts it, "it is difficult to imagine what early modern natural history or natural philosophy would look like without that component contributed by travelers, navigators, merchant-traders, soldiers, and adventurers."[26] Intelligence regarding Spanish-controlled regions such as the Canaries proved especially coveted, given the shroud of secrecy with which they guarded their colonies.[27]

By the time Sprat included the "Relation" in his *History of the Royal Society of London*, it was common for travelers to claim that the Indigenous

Guanche inhabitants of the Canary Islands no longer existed. Even more common was the collapsing of the islands' distinct Indigenous groups under the single ethnonym "Guanche," which originally signified the inhabitants of Tenerife specifically.[28] This imprecision likely results, at least in part, from the scarcity of physical archives concerning Indigenous Canarians, many of which were destroyed in the early years of conquest.[29] However, as is the case with so many Indigenous communities, the Guanches have endured, as evidenced both by Sprat's account and by their descendants' uninterrupted presence on the Canary Islands. Today, most scholars consider the Guanches among the ancestors of the contemporary Amazigh community, which traces its roots to pre-Islamic North Africa and which has seen a significant cultural, linguistic, and literary renaissance in the last several decades.[30] Even more pertinently, despite its "ghostly" presence in the Spanish literary canon, contemporary Canarian literature has seen its own revitalization, especially with the help of social media and other nontraditional forms of publication and circulation, as Rhian Davies powerfully demonstrates.[31] The Guanche whistling language, Silbo Gomero, colloquially known as El Silbo, still exists today thanks to preservation efforts and educational reforms in the 1990s.[32] Mimicking the vowel sounds and inflections of the Canarian Spanish spoken in the islands, El Silbo can communicate across great geographic distances, which, given the area's steep volcanic mountains and wide valleys, saved early inhabitants days of treacherous travel.[33] Like all Indigenous peoples, the Guanches had intimate knowledge of the resources and dangers of their lands, be they medicinal plants or safe routes of passage. They harnessed this knowledge for strategic ends and created numerous site-specific innovations, or what Marcy Norton calls "subaltern technologies," examples of which, including El Silbo, can be found throughout the "Relation" and on the islands today.[34] The Guanches and their ancestral lands carry millennia of embodied and often unrecorded know-how, much of which the merchants in the "Relation" were eager to extract, disavow, and repackage in the form of a written travelogue.[35]

In what follows, I trace the presence of seventeenth-century Guanche knowledge as it appears in the "Relation." Much like Nicole Aljoe and Elizabeth Maddock Dillon do in their Early Caribbean Digital Archive, I sift through the language of a colonial document to find evidence of an effaced Indigenous presence.[36] Settler-colonial knowledge of and survival in distant lands always depended on local informants, and we must approach any text written by a settler as what Ralph Bauer and Marcy Norton call an "entangled history"—that is, we must "attend to the multiplicity of sources, agencies, directions of influence, and modalities of intercultural connectedness," rather than presuming that European settlers always held power over colonized

Indigenous populations.[37] Taking up the challenge posed by James Delbourgo and Nicholas Dew, I am moving away from "preoccupations with alterity and the textual erasure of indigenous presence," which risk reinforcing an oversimplified binary between colonizers and the colonized, and "toward a social history of the interconnections between the radically different peoples that made and circulated early modern knowledge."[38] This means crediting specific Guanche knowledge by reading for archival gaps and grammatical exclusions to then situate them in an "entangled" or "interconnected" network of empiricism and local know-how alike.

Ultimately, rather than considering the Guanches in the "Relation" in terms of their relevance to European imperial history, this essay instead relies on the methods of Black and Indigenous studies to develop a different approach to reading colonial documents. Seeing archival gaps merely as injustices inflicted by the pens of colonial writers and trying to know with certainty the precise shape of the knowledge that those writers erased effectively recreates the power relations and empirical methods that I am striving to critique. Instead of "disembedd[ing] native literatures from their traditions" and imposing a single, colonially rooted analytical method, my readings of Guanche knowledge steer us away from universal legibility and toward something undetermined and entangled.[39] Nathaniel Mackey might call such an approach a "discrepant engagement," which, "rather than suppressing resonance, dissonance, [and] noise, seeks to remain open to them," refusing neat, resolute answers.[40] This approach attempts to read Guanche knowledge in the spirit in which the Guanches themselves offered it—that is, provisionally and with irreconcilable elisions that defy written documentation and reproduction. Within this paradigm, the Guanches' silences, like those that Sharpe traces throughout African diasporic literature, can have positive value by demonstrating Indigenous resistance and indifference to colonial powers.[41] They can point toward Indigenous expertise in even the most antagonistic of documents, much as Saidiya Hartman has been able to read for or imagine the presence of Black women in texts about chattel slavery.[42] They allow us to imagine, as Kelly Wisecup argues was the case for eighteenth- and nineteenth-century Indigenous communities in the United States, how the Guanches may have manipulated and reorganized colonial archives to serve their own purposes.[43]

Reframing archival gaps as Guanche-induced lets us see how, as Michel de Certeau suggests was the case for Indigenous peoples of the Americas, seventeenth-century Guanches made of the "laws imposed on them something quite different from what their conquerors had in mind ... by using them with respect to ends and references foreign to the system they had no choice but to accept."[44] Operating amid the twin systems of colonization and of scientific extraction and commercial exploitation that were thrust upon them, the Guanches of the "Relation" masterfully control the amount of information any European traveler could ever hope to take away. As a result, they enforce a bewildering epistemological silence that disorients Enlightenment empiricism, pushing readers to embrace an analytical method in which such bewilderment and disorientation are themselves the point.

The "Relation" makes no secret of the fact that the "Merchants and Men worthy of Credit" charged with recording their excursion to one of the peaks of Tenerife relied on Native knowledge.[45] Indeed, as the informants confess in the very first sentence, they can only "set out from *Oratava*, a Port Town in the Island of *Teneriffe*" after "having furnished [them]selves with a Guide, Servants, and Horses" to carry their many provisions.[46] A knowledgeable guide is a necessary precondition for any fact-finding mission, given the island's dangerous volcanic terrain, and evidence of those guides' expertise appears in virtually every moment of the narrative, despite their frequent grammatical eradication.[47] For example, after suffering what sounds like altitude sickness and losing one member of their company, the remaining men in the expedition finally reach "the *Sugarloaf*," an especially steep and sandy section of the mountain. There, despite the difficulties of the terrain, they "begin to travel again in a white sand, being fore-shod with shooes whose single soles are made a finger broader than the upper leather, to encounter this difficult and unstable passage."[48] Only with the help of a specially made shoe with extra surface area on its sole can the English merchants cross the "unstable" sandy passage. Given the other documented examples of specialized clothing being used in the Canaries, including the *tenique*—a cape with stones sewn into its seams to keep it from catching too much wind and causing its wearer to be blown over—as well as *mahos* (goatskin shoes worn primarily by inhabitants of the eastern islands), these broad-soled shoes that the Guanches supplied to their European charges are most definitely an invention rooted in local know-how and an example of "subaltern technology" at work.[49] However, the Native artisans who would have made these shoes and the expert guides who would have required or provided them are absent in the sentence. The British merchants are passively "fore-shod" and the soles "are made," with no grammatical attribution to a subject who actually performed these actions or possessed this expertise. According to Pratt, this is a common habit in settler travel writing.[50] It constitutes a colonial erasure, to be sure, and one that results in a peculiar, syntactically distorted sentence in which the shoes seemingly appear out of thin air. However, the brevity of this detail could just as likely reflect a conditional exchange in which the Indigenous guides never made the merchants privy to the skilled work of their local artisans. Or, perhaps the merchants never thought to ask about this technology, not having registered it as such. In either case, one could speculate that the passive voice evidences a strategic wielding of knowledge on the part of Guanches in which they allow their practical expertise to fly below the empirical radar, indifferent to settler curiosity and set on simply accomplishing the task they had been hired to do.

Such a reading becomes even more likely when paired with a similar instance later in the "Relation," when yet another subaltern technology comes to the rescue of the group of European explorers. After climbing to the summit and making various observations about small springs fed by the snowmelt and pools of water that have collected within the mountain's caverns, the merchants turn back and begin their descent to Oratava. Their Indigenous guides—whom they continue to refer to as their "Servants"—remain in sight, holding ropes for the Englishmen as they spelunk into a frozen cave. Despite an impressive array of icicles, the men grow "quickly weary of this excessive cold place" and continue down the mountain, arriving "from whence [they] set forth, [their] faces red and sore." As with the specialized shoes, the informants at once detail and efface the solution to their woes, seemingly in a single breath. To "cool" their wind-burned and possibly frostbitten faces, the narrator notes, "we were forced to wash and bathe them in Whites of Eggs, &c."[51] The elision here is twofold: again, the informants share this detail in the passive voice, grammatically eliminating the person who "forced" such treatment upon them. Further, in a curious bit of typographical erasure, the specific ingredients of the salve are also abbreviated as "&c."—a shorthand for "etc.," the truncated version of the Latin phrase "et cetera."

Appearing in any number of early modern and eighteenth-century European genres, "&c." can signal, among other things, aposiopesis, or the sudden breaking off of speech. As Laurie Maguire explains, this multipurpose mark—which shares roots with the ellipsis—does not only abbreviate lists and curtail speech; it can also indicate the interruption or silencing of forbidden, unknown, or even bawdy information. It "plays a conceptually sophisticated game with boundaries and cusps, with abruption and continuation, with suspension and extension of meaning."[52] In this sense, we could see this "&c." as a sort of "abruption" similar to the use of passive voice, a device that removes Indigenous knowledge producers from colonial narratives. However, the mark also suggests the incomplete nature of the informants' own knowledge. And this is not necessarily because they have failed as empiricists, but rather, I would argue, because of the Guanches' strategic withholding of local knowledge. In this reframing of the situation, the abbreviated list of ingredients for the egg-white-based balm stands less as evidence of colonial domination than of complex Indigenous expertise that cannot be fully rendered in the language available to the author of the "Relation" or to Sprat and his Royal Society associates. Even more interestingly, the "&c." invites readers both then and now into a moment of what Maguire would call "suspended" meaning making, in which we can "extend" and productively reimagine Indigenous knowledge forms in contexts in which they have been assumed to have been lost or silenced. Teetering on the cusp of legibility, this "&c." not only announces entangled, unwritten, and unwritable Indigenous Guanche epistemologies; it also inadvertently produces them. It offers readers an opportunity to co-create meaning, while simultaneously withholding the explicit, empirical descriptions that would allow them to know what that meaning was supposed to be.

While these first few moments of productive silence function mostly at the grammatical level, it helps to think of them in relation to later, more overt examples of entangled knowledge exchange that appear in the text, such as the scene at the Guanche burial caves with which I began. To return briefly to the physician's account, the Guanches' "favour" is not without its limits. They grant him access to select locations under specific, bartered conditions; but they also announce to him "that they have above twenty Caves of their Kings and great Persons, with their whole Families, yet unknown to any but themselves, and which they will never discover."[53] Furthermore, they frame their secrecy as a response to previous waves of Spanish colonization. Despite the physician taking "great care ... to enquire of these people" regarding their traditions for embalming bodies, he is met with this answer from the oldest among his Guanche guides (who is said to be "above a hundred and ten years of age"): "They had of old one particular Tribe of men that had this Art amongst themselves only, and kept it as a thing sacred, and not to be communicated to the Vulgar: These mixt not with the rest of the inhabitants, nor married out of their own Tribe, and were also their Priests and Ministers of Religion: That upon the Conquest of the *Spaniards* they were most of them destroy'd, and the Art lost with them, only they held some Traditions yet of a few Ingredients, that were made use of in this business."[54] As if throwing the consequences of colonization back in the face of yet another colonizer, the Guanche elder here gives voice to the silencing of his culture centuries earlier. In undoing this silence and, as it happens, adding what had been silenced to the textual archive, he dictates the flow and quality of whatever information remained after the Spanish conquest of the Canaries in the fifteenth and sixteenth centuries. Indeed, even as the elder recounts his knowledge of the "few Ingredients" involved in embalming that were not "lost" with "the Tribe of men" killed or enslaved by Spanish settlers, he mars that knowledge (which the physician has taken such "great care" to learn) by detailing its historic dismantling at the hands of other Europeans. While the physician goes on to provide a sort of recipe for an embalming cream described to him by the elder, which involved boiling native herbs in goat-milk butter and hog grease, the physician and, later, the readers of the "Relation" cannot escape the fact that this information is only partial. The settler-colonial projects of the past have disrupted the empirical transparency of Indigenous knowledge in the present of the "Relation." Guanche leaders insist that this reality must frame any information about their sacred customs.

A similar sort of elision occurs in relation to the Guanches' methods for predicting weather patterns. After reaching the peak of Tenerife, the informants for the "Relation" stare out at the panorama above the clouds and then punctuate their wonder with a note of uncertainty: "Whether these Clouds do ever surmount the *Pico* we cannot say, but to such as are far beneath, they sometimes seem to hang above it, or rather wrap themselves about it, as constantly when the North-west Wind blows."[55] The informants "cannot say" with certainty what patterns the weather usually follows beyond how it "seems" to them, since they are but visitors to the region. By contrast, the Guanches apparently *do* have an intimate knowledge of and explanation for this phenomenon. Indeed, they have a specific name for it: "this [North-west Wind] they call the *Cappe*, and [it] is a certain prognostick of ensuing Storms."[56] With such expert knowledge of their native climate, the Guanches, as the informants render them in the "Relation," can predict the weather—yet another example of a subaltern technology and, in this case, one that is actually legible to European observers.

The merchants know and record the name "Cappe" and understand its place in a "prognostick" system, but the absence of any more empirical or practical observations may speak to the fact that such details were never shared. Like the Guanche elder who explicitly limited the information he would share with "the Vulgar" European physician, the guide on the expedition to the top of the mountain shares a measured amount of information without elucidating their entire system for weather prediction. Further still, the relative absence of the belabored measurements so common in early modern travel writing may suggest that Indigenous knowledge of weather patterns actually *cannot* be shared, perhaps because it relies upon an epistemological system, embodied or otherwise, that was illegible to European eyes and capabilities. As compared to the description in the "Relation" of the "Pit called *Caldera*," a concave span of land that the informants measured using numbers and comparisons ("a Musquet-shot across, and neer fourscore yards deep, in shape like a *cone*, within hollow like a Kettle or Cauldron"), Indigenous knowledge of the wind patterns endures through means and experiences that are difficult, if not impossible, to capture in writing.[57]

In each of these instances, the Indigenous community interacts with the settler merchants and the physician in direct ways, either guiding them through Canarian lands or communicating with them through spoken words, likely mediated by a translator. However, in the closing moments of the "Relation," the Guanches enact yet another sort of silence that eludes English comprehension. Relaying the physician's observations, the informants explain: "He told also (and the same was seriously confirmed by a *Spaniard*, and another *Canary* Merchant then in the company) That they [the Guanches] whistle so loud as to be heard five miles off. And that to be in the same Room with them when they whistle, were enough to indanger breaking the *Tympanum* of the ear, ... [the physician] (being in Company of one that whistled his loudest) could not hear perfectly for fifteen dayes after, the noise was so great."[58] To call this whistling "noise" indicates that the physician—as well as the Spaniard and the other merchant who appear, parenthetically, to endorse his account—has either failed or refused to register the sounds before him as language.[59] While Julien Meyer explains that documented evidence of whistling languages in the Canaries can be found as early as the beginning of the fifteenth century, when two Franciscan priests made note of the inhabitants' peculiar wordless speech as "le plus estrange langaige de tous les autres païs de pardeçà" ("the strangest language of all other countries around"), the physician in the "Relation" hears nothing but an eardrum-shattering racket.[60]

One could read this as an erasure in the colonial archive, in which settler merchants are flattening a complex Indigenous language into mere "noise." Yet, given the Guanches' subtle forms of resistance elsewhere in the "Relation," we could also read it otherwise. First, the whistling could be something more akin to clandestine resistance. The Guanches communicate in a language twice removed from what the English physician would understand—El Silbo, at its inception, mimicked the tonal qualities of the Indigenous languages spoken on the Canary Islands, although those individual idioms would later be collapsed into the colonizers' Spanish.[61] As a result, the Guanche man in this scene not only evades the eyes and ears of his observers, to which he is seemingly indifferent, but manages to inflict bodily harm on a European settler.[62] Second, and as Mackey would urge, we might simultaneously engage with this "noise" in our own discrepant way, neither taking it in the marginalizing spirit in which the colonial informants offer it, nor attempting to "suppress or silence" it, decode it, or thrust it into the realm of accessibility.[63] Instead, we can let it exist *as noise*, in all of its irreconcilable and productive obscurity. A rather loud sort of silence,

Guanche whistling hints at the limits of written archives, announcing its presence without conceding to colonial demands for legibility.

The "Relation" makes up but a fraction of the longer *History of the Royal Society*, and these brief moments of Indigenous presence constitute an even smaller portion still. Yet it is paradoxically the brevity and lack of information about the Guanches that points toward their sustained presence and expertise through the centuries of colonization. Of course, any act of archival recuperation, including what I am offering here, must be treated with skepticism. In particular, it must resist what Stephen Best calls "the recovery imperative"—that desire to "give 'voice to the voiceless,' [or] to write the 'hidden history' of resistance."[64] To indulge such ambitions risks supplanting seventeenth-century colonial ethnography with a well-meaning, but nonetheless misleading, contemporary counterpart. However, by shifting our focus away from what the "Relation" and its readers could have known and recorded about the Guanches, and instead considering the ways in which these Indigenous actors may or may not have allowed their knowledge to be legible, we can use the "Relation" as a minor case study with which to open new methodological doors. Silence and unknowing become meaningful ends in and of themselves. By sitting with the archival gaps in the text, we can get closer to Best's proposed solution of a "melancholy historicism," in which "history consists in the *taking possession* of such grievous experiences as archival loss."[65] To feel the melancholy absence of Guanche knowledge is to feel the consequences of settler colonialism and its attendant genocides, which nearly annihilated the Indigenous cultures of the Canary Islands. For me, as a Lebanese woman who grew up in the heart of United States empire, and who is currently living on occupied Anishinaabe land in Chicago, to feel this absence is to accept its contradictions. Without collapsing difference, it is to acknowledge or "take possession of" a shared experience of diaspora, displacement, and loss, and to then build solidarity across communities without laying claim to them. In very real terms, it is to be in and to embrace the darkness of Édouard Glissant's "right to opacity" and live out its liberating potentials.[66]

Global eighteenth-century studies, and especially Indigenous studies, have recently moved away from the sort of counter-archival readings of colonial documents offered here and rightly turned toward Indigenous sources to give voice to Indigenous perspectives. As part of this, scholars have pushed for an expanded sense of what qualifies as literature and culture, making space for the nontextual and the paratextual in the archive broadly construed.[67] For global eighteenth-century studies to live up to its name, globalization must happen at a geographic scale, which is to say that we must read, teach, and write about literature produced outside of Europe. But it must also happen on a methodological scale, by which I mean we must ask what the appropriate modes of reading, teaching, and writing actually are for cultural objects coming out of diverse traditions. Embracing archival gaps as irreparable silence and reimagining that silence positively—as both Sharpe and the Guanches of the "Relation" do—is one possible answer to this question, and one which allows us to see ambiguity as more than just colonial erasure. It teaches us to resist the empirical drive toward legibility passed down through the humanities since the Enlightenment.[68] Other answers, which will be as vast and varied as the global eighteenth century itself, must emerge out of conversations with and guidance from Indigenous communities. Rather than attempting to have the last word on the Guanches of Tenerife, or even on the reading practices that world literatures require more broadly, my hope is that this essay invites collaboration and participation well beyond the academy, where ways of knowing and caring for the world far exceed those most readily available in many of our disciplines.

Notes

1. Sprat, *The History of the Royal Society of London for the Improving of Natural Knowledge by Tho. Sprat* (London, 1667), 209. Subsequent mentions in the main text will be made as *History* when referring to Sprat's volume as a whole and as "Relation" when specifically referring to "A Relation of the Pico Teneriffe." However, all citations in the notes will be made as *History*.

2. Sprat, *History*, 209.

3. Sprat, *History*, 209.

4. For a helpful primer on the founding of the Royal Society, as well as on the specific role of Sprat's *History* in consolidating the group's identity and mission, see William T. Lynch, *Solomon's Child: Method in the Early Royal Society of London* (Stanford: Stanford University Press, 2001), especially chapter 5; see too J. Ereck Jarvis, "Thomas Sprat's 'Mixt Assembly': Association and Authority in *The History of the Royal Society*," *Restoration: Studies in English Literature and Culture, 1660–1700* 37, no. 2 (2013): 55–77.

5. Sprat, *History*, 20, 209.

6. Sprat, *History*, 72.

7. Ann Laura Stoler, *Along the Archival Grain: Epistemic Anxieties and Colonial Common Sense* (Princeton: Princeton University Press, 2009), 20–21, 50–53.

8. Ahmed, *Archaeology of Babel: The Colonial Foundation of the Humanities* (Stanford: Stanford University Press, 2018), 39.

9. Tamazgha is a span of land now understood to include all of the North African Maghreb, the Canary Islands, and parts of sub-Saharan Africa. See Brahim El Guabli, "Where Is Amazigh Studies?," *Journal of North African Studies* 27, no. 6 (2022): 1093. El Guabli identifies as Amazigh, Black, and Sahrawi. See "My Amazigh Indigeneity (the Bifurcated Roots of a Native Moroccan)," *The Markaz Review*, 15 September 2021, https://themarkaz.org/my-amazigh-indigeneity-the-bifurcated-roots-of-a-native-moroccan/.

10. Sharpe, *Immaterial Archives: An African Diaspora Poetics of Loss* (Evanston: Northwestern University Press, 2020), 13.

11. See Bertrand Westphal, "The Canaries: Between Mythical Space and Global Drift," in *A Comparative History of Literatures in the Iberian Peninsula*, ed. Fernando Cabo Aseguinolaza, Anxo Abuín González, and César Domínguez, 2 vols. (Philadelphia: John Benjamins, 2010), 1:292.

12. For example, in his 1664 *Mundus Subterraneus*, Athanasius Kircher framed the Guanches as the last remaining Atlanteans, and their Indigenous islands, the Canaries, as the visible peaks of what was once Atlantis. Other European writers, from the early modern period through the late nineteenth century, echoed his observations in various genres. See Westphal, "Canaries," 296–97, for a thorough tracing of the origin myths. See also Eyda M. Merediz, *Refracted Images: The Canary Islands through a New World Lens* (Tempe: Arizona Center for Medieval and Renaissance Studies, 2004), especially 1–2; and her "Estudio crítico," in Lope de Vega's *Comedia la famosa de Los guanches de Tenerife y Conquista de Canaria*, ed. Eyda M. Merediz (Newark: Juan de la Cuesta, 2003), 10.

13. Merediz, *Refracted Images*, 8.

14. Gutiérrez de Armas, "Archival Practices in Early Modern Spain: Transformation, Destruction and (Re)Construction of Family Archives in the Canary Islands," *Archives and Manuscripts* 48, no. 1 (2020): 8.

15. See John Mercer, *The Canary Islanders: Their Pre-History, Conquest, and Survival* (London: Collings, 1980), 155–59, 222–40. Capturing and enslaving Native people was common practice when the French invaded the Canary Islands in the fourteenth and fifteenth centuries, and it continued under Spanish colonization in the sixteenth and seventeenth centuries. Particularly under the Spanish, Indigenous Guanches were removed from their homelands and sold in Europe or to neighboring islands like Portuguese-controlled Madeira, where they typically labored on sugarcane plantations.

16. See Merediz, *Refracted Images*, 18–21; and Mercer, *Canary Islanders*, 184–209.

17. Merediz, *Refracted Images*, 13. Merediz's first chapter provides a thorough account of the stages of colonization of the Canary Islands, with particular attention given to the role of literary and historiographic sources in recording and imagining the Spanish colonial presence in these lands. For a list of European interventions in the Canaries, see Isacio Perez Fernandez, "Registro Historico: Intervenciones Europeas en Canarias y Africa Hasta el Siglo XVI," in Bartolome des las Casas, *Brevisima Relacion de la Destuccion de Africa: Preludio de la Destrucción de Indias*, ed. Isacio Perez Fernandez, (Salamanca: Viceconsejeria de Cultura y Deportes del

Gobierno de Canarias, 1989): 145-187. For further historical context on the long trajectory of Spanish colonization of the Canaries, see J. H. Elliott, *Imperial Spain: 1469–1707* (New York: Penguin Books, 2002), especially chapter 2.

18. Merediz, *Refracted Images*, 14–17, 38–44.

19. One of the most readily available examples of such work is Lope de Vega's *Los guanches de Tenerife y conquista de Canaria* (1606–7), a comedy that recounts the late fifteenth-century conquest and defeat of Tenerife and the marriage of a Spanish captain to a Guanche princess. Lope's play is a dramatic retelling of Antonio de Viana's 1604 epic poem *Antigüedades de las Islas Afortunadas de la Gran Canaria, conquista de Tenerife y aparición de la santa imagen de Candelaria en verso suelto y octava rima*, which is itself based on a historical account, *Del origen y milagros de la imagen de nuestra señora de la Candelaria, que apareció en Tenerife, con la descripción de esta isla* (1594), written by a Dominican friar, Alonso de Espinosa, who was dispatched to Tenerife to document the miracles attributed to the Virgin of Candelaria, who appeared to the Indigenous Guanche inhabitants. On this genealogy, see Merediz, *Refracted Images*, especially her second and fourth chapters, as well as her critical edition of Lope de Vega's play, cited above in note 12.

20. Said, *Orientalism* (New York: Vintage, 1979), especially 6, 176–82, 201.

21. Mercer, *Canary Islanders*, 215. Mercer also notes that a majority of the land in the Canary Islands is still controlled by a small number of wealthy Spanish elites to this day (217).

22. Westphal, "Canaries," 294. The precise number of remaining Guanche families may have differed from what is officially recorded, which we must approach as critically and skeptically as we would any other colonial archive. However, given the long history of dispossession and displacement of Indigenous Guanches, both before and after the turn of the sixteenth century, the general trend implied by these records, no matter how imprecise, seems highly plausible.

23. Pratt, *Imperial Eyes: Travel Writing and Transculturation* (London: Routledge, 1992), 7, 38–67.

24. See Daniel Carey, "Compiling Nature's History: Travellers and Travel Narratives in the Early Royal Society," *Annals of Science* 54, no. 3 (1997): 276.

25. See James Delbourgo and Nicholas Dew, "The Far Side of the Ocean," in *Science and Empire in the Atlantic World*, ed. James Delbourgo and Nicholas Dew (New York: Routledge, 2008), 13. For more on the practice of sending questionnaires to guide observation, see Antonio Barrera-Osorio, "Empiricism in the Spanish Atlantic World," in *Science and Empire*, 177–202.

26. Shapin, *A Social History of Truth: Civility and Science in Seventeenth-Century England* (Chicago: University of Chicago Press, 1994), 245.

27. See Alison Sandman, "Controlling Knowledge: Navigation, Cartography, and Secrecy in the Early Modern Spanish Atlantic," in *Science and Empire*, 31–51.

28. Mercer, *Canary Islanders*, 237. See also A. José Farrujia de la Rosa, *An Archaeology of the Margins: Colonialism, Amazighity and Heritage Management on the Canary Islands* (New York: Springer, 2014), 3n2.

29. The archives of Gran Canaria and La Palma, for example, were destroyed in the sixteenth century by fires and pirates. See Mercer, *Canary Islanders*, 215; and El Guabli, "Where Is Amazigh Studies," 1094.

30. I use the term "Amazigh," as generally preferred by this community itself, over the now obsolete "Berber" (in Arabic, بربر, *barbar*), which was first imposed by Arab writers during the seventh-century conquests. For a helpful outline of the history and constructed nature of this ethnic category, see Ramzi Rouighi, *Inventing the Berbers: History and Ideology in the Maghrib* (Philadelphia: University of Pennsylvania Press, 2019); James McDougall, "Histories of Heresy and Salvation: Arabs, Berbers, Community, and the State," in *Berbers and Others: Beyond Tribe and Nation in the Maghrib*, ed. Katherine E. Hoffman and Susan Gilson Miller (Bloomington: Indiana University Press, 2010), 15–37; and Farrujia de la Rosa, *Archaeology of the Margins*, 11. On the Amazigh studies movement more broadly, see El Guabli, "Where Is Amazigh Studies?" and "Literature and Indigeneity: Amazigh Activists' Construction of an Emerging Field," *Los Angeles Review of Books*, 28 October 2022, https://lareviewofbooks.org/article/literature-and-indigeneity-amazigh-activists-construction-of-an-emerging-literary-field.

31. Davies, "A Journey through Uncharted Territories?: Reassessing Canarian Literature and the *Novela Negra* through an Analysis of Identity, Solitude, and Place in Miguel Aguerralde's *Claro de Luna* (2009)," *Journal of Iberian and Latin American Studies* 26, no. 1 (2020): 83–105.

32. For more on Silbo Gomero, see Julien Meyer, *Whistled Languages: A Worldwide Inquiry on Human Whistled Speech* (New York: Springer-Verlag, 2015), particularly chapters 2 and 4.

33. Meyer, *Whistled Languages*, 35.

34. Norton, "Subaltern Technologies and Early Modernity in the Atlantic World," *Colonial Latin American Review* 26, no. 1 (2017): 28; Sprat, *History*, 201.

35. For this process of "disavowal," see Norton, "Subaltern Technologies," 20–25.

36. Aljoe and Dillon, "Decolonizing the Archive: Remix and Reassembly," Early Caribbean Digital Archive, accessed August 16, 2023, https://ecda.northeastern.edu/home/about/decolonizing-the-archive/.

37. Bauer and Norton, "Introduction: Entangled Trajectories: Indigenous and European Histories," *Colonial Latin American Review* 26, no. 1 (2017): 3. For other notable examples, see also Norton, "Subaltern Technologies"; Londa L. Schiebinger, *Plants and Empire: Colonial Bioprospecting in the Atlantic World* (Cambridge: Harvard University Press, 2004); and Susan Scott Parrish, *American Curiosity: Cultures of Natural History in the Colonial British Atlantic World* (Chapel Hill: University of North Carolina Press, 2006).

38. Delbourgo and Dew, "Far Side of the Ocean," 12.

39. Ahmed, *Archaeology of Babel*, 39.

40. Mackey, *Discrepant Engagement: Dissonance, Cross-Culturality, and Experimental Writing* (Cambridge: Cambridge University Press, 1993), 20.

41. See Sharpe, *Immaterial Archives*, 3–18.

42. Hartman, "Venus in Two Acts," *Small Axe* 26 (2008): 1–14.

43. Wisecup, *Assembled for Use: Indigenous Compilation and the Archives of Early Native American Literatures* (New Haven: Yale University Press, 2021), especially 2–6.

44. Certeau, *The Practice of Everyday Life*, trans. Steven Rendall, 3rd ed. (Berkeley: University of California Press, 2011), xiii.

45. While it is difficult to be certain, the mountain that the informants of the "Relation" write about is likely Mount Teide, a volcanic peak in the center of Tenerife that rises 3,715 meters above sea level.

46. Sprat, *History*, 200.

47. For a thorough consideration of the importance of Indigenous guides in a similar context, see Kimberly Takahata, "'Follow me your guide': Poetic Empire in John Singleton's *A General Description of the West-Indian Islands*," *Studies in Eighteenth-Century Culture* 49 (2020): 45–64.

48. Sprat, *History*, 201.

49. On specialized clothing in the Canaries, see Mercer, *Canary Islanders*, 249; and Norton, "Subaltern Technology," 28.

50. Pratt, *Imperial Eyes*, 51–52.

51. Sprat, *History*, 204.

52. Maguire, *The Rhetoric of the Page* (Oxford: Oxford University Press, 2020), 111.

53. Sprat, *History*, 211.

54. Sprat, *History*, 210.

55. Sprat, *History*, 203.

56. Sprat, *History*, 203.

57. Sprat, *History*, 202.

58. Sprat, *History*, 213.

59. See Meyer, *Canary Islanders*, 254, for a brief discussion of this scene.

60. The broader passage from which this quotation comes reads: "Est l païs habité de grand peuple qui parle le plus estrange langaige de tous les autres païs de pardeçà; & parlent des baulievres ainsi que si feussent sans langue" ("It is the country inhabited by large people who speak the strangest language of all other countries around, and they speak with two lips as if they were without a tongue"). Pierre Bontier and Jean Le Verrier, *Le Canarien; livre de la conquête et conversion des Canaries (1402–1422) par Jean de Bethencourt*, ed. Gabriel Gravier (Rouen, 1874), 125. See also Meyer, *Whistled Languages*, 12–13n3, for an explanation of "baulievres."

61. See Meyer, *Whistled Languages*, 13.

62. On this topic more broadly, see Namwali Serpell, "Unbothered: On Black Nonchalance," *Yale Review* 108, no. 4 (2020): 44–65.

63. Mackey, *Discrepant Engagement*, 19.

64. Best, *None Like Us: Blackness, Belonging, Aesthetic Life* (Durham: Duke University Press, 2018), 84.

65. Best, *None Like Us*, 15.

66. Glissant, *Poetics of Relation*, trans. Betsy Wing (Ann Arbor: University of Michigan Press, 1997), 189–94.

67. For two representative examples of this work, see Daniel Heath Justice (Cherokee Nation), *Why Indigenous Literatures Matter* (Waterloo: Wilfred Laurier Press, 2018); and Diana Taylor, *The Archive and the Repertoire: Performing Cultural Memory in the Americas* (Durham: Duke University Press, 2003).

68. See Sharpe, *Immaterial Archives*, 13; and Ahmed, *Archaeology of Babel*, 39.

The Question of I'tisam-ud-Din: An Indian Traveler in Eighteenth-Century Europe

SANJAY SUBRAHMANYAM

> On the Continent learned persons love to quote Aristotle, Horace, Montaigne and show off their knowledge; in England only uneducated people show off their knowledge, nobody quotes Latin and Greek authors in the course of a conversation, unless he has never read them.
> —George Mikes, *How to Be an Alien* (1946)

The Context

European overseas empire building in the early modern period notoriously proceeded in fits and starts. After substantial territorial gains in the Atlantic world and the acquisition of some footholds in the Indian Ocean during the first half of the sixteenth century, the seventeenth century saw a distinct slackening of the European imperial drive, as bloody and debilitating internecine conflicts within Europe, such as the Thirty Years' War, took precedence. Nevertheless, the Dutch managed to make inroads into Island Southeast Asia, while the English set up their colonies on the North American East Coast. A second major wave of overseas expansion followed in the latter half of the eighteenth century, with the British push into South Asia compensating for their loss of a good part of their American colonies.[1] By around 1800, although the Spanish, Portuguese, and French were all significant imperial powers, it was the British Empire that had emerged as the *fer-de-lance* of European overseas ambitions, and it consolidated its preeminence in 1815 with the defeat of the rival Napoleonic project. The emergence of this new incarnation of the British caused some consternation in various polities of the Islamic world, which had grown used to seeing them as mere merchants, even if some British visitors were given to bouts of surly and aggressive behavior, like the infamous Sir Josiah Child (1630–99).[2] For intellectuals in the Islamic world, understanding the British—their politics, their society, and their mentality—was no longer a luxury in the eighteenth century, but rather a pressing existential question.[3]

This essay focuses on one of the earliest South Asian authors of a first-person account of the West, Shaikh I'tisam-ud-Din from Bengal, who wrote the *Shigarf-nama-yi wilayat* (Wonder-Book of England; see Figure 1).[4] By around 1730, roughly the year of his birth in *qasba* Panchnur (or Pajnaur) in the Nadia region of western Bengal, Europeans had been significant actors in the Bay of Bengal for well over two centuries.[5] The Portuguese had first arrived in the late 1510s, when the region was still under the control of the Husain Shahi Sultanate, and proceeded to establish themselves in two areas: Chatgaon to the east, near the frontier with Burma, which they termed Porto Grande, and Satgaon to the west, which they termed Porto Pequeno.[6] Although this presence was largely a decentralized affair run by private traders, mercenaries, and freelancers, the Portuguese were nevertheless able to gain some influence over trade from the ports of the Ganges delta, without ever really dominating it, in the sixteenth century. Eventually they were joined by Catholic priests (from both the secular clergy and the missionary orders, like the Jesuits and Augustinians), who made modest efforts at conversion among both the peasants and the townsmen.[7]

The Portuguese were thus witnesses when the Mughals made their first incursions into the region in the 1530s, during the reign of Humayun, although they were initially unable to consolidate their power. As a consequence, the middle decades of the sixteenth century led to political fragmentation in the region, with local and regional dominance being largely in the hands of powerful magnates called zamindars, some of whom were from locally entrenched families, while others belonged to migrant groups from the west, such as the Afghans. Later, in the 1570s, the Mughals under Akbar (r. 1556–1605) returned to the charge and proceeded to occupy the western part of Bengal, partly (but not entirely) displacing their Afghan rivals, such as the Karranis.[8] However, their expansion further east proved to be a long and painful affair, carried out in campaign after campaign in

Figure 1. The portrait frontispiece of Shaikh I'tisam-ud-Din, *Shigurf namah i Velaët, or, Excellent intelligence concerning Europe: Being the travels of Mirza Itesa Modeen in Great Britain and France* (London, 1827). From the author's personal collection.

what their disenchanted commanders viewed as the watery maze of the Ganges delta; the conquest of the easternmost Chatgaon region of Bengal was only accomplished in the 1660s during the reign of Aurangzeb. One of these campaigns, in 1632, led to the expulsion, by the Mughal general Qasim Khan Juwaini, of the Portuguese from their fortified town of Hughli, which had succeeded Satgaon as the preferred port on the western end of the Ganges delta.

By the second half of the seventeenth century, the Dutch and the English had overtaken the Portuguese in the markets of Bengal and maintained regular contacts with the Mughal government in the region, which was now based in the provincial capital of Jahangirnagar (now Dhaka). They had also set up trading outposts, or factories, in other parts of the Mughal Empire, most notably in Gujarat, where the port city of Surat dominated trade between India on the one hand, and the Red Sea and the Persian Gulf on the other. While the Dutch used their privileged situation in Southeast Asia and Japan to trade in spices, copper, and other goods, the English were mostly concerned with exporting Indian textiles from both Gujarat and Bengal into Europe. However, traders from both nations were generally unable to obtain permission from the Mughals to fortify their factories. This meant that the first English and Dutch forts in India were built beyond the reach of the Mughals in the southern part of the subcontinent, in sites such as Armagon, Madras, Nagapattinam, and Pulicat. Even the weaker European powers, like the French and the Danes, managed to build small fortresses on the southeastern—or Coromandel—coast of India.

Texts written in India concerning the gradual emergence of European maritime power remained limited in their number and extent in the sixteenth and seventeenth centuries. Perhaps the most significant are the writings in Arabic from Kerala, in both prose and poetry, that denounce the Portuguese and their violence in no uncertain terms and call for jihad against them.[9] These texts are part of a corpus written in Arabic along different parts of the coast of the Indian Ocean: the Hijaz, the Hadramaut, and other sites. By contrast, the Indo-Persian chronicling tradition paid only limited attention to the "Frankish hat-wearers" (*kulah-poshan-i firang*), except when they engaged in striking acts of violence, such as the drowning of Sultan Bahadur of Gujarat when he went to meet the Portuguese governor, Nuno da Cunha, in 1537. Often, Europeans were regarded as no more than amusing bearers of curiosities, such as musical instruments, clocks, or turkeys, or of new products of debatable worth, such as the tobacco plant. One Mughal intellectual who took them more seriously was a certain Tahir Muhammad Sabzwari, who had been sent by Akbar to Goa to negotiate with the Portuguese in the early 1580s. In his *Rauzat al-Tahirin*, Tahir Muhammad devotes some attention to the Franks, especially the Portuguese, and their activities in various parts of the Indian Ocean; somewhat unusually, he also shows some knowledge of the contemporary state of politics in Portugal, Spain, and the Maghreb.[10]

During the first half of the seventeenth century, other intellectuals at the Mughal court went on to accumulate a more bookish form of knowledge regarding Europe, often through contacts with the Jesuits. The most accomplished among them was probably Mulla 'Abdus Sattar ibn Qasim Lahauri, who was the collaborator and translator of the well-known Spanish Jesuit Jerónimo Xavier. 'Abdus Sattar helped Xavier translate a number of Christian texts into Persian, but also effectively coauthored others, such as a mirror of princes entitled *Adab al-saltanat,* presented to the ruler Jahangir.[11] At the same time, he acquired a sufficient knowledge of written Latin as to be able to consult the limited library that the Jesuits had at their disposal, and thereby produce an abridged and schematic account of European history, which he called (at least in some versions) *Ahwal-i Firangistan* (Account of the land of the Franks). 'Abdus Sattar was not able to paint an up-to-date picture of European politics and society, however, because his main sources ended in the fifteenth century. It may also have been the case that his Jesuit interlocutors did not want to reveal too much to him, even though some references to more recent figures, such as Christopher Columbus, Hernán Cortés, Dom Sebastião of Portugal, and Philip II of Spain, made their way into the *Adab al-Saltanat.*

The various East India Companies also provided the Mughal court with some knowledge of Europe through cartography. The celebrated atlas of Abraham Ortelius had already made its way to Akbar's library around 1580, as a gift brought from Goa by the Jesuits. In the 1610s and 1620s, both the English and the Dutch were told several times that maps and other cartographic representations would find a positive reception in elite Mughal circles, as we learn from the accounts of Sir Thomas Roe and Francisco Pelsaert. An adaptation of one of those maps for political purposes can be found in the well-known allegorical painting by Abu'l-Hasan of the embrace of Jahangir and Shah 'Abbas, dating to roughly 1618, in which the two rulers are placed on a terrestrial globe with a significant number of places clearly marked, including sites in Europe such as Venice, Hungary (Magyar), Moscow, Portugal, and France.[12] As might be expected, Ottoman knowledge of these regions (as reflected in the writings of someone like Katip Çelebi) far exceeded what the Mughals possessed at this time, but we cannot assume that this necessarily implies a Mughal indifference to these questions. Much the same seems to have been the case in the second half of the seventeenth century. In his comments on the Mughal court in the 1660s, François Bernier mentioned that men like his own patron, Danishmand Khan, and a certain Rustam Khan ("who speaks Portuguese and Latin") were quite well informed about the Europeans and their affairs.[13] When the English East India Company's ambassador, Sir William Norris, visited Aurangzeb in the Deccan in the early eighteenth century, he was somewhat nonplussed to be questioned by well-placed courtiers, like the *bakhshi ul-mamalik* Ruhullah Khan, about the current state of political relations between England, France, and the Dutch Republic.[14]

Thus, even if the knowledge did not always take textual form, members of the lettered classes in various Indian states seem to have possessed, by the first half of the eighteenth century, some knowledge not only of the Europeans as they presented themselves in the waters of the Indian Ocean, but also of Europe itself. But this knowledge was unsystematic and often anecdotal. The polities of peninsular India—such as the Nayaka states that had succeeded Vijayanagara, and the Marathas—had also had relations with various groups of Europeans from the sixteenth century onward, and even represented them through the visual arts, but did not write a great deal about them until 1700. This is striking because we know that several Indians traveled to Europe via the Cape Route in the years after Vasco da Gama's initial voyage, some as slaves or servants, but others as diplomatic envoys or commercial agents. Let's consider three significant examples. The first of these was a young man of the Chetti community, sent by the Samudri Raja of Calicut to the Portuguese king as his envoy in the 1510s, who converted to Christianity while in Portugal and took the name João da Cruz. On his return to India, he was apparently rejected by his natal community on account of his conversion, but continued to serve as a cultural go-between in southern India until at least the late 1530s, when we find him with the Parava fishing community in southern Tamilnadu. More than half a dozen of his letters can be found in the archives, all written in Portuguese and directed to addressees in Portugal.[15] However, so far as we know, he never wrote an account of his travels to Europe for the edification of his compatriots.

A second example comes from slightly later in the same century and concerns a Tamil-speaking Srivaishnava Brahmin named Sri Radharaksha Pandita, who was employed by the rulers of Kotte in western Sri Lanka. The Brahmin, despite the obvious difficulties for a high-caste man to make such an extended sea voyage, was sent first to India in 1541 and then set sail early in 1542 to Portugal, along with the returning governor, Estêvão da Gama, with the intention of negotiating directly with the Portuguese court on behalf of his master, King Bhuvanekabahu. We are aware that Sri Radharaksha was offered high dignities and met ceremonially at the quay in Lisbon by a party of high nobles, including the king's own brother. He was later taken to the palace, where he presented a lavish gift to the Portuguese ruler and participated in a number of ceremonies intended to formalize the ties between Kotte and Portugal. In March 1543, he boarded a ship back to India, and we are informed that by November of that year he was home and reporting to his monarch on the visit.[16] However, despite the fact that he remained engaged in diplomatic activities for at least another decade and eventually converted, under Portuguese pressure, to Christianity while visiting Goa in 1552, he too does not seem to have left behind an account of his visit to Europe.

Our third example concerns the Sultanate of Bijapur in the Deccan, with which the Portuguese in Goa had had difficult relations since at least 1510, including several frontier wars. At the conclusion of one of these periodic outbursts of violence, the Sultan 'Ali 'Adil Shah decided to send an envoy to Lisbon to negotiate a more stable agreement. The dignitary chosen for the task was a certain Zahir Beg, who set out from Goa in January 1575 and arrived in Lisbon that August, accompanied by a Jewish interpreter, Khoja Abraham. After a tactical delay of some months, he was finally received by the young Portuguese king at his palace in Sintra and treated with honor. In turn, he offered King Sebastião some rather lavish presents, including a jeweled dagger and a number of precious stones and pearls.[17] Returning to Goa the following year, Zahir Beg then signed a treaty with the Portuguese governor in Goa, which inaugurated a rather long phase of relative peace in Bijapur-Portuguese relations. Once again, though, the diplomatic visit did not produce a written account of Zahir Beg's experiences in Portugal. A similar silence was characteristic of other visitors to Europe from the Indian subcontinent through the seventeenth century, no matter their status.

In sum, the Indian and Indo-Islamic polities of the eighteenth century that confronted the growing power of the East India Company around 1750 were neither entirely ignorant nor particularly well informed concerning their European interlocutors. In the second half of the eighteenth century, however, they found themselves obliged to inform themselves far more expeditiously. We see this even in a minor chronicle like the *Tuzak-i Walajahi*, written for the rulers of Arcot in south India in the early 1780s. Its author, Burhan Khan Handi, writes:

> Some generations ago, five groups from among the people of the Frankish community [*ahl-i firang*] established their respective centers on the seacoast in the districts belonging to Arcot with the permission of the then rulers [*hukkam*] of the country of Payanghat. I describe each group below. Three hundred years ago, none of the Frankish merchants [*tajirat-i qaum-i firang*] came to the coast of Hindustan [*sawahil-i Hindustan*] for the purpose of trade because in those days travel by sea and the manning of

ships were not so advanced as they are at present. The Frankish merchants did not attempt a journey by sea which lasted more than two or three days along the coast. In those days, the trade of Hind and 'Iraq was in the hands of the Arab merchants [*tujjar-i 'arab*]. The Frankish merchants, especially those who lived in the cities of Venice and Genoa [*shahr-i Vinas wa shahr-i Jiva*], as far as Iskandariyya, Misr, and in other places on the coast of the Red Sea, travelled by the land route. They supplied the rare commodities of Firangistan to the Arab merchants with whom they had concluded treaties or covenants that they would not sell or buy except through them.[18]

Burhan goes on to lay out his own version of the adventures of Columbus, whom he describes as "an expert in the science of astronomy [*'ilm-i nujum*] and geometry ... the first to understand the qualities of a magnet, the maker of the mariner's compass, who was well acquainted with the rules by which to find his way in all four directions at sea, even in cloudy weather or in the darkness, and who put down all his discoveries in writing." Columbus, he notes, overcame his opponents and went on to discover lands in which "the inhabitants were of a black color" and, finally, the mainland of America itself. He is said to have died in prison because of jealous rivals, but "from that time, travel by sea became popular in Firangistan." It was because of him that the Portuguese decided to "come by ships to the coast of Hindustan and establish[ed] their trade," and they were then followed by others, such as the Danes, the Dutch, the French, and, not least of all, the English.[19] Burhan considered it important to provide his readers with a brief history of England from its origins to the reign of George III, including the "conversion" of the population "to the religion of Jesus (peace be upon him), the beginnings of their administration [*intizam-i saltanat*], and the genealogy of their kings." This is followed by a short account of the papacy (*bayan kaifiyat-i Papa*), which resided in the city of Old Rome (*Rum-i qadim*). The real mystery for him, as for so many others, remained how these traders, who had "made a covenant with their own Padshah," had become the rulers of so many strange and distant lands.[20]

An Author and His Text

The same questions and preoccupations would also trouble I'tisam-ud-Din, as we shall see from a close reading of his account. After some initial religious invocations, throat clearing, and the citation of some appropriate verses, here is how I'tisam-ud-Din begins his text:

To the travelers of the times and those who have seen the world [*siyyahan-i ruzgar wa jahandidagan*], it will be written that this lowliest of men traveled to the Wilayat of England due to destiny and the necessities of life. The rare facts and features I saw and heard on land and sea comprise strange tales and narratives full of wonders [*dastani ast gharib wa hikayati ast bas shigarf*]. It was in the year 1199 Hijri [1785], after returning to the sacred land of Bengal, as my mind drifted to the farthest places and I suffered distress from the turn of my fate, and the chaos and upheaval of the times, that I turned to the beneficial effects of the pen and the story. It was at the insistence of friends that this most guilty of sinners, I'tisam-ud-Din, the son of the late Shaikh Taj-ud-Din, an inhabitant of the *pargana* of Panchnur, put pen to paper to write an account of this wondrous journey. Because the purpose of this book is to inform and be useful to the reader, and since I lack literary talent, I have refrained from ornamenting it with complex language and colorful phrasing. I have gathered these stories in a collection and called it *Shigarf-nama-yi wilayat*, so that it may be remembered in the pages of our times. (3)[21]

We must therefore bear in mind that the text was completed in the mid-1780s, whereas the travels themselves took place a good deal earlier, in the late 1760s. Nevertheless, given the remarkable detail with regard to persons and places that can be found in the text, we should assume that I'tisam-ud-Din—even if he was endowed with a prodigious memory—must have maintained some notes (or perhaps a daily account, or *ruznamcha*) that he then made use of at a later date.

We can be certain that even if I'tisam-ud-Din was somewhat plagued by melancholy and self-doubt, as the opening lines just quoted suggest, he did not lack self-esteem, which stemmed from several distinct sources. One of these was genealogical, as reflected both in the *Shigarf-nama* and in another text called the *Nasab-nama*, or "lineage-book," which presented the genealogy of his own family as high-status Sayyids who possessed a long pedigree of both learning and service to the state.[22] However, given the proliferation of pseudo-Sayyids in the post-Mongol world, these claims should perhaps be taken with a grain of salt. But they were crucial in many ways to I'tisam-ud-Din's self-presentation and served as a bulwark against the mockery to which his European interlocutors sometimes subjected him. A second source, possibly even more important, was the fact that I'tisam-ud-Din possessed both cultural capital (*adab*) and the scribal and secretarial skills of a member of the literati (*munshi*) class. These skills included penmanship, a knowledge of grammar, an understanding of Islamic religious traditions, and the mastery of a body of historical and literary materials in

Persian and, to a lesser degree, in Arabic. To be sure, there were hundreds, if not thousands of such munshis in the 1760s and 1770s scattered across the length and breadth of South Asia, many of them Muslims, but also some Persianized Hindus, especially ones belonging to a handful of scribal castes. On the other hand, few Europeans could claim a high degree of comfort with such skills, a fact that rendered them fairly dependent on the mediation of the munshis in the period prior to 1830. The text of I'tisam-ud-Din is in part a reflection of the discomfort inherent in such a relationship between a socially superior but dependent European sahib and an inferior but more skilled Persianate munshi.

Mughal rule in Bengal had been progressively consolidated from the time of Akbar in the 1570s, but still remained fragile through much of the seventeenth century. It was only in the decades immediately preceding I'tisam-ud-Din's birth that the terms of Mughal government in Bengal shifted. This is a transformation often associated with the figure of Murshid Quli Khan (d. 1727), who was first brought into the province as *diwan* (financial intendant) and later became governor (*subadar*). His entry into the Bengal political scene in 1700 followed a period of serious turbulence in western Bengal, caused by various rebellions.[23] These uprisings targeted not only the large Burdwan zamindari, but also the European factories in the region, and eventually led the emperor Aurangzeb to take firm measures to ensure that such turbulence did not recur. The new policies favored the consolidation of certain zamindaris, but they also led to the building up of a considerable bureaucratic apparatus, the purpose of which was to deepen Mughal knowledge of the resources of the province, sweep more revenue into the treasury, and curb zamindari power.[24] The expansion of a class of what Mughal chroniclers termed "knowledgeable revenue-collectors" (*'ummal-i waqif*), in turn, represented a window of opportunity for the Persian-educated gentry of petty urban centers.

I'tisam-ud-Din is somewhat reticent about his early life, education, and incorporation into this provincial Mughal bureaucracy. He only begins his account of himself after the East India Company's victory at Palashi (Plassey) in 1757, when he would have already been in his late twenties, and he states that at the time of Mir Ja'far 'Ali Khan, he was patronized by the mir munshi Mirza Muhammad Qasim and by Munshi Salim-Allah. It is, however, evident that before this, he would already have received the training of the Persianate gentry of the time, whether Muslim or Hindu, in belles lettres, accountancy, and the Mughal legal system. An interesting comparison would be the career of his almost exact contemporary and bête noire, the Kayastha entrepreneur Nabakrishna Deb, who was born around 1733 and raised in Muragachha, which is also in the Nadia region.[25] Nabakrishna's father, Ramcharan, was first involved in the management of a zamindari and then obtained his own revenue farm, only to be killed by the Marathas in the 1730s in the course of an expedition to Odisha. Though he was left somewhat to fend for himself, Nabakrishna obtained an acceptable Persianate education and by the early 1750s was employed by Warren Hastings as a Persian preceptor. It was his entry into a spectacular political career under early colonial rule that enabled him to create the Shobhabazar zamindari and maneuver his way to elevated titles by the end of his life in 1797.

I'tisam-ud-Din, by contrast, is quite discreet about his activities during the time of the nazim 'Ali Vardi Khan (1740–56) and the years immediately succeeding the battle of Palashi, in which Siraj-ud-Daula was defeated and subsequently killed. However, like some other members of the munshi class, including his erstwhile mentor Salim-Allah, he seems to have sensed that a full-fledged change of regime was in the air, and so acted accordingly, no matter how sentimentally attached he may have been to the Mughals. By the early 1760s, he had attached himself to the entourage of Major Martin Yorke and accompanied him on his successful campaign against Asad-uz-Zaman, the Raja of Birbhum. He explains: "When Yorke Saheb was leaving for England, he gave me a recommendation letter for Major [Thomas] Adams, and a map of the journey from Birbhum to 'Azimabad [Patna], as well as one or two Afghan hounds [*sag-i tazi*]. But on account of the intrigues of Munshi Nabkissan, who nowadays is called Raja, this employment did not materialize. Eventually, I was employed in the offices of Mr. [William] Steers, who was the army paymaster stationed in Chakla Jalesar, under Captain [Lauchlin] MacLean. After that, I accompanied the army during the battles against Qasim 'Ali Khan in Giria and Udaynala" (5).[26] These battles took place in the neighborhood of Rajmahal in August and September 1763, and the company forces, led by Major Adams, emerged victorious. I'tisam-ud-Din continues: "From Rajmahal, I returned with my own Sahib and arrived in Medinipur, where in the jurisdiction of Mr. [John] Burdett I held the post of *tahsildar* of pargana Qutbpur for one year. Steers Saheb was a generous and virtuous man. Indeed, after him, I could never find a Sahib who was as affectionate to me. After his death, I wept for a month. Then, for a whole year, I kept sighing from sorrow. Even today, whenever I think back on him, the wound remains fresh" (5).[27]

It was around this time that I'tisam-ud-Din found a new employer in the form of Colonel (later Brigadier) John Carnac (1716–1800), a close associate of Robert Clive. Educated at Trinity College in Dublin, Carnac had a long and convoluted career, including several stints in India, where he first arrived in 1754. Since substantial bodies of private papers relating to him have survived, it is possible for us to gain a sense of what it would have been like to work as a munshi in his establishment in the 1760s.[28] Carnac had an extensive network of informants and correspondents stretching across much of Hindustan, with whom he engaged in dealings conducted in English, French, Persian, and, occasionally, Bengali. I'tisam-ud-Din appears to have been one of two munshis assigned to deal with the Persian materials; the other was Muhammad Mu'izz. The work here would have consisted of receiving and orally summarizing the contents of letters and writing responses when necessary, usually in the more efficient *shikasta* script preferred for these purposes. It would also have meant the processing of news that arrived in the form of *akhbarat,* or newsletters, regarding political changes in courts, the movements of armies, and the like.[29] Quick copies for the record of letters that had to be forwarded to another party were also sometimes made. Periodically, complaints and petitions in Persian were addressed to Carnac by parties from as far away as Benares, and mixed with correspondence in English.[30] Carnac apparently had some knowledge of Persian, as is evidenced by the fact that he accumulated a collection of manuscripts in that language, some of which later passed into the possession of his friend William Jones.[31] But we cannot rule out the distinct possibility that he, like many other East India Company officials, primarily communicated with his Indian employees in some form of Hindustani (or zaban-i urdu, as it was increasingly called in the period). At any rate, he would not have possessed the requisite level of adab (or etiquette) that was needed to deal directly with members of the Indo-Islamic aristocracy in writing, let alone with the emperor Shah 'Alam, with whom he exchanged letters in the mid-1760s.[32]

It was through Carnac that I'tisam-ud-Din made the acquaintance of a Scotsman, Archibald Swinton (1731–1804), whom he eventually accompanied to England in the mission that is at the heart of the *Shigarfnama*. Trained as a surgeon, Swinton had first arrived in southern India in 1752, before making his way to Bengal in 1759. Within a few years, he was apparently well regarded in the British community for his command of spoken Persian and went on to play a significant role in the tumultuous events of the *nizamat* of Qasim 'Ali Khan, in the course of which he was wounded in battle and had to have one of his arms amputated. In the aftermath of the Battle of Baksar in October 1764, he was chosen by Carnac to aid in his negotiations with the Mughal court and with Shuja'-ud-Daula of Awadh. Here is what Carnac wrote to John Spencer in January 1765: "I purpose appointing Captain Swinton my Persian interpreter provisionally, till the Board's pleasure is known, and I request you will procure me the confirmation of that appointment. I will boldly pronounce there is no person at present in Bengal so capable of that Employ, he being as well as any, in the country language, and superior to all, in the knowledge of the manners of the

Natives, and how we are to conduct ourselves towards them, for which he is peculiarly qualified, by the mildness and calmness of his temper, besides as we must have much intercourse with the King, he is fittest of anybody to be about him, His Majesty being so much pleased with his behavior formerly, as to conceive an extreme liking to, and to have an entire confidence in him."[33]

Swinton thus found himself present and playing an active role at the time of the signing of the fateful Treaty of Allahabad of August 1765, through which the East India Company extorted from the Mughal emperor major fiscal rights in the eastern provinces of the empire (see Figure 2).[34] I'tisam-ud-Din accompanied Carnac to Allahabad and participated in the writing of the Persian version of the bilingual text of the treaty (see Figure 3). Soon thereafter, in the final months of 1765, he entered for a brief period into direct Mughal service and gained sufficient trust that he was appointed as munshi to Swinton, perhaps at the behest of the important noble Munir-ud-Daula, after Swinton was himself appointed as Shah 'Alam's envoy to George III (he was to deliver a petition and a sizable tribute).[35] By all accounts, I'tisam-ud-Din seems to have imagined that this would be a significant stepping-stone in his career at the Mughal court. As it turned out, both Clive and Swinton had other plans, and the mission was destined to fail from the outset.

Swinton and I'tisam-ud-Din set sail for Europe in early 1766, departing from Hijli in a French vessel commanded by a Monsieur Courville. Their destination was the French Atlantic port of Nantes, well known for its role in the eighteenth-century slave trade. En route, the ship stopped in Mauritius, which allowed I'tisam-ud-Din to add a section on the Indian Ocean to his book, much of which was a gloss on the earlier account of Tahir Muhammad, *Rauzat al-Tahirin*, of which Swinton had acquired a manuscript copy.[36] Over the long voyage, the munshi and the Scotsman seem to have had extended conversations on a variety of subjects. Swinton was eager to improve his knowledge of the Persian language and delve deeper into its literary culture, and he consequently read texts like the *Kalila wa Dimna* (a well-known set of animal fables) under the munshi's tutelage. At the same time, he wished to influence I'tisam-ud-Din's view of Europe even before he arrived there, insisting in particular on the superiority of the British over all other Europeans. Some of this propaganda fell on fertile ground since the munshi already had strong prejudices against the Portuguese, whom he associated with gratuitous maritime violence and the slave trade in the Bay of Bengal. This helps explain why he insisted that the 1755 Lisbon earthquake was God's chastisement of the accumulated sins of the Portuguese. Swinton's campaign was successful, and I'tisam-ud-Din learned to reproduce the British contempt for the French, as can be seen in his description of Nantes. While admitting that the French had once enjoyed cultural superiority over the

Figure 2. Benjamin West, *Shah 'Alam Conveying the Grant of the Diwani to Lord Clive, August 1765.* c. 1818. British Library, London, BL1547012. From the archive of the British Library / Bridgeman Images.

Figure 3. A detail from the Treaty of Allahabad (1765) showing the seals and signatures of the parties. British Library, MSS Eur. G. 49. From the archive of the British Library.

English, I'tisam-ud-Din portrayed them as currently backwards and poor, and yet "a conceited race, whose conversation was always an attempt to display their own superiority and to unfairly belittle other nations" (61–62).[37]

Briefly separated from Swinton at Nantes, I'tisam-ud-Din eventually made his way to London, via Calais and Dover. The city seems to have immediately left a strong impression on him. All in all, he would spend eighteen months in Britain, eventually returning to Bengal in late 1768 or early 1769. The extended section of the text that begins with his arrival in Dover and continues through his stay in England and Scotland is, however, not limited to a single register and does not possess a clear organization. Rather, it is characterized by abrupt shifts in both tone and content. Besides the odd anecdote emphasizing the strange and wondrous (*'aja'ib-o-ghara'ib*) aspects of Britain, there are certainly a good number of passages devoted to specific social and political institutions (libraries, museums, orphanages, gardens) and to subjects like agriculture and hunting. But these are interspersed with the personal experiences of the author in his travels and his encounters with a variety of people.

Yet another component of the *Shigarf-nama* is the space that is devoted to debates and disputes between I'tisam-ud-Din and a variety of interlocutors, in which he usually wins the argument. But this does not make of him a sort of V. S. Naipaul *avant la lettre*, whose purpose is to constantly and insistently assert his own cultural superiority. On the contrary, we shall see that I'tisam-ud-Din uses "wilayat" as a mirror to hold up to what he sees as the political problems and cultural failures of the Mughal Empire. It is this curious mixture of self-assertion and self-abnegation that lends the text an intriguing quality. A further tension is produced by his underlying realization of the questionable motives of both Robert Clive and his own immediate patron, Archibald Swinton, in their role as mediators between the Mughal emperor and George III.

Nevertheless, the first impression one gets from the text is certainly the contrast between English order and unity and Mughal disorder and disunity. Underlying this is a theory of Mughal decline, rather than a simple juxtaposition of unchanging national characters, because I'tisam-ud-Din believes that in its glory days of the sixteenth and seventeenth centuries, the Mughal Empire was more than a match for the Europeans. But then decadence began to take hold:

> At the death of Hazrat Khuld Makan [Aurangzeb], slackness and indiscipline became rife in the Sultanate of Hindustan under the later Padshahs, and particularly Muhammad Shah who spent his time in tumultuous revelry and seances of pleasure

> and intoxication [*majlis-i 'aish-o-nashat*], not caring for the running of the kingdom. The manners and dress of the women's quarters overtook the palace. The sounds of the *barbat* and *tanbur* [musical instruments] were what gave pleasure. The shrill voices of women came to be heard over the grave voices of men. The business of courtesans thrived in the bazaar, and the pious were disturbed at their prayers. Impostors [*muqallidan*] rose up to be *umara'* and the true *amirs* fell into decadence. The governors of each province managed the administration and finances at their pleasure and neglected the maintenance of armies, so that rebels and criminals became more and more daring in their depredations. (23)[38]

This passage occurs quite early in the text, and although it is not particularly original in its lament, it nevertheless announces a leitmotif to which the traveler will return time and time again. In contrast to the Mughal (and, more generally, the Indian) way of bringing up male children, which he believes has led to effeminacy and decadent vanity, he claims the English teach their sons to incarnate robust masculine values, as well as a love of frugality and material gain:

> Having given material considerations priority over spiritual ones, the English have devised such rules and procedures for making all endeavors simple and orderly that people cannot but devote themselves to the pursuit of worldly success. From youth till old age their time is spent in study, thoughts of earning a livelihood, and in increasing their wealth. Worldly success attends knowledge of the arts and sciences. Even if there is someone who is indifferent to the acquisition of knowledge, or despite his having the intelligence and means, willfully avoids taking up any occupation and like Indian youths spends day and night in pursuit of pleasure or divides his time between feasting and sleeping, the guardians of the law advise him to mind his ways, and if this produces no result, point out the right path with the help of the rod. Even if someone inherits much wealth from his father, he doesn't regard the moiety as his own and doesn't spend it for his everyday needs; he sets it apart as savings. He will never spend his inherited capital and will run his household on his own earnings. (173)[39]

No wonder then that a handful of men from such a culture had been able to overrun and seize a large chunk of the once-mighty Mughal Empire!

But there was also a troubling aspect to this relentless pursuit of profit and material advancement in I'tisam-ud-Din's eyes, especially as his initially somewhat positive understanding of Protestantism frayed. There were real questions to be asked, he felt, about the honesty and reliability of the English, a nation that "condemn[s] the poor and consider[s] the rich illustrious." An example of this can be found in his dealings with William Jones, whom he and Swinton met in Oxford:

> There were a number of Persian books in that place. I saw a translation of *Kalila wa Dimna*, and I made a copy of the epilogue to the *Farhang-i Jahangiri* for Captain Swinton. I also met Mr. Jones, who is now one of the high court judges in Calcutta. He and Captain Swinton took this contemptible author along with them to a library [the Bodleian]. There I saw books in both Persian and Arabic. Among them were three different letters, written in Persian and Turkish by the Pasha of the kingdom of Algeria—which is among the dependencies of the Ottoman Empire [*mulk-i Rum*] on the seashore—addressed to the King of England [*Shah-i wilayat*]. Since at that time there was no one in *wilayat* who was fluent in reading Persian, he had not fully and perfectly comprehended the meaning and intent of the letters, and had placed markers of doubt in various places, and showed them to this contemptible one. I provided the correct readings. He also produced other books in order to test and ascertain this worthless one's skills. At any rate, after I clarified the substance and meaning of those [texts] to the extent of my competence and capability, he was impressed. ... [Previously,] while on board the ship [from Bengal to France], Captain Swinton had read the entire text of *Kalila wa Dimna* with this contemptible one and had also translated the twelve *a'ins* of the *Farhang-i Jahangiri*, which illustrate the principles of the Persian language. Mr. Jones in London, with the aforementioned Captain's permission, adapted that translation into a treatise called *Shakaristan*, printed it, made it available for purchase, and made a handsome profit. Even now, the *Shakaristan* remains popular with the [British] sahibs [see Figure 4]. (94–95)[40]

The implication is that it was I'tisam-ud-Din's work on the *Farhang-i Jahangiri* (a celebrated dictionary from the early seventeenth century compiled by Jamal-ud-Din Inju Shirazi) that has been appropriated for commercial profit by the slippery Mr. Jones, perhaps with the connivance of Captain Swinton.[41] [see Figure 5]

Early in his stay in England, while living near the Haymarket in London, I'tisam-ud-Din appears to have been fascinated by the theater and attended a number of performances (he also went to the circus). On account of his limited command of English, he seems to have partially misunderstood

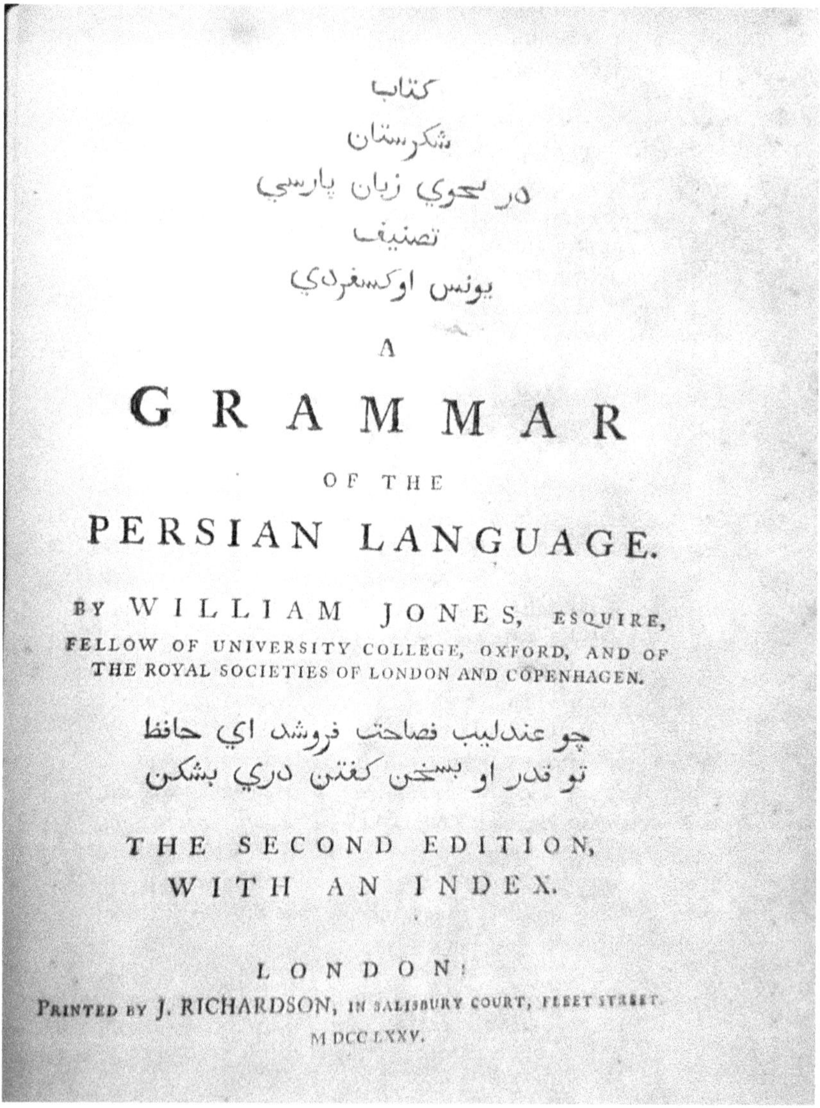

کتاب
شکرستان
در نحوي زبان پارسي
تصنیف
یونس اوکسفردي

A
GRAMMAR
OF THE
PERSIAN LANGUAGE.

BY WILLIAM JONES, ESQUIRE,
FELLOW OF UNIVERSITY COLLEGE, OXFORD, AND OF
THE ROYAL SOCIETIES OF LONDON AND COPENHAGEN.

چو عندلیب فصاحت فروشد اي حافظ
تو قدر او بسخن گفتن دري بشکن

THE SECOND EDITION,
WITH AN INDEX.

LONDON:
PRINTED BY J. RICHARDSON, IN SALISBURY COURT, FLEET STREET.
M DCC LXXV.

Figure 4. The title page of William Jones, *A Grammar of the Persian Language*, 1775 (originally published in 1771). Author's personal collection.

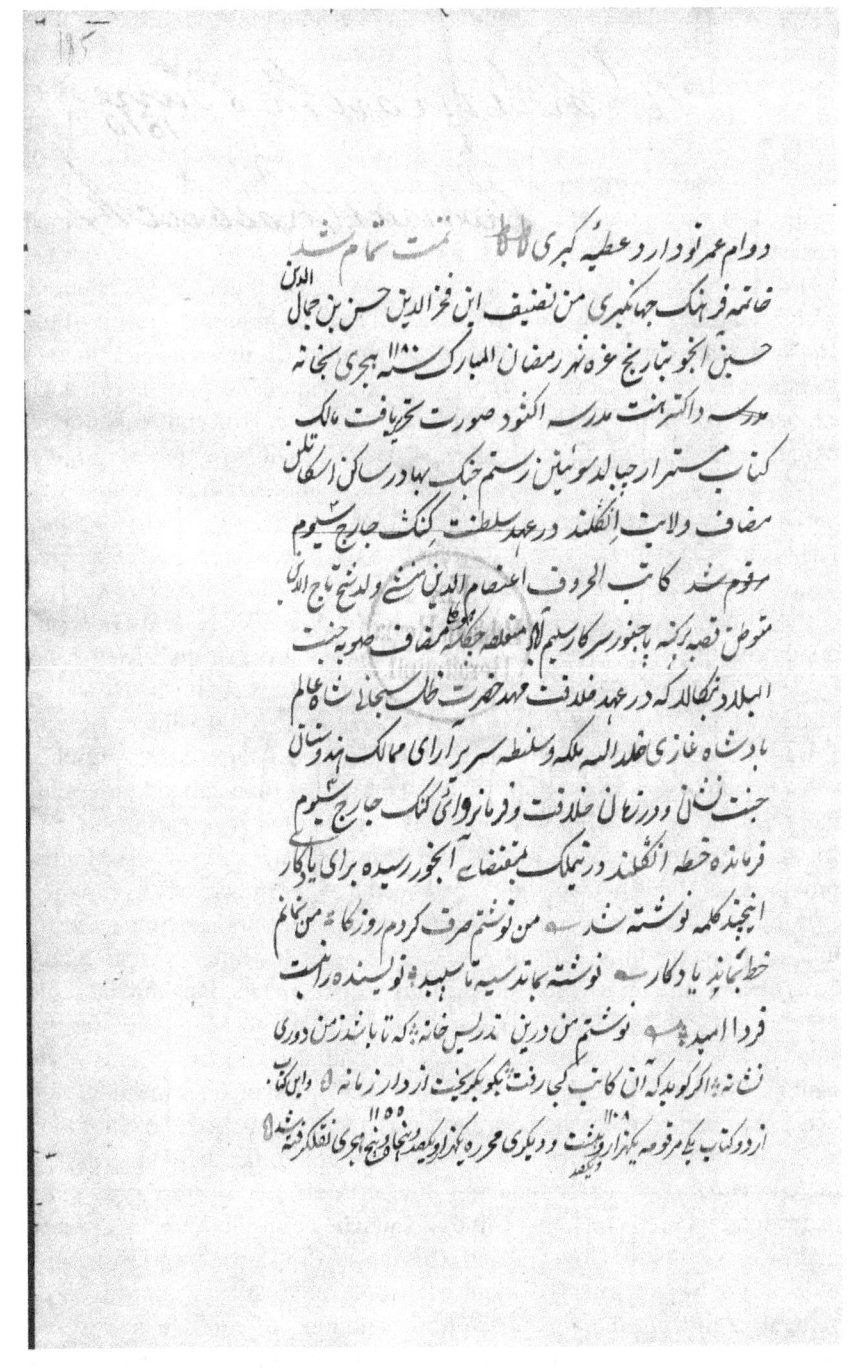

Figure 5. A page from the copy of Jamal-ud-Din Inju Shirazi's *Farhang-i Jahangiri* that I'tisam-ud-Din made during his visit to Oxford. Staatsbibliothek zu Berlin, MS Orient. fol. 503 (Pertsch no. 128), fl. 185a. Courtesy of the Staatsbibliothek zu Berlin.

the plays he saw, as we see from the rather peculiar plot summaries that he provides. However, the plays also confirmed his rather skeptical view of English mores, which is hardly surprising given that they included a version of John Gay's *The Beggar's Opera* and a weak abridgment of *King Lear* (with the incongruous happy ending added by Nahum Tate). In the first of these, the main character is saved from execution by royal intervention, despite his immoral deeds, while in the latter, the good daughter's triumph nevertheless exposes the inherent flaws of the polity.[42]

I'tisam-ud-Din's stay in Britain was to end on a sour note, as his relations with Swinton progressively deteriorated. This was in part the result of the constant jockeying for status between the two men: the munshi was reluctant to accept that he was a mere employee, and Swinton, despite his extended exposure to India, often exhibited a scarcely disguised contempt for its culture and seems to have expected I'tisam-ud-Din to embrace English habits and customs. There had, of course, been a long-standing cut and thrust between the two on matters of religion and the relative superiority of Sunni Islam and Protestant Christianity. At first, some of these cracks were papered over by their adopting a similarly patronizing attitude to their respective cultural enemies: the Hindus and the Catholics. Later, I'tisam-ud-Din made good use of the *Mir'at al-Quds*, the Persian rendering of the life of Jesus by Jerónimo Xavier and 'Abdus Sattar, to score some points.[43] However, as the two traveled together, Swinton became increasingly impatient with I'tisam-ud-Din's habits and demands, which included the constant presence of an Indian body servant in order to prepare halal food and aid him in his daily routine and ablutions. Swinton even began to mock I'tisam-ud-Din for his abstemiousness, reminding him that in private, many of the Mughal provincial officials he had known had been heavy drinkers of alcohol.

As a result of this constant barrage of petty insults, accompanied by mocking suggestions that no respectable Englishwoman would marry him, I'tisam-ud-Din became increasingly resistant to the idea that he settle down in England and become a tutor in Persian and Mughal culture to English East India Company officials. He had also become aware, while visiting Scotland, that Swinton had a number of skeletons in his closet, and even claimed that when Swinton was a young surgeon, he had killed a man in a botched experiment and been obliged to flee Britain to escape the consequences.[44] After spending time in Melaka and Burma, Swinton had wound up in Madras, met Clive and attached himself to him in order to make a career. As for Clive himself, I'tisam-ud-Din shows some awareness of the 1766–67 parliamentary inquiry into both Clive and the company more generally, although he was unaware that nothing of consequence would come of the matter.[45] The attempts of Shah 'Alam, to whom I'tisam-ud-Din remained loyal, to shore up his status by appealing to George III against his representatives in India were to prove of no consequence, as the Mughal Empire continued its slow downward slide.

Toward a Conclusion

When I'tisam-ud-Din returned to Bengal in 1769, the province was in the midst of a disastrous famine, which may have claimed as many as two million lives.[46] While he passes over this dismal event in silence, it was remarked upon by many other contemporaries, who noted that whatever the causes, the East India Company's administrative incompetence considerably exacerbated the effects. Devoted to the cult of revenue extraction, the company and its intermediaries largely abandoned the sort of relief measures and emergency loans that had long characterized Mughal practices when faced with such disasters. Given the political outcome of his travels, I'tisam-ud-Din was in no position to return to the court of Shah 'Alam as a supplicant in search of further advancement. Instead, he continued to work for some years for the East India Company, accompanying Colonel John Upton from Bengal to Pune in 1775–76 to negotiate a controversial treaty with Nana Phadnavis and other Maratha leaders.[47] By the time he was writing in the 1780s, I'tisam-ud-Din had come to constantly lament his "present misfortune," which accounts for the mournful and even bitter tone that periodically creeps into the *Shigarf-nama*. There are hints, too, that some of his contemporaries treated him with scarcely concealed disdain. On the other hand, his text did reach the hands of British readers, and once it had been selectively translated and deftly cleansed of its criticisms of Britain and the British, could be read as an unalloyed tribute from a native subject.[48]

In contrast, Archibald Swinton spent the last four decades of his life in prosperity, thanks in large part to the wealth, rich objects, paintings, and manuscripts that he had accumulated in his Indian years; the manuscripts are today dispersed across collections in London, Oxford, Edinburgh, and Berlin (see Figure 6 for a portrait from his collection).[49] For his part, Clive—with whom Swinton eventually fell out—died by his own hand in London in 1774, in circumstances that remain murky. But he too had made a vast fortune (around £400,000) and was able to leave a substantial estate to his heirs.[50] It is undoubtedly difficult to decide what the overall judgment of I'tisam-ud-Din, a member of the provincial Mughal gentry who worked quite closely with such men and participated willy-nilly in their projects, might have been toward company rule.[51] It is certain that he saw himself to some extent as their victim and dupe, and his critique of British chicanery extended even further to include intellectual figures like William

Figure 6. Portrait of the Bengal Nawab Siraj-ud-Daula (d. 1757). 1756. National Museums of Scotland, Edinburgh, Archibald Swinton Collection, V.2021.34 / PF1077410. Image © National Museums of Scotland.

Jones. Faced with a bewildering set of circumstances and a world that was being rapidly transformed, he did not resort to desperate maneuvers such as feigning insanity, unlike Jonathan Spence's Chinese antihero John Hu on his visit to France in the 1720s.[52] However, it may still be said that his attitude ultimately reveals a profound ambivalence in the face of cultural and political circumstances that he obviously found difficult to grasp, let alone master. This ambivalence, I would suggest, lies at the heart of the *Shigarf-nama* and its organizing conceit of "wonder."

Notes

I am grateful to Abbas Amanat, Ali Anooshahr, Rajeev Kinra, and Umid Sipihrirad for their assistance with this essay. Particular thanks to Muzaffar Alam for his help with reading I'tisam-ud-Din's original text and other Persian documents.

1. For a quick overview, see Charles H. Parker, *Global Interactions in the Early Modern Age, 1400–1800* (Cambridge: Cambridge University Press, 2010), 13–38.

2. Margaret R. Hunt, "The 1689 Mughal Siege of East India Company Bombay: Crisis and Historical Erasure," *History Workshop Journal* 84 (2017): 149–69.

3. Gulfishan Khan, *Indian Muslim Perceptions of the West during the Eighteenth Century* (Karachi: Oxford University Press, 1998); Juan R. I. Cole, "Invisible Occidentalism: Eighteenth-Century Indo-Persian Constructions of the West," *Iranian Studies* 25, nos. 3–4 (1992): 3–16; Mona Narain, "Eighteenth-Century Indians' Travel Narratives and Cross-Cultural Encounters with the West," *Literature Compass* 9 (2012): 151–65.

4. For an edition of the text, see I'tisam-ud-Din, *Shigarf-nama-yi wilayat: Safarnama-yi Munshi Mirza I'tisam-ud-Din Jaunpuri bi Inglistan*, ed. Umid Sipihrirad (Bujnurd: Bizhah Yavard, 1397 [2018–19]), which is based upon the manuscript at the National Library and Archives of Iran in Tehran. Subsequent citations will be made parenthetically. An abridged modern translation into English (via Bengali) is to be found in Mirza Sheikh I'tesamuddin, *The Wonders of Vilayet: Being the Memoir, Originally in Persian, of a Visit to France and Britain in 1765*, trans. Kaiser Haq (Leeds: Peepal Tree Press, 2001). An older translation, with myriad problems, is *Shigurf namah i Velaët, or, Excellent intelligence concerning Europe: Being the travels of Mirza Itesa Modeen in Great Britain and France*, trans. James Edward Alexander (London, 1827). There is also a good translation into Urdu: Munshi I'tisam-ud-Din, *Shigarf-nama-yi wilayat*, trans. Amir Hasan Nurani (Patna: Khuda Bakhsh Library, 2008). All translations in this essay are mine (with the aid of Muzaffar Alam) and follow the Sipihrirad edition. However, I will also cite the Haq translation (as *Wonders of Vilayet*), noting when it is inaccurate, because it has usually been cited in the scholarship on I'tisam-ud-Din.

5. The location of Panchnur (or Pajnaur) may be found in Irfan Habib, *An Atlas of the Mughal Empire* (Delhi: Oxford University Press, 1982), map 11A.

6. Geneviève Bouchon and Luís Filipe Thomaz, eds., *Voyage dans les Deltas du Gange et de l'Irraouaddy: Relation Portugaise Anonyme (1521)* (Paris: Centre Culturel Calouste Gulbenkian, 1988).

7. For more, see my "Notes on the Sixteenth-Century Bengal Trade," *Indian Economic and Social History Review* 24, no. 3 (1987): 265–89.

8. Richard M. Eaton, *The Rise of Islam and the Bengal Frontier, 1204–1760* (Berkeley: University of California Press, 1996), 137–50.

9. Ayal Amer, "The Rise of Jihādic Sentiments and the Writing of History in Sixteenth-Century Kerala," *Indian Economic and Social History Review* 53, no. 3 (2016): 297–319; P. K. Yasser Arafath, "Malabar Ulema in the Shafiite Cosmopolis:

Fitna, Piety and Resistance in the Age of Fasad," *Medieval History Journal* 21, no. 1 (2018): 25–68.

10. Muzaffar Alam and Sanjay Subrahmanyam, "Southeast Asia as Seen from Mughal India: Tahir Muhammad's 'Immaculate Garden' (ca. 1600)," *Archipel* 70 (2005): 209–37. The two principal manuscripts are Bodleian Library, Oxford, Elliot 314 (Sachau-Ethé cat. no. 100), which earlier belonged to Archibald Swinton, and British Library, London, Or. 168 (Rieu cat., vol. 1, 119b).

11. Muzaffar Alam and Sanjay Subrahmanyam, "Mediterranean Exemplars: Jesuit Political Lessons for a Mughal Emperor," in *Machiavelli, Islam, and the East: Reorienting the Foundations of Modern Political Thought*, ed. Giuseppe Marcocci and Lucio Biasiori (Basingstoke: Palgrave Macmillan, 2018), 105–29.

12. Ebba Koch, "The Symbolic Possession of the World: European Cartography in Mughal Allegory and History Painting," *Journal of the Economic and Social History of the Orient* 55, nos. 2–3 (2012): 547–80.

13. For Bernier's views, see Sanjay Subrahmanyam, *Europe's India: Words, People, Empires, 1500–1800* (Cambridge: Harvard University Press, 2017), 1–7.

14. See British Library, London, IOR/E/3/61, O.C. 7561 (1701), as well as other documents in the same volume concerning Norris's discussions with the Mughal court. For a description of this embassy and its issues, see Georgia O'Connor, "'For Nation, King, and Company': William Norris, Two English East India Companies, and a Forgotten Embassy to Mughal India, 1699–1702" (PhD diss., Monash University, 2021).

15. See, for example, his letter dated 1537 in António da Silva Rego, ed., *Documentação para a História das Missões do Padroado Português do Oriente: Índia*, 12 vols. (Lisbon: Agência Geral das Colónias, 1949–58), 2:256–61. For a general list of his letters, see Georg Schurhammer, "Letters of D. João da Cruz in the National Archives of Lisbon," *Kerala Society Papers* 6 (1930): 304–7.

16. Jorge Manuel Flores, *Os Portugueses e o Mar de Ceilão: Trato, diplomacia e guerra (1498–1543)* (Lisbon: Edições Cosmos, 1998), 189–91.

17. Joseph Wicki, ed., *Documenta Indica X (1575–1577)* (Rome: Monumenta Historica Societatis Iesu, 1968), 1057–62.

18. Munshi Burhan Khan Handi, *Tuzak-e Walajahi*, ed. T. Chandrasekharan and Syed Hamza Hosain Omari (Madras: Government Oriental Manuscripts Library, 1957), 88–89; Burhan, *Tuzak-i Walajahi of Burhan ibn Hasan*, trans. S. Muhammad Husayn Nainar, 2 parts (Madras: University of Madras, 1934–39), 1:85–86.

19. Burhan, *Tuzak-i Walajahi*, 1:87–89.

20. Burhan, *Tuzak-i Walajahi*, 1:97–98.

21. I have slightly modified the translation given in Arash Khazeni, *The City and the Wilderness: Indo-Persian Encounters in Southeast Asia* (Berkeley: University of California Press, 2020), 25–26.

22. Qazi Mohammed Sadrul Ola, trans., *History of the Family of Mirza Itesamuddin of Qusba Panchnoor: The First Educated Indian and Bengali Muslim to Visit England in 1765 A.D.*, (Dhaka: Q. A. Zaman, 1984).

23. See John McLane, *Land and Local Kingship in Eighteenth-Century Bengal* (Cambridge: Cambridge University Press, 1993), 34–35, 138–42.

24. See Muzaffar Alam and Sanjay Subrahmanyam, introduction to *The Mughal State, 1526–1750*, ed. Muzaffar Alam and Sanjay Subrahmanyam (Delhi: Oxford University Press, 1998), 46–53.

25. S. C. Hill, "Account of Late Maharaja Nubkissen Bahadur," *Journal of the Asiatic Society of Bengal* 71, no. 1 (1902): 1–13.

26. On MacLean, see the letter dated 29 September 1763 in *Fort William–India House Correspondence, Vol. III (1760–1763)*, ed. R. R. Sethi (New Delhi: National Archives of India, 1949), 529–30.

27. Steers's death from fever is reported in a letter dated 26 November 1764, in *Fort William–India House Correspondence, Vol. IV (1764–1766)*, ed. C. S. Srinivasachari et al. (New Delhi: National Archives of India, 1962), 275.

28. British Library, London, Sutton Court Collection, MSS Eur. F128; National Library of Wales, Abersytwyth (henceforth NLW), "The Correspondence of Brigadier-General John Carnac, 1760–1769."

29. NLW, Carnac 04/9/25, report on Qasim 'Ali Khan.

30. NLW, Carnac 06/15/19 (i)–(k), for petitions from the kotwal of Benares and others that also involved William Bolts.

31. See Jonathan Lawrence, "Building a Library: The Arabic and Persian Manuscript Collection of Sir William Jones," *Journal of the Royal Asiatic Society* 31, no. 1 (2021): 1–70.

32. NLW, Carnac 05/1/11 (1764) and 05/7/39 (1764). The latter exchange was conducted in the lead up to the Battle of Baksar.

33. A. C. Swinton and J. L. Campbell Swinton, *Concerning Swinton Family Records and Portraits at Kimmerghame* (Edinburgh: John Lindsay, 1908), 105.

34. On the circumstances of these coerced negotiations, see Robert Travers, "A British Empire by Treaty in Eighteenth-Century India," in *Empire by Treaty: Negotiating European Expansion, 1600–1900*, ed. Saliha Belmessous (New York: Oxford University Press, 2014), 132–60.

35. The original of the petition from Shah 'Alam, which was eventually brought to England by Robert Clive in 1767, is untraceable. A damaged copy may be found in the Royal Asiatic Society, London, Codrington/Reade No. 69 (9), Box 33. For an English translation, see A. B. M. Habibullah, "Shah Alam's Letter to George III," *Proceedings of the Indian Historical Records Commission* 16 (1939): 97–98.

36. See Khazeni, *The City and the Wilderness*, 33–34.

37. Cf. *Wonders of Vilayet*, 52.

38. Cf. the inaccurate translation in *Wonders of Vilayet*, 21.

39. Cf. *Wonders of Vilayet*, 123. See also Humberto Garcia, *England Re-Oriented: How Central and South Asian Travelers Imagined the West, 1750–1857* (Cambridge: Cambridge University Press, 2020), 111.

40. Cf. *Wonders of Vilayet*, 71–72 (which omits some crucial parts).

41. For a full discussion of this passage, on which I have drawn, see Rajeev Kinra, "William Jones and Indo-Persian Scholarship," *Global Intellectual History*, May 2024; https://doi.org/10.1080/23801883.2023.2184410

42. For more, see Garcia, *England Re-Oriented*, 88–96.

43. Xavier and Sattar, *Mir'āt al-quds (Mirror of Holiness): A Life of Christ for Emperor Akbar*, ed. and trans. Pedro Moura Carvalho and Wheeler M. Thackston (Leiden: Brill, 2012).

44. See I'tisam-ud-Din, *Shigarf-nama-yi wilayat*, 104. Cf. *Wonders of Vilayet*, 71–72.

45. For more on the inquiry, see Spencer A. Leonard, "'The Capital Object of the Public': The 1766–7 Parliamentary Inquiry into the East India Company," *English Historical Review* 132, no. 558 (2017): 1110–48.

46. Rajat Datta, *Society, Economy, and the Market: Commercialization in Rural Bengal, c. 1760–1800* (New Delhi: Manohar, 2000), 260–68. Datta argues for a far lower mortality figure than earlier authors, and his reasoning remains speculative.

47. The passage on the embassy to Pune does not appear in the Tehran manuscript and so is not included in Umid Sipihrirad's edition. It is, however, part of the other main manuscript of the text: British Library, Or. 200. For more on the embassy, see William Charles Macpherson, ed., *Soldiering in India, 1764–1787: Extracts from Journals and Letters Left by Lt. Colonel Allan Macpherson and Lt. Colonel John Macpherson of the East India Company's Service* (Edinburgh: William Blackwood, 1928), 230–91. Allan Macpherson was the official Persian interpreter of the embassy and was accompanied by his own munshi, Ghulam 'Ali.

48. See the discussion of James Alexander's interventions in Norbert Schürer, "Sustaining Identity in I'tesamuddin's *The Wonders of Vilayet*," *The Eighteenth Century* 52, no. 2 (2011): 137–55.

49. Jeremiah P. Losty, "Eighteenth-Century Mughal Paintings from the Swinton Collection," *The Burlington Magazine* 159 (2017): 789–99; see also *A catalogue of a very valuable collection of Persian, and a few Arabic Mss., selected many years ago, in the East, by Archibald Swinton Esq.* (London, 1810).

50. For the complex nature of Clive's financial affairs, see Bruce Lenman and Philip Lawson, "Robert Clive, the 'Black Jagir,' and British Politics," *Historical Journal* 26, no. 4 (1983): 801–29.

51. For two somewhat different interpretations, see Michael H. Fisher, *Counterflows to Colonialism: Indian Travellers and Settlers in Britain, 1600–1857* (Delhi: Permanent Black, 2004), 86–92; and Partha Chatterjee, *The Black Hole of Empire: History of a Global Practice of Power* (Princeton: Princeton University Press, 2012), 67–73.

52. Spence, *The Question of Hu* (New York: Alfred A. Knopf, 1988).

Turning the Crank: The Performance of Empire through Tipu's Tiger

VINCENT PHAM

The record of English expansion in India is often traced through the Battle of Buxar in 1764, Warren Hastings's impeachment and trial (1785–97), or the defeat of the Maratha Empire in 1818. This essay seeks to shift the scale of colonization down to a more human level through an examination of the iconography, display, and performance of Tipu's Tiger, an automaton toy organ built around 1795. The organ takes the form of a Bengal tiger straddling a British East India Company soldier; it is operated by playing a set of keys located inside the flank of the tiger, while simultaneously turning the crank near its shoulder to push air through the instrument's bellows. The organ was commissioned by Tipu Fath Ali Khan, more commonly known as Tipu Sultan. Tipu and his father, Hyder Ali, had usurped control of Mysore from Krishnaraja Wadiyar II, shifting the balance of religion and power in the kingdom from Hindu to Muslim.[1] Tipu and his father fought the East India Company in the four Anglo-Mysore Wars (1766–69, 1780–84, 1790–92, and 1798–99), each of which offered substantial resistance to the British colonial project in India. After Tipu's death and the fall of the Mysorean capital at Srirangapatna in 1799, Tipu's Tiger was confiscated by the East India Company. In 1808, the automaton was put on display adjacent to the library at East India House, the headquarters of the company in London. The premises were public and the company's museum served as a showcase for objects acquired from the far reaches of the world. Records confirm that visitors were invited to play the organ and that they often chose British nationalist songs. An instrument that was once used to perform at Tipu's court was thus apparently repurposed, its function and symbolism reversed in order to celebrate the East India Company's triumph and subsequent rule.

Most of the scholarship on Tipu's Tiger has tended to emphasize its iconography, its use in imperial self-fashioning, and the theatricality of its sound or display.[2] Indeed, its display as a trophy is an early form of what Tony Bennett has described as Britain's "exhibitionary complex," in which an entity in power shows off previously private objects to the public, thereby allowing those objects to become vehicles for wielding cultural power and conditioning the bodies of their viewers.[3] If we follow that line of thought, Tipu's Tiger could be regarded as an imperial tool that trapped and declawed one of the principal symbols of colonial resistance. Yet playing the organ was both difficult and cacophonous and so effectively required its would-be users to align themselves with the very resistance over which they thought they were triumphing. Accordingly, I propose that we should regard the organ as a "scriptive thing" that asks its users to remain open to a multitude of responses, rather than conform to a "rigid dictation of performed action."[4] It is through this conflict of imperial interests that we can best discern how the sonic can also serve as a material trace of empire.

Tipu's Tiger emerged toward the end of thirty-three years of Mysorean resistance to the East India Company's incursions. The Second Anglo-Mysore War had shown Mysore to be a valid threat; they humiliated the East India Company's troops in battles at Pollilur (1780), Annagudi (1782), and Bednore (1783). To make matters worse (as far as the British were concerned), between 1780 and 1784, Mysore was directly supported by the French with *materiel* and tactical training, which put them technologically on par with the East India Company's forces. They were equipped with contemporary firearms, artillery, and iron-cased rockets, which were key to their victories. However, those victories would only last into the first part of the next Anglo-Mysore war in this most protracted of Britain's imperial campaigns.

A plethora of visual productions reveal the British public's keen interest in the extent and limits of Mysorean power. In the Third Anglo-Mysore War, for example, James Gillray's *The Coming on of the Monsoons; or The Retreat from Seringapatam* commemorates the routing of East India Company troops under General Charles Cornwallis at the first siege of Srirangapatna in 1791. With his provisions running low and no reinforcements in sight, Cornwallis was forced to withdraw his forces from Tipu's walls. Gillray, ever the caricaturist, pointedly depicts the young Tipu triumphally urinating on a terrified Cornwallis, who retreats, riding a donkey, at the heels of his army (see Figure 1). Toward the bottom of the print, Gillray includes a

Turning the Crank: The Performance of Empire through Tipu's Tiger / 227

Figure 1. James Gillray, *The Coming on of the Monsoons; or The Retreat from Seringapatam*, 1791. Hand-colored etching, 22.1 x 27.5 cm. Courtesy of the Lewis Walpole Library, Yale University.

passage from William Shakespeare's *Henry IV, Part I*. The scene quoted is one in which Falstaff concocts an outrageous lie regarding his heroism and martial prowess. Gillray implies that Cornwallis is a similar sort of coward. The depiction of Cornwallis in retreat played to the British public's general anxiety regarding the prospects of victory in India. However, the outcome of the conflict was more sobering than Gillray's print suggests. While Tipu was able to hold the capital, a renewed siege by the East India Company and its allies ultimately compelled him to sue for peace. That peace cost Mysore about half of its territory and forced Tipu to surrender his second and third sons to the East India Company as hostages until he paid reparations for the allied war costs.

However, Gillray's print was only one of a host of visual productions relating to the conflict. The British public's fascination with Indian resistance created a "Tipumania" that continued well into the nineteenth century and included paintings, plays, mezzotints, and panoramas. Consider Robert Home's paternalistic history painting, *The Reception of the Mysorean*

Hostage Princes by Marquis Cornwallis, which depicts the taking of Tipu Sultan's sons—Abdul Khaliq and Muhin-ud-din—as hostages until Tipu could pay the company's terms in full. Cornwallis's demand that Tipu's sons serve as sureties was an act of calculated retribution for his previous humiliation at Srirangapatna. The subservience of the Mysorean contingent is clear in Home's painting as they hand over the crown princes to the beneficent-seeming Cornwallis (see Figure 2). This is representative of the atmosphere in Britain after the news of the shift in British fortunes in the Third Anglo-Mysore War had arrived. Tipu's hostage sons went on to be represented in a similar spirit of imperial triumphalism in sculpture, embroidery, home furnishings, pocket journals, and commemorative coins.[5] Other paintings by Mather Brown, Henry Singleton, and Charles Turner similarly celebrated the hostage exchange as a significant compensation for the defeats that the British had suffered in the Second Anglo-Mysore War and in the American Revolution.

Images along these lines were key to the rehabilitation of the public's perception of British imperial rule. At a time when George III and Warren Hastings were being lambasted in the press and Parliament, paintings like Home's were, as Daniel O'Quinn argues, designed to consolidate public opinion on the extended martial conflicts in India.[6] This comes across in the presentation of the Indian princes as serene, placating, and deferential to the benevolent retinue accompanying Cornwallis. As Sean Willcock points out, such depictions are "symptomatic of a persistent anxiety over the morality and … motives of the capture" of children.[7] The propagandistic imagery created by the company around Tipu was an attempt to maintain the moral high ground by insisting that the use of children as hostages was not only palatable, but necessary to achieving the greater good of peace with Mysore.

Tipu's children were reportedly unharmed while they were in captivity, and Tipu would later secure their return after paying his reparations in Madras. Signing the Treaty of Srirangapatna in 1792 meant that Tipu ceded half of the overall territory of Mysore to the East India Company and its allies (Nizam Asif Jah II of Hyderabad and Peshwa Madhavrao II of the Maratha Empire). However, the fate of British dominion in India was still uncertain at the close of the eighteenth century. The volatility of the Anglo-Mysore Wars prompted the East India Company and its propagandists to play up the dangers of oriental despotism (in part by framing Tipu as a dark, rapacious usurper). The company's methods, including its early museological institutions, proved crucial in the recontextualizing of the single most intriguing object that came out of these conflicts: Tipu's Tiger (see Figure 3).

When Hyder Ali and his son Tipu wrested control of Mysore from Krishnaraja Wadiyar II, they took steps to legitimate their rule. One of those

Turning the Crank: The Performance of Empire through Tipu's Tiger / 229

Figure 2. Robert Home, *The Reception of the Mysorean Hostage Princes by Marquis Cornwallis, 26 February 1792*, 1793. Oil on canvas, 149.2 x 202.5 cm. Courtesy of the National Army Museum, London.

included the adoption of particularly powerful symbols, especially that of the Bengal tiger. British commentators were quick to ascribe a synecdochic relationship between Tipu and the tiger (with the latter standing in for India as a wild and savage place in need of taming by the East India Company). But Muslim rulers had often used the imagery of tigers to reinforce their reigns (and the Wadiyars did not, which allowed Hyder and Tipu to distinguish themselves from the kingdom's previous dynasty). Indeed, Kate Brittlebank's examination of the motif finds that the Bengal tiger appeared on Tipu's weapons, military uniforms, palatial murals, coins, and throne.[8]

The organ for Tipu's Tiger was built by French or Dutch craftsmen in the 1790s. The shell and British soldier being mauled were added shortly thereafter in Channapatna, along with the crank. When the latter is rotated continuously, the two bellows hidden inside the tiger pump air through thirty-six organ pipes. Simply turning the crank moves the soldier's hand and produces two distinct sounds: a high, flute-like wail from the mouth of the man and a less frequent and lower-pitched grunt from the tiger's head. For every eight wails, there is one grunt. To the wails and grunts can be added a

230 / PHAM

third kind of sound. Opening the flank of the tiger reveals a set of eighteen ivory keys that can be played in semitones, like a piano. The wailing and grunting are independent of (and prior to) the sounds made when the keys are depressed, so playing the Tiger can be a quite cacophonous enterprise with the three kinds of sound all competing for attention.

When considering the overall design of Tipu's Tiger, an argument might be made for the power of its imagery. The carved tiger straddles the British soldier in a dominant position, sinking its fangs into the neck of the man. Its front claws are buried deep into the shoulders, while its hind legs are conspicuously close to the soldier's crotch, an area of the body that had become strongly associated with Mysorean cruelty. Linda Colley recounts how East India Company soldiers taken prisoner by Tipu's forces underwent forced circumcision, often without anesthesia.[9] While this was probably intended as way of incorporating the prisoners into Muslim society, for the British public it was unmistakably a punishment—an extended, national emasculation akin to the defeats of the first two Anglo-Mysore Wars. The tiger offers a similar kind of sexual reversal as it, a symbol of Indian power, mauls and mounts the East India Company soldier. Tipu clearly relished

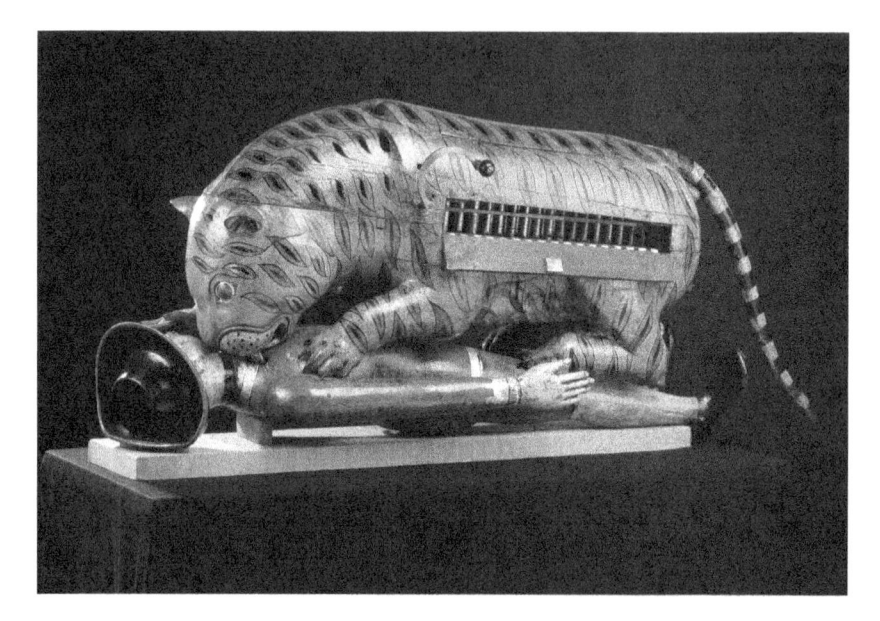

Figure 3. Tipu's Tiger, c. 1790. Semi-automaton mechanical organ. Painted wood with metal and ivory fixtures, 178 x 71 x 61 cm. Courtesy of the Victoria and Albert Museum, London.

the terror that such inversions induced, since murals of tigers consuming Europeans appeared throughout his realm.

The fall of Mysore in 1799 was a seismic geopolitical event: one of the last barriers to company rule was removed, and the British would make steady inroads into South Asia after the turn of the nineteenth century. For the British soldiers who stormed Srirangapatna, no good deed went unrewarded: fifty thousand medals were minted in gold, silver, bronze, and tin to commemorate the battle and were distributed to the soldiers based on their rank. The oppositional relationship between Tipu and the British was captured in a medal design by Conrad Heinrich Küchler (see Figures 4 and 5). The obverse side of the medal depicts the British lion roaring over and mounting the Bengal tiger—a reversal of what we get in Tipu's Tiger. There is an inscription above the two in Arabic: "Asadullah al-Ghaleb" ("the conquering lion of God"). It is difficult to avoid the conclusion that the medals were meant to overwhelm and replace imagery of Indian dominance, such as in Tipu's Tiger.

After the death of Tipu Sultan at the hands of the East India Company, Tipu's Tiger was looted from his Rajmahal, or music room. Accounts of the organ highlighted Tipu's supposed sadistic delight in the tiger's primal power and hostility toward Europeans. A firsthand description by Richard Wellesley, the governor general of Bengal (and brother of the future Duke of Wellington), recalls that "in a room for musical instruments was found an article which merits particular notice, another proof of the deep hate, and extreme loathing of Tipu Sahib towards the English. This mechanism represents a royal tiger in the act of devouring a prostrate European. There are some barrels in imitation of an organ within the body of the Tiger. The sounds produced are intended to resemble the cries of a person in distress intermixed with the roar of a tiger. The machinery is so contrived that while the organ is playing, the hand of the European is often lifted up, to express his helpless and deplorable condition."[10] From there, the tiger avoided the fate of the sultan's jewels and other possessions after the siege of Srirangapatna. Most of the valuables in Tipu's palace were divided among the victorious soldiers as spoils of war, with some ending up in the hands of individual British collectors.[11] However, the organ presented an opportunity for the East India Company to reverse the iconography of the tiger that had been deployed so effectively against them. Joshua Ehrlich describes this as the "symbolic power of plunder."[12] Wellesley sent Tipu's Tiger to London in 1799. However, in spite of calls for it to be displayed at the Tower of London, it was instead placed into storage for nine years until the company included the organ in its own displays at East India House in 1808.

Figures 4 and 5. Conrad Heinrich Küchler, obverse and reverse of *The Seringapatam Medal*, nineteenth century. Silver, 4.8 cm diameter. Courtesy of the Victoria and Albert Museum, London.

Susan Stronge has found that the company's collections were open to the public and that visitors could not only view Tipu's Tiger but were also "allowed" to "open the flap and play patriotic songs like 'Rule Britannia' or 'God Save the King.'"[13] Tipu's automaton, which had been created as a symbol of his hatred for the East India Company, was thus uprooted and put on display, used to play the imperialist songs of a people both unfamiliar with and unsympathetic toward Indian objections to the British presence in South Asia. This trivialized reuse of Tipu's Tiger, divorcing the organ from its original Mysorean context and using it to champion British nationalism, was one of the ways in which the East India Company attempted to defang the tiger. In essence, they put the symbol of what had been plaguing them for years in a pillory for public view and humiliation. Once it was at East India House, the toy organ allowed visitors to turn the crank without fear of reprisal from this once fearsome but now subdued enemy. What was once a stand-in for an apex predator had become a curiosity tinged with moral judgment that, in effect, justified the British conquest. Tipu's Tiger was put on display so that the British public could see (and hear) the power of empire at work. Not only could the enemies of the East India Company be physically defeated, but their symbols could be as well (by being appropriated and repurposed).

Turning the Crank: The Performance of Empire through Tipu's Tiger / 233

My emphasis so far has been upon the symbolic inversion of Tipu's Tiger: how a musical instrument that signified resistance to British imperial incursion got subverted into a means of celebrating the East India Company's victory over Mysore. The looting of the organ and its removal to East India House transformed the object into a trophy to be shown off in the very seat of the company's power. I propose, however, that performers on the organ, even when they were playing nationalist songs to humiliate and efface the Indian power represented by Tipu's Tiger, were unable to escape the other sounds it made. Those other sounds (the wailing and grunting) effectively act as a material trace of empire, a reenactment of the noisy battle between the forces represented by its two caricatural figures.

Eighteenth-century automata often performed a semi-automated task that, once complete, supposedly showed the relationship between the task (which has been accomplished mechanically) and a larger system. For example, Jacques de Vaucanson's Canard Digérateur (Digesting Duck) demonstrates how an automaton can mechanize physiological or natural processes. Vaucanson's duck entered into the scientific debate over whether digestion was a chemical or a mechanical process. It appeared to simulate the consumption of food (pelleted grain) and then, after a pregnant pause, the duck excreted a pre-prepared pellet of simulated excrement, painted to match the color of the grain the duck had "eaten." However, a close observer might note that the food fed to the Canard Digérateur could not have been processed biologically in such a short amount of time. The duck's ability to simulate a process in an at least initially convincing manner and simultaneously to engage in fraud opens up similar questions for other automata, including Tipu's Tiger. If Vaucanson's duck was built to show how digestion works, then the organ, once it was ensconced at East India House, might be inadvertently doing something similar: demonstrating how small-scale power works. As a "scriptive thing," Tipu's Tiger relies upon a shared animosity: even as its performers triumph over its Indian makers, it exerts what Michel Foucault would call "a subtle coercion" on those very performers through its cacophony. Indeed, Foucault has argued that automata were one of the means through which small-scale power worked in the eighteenth century, and that they did so not "'wholesale'" but "'retail,' individually, ... obtaining holds upon [the body] at the level of the mechanism itself—movements, gestures, attitudes, rapidity: an infinitesimal power over the active body."[14] In order for the organ to have such power, it needed to engage individual bodies as an apparent plaything.

Because of the need to continually crank the organ in order to operate the bellows and give it voice, playing Tipu's Tiger required at least two people: one to turn the crank for air and another to press the keys. And yet, once it was sounding, a third person became part of the situation. In light of Gayatri Chakravorty Spivak's meditations on the concept of "dvaita"—the twoness, or dualism, through which the supernatural is occasionally made manifest in the natural world—we can recognize how, as performers turn the crank and press the keys, the long-dead Tipu takes on a liminal presence: erased by the jingoistic tunes being played and yet ever present because of the object's origins and iconography.[15] With a turn of the crank, the organ becomes an echo of Tipu himself: it remains associated with him and retains his name, despite the sacking of Srirangapatna, and it makes the wail and the grunt whether or not the keys are producing any music. Indeed, users of the East India Company's library grew increasingly frustrated by the cacophony—so much so that *The Athenaeum* happily reported that the organ had been silenced after someone intentionally hid the handle of the crank.[16]

The display of Tipu's Tiger at East India House and the nationalist songs performed on it all point to how the organ was used to justify the company's military actions in Mysore (and, by extension, those of the British Empire more generally). However, the cacophonous disruption of the company's reading room every time the organ was played must have pleased Tipu's spirit in some regard. Yet preventing such disruptions meant forgoing the easy feelings of triumph that visitors could get from playing the organ. One had to either endure the cacophony (as a sonic trace of the unpleasant complexities of empire) or be silent and so deny oneself the opportunity to further defang the tiger.

After being on display at East India House for several decades, Tipu's Tiger passed into the keeping of the India Office when the East India Company was absorbed by the Crown in 1858. When the India Office's museum was dissolved in 1879, and the collections that used to belong to the company were dispersed among other institutions, the South Kensington Museum (now the V&A) took in the organ. There, what had been a symbol of Tipu's imagined victory was overwritten yet again as it was absorbed into the museum's holdings as part of what Queen Victoria called "a monument for discerning Liberality and a Source of Refinement and Progress."[17] Its display as yet another attempt to justify the colonial project and its violence in India were part of what Maya Jasanoff calls the "imperial arrogance" of the time.[18]

In the twenty-first century, the display of Tipu's Tiger at the V&A continues to change. It was situated in its own vitrine in 2012 but has since been folded into a larger display featuring regalia from South Asia, which diminishes the individual object's felt uniqueness. One can see the organ in the galleries (South Asia, Room 41), but the busyness of the display and the inability of viewers to move completely around the tiger prevent the full experience of its three-dimensionality, much less of hearing it or seeing the organ in motion. Tipu's Tiger, then, is flattened, its sculptural, sonic, and mechanical qualities restricted in favor of its presentation as a part of a patchwork display of early Indian decorative arts.

There have been no official requests for repatriation of the objects taken when Srirangapatna was stormed in 1799, but as we learn more about Tipu's Tiger and its complicated and embodied past, perhaps such requests will come. For all the ways in which it has been treated as a toy or curiosity or spoil of war, not much different than the caged tigers that symbolized the "natural" absorption of Indian domains into the British Empire, this tiger may still have claws and fangs.[19] Tipu's Tiger retains its mystique to this day: it was the object that supposedly best revealed Tipu Sultan's "savage" nature, and by making it a public attraction, the East India Company was able to claim moral justification for their conquest. And yet it—and the cacophony it can produce—has outlasted not only the company, but almost the entire British Empire.

Notes

I would like to thank the American Society for Eighteenth-Century Studies for its generous grants to non-tenure-track faculty, one of which allowed me to present an earlier version of this project at their 2022 Annual Meeting. This essay would not exist without the feedback and support of colleagues like Jason Shaffer, Michael Witte, and the anonymous reviewers for the journal. I would also like to thank Thanh and my parents and friends for their unwavering support.

1. I will be referring to the central object considered in this essay as "Tipu's Tiger." However, some historical records and the V&A, which now has the organ in its keeping, refer to it as "Tippoo's Tiger," which is more likely to return results when searching. The (often misleading or disrespectful) transliteration of names is part of the history of empire. My decision to refer to Tipu Sultan in a different manner than the East India Company referred to him is consonant with my analysis of his tiger as an extension of its former owner's life and times.

2. See, for example, Maya Jasanoff, "Collectors of Empire: Objects, Conquests, and Imperial Self-Fashioning," *Past and Present* 184 (2004): 109–35; Ryan McCormack, *The Sculpted Ear: Aurality and Statuary in the West* (University Park: Pennsylvania State University Press, 2020), 63–86; and Daniel O'Quinn, *Staging Governance: Theatrical Imperialism in London, 1770–1800* (Baltimore: Johns Hopkins University Press, 2005), 312–48.

3. Bennett, "The Exhibitionary Complex," *New Formations* 4 (1988): 74.

4. Robin Bernstein, "Dances with Things: Material Culture and the Performance of Race," *Social Text* 27, no. 4 (2009): 68. Bernstein's approach allows for a more long-form means of re-embodying the experiences of the past. Things shape human behavior and activate a kinesthetic imagination that leads to determined or implied scripts.

5. See Sean Willcock, "A Neutered Beast? Representations of the Sons of Tipu Sultan—'The Tiger of Mysore'—as Hostages in the 1790s," *Journal for Eighteenth Century Studies* 36, no. 1 (2012): 135.

6. O'Quinn, *Staging Governance*, 313. The images of artists like Home were used to help persuade the public that the East India Company's actions in the colonies were justified, despite the repeated revelations, particularly in the Hastings trial, of their abuses of power.

7. Willcock, "A Neutered Beast?," 124.

8. See Richard H. Davis, *Lives of Indian Images* (Princeton: Princeton University Press, 1999), 150; and Kate Brittlebank, "Sakti *and* Barakat: The Power of Tipu's Tiger; An Examination of the Tiger Emblem of Tipu Sultan of Mysore," *Modern Asian Studies* 29, no. 2 (1995): 257–69.

9. Colley, *Captives* (New York: Pantheon Books, 2002), 288.

10. Quoted in Susan Stronge, *Tipu's Tigers* (London: Harry N. Abrams, 2009), 65.

11. "William Beckford added Tipu's jade hookah to the extravagant clutter of Fonthill; Sir John Soane furnished a sitting room with Tipu's ivory table and chairs; one collector ingeniously adapted a gold tiger's foot from the base of Tipu's throne into a snuff box; and the 10th earl of Lindsey enjoyed the singular privilege of being baptized in one of Tipu's Sevres tureens. ... Lady Henrietta Clive, whose husband Edward was governor of Madras, and Robert Clive's son and heir," came into possession of Tipu's personal tent, a gold finial tiger head, and, allegedly, his sword: Jasanoff, "Collectors of Empire," 127. See also Kieran Hazzard, "The Clives at Home: Self-Fashioning, Collecting, and British India," in *Politics and the English Country House, 1688–1800*, ed. Joan Coutu, Jon Stobart, and Peter N. Lindfield (Montreal: McGill-Queen's University Press, 2023), 236–37.

12. Ehrlich, "Plunder and Prestige: Tipu Sultan's Library and the Making of British India," *South Asia: Journal of South Asian Studies* 43, no. 3 (2020): 485.

13. "Spotlight on V&A India Collections," V&A Museum, 30 September 2015, YouTube video, 1:16–27, https://youtu.be/jVPq_7kIufw. McCormack notes the glee with which Nigel Bamforth "jokingly play[ed] 'Rule Britannia!' and 'God Save the Queen'" in a different video, after which he and two conservationists for the V&A "grin widely and slowly turn to look at the camera" (*Sculpted Ear*, 85). The V&A has since taken down the video, but its page has been archived: https://web.archive.org/web/20160915100150/https://vimeo.com/6699473.

14. Foucault, *Discipline and Punish: The Birth of the Prison*, trans. Alan Sheridan (New York: Vintage, 1995), 137.

15. Spivak, "Moving Devi," *Cultural Critique* 47 (2001): 124. Spivak explains "dvaita" as "a participation without belonging, a taking part of without being a part of."

16. Arthur W. J. G. Ord-Hume, "Tipu's Tiger and Its History and Description, Part 2," *Music and Automata* 3, no. 10 (1987): 79, citing *The Athenaeum*, 5 June 1869, p. 766.

17. *London Gazette*, 19 May 1899.

18. Jasanoff, *Edge of Empire: Lives, Culture, and Conquest in the East, 1750–1850* (New York: Knopf, 2005), 177–80.

19. McCormack, *Sculpted Ear*, 68.

The Principle of Neutrality and the Evidentiary Patterns of Conspiratorial Thought in the Early United States

NAN GOODMAN

From the American Revolution through the end of George Washington's second term as president in 1797, American political and legal thought was centrally concerned with the definition and enforcement of the principle of neutrality. An important building block of American domestic policy, neutrality was enshrined in the Constitution—in the Establishment and Free Exercise clauses of the First Amendment—and in the general principle that the "government . . . must be impartial."[1] It was also at the heart of the new American experiment in federalism. The Constitution, James Madison wrote, would serve as a "disinterested & dispassionate umpire in disputes between different passions & interests in various states."[2] As the cornerstone of American foreign policy, neutrality's role was arguably even more critical. It was, for example, fundamental to the Declaration of Independence from Great Britain in 1776, Washington's Neutrality Proclamation in 1793, and the "Treaty of Amity, Commerce and Navigation between His Britannic Majesty and the United States of America," more commonly known as the Jay Treaty, in 1794.

Unsurprisingly, given its central role in the development of the nation, neutrality has been the subject of much scholarship. Largely overlooked in the many studies of neutrality, however, is the role it played as a source of early American conspiracy theories. Conspiracy theories were first linked to neutrality during the Revolutionary War, when many of the so-called neutrals, who resisted taking up arms for the Patriot or Loyalist side, were arrested, banished, or confined for harboring what were said to be "suspicious and equivocal" characters. Neutrality also gave rise to conspiracy theories during the debates over the Neutrality Proclamation and the Jay Treaty. In these discussions, both George Washington and John Jay, who negotiated the Jay Treaty, came under fire. As news of the terms of the Jay Treaty were made public, for example, Jay was hanged in effigy throughout the country and Washington was said to be "dangerous," "treasonous," and in one unforgettable articulation of the perils of neutrality, in possession of "a cold hermophrodite faculty ... [that] was credited for a while by enemies as by friends, for ... impartiality."[3]

To be sure, neutrality was not the first or even most important source of conspiratorial thinking in early America. From the American Revolution, which Bernard Bailyn believed was inspired by fears of "a conspiracy against liberty ... nourished by corruption," to the rise of the secret societies of Masons and Illuminati that Richard Hofstadter identified as a source of early American "paranoid" thought, scholars have long associated the early United States with conspiracy theories.[4] Driving these theories, these scholars argue, was a mindset steeped in the increasingly polarized and Manichean terms that governed relations between Great Britain and the American colonies and an accompanying tendency to think apocalyptically.[5] Indeed, thinking conspiratorially was so pervasive in this period that almost all the major issues, including the creation of the Bank of the United States, the repayment of the Revolutionary War debt, and the location of the nation's capital, were affected by it in some way.

While the conspiracy theories generated in the context of neutrality also featured Manichean and apocalyptic beliefs, they arose in a context not of political polarization and paranoia, but of disengagement from partisan politics and an embrace of rational thought. As such, they offer a counterpoint to the affective and psychological approaches that characterize Bailyn's and Hofstadter's theses about early American conspiracy theories. Indeed, in shifting my focus away from the affective and psychological origins of early American conspiracy theories and toward their intersection with rational thought, I take my cue from Gordon Wood, who, contra Bailyn and Hofstadter, associated early American conspiracy theories not with the Manichean or apocalyptic imaginings of an unsettled eighteenth-century populace, but with Enlightenment thought. For Wood, conspiratorial thought was a natural outcome of the Enlightenment's emphasis on the explanatory power of human agency, as opposed to God's. Instead of attributing one's circumstances to God or Providence, Wood argues, people began to believe in the eighteenth century that what "happened in society" was the result of "the strictly human level of men's motivations and goals," from which the intrigues and plots of conspiracy theories were born.[6]

Although, like Wood, I attribute the spread of conspiratorial thinking in this period to the rise of rational, human-centered thought, my focus on neutrality shifts our attention once again—in this case, from a discourse on causation and human agency to a discourse on evidence or how the conditions of neutrality were to be assessed. Rather than being concerned with "men's motivations and goals," the conspiracy theorizing that emerged from the neutrality debates revolved around questions of evidence and procedure.[7] To be sure, neutrality was never the transcendent, value-free principle it was often proclaimed to be. Yet it consistently promoted the ideal of a clear and open mind whose capacity to assess the truth was grounded in the rule-guided procedures by which Americans learned how to weigh evidence.[8] In short, neutrality was not just rooted in the paradigm of rational thought that emerged from the Enlightenment, but also constitutive of it.

In tying the evidentiary assumptions behind rational thought to conspiracy theories, I build on the recent work of social epistemologists who seek to understand conspiracy theories in terms of their evidentiary assumptions. How conspiracy theorists use evidence, they argue, reveals the epistemic "routes to knowledge": "the social processes and practices that inculcate [conspiratorial] belief."[9] "Conspiracy theories," Michael Barkun explains, "purport to be testable by the accumulation of evidence about the observable world. Those who subscribe to such constructs do not ask the constructs to be taken on faith."[10] Jovan Byford reinforces Barkun's description by pointing to the lengths to which conspiracy theorists often go to "corroborate" and "verify" their arguments, while Matthew R. X. Dentith notes that "what will make a conspiracy theory a rational or reasonable belief ... depends on the evidence."[11]

In addition to being intrinsically structured by and oriented around evidentiary assessments that are crucial to rational thought, neutrality offers an especially telling vantage point on the "routes to knowledge" because of its evidentiary ambiguity.[12] First expounded by Hugo Grotius and Alberico Gentili in their early modern treatises on the law of nations and the rules of war, neutrality was conceptually fraught and difficult to prove from the start. Under the just-war theory of the Middle Ages, for example, neutrality was seen as morally and legally unacceptable. By the late sixteenth and early seventeenth centuries, however, Grotius and Gentili, who were heirs to that tradition, acknowledged that neutrality had a place in the law of war. Because so little had been formulated about neutrality in the past, however, their explanations of the rights and duties of neutral parties were only partially fleshed out. Perhaps the biggest problem from an evidentiary point of view was that the rules governing neutrality had never been institutionalized. Instead, the law of neutrality grew from a practice that was in constant flux. From this theoretical and practical disarray, Stephen Neff explains, two rules, each highly problematic, emerged to guide the evidentiary inquiry into whether neutrality had been adequately observed or violated: the first was "abstention from participation in the hostilities" and the second was "impartiality as between the belligerents."[13] Although he does not discuss it, Neff also points to a "grey area" "between abstention and impartiality" in which, I would argue, a third problem arose: that of self-evidence, or the assumption that neutrality, when it was achieved, was so blatantly obvious that it required no proof at all.[14]

To explore the critical role played by the patterns of thought that characterized evidentiary assessments of neutrality, I begin with a brief review of the state of early American evidence law. Following this review, this essay is divided into three sections that each address the specific evidentiary problematics that characterized neutrality in the legal proceedings, congressional debates, newspaper accounts, and political pamphlets through which it was then being defined. In the first section I examine abstention, which became salient during discussions concerning the neutrals in the Revolutionary War and particularly emerges in the reports of the Committees for Detecting and Defeating Conspiracies in New York and in the safety committee reports of other states. In the second section I explore impartiality, which emerged during the crises over the Neutrality Proclamation and the Jay Treaty. In the third and final section I consider the claims of self-evidence brought forward in the debates about those same documents. Of course, no single one of these issues or evidentiary problematics is directly responsible for any given conspiracy theory at the time, but taken as a whole, I argue, they give us a more complete picture of how the evidentiary inquiries from which early Americans drew inferences about neutrality created some of the "epistemic routes" that marked the conspiracy theories of the early American period as much as they do our own.

Early American Evidence

Since the Enlightenment, empirical evidence has been considered the most reliable source of the truth. Needless to say, at the heart of this consideration is a general assumption about the probative value of empirical evidence; but as legal disputes soon revealed, even empirical evidence could be ambiguous and unreliable. This was why rules of evidence were devised:

to alert people to the manifestations of unreliability and to guide them toward more reliable and justifiable sources of knowledge and truth. These rules—about relevance, authenticity, voluntariness, and competency, among other things—were designed to safeguard the production of knowledge in laboratories, public and private venues, and courts of law. Of course, the rules of evidence that first appeared in the legal treatises of the eighteenth century drew heavily on the general theories of knowledge being developed at the time, including preeminently those of John Locke. Citing Locke, Geoffrey Gilbert, for example, author of the first English book on evidence (published in 1754), explained that weighing evidence was a matter of determining the probability of truth "from perfect certainty and demonstration, quite down to Improbability and Unlikeliness."[15] Each determination, Gilbert explained, depended on "acts of mind proportion'd to these Degrees of Evidence, which may be called Degrees of assent, from full assurance and Confidence, quite down to Conjecture, Doubt, Distrust, and Disbelief."[16] To be sure, while these "degrees of assent" were germane to ways of knowing in all areas of inquiry, Gilbert recognized that weighing evidence in legal contexts required special consideration. What Gilbert was among the first to acknowledge, Barbara Shapiro explains, was that "the law did not have access to certain knowledge because litigation depended on transient events 'retrieved by Memory and Recollection' ... [and] therefore of necessity 'determined by Probability,' not by demonstration."[17] Put another way, the core elements of legal evidence—namely, those of witnessing and testimony—were in contrast to most other manifestations of evidence predicated "on the epistemic experience of a prior event."[18]

What emerged from Gilbert's treatise, and those that followed in its wake, was a growing awareness of the need to distinguish between certainty—a possibility only in the case of observations and experiences that happened concurrently—and probability, which was the closest one could come to certainty when the narration of an event was removed in time from the observation or experience of it. The legal standard of requiring proof "beyond a reasonable doubt," but no more, was invented to fill this gap. To be sure, there was still a lot of uncertainty about the rules of evidence throughout the eighteenth century; but as John Henry Wigmore, one of the foremost early twentieth-century experts on the history of evidence, pointed out, by the later eighteenth century (that is, when the debates over the Neutrality Proclamation and the Jay Treaty were taking place), the rules of evidence had attained an unprecedented level of detail and fixity.[19] Most of this detail concerned procedures for cross-examining witnesses, including rules for impeachment and corroboration, confessions, leading questions, ordering testimony, and authenticating documents.[20] Central to most legal proceedings of the period, these rules arguably took on an even greater prominence in the United States, where, as Lawrence Friedman suggests, an especially distrustful public paid close attention to what evidence was admissible and what was not.[21]

Of course, while the early legal procedures on evidence did not address the issue of conspiracy directly, the preoccupation with assessing evidence with what Gilbert called the proper "degree of assent" suggests a corresponding awareness of the dangers of developing patterns of thought based on erroneous reasoning. Indeed, in the context of neutrality, where adducing evidence posed a particular challenge, the evidentiary contradictions, inconsistencies, and uncertainties that have long fueled conspiratorial thought are hard to miss.

Abstention and the Absence of Evidence

The first challenge in assessing the evidence of neutrality revolved around the unverifiability of abstention. In a system like that of Anglo-American law—which is based on acts of commission, as opposed to omission—proving a principle by looking to the absence of action was incongruous at best. This incongruity came to the fore during the revolutionary period when so-called neutrals or persons of "equivocal character" who had committed no discernible crime were rounded up, questioned, and often confined. Toward this end, the Continental Association, operating under the authority of the Continental Congress, established committees of safety whose mandate was to surveil and imprison not only those who identified as Loyalists, but also those who identified with neither the Loyalists nor the Patriots.[22] There were, of course, people at the time who were actually conspiring against the revolutionaries, plotting ways of assassinating George Washington, aiding the British army by supplying them with arms, or undermining the Continental army by selling secrets to the other side. The neutrals, however, were unaffiliated and had never taken up arms for either side. Holding fast to their abstention from action, which they believed would protect them from accusations or arrests, they were nevertheless seen as suspicious, and their abstention was taken as proof of their potential to conspire against the United States.

These suspicions about the neutrals arose in part because of the way that neutrality was then understood. Once seen as the civic virtue it would again become, neutrality as a personal attribute had fallen into disrepute in the early modern period. Virginia Cope describes how "from Hobbes onward, theories developed that posited self-interest as the driving force of human nature and consequently of economic and political regulation, concepts that rendered disinterest as impossible, insidious, or, most damningly, irrelevant."[23] To "impossible," "insidious," and "irrelevant," we can add "potentially conspiratorial," for neutrality blurred the lines of allegiance in a way that made people quite uncomfortable. As Judith Van Buskirk explains, murky political allegiances were to be found up and down the Eastern Seaboard, creating an environment in which no one really knew where anyone stood.[24] Aaron Sullivan adds that "many Americans remained uncertain of their neighbor's actual allegiance. Many remained uncertain of their own."[25]

Among the many neutrals were groups like the Shakers, who remained neutral because they abhorred war on principle. But there were also people actively struggling to situate themselves with respect to the growing hostilities. As Kariann Akemi Yokota points out, while the process of "unbecoming British" made many people question their lifetime loyalties, it didn't always result in an affiliation with the opposition.[26] For many others, neutrality meant sometimes siding with one side and sometimes with the other. For these neutrals, affiliation was in constant flux. As Brendan McConville explains, "Men answered some militia mobilizations, and then ignored others; resisted drafts; or fought for both sides."[27] Women were also often of two minds, especially when family members found themselves on both sides of the struggle. In at least one case, the danger of these fluctuating affiliations was acknowledged in a law targeting people who had "advocated the American Cause till it became serious."[28]

Thus, while only one state, New York, established a committee that explicitly targeted neutrals as potential conspirators (the Committee for Inquiring into Detecting and Defeating all Conspiracies), many states, including New Jersey and Pennsylvania, deployed their safety committees in similar ways, imprisoning neutrals and forcing them to sign oaths of allegiance to the Patriot cause or, failing that, stripping them of their liberties as citizens or banishing them from the state altogether.[29] That so many states regularly resorted to such drastic action suggests a widespread fear that neutrals were merely Loyalists in disguise waiting for the right opportunity to show their true colors. "One could never," Van Buskirk writes, "rule out a general uprising" of the people who "appeared dormant one day, and then erupted the next."[30]

In large part because it made no effort to conceal its pursuit of neutrals, New York's committee provides the clearest window into the legal complexities that arose as a result of making the absence of action grounds for arrest. Indeed, the language of the New York committee's standard summons reveals the strain such actions put on the evidentiary assumptions fundamental to the law. Instead of targeting individuals for what they had done, it named specific forms of abstention, targeting people who "from having neglected or refused to associate with their fellow citizens for the defence of their common rights" or "from their having never manifested, by their conduct, a zeal for, and attachment to the American cause—or from their having maintained an equivocal neutrality, have been considered by their countrymen in a suspicious light."[31] In three distinct yet oddly similar articulations of the suspect nature of their behavior (their "neglect," their failure to "manifest ... a zeal," and their "equivocal neutrality"), the committee criminalized the neutrals' abstention from action in violation not only of the rules of evidence, but also, even more conspicuously, of the most fundamental principle of criminal law: that of legal causation. Significantly, subsequent efforts to criminalize abstention, perhaps in recognition of these problems, insisted on some evidence of action, no matter how small. Thus a New York law from 1778 suggests that evidence of action in a context otherwise devoid of it might be found by conflating the failure to act ascribed to some neutrals with the actual acts and betrayals of others who, once professing neutrality, had gone on to join the enemy's forces: "Inasmuch therefore as it is reasonable to suppose that many persons who affect a similar neutrality of principal only wait an opportunity of persuing a similar Conduct with those who have at length thrown off the mask and taken an *active* part with our open enemies."[32]

With this language, the New York state legislature conflated inaction with action and fact with probability. Perhaps even more importantly, however, the legislature's language also replaced the law's need for empirical evidence (the observation of things) with character evidence (the observation that there are different kinds of people, some of whom are less trustworthy than others). This substitution soon became commonplace for both conspiracy theorists and their detractors.[33] In this context, being neutral was considered tantamount to being the kind of person who would conspire against the nation if given the chance. This false equivalence entered the evidentiary calculus of the detection and safety committees and circulated widely in political and popular publications. In one salient example, a series of seven letters written in 1776 and falsely attributed to George Washington depicted Washington—then the general of the Continental army—as dangerously neutral, unsure of his army's capability, and longing for peace. While they carried little weight at the time, these characterizations came back to haunt Washington during the debates over the Neutrality Proclamation and the Jay Treaty, when the assumption that he had been "neutral in the Revolution" and "frigid in regard to independence" marked him as the kind of person who would be neutral again.[34]

"Too Many Factors" and the Evidence of Impartiality

If the evidentiary arguments that surfaced in the context of abstention paved the way for certain "acts of mind" that were obviously not "proportion'd to the evidence," to use Gilbert's phrase, the evidentiary arguments that emerged during the debates over the Neutrality Proclamation of 1793 and the Jay Treaty of 1794 modeled still other epistemological pitfalls that paved the way for conspiratorial thought. Some of these pitfalls revolved around the idea of impartiality.[35] Unlike the "acts of mind" associated with abstention, however, which prohibited action, impartiality allowed for and even encouraged it, "provided, crucially that it ... [was] done equally for each belligerent."[36] Basing impartiality on an act of commission made it legible under the evidentiary conventions of American law. It nevertheless remained difficult to prove because the concept was indeterminate and subject to multiple interpretations. If the parties to a declaration of neutrality, for example, agreed that providing humanitarian assistance to the belligerents qualified as impartial, the question of what counted as humanitarian remained unaddressed. If the parties further agreed that trade could continue with both belligerents so long as it was "done equally for each," the question of how to measure equality stood in the way. Nor was it clear whether equality in this context meant equality of intention or equality of outcome. What if, for example, the intention was to trade with or provide resources equally for both belligerents, but the result of that intention was unequal?

In short, what appeared to be a principled and straightforward decision—to remain impartial—was contingent on assessing the evidence of a given action at a given time in a given place. As Hans J. Morgenthau puts it, neutrality cannot be "deduced from the abstract concept ... of 'impartiality,'" but rather had to be assessed on a case-by-case basis.[37] Impartiality, then, invited endless questions into the historical and geopolitical contingencies that determined what would or would not count as impartial, and these questions complicated the evidentiary calculus surrounding the concept of neutrality. Such questions, as Sandra Moats points out, "set the future of foreign policy" in the United States; I argue, however, that they also played a part in "setting the future" of evidentiary inquiry.[38] In the case of an ideal that was thought to be attainable regardless of perspective or location, the sheer range of circumstances that might qualify as impartial in a given context cast suspicion on almost every evidentiary inquiry into them. By examining the depth and frequency of the evidentiary manipulation and misinterpretation that made the guidelines for assessing impartiality epistemologically problematic, we gain additional insight into how the evidentiary underpinnings of conspiratorial thought became so commonplace in American culture and history.

An example of how some of these endless contingencies generated suspicion can be seen in the events leading up to the Proclamation of Neutrality of 1793. As soon as war was declared between the United States' two closest allies, Great Britain and France, President Washington sought to articulate a position of neutrality in order to preserve US independence. Although many people questioned whether neutrality was the right decision under the circumstances, the more immediate question among Washington's advisors was whether neutrality was a legally viable position, given the earlier promise of neutrality that had been given to France at the end of the Revolutionary War. When the minister of France told Thomas Jefferson in August 1792, for example, that France had declared war on Hungary and Bohemia, Jefferson, then the secretary of state, assured France that the United States would remain friendly "and render all those good offices which shall be consistent with the duties of a neutral nation," referring to the earlier neutrality agreement that the United States had signed with France.[39] When Great Britain and Holland, both important trading partners for the United States, joined the war against France, however, "the good offices ... [that were] consistent with a neutral nation" took on another meaning altogether. When the only parties to the conflict with France were nations with which the United States did little to no business, the earlier neutrality with France took precedence. When rendering the same "good offices" threatened Great Britain, however, actions formerly deemed impartial and "consistent with a neutral nation" needed to be reassessed.[40] It was just such a reassessment that seemed to impel Washington, on hearing that Great Britain had joined the war, to ask his cabinet for advice: "The posture of affairs in Europe, particularly between France and Great Britain, places the United States in a delicate situation and Requires much consideration of the measures which will be proper for them to observe in the War between those Powers."[41]

Seeking guidance on how to craft a policy of neutrality, Washington sent his cabinet a lengthy set of questions. The most important were (1) whether he should issue a neutrality proclamation; (2) whether under the terms of such a proclamation he could still receive France's new minister, Edmond Genet; and (3) whether the United States still needed to honor the treaty it had signed with France in 1778. This treaty, notably, had given preference to France and its ships in the event of a future war and had pledged to help defend the French colonies in the West Indies. Aware that this was a time-sensitive matter, the cabinet ministers sent an immediate but brief response: Washington should issue the proclamation and receive Genet. The minutes of this cabinet meeting note only that "the remaining questions were postponed for further consideration."[42]

If the cabinet thought that they could safely put off the question of how the 1778 treaty with France might affect the 1793 Neutrality Proclamation until after the latter was issued, however, they were sorely disappointed. If anything, the proclamation, which required that the United States "should with sincerity and good faith adopt and pursue a conduct friendly and impartial toward the belligerent Powers," made matters much worse, bringing the revolutionary and early republican understandings of neutrality in a foreign-policy context into conflict.[43] Under his interpretation of the 1778 treaty, for example, Genet, who had arrived in the United States long before Washington officially received him, was actively commandeering American ships and recruiting Americans to fight for the French cause.[44] Republican newspapers also contributed to the conflict, framing the proclamation as a betrayal of the alliance with France and an act of ingratitude. France, of course, was going through its own revolution and many thought the United States should have joined forces with the French as recompense for their help during the American fight for independence. "The cause of France is the cause of man," an anonymous individual wrote to Washington, "and neutrality is desertion."[45]

Developing into a wedge issue between the Democratic-Republicans and the Federalists, the proclamation exposed just how historically and geopolitically contingent the evidentiary terms of neutrality could be. For Jefferson and James Madison, for example, who originally supported the proclamation but quickly changed their tune, neutrality was not simply a required pivot in foreign policy in light of new circumstances, but evidence of a government conspiracy. The proclamation, the Democratic-Republicans argued, was deliberately designed to create conflict between the United States and France and to undercut revolutionary principles. In other words, what the president took as proof of neutrality was not neutral at all. Washington was accused of "double dealing," "monarchical mystery," and "court intrigue."[46] Jefferson went on to say that if the United States refused to comply with its previous treaty obligations, that would in itself amount to a breach of neutrality with France.[47] The French Minister, Jean-Antoine-Joseph Fauchet, raised this point as well, wondering whether the US Proclamation of Neutrality could be fulfilled, insofar as it pertained to France, if the neutral party refused to abide by its preexisting treaty obligations.[48]

If Washington's response to the Franco-American Treaty gave Jefferson reason to mistrust the president, Alexander Hamilton's argument in favor of the proclamation only further fanned the flames of suspicion. More concerned with the possibility of alienating the British than the French, Hamilton looked on the treaty with France as peripheral, if not irrelevant, to the determination of American neutrality. Writing as "Pacificus" in *the*

Gazette of the United States, the Federalist rival to *the National Gazette*, Hamilton argued that while the Franco-American Treaty had committed the United States to come to France's aid, it did so in a way that remained consistent with the proclamation: "The guarantee clause of the Treaty with France relates merely to defence and preservation of her American colonies" and was therefore well within the parameters of impartiality. That Hamilton came to such a different conclusion than Jefferson regarding the same historical and geopolitical situation only further confused the evidentiary standards surrounding impartiality and aroused more suspicion about what a stance of neutrality might reveal.

Additional challenges to assessing the evidence of impartiality arose outside the context of the 1778 treaty. These problems demonstrated the difficulty of weighing the evidence of impartiality when there were, as one senator put it almost two hundred years later, "too many factors ... to justify a stand on the simple basis of impartial intent."[49] Actions on either side of impartiality could take many forms and the language of the Neutrality Proclamation did not distinguish among them. For one thing, at Jefferson's insistence the proclamation omitted the term "neutrality" itself, which left the even vaguer term "impartiality" to do the signifying. Admittedly, a more specific instruction for citizens to "avoid all acts and proceedings whatsoever, which may in any manner tend to contravene such disposition" followed the initial proclamation that the United States would be pursuing "a conduct friendly and impartial toward the belligerent Powers," but the added clauses shed little light.[50] If the proclamation's language remained vague, however, it was clear from his correspondence that Washington had a specific violation of neutrality in mind: namely, the act of privateering. On hearing "that vessels [at Genet's behest] are already designated as Privateers," Washington urged Jefferson to adopt "such measures as shall be deemed most likely to effect" neutrality.[51]

Before any specific amendments to the proclamation were passed, however, the consequences of failing to prohibit privateering became all too apparent when a case involving one of Genet's privateers landed in court. *Henfield's Case*—which altered the evidentiary landscape around neutrality yet again and revealed how easy it was not only to manipulate evidence, but also to dismiss it altogether—concerned an American citizen, Gideon Henfield, who found work as a sailor on a French privateer named, after the minister himself, the Citoyen Genet.[52] When the Citoyen Genet seized a British ship, the William, at sea, Henfield became its prize master and sailed it back to Philadelphia as a French possession. As soon as the ship arrived, however, George Hammond, the British minister to the United States, complained to Jefferson that the act breached "that neutrality which the United States profess to observe."[53]

Henfield's Case demonstrated the dangerous ambiguity of Washington's neutrality on several levels. For one thing, it raised a number of administrative questions that the proclamation left unanswered, including which court should hear the case and which branch of the federal or Pennsylvania state government should enforce the policy or judgment.[54] But the evidentiary significance of *Henfield's Case*, which was closely watched by large numbers of Americans, was arguably even greater because the claims that both sides made focused not on the intricate details of what had happened, but rather on how little the evidence of what had happened mattered in the first place.[55] For example, Justice Wilson, who addressed the grand jury in the indictment phase of the case, asserted that Henfield's guilt was so obvious that there was no need for any evidence at all: "That a citizen, who in our state of neutrality, and without the authority of the nation, takes a hostile part with either of the belligerent powers, violates thereby his duty, and the laws of his country, is a position so plain as to require no proof."[56] Of course, despite this charge to the jury, evidence of Henfield's guilt was presented at trial, and, as Wilson had proclaimed, it proved undeniable. The defense, of course, denied the claim that Henfield had remained an American citizen, while also arguing that even if the court chose to see him that way, at the time of the seizure he was not on American soil and therefore not subject to American law. Needless to say, both arguments were unsuccessful.

Regardless of the proof of Henfield's culpability, however, the jury found him not guilty. This finding mystified the nation on political grounds because the policy of American neutrality was, despite its prominent critics, looked on favorably by the population at large. The jury's finding, however, was arguably even more mystifying from an evidentiary point of view because it was clear from the evidence that Henfield had violated the law. The only explanation for the verdict came from a single juror who, when questioned after the trial, revealed that he had voted for acquittal because he believed that Henfield had committed the crime but didn't intend to do so.[57]

Whether or not this juror's account is trustworthy, it suggests that in handing down an acquittal, the jury in *Henfield's Case* effectively nullified the law—acknowledging both the facts and the law but dismissing their relevance. To be sure, jury nullification was not uncommon in this period and juries often acted "lawlessly," as Lawrence Friedman observes, but they tended to do so by altering the facts to arrive at a different understanding of the law—finding stolen goods to be worth far less than they clearly were, for example.[58] In *Henfield*, however, the determining factor appeared to be the ambiguity of the evidence required to make the law comprehensible in the first place. If the interviewed juror is to be believed, the jury voted to nullify because it was hopelessly unclear from the infinite number of circumstances that might or might not count as evidence of impartiality how an ordinary citizen was to comply with the law. Such a decision furthered the disconnect between the mandate to interpret evidence and the ability to draw the right inferences from it, for which the neutrality debates and the conspiracies they generated were becoming known.

The ambiguity of evidence featured in the debates over the Proclamation of Neutrality also informed the lengthy controversy concerning the Jay Treaty, which further reinforced the suspicion that determinations about neutrality were a cover for partisan politics. Indeed, in 1794, when Washington dispatched John Jay, then the chief justice of the Supreme Court, to negotiate a treaty with Great Britain, the terms of the (then) present neutrality were once again encumbered by the terms of a previous neutrality—in this case, the 1783 Treaty of Paris that ended the Revolutionary War.[59] Unlike the proclamation, however, which had no status as law, the Jay Treaty, by virtue of Article II, Section 2 of the Constitution, was incorporated into "the supreme law of the land," which made the stakes of interpreting it as evidence of neutrality considerably higher. The Senate—whose job, according to that same Constitutional Article, was to offer "advice and consent" to the treaty-making executive—took up the task of weighing the evidence of and in the Jay Treaty in June of 1794.

The Jay Treaty had twenty-seven provisions, each of which posed its own evidentiary challenge. The Senate's overarching concern, however, had to do with whether Jay had failed to maintain the sovereignty and neutrality guaranteed to and pledged by the United States in the Treaty of Paris, thereby pitting the meaning of neutrality in the past against its meaning in the present. To be sure, the Jay Treaty maintained neutrality, insofar as it successfully averted war, but many Democratic-Republicans doubted whether the peace that had been achieved—a peace in which the United States made far more concessions than Great Britain—was consistent with American neutrality. Of particular interest to the Democratic-Republicans were provisions concerning the Canadian-Maine boundary, compensation for prerevolutionary debts, and the persistent seizure of American ships by the British.

Reading the failure of various individual provisions to secure American interests as the failure of neutrality overall, the Democratic-Republicans pursued another tactic common to conspiracy theorists: equating their sense of the relevant facts with carefully selected pieces of evidence, rather than with the treaty as a whole. Harping on the most disappointing of the provisions, one of Washington's most conspiracy-minded detractors, Benjamin Franklin Bache, editor of the *Aurora*, described the Jay Treaty as the president's "pact with the devil."[60] Fisher Ames, the eminent congressman from Massachusetts, decried this strategy of condemning the whole treaty on the basis of a critique of individual provisions. Those who wanted to vote against the Jay Treaty, he argued, should be confident that it was "bad not merely in the petty details, but in its character, principles, and mass."[61]

On 24 June 1795, after much debate, the Senate ratified the treaty, but the evidentiary aspects of the neutrality debates were far from over. Many senators wanted to see more evidence that the neutrality of the treaty had been achieved in good faith before they voted to appropriate funds for its enforcement. Toward this end, a Democratic-Republican congressman from New York, Edward Livingston, introduced a resolution requesting that more evidence be provided before the House took a vote. Washington noted that Livingston had asked him to give the House "a copy of the instructions to the minister of the United States, who negotiated the treaty with the king of Great Britain ... together with the correspondence and other documents relative to the said treaty."[62]

In the ever-changing evidentiary landscape around neutrality, this request for additional evidence was arguably more indicative of the conspiratorial thought patterns embedded in the assessment of neutrality than any other request or inquiry. For no matter how compelling the available counterevidence might be, Mark Fenster explains, conspiracy theorists will never stop looking for the smoking gun. For the conspiracy minded, "there is always something more to know about an alleged conspiracy," and the more the desired information is withheld, the more distrustful the conspiracy minded can become: "The very attempt to shut interpretation down is itself a suspicious act."[63]

Challenged by several of his colleagues for making a request that was itself so vague, Livingston concealed his partisan motives. Addressing "the gentleman from Connecticut who wished to know why ... [he] had brought this resolution before the House," Livingston said only that "he did it for the sake of information."[64] When asked a more specific question about which points he wanted to investigate more closely, Livingston reverted to tautology, another common tactic among conspiracy theorists, observing that "it was impossible to say to which or how many of these points without a recurrence to those very papers."[65] In the face of such responses, Ames took Livingston's request to task for its logical weakness: "Suggestions of this kind will not yield to argument for as they were not reasoned up, they cannot be reasoned down."[66] In spite of this and other objections, many congressmen remained suspicious and Livingston's proposal narrowly passed. When Washington refused to comply with it, however, the final battle over the evidence of neutrality in the early republic began.

The Self-Evidence of Neutrality

In recognition, perhaps, of the evidentiary ambiguity and uncertainty that surrounded the inquiries into abstention and impartiality in the context of neutrality, those arguing for neutrality often resorted to a form of circular reasoning familiar to many conspiracy theorists. This reasoning was especially visible during the Jay Treaty debates in which the treaty itself was offered as sufficient evidence of the neutrality it had been designed to achieve. The argument in this case was that the neutrality of the treaty was self-evident: something that could be discovered after the fact in the terms it set, regardless of whether those terms had run afoul of the rules. Like all versions of self-evidence, neutrality in this case concealed the conditions of its own production, relying for its legality on the expression in which it was itself conveyed.

Washington's rejection of the House's request for more information about the treaty negotiations was the first volley in this new evidentiary approach to neutrality. Because the Jay Treaty had been ratified by the Senate and signed into law, Washington argued, there was no need for further proof of its positive contribution to the law and policy of neutrality. Although Washington and other supporters of the treaty did not say so explicitly, the underlying premise of this argument was that the treaty was neutral on its face or, to use a term that had resonance from its prominent place in the Declaration of Independence, that it was self-evident. In the words of a philosopher from earlier in the century, an act or proposition was self-evident when just "a bare attention to the ideas themselves provides full conviction and Certainty," and when it was not "possible to call in anything more evident."[67] The implication, of course, was that rational people would recognize the truth of something that was self-evident and, crucially, do so without the need for further proof. Self-evident acts or propositions, in short, were "not the fruit of supporting evidence, inference, and argument" (i.e., the standards that otherwise characterized the established practices for weighing evidence in the law).[68]

Scholars have long noted how the logical problems associated with self-evidence continued to dog the American legal and political system after the Declaration of Independence, but they have overlooked their salience in the Jay Treaty debates, in which they played an important part in the development of conspiracy theories about Jay, Washington, and the treaty negotiations themselves. A strategy of last resort, arguments for the self-evidence of the Jay Treaty rested on several interrelated grounds. The first was its authority as law. "The course which the debate has taken on the resolution of the House," Washington wrote after receiving Livingston's request, "leads to some observations on the mode of making treaties under the *Constitution of the United States.*" Offering a brief civics lesson, Washington reminded the members of the House that, according to the Constitution, "the power of making treaties is exclusively vested in the President, by and with the advice and consent of the Senate, provided two-thirds of the Senators present concur." This reminder is telling in many ways, but primarily for its invocation of what Washington considered the self-evidence of the Constitutional provision in support of the self-evidence of the Jay Treaty provisions: "If other proofs than ... the plain letter of the Constitution itself be necessary to ascertain the point under consideration," the House could consult the relevant—and equally self-evident—legislative history.[69] This history, he noted, showed that a proposal to require the House's approval in making treaties had been considered during the drafting of the Constitution and rejected definitively.

That the Jay Treaty had a legal authority that the Proclamation of Neutrality lacked reinforced Washington's rejection of Livingston's request for further evidence of its validity. This was the case, he confessed, even though he didn't like the treaty himself. "My opinion respecting the treaty," he wrote, just before he signed it into law, "is the same now that it was: namely, not favorable to it." But, he continued, "it is better to ratify it in the manner the Senate have advised ... than to suffer matters to remain as they are, unsettled."[70] Thus Washington's desire to ratify the treaty was largely pragmatic. However, the implications of his public position for the inquiry that Livingston proposed meant that at a certain point the government could, in what the Democratic-Republicans believed was an arbitrary and potentially monarchical move, cut off the production and interpretation of further evidence. "Are we to explain the Treaty by private and confidential papers, or by anything extraneous to the instrument itself?," a Federalist congressman asked in the debate over Livingston's proposal: "I conclude not. The instrument is then before us; let us compare it with the Constitution and see if there is one article, sentence, word or syllable in the Treaty, which clashes with, or is contradictory to, the Constitution."[71] In a similar vein, another congressman cast even more suspicion on Livingston's request: "Gentlemen complain of want of information," he began. "Admitting their complaint to be well founded, let them resort to the proper sources of information. What are those sources? If information be wanted to enable them to judge of the constitutionality of the instrument, let them take the Constitution in one hand and the Treaty in the other, compare them, and then decide."[72]

The exhortation to read the Constitution and the Jay Treaty side by side offers a second ground for considering the treaty as self-evident, one that redirected the evidentiary inquiry away from fact gathering and toward close reading. If supporting evidence were needed, the theory went, the language of the document would be adequate to the task. Washington, after all, had referred the congressmen to the "Plain Letter" of the Constitution. It followed that the plain letter of the treaty would yield the truth as well. Thus, in his published defenses of the treaty, Hamilton argued that if people read the treaty carefully, they could not help but see it as reasonable. Toward this end, he provided a close reading of each provision of the treaty to show that "it closes and upon the whole as reasonably as could have been expected the controverted points between the two Countries."[73] Similarly, John Fenno, publisher of the *Federalist Gazette*, argued that "the more the treaty is read, the better it is understood, the less objectionable it appears." Reading it carefully, Fenno urged, would also tamp down what he called the "frantic enthusiasm" of the treaty's critics.[74] Describing his own process of reconciling himself to the treaty, Congressman William Lyman of Massachusetts also pointed to the power of close reading as a means of assessing the treaty: "I have read the treaty with care and attention and I am free to own that upon the first perusal of it I had a prejudice against it; it appeared to me that some of its stipulations were too favorable for Britain, and too disadvantageous to ourselves; but ... the more I have attended to the subject, the more I am reconciled to it."[75]

Grounded in political expediency, on one hand, and linguistic self-sufficiency, on the other, these arguments about self-evidence aroused suspicion among conspiracy-minded congressmen who saw them as unconstitutional prohibitions on their fact-finding mission and smoke screens to conceal the truth. While Washington argued that House members should turn their attention to "the treaty that is," not the "treaty that ought to be," the Democratic-Republicans persisted in arguing that they had a "right to judge of the expediency or inexpediency of carrying it into effect." "This right," they argued, "depended on its merits."[76] Without the information that the president had denied them, William Maclay of Pennsylvania observed, members of the House "were left to take their measures in the dark; or in other words, they were called upon to act without information."[77]

When it became clear that people like Maclay were growing more, rather than less, suspicious as a result of Washington's refusal to provide additional evidence, the argument for the self-evidence of the treaty shifted to the political and legal futility of resisting its authority. In an information hierarchy, Washington, Hamilton, and other Federalists observed, the treaty was at the top. Insisting that the Jay Treaty was "a treaty in the eyes of the Constitution, and the law of nations," William Murray, a representative from Maryland, reminded his colleagues that there was "nothing that we can rightfully do, or refuse to do, [that] will add or diminish its validity, under the Constitution and law of nations."[78] To act otherwise would not simply reverse the inferences drawn from its evidence, but overturn the evidentiary system as a whole. John Jay himself reiterated the futility of providing additional evidentiary assessments by projecting the treaty into the written record of a future history: "The treaty is as it is, and the time will certainly come when it will very universally receive exactly that degree of commendation or censure which, to candid and enlightened minds, it shall appear to deserve."[79] Still concerned with the treaty's largely negative reception two months later, Jay added, "As to the treaty no calumny on the one hand nor eloquence on the other, can make it worse or better than it is. At a future day it will be generally seen in its true colors and in its proper point of view."[80]

Jay's effort to reserve any further evidence-based inquiries into the Jay Treaty for a later date not only closes out the arguments put forward for the treaty's self-evidence ("it is as it is"), but also provides a productive ending point for the argument I've been making. For it was ultimately the challenge of assessing the evidence of neutrality in the moment that encouraged the founding generation in many of its conspiratorial beliefs. With respect to abstention, as we have seen, the evidence simply didn't exist. This made the arguments both for and against neutrality susceptible to fallacious acts of fabrication. When it came to impartiality, there was an overabundance of potential evidence, but this made the arguments for and against neutrality susceptible to inferences that selected or manipulated the available evidence or dismissed it, as in *Henfield*, altogether.

Of course, none of these evidentiary quagmires were peculiar to the concept of neutrality, but as one of the most contentious issues in the revolutionary and early republican periods, neutrality proved an especially fertile field for the development and spread of unreliable approaches to evidence. If to foster sound conclusions, as Gilbert's treatise on evidence proposed, "acts of mind" were to be proportioned to the evidence in question, the "acts of mind" on display in the neutrality debates fell far short of the mark, revealing what Dentith calls "the epistemic warrant of conspiracy theories" that have helped make them an enduring piece of how Americans think.[81]

Notes

I would like to thank my colleagues who commented on a draft of this paper at a works-in-progress session at the University of Colorado Boulder, as well as the anonymous readers for *SECC*.

1. See Cass R. Sunstein, "Neutrality in Constitutional Law (with Special Reference to Pornography, Abortion, and Surrogacy)," *Columbia Law Review* 92, no. 1 (1992): 1.
2. Madison to George Washington, 16 April 1787, Founders Online, National Archives, https://founders.archives.gov/documents/Madison/01-09-02-0208.
3. Thomas Paine to Washington, 30 July 1796, Founders Online, National Archives, https://founders.archives.gov/documents/Washington/05-20-02-0329.
4. Bailyn, *The Ideological Origins of the American Revolution* (Cambridge: Harvard University Press, 1967), xiii; Hofstadter, *The Paranoid Style in American Politics and Other Essays* (Cambridge: Harvard University Press, 1952), 4.
5. For an innovative view of the history of conspiracy theory scholarship, see Ed White, "The Value of Conspiracy Theory," *American Literary History* 14, no. 1 (2002): 1–31.
6. Wood, "Conspiracy and the Paranoid Style: Causality and Deceit in the Eighteenth Century," *William and Mary Quarterly* 39, no. 3 (1982): 414.
7. Bruce Ackerman argues that neutrality is in this sense an "ideal decision procedure." See his "What Is Neutral about Neutrality?," *Ethics* 93, no. 2 (1983): 377. Of course, Ackerman was discussing neutrality not as a principle of foreign policy, but rather of dialogue in a liberal state. For more on this, see Ackerman, "Neutralities," in *Liberalism and the Good*, ed. R. Bruce Douglass, Gerald M. Mara, and Henry S. Richardson (London: Routledge, 1990), 29–43.
8. See Alfred Moore, "Conspiracy and Conspiracy Theories in Democratic Politics," *Critical Review* 28, no. 1 (2016): 5.
9. See Ronald J. Allen and Brian Leiter, "Naturalized Epistemology and the Law of Evidence," *Virginia Law Review* 87, no. 8 (2001): 1497.
10. Barkun, *A Culture of Conspiracy: Apocalyptic Visions in Contemporary America* (Berkeley: University of California Press, 2003), 22–23.
11. Byford, *Conspiracy Theories: A Critical Introduction* (Basingstoke: Palgrave Macmillan, 2011), 90; Dentith, *The Philosophy of Conspiracy Theories* (Basingstoke: Palgrave Macmillan, 2014), 37.
12. Psychologists often describe ambiguous evidence as particularly prone to fallacious reasoning, including interpretations based on confirmation heuristics. See, for example, J. Klayman and Y-W Ha, "Confirmation, Disconfirmation, and Information in Hypothesis Testing," *Psychology Review* 94, no. 2 (1987): 211–28.
13. Neff, *The Rights and Duties of Neutrals: A General History* (Manchester: Manchester University Press, 2000), 13.
14. Neff, *Rights and Duties of Neutrals*, 13.
15. Gilbert, *The Law of Evidence* (London, 1760), 1.
16. Gilbert, *Law of Evidence*, 1.

17. Shapiro, *"Beyond Reasonable Doubt" and "Probable Cause"* (Berkeley: University of California Press, 1991), 26.

18. See Andrea Frisch, *The Invention of the Eyewitness: Witnessing and Testimony in Early Modern France* (Chapel Hill: University of North Carolina Press, 2004), 27.

19. Wigmore, "A General Survey of the History of the Rules of Evidence," in *Select Essays in Anglo-American Legal History by Various Authors*, 3 vols. (Boston: Little, Brown, 1907–9), 2:696.

20. Wigmore, "General Survey," 2:695.

21. Friedman, *A History of American Law* (New York: Simon and Schuster, 1985), 153.

22. For more on these committees, see Joshua Canale, "When a State Abounds in Rascals: New York's Revolutionary Era Committees for Public Safety, 1775–1783," *Journal of the Early Republic* 39, no. 2 (2019): 203–38.

23. Cope, *Property, Education, and Identity in Late Eighteenth-Century Fiction: The Heroine of Disinterest* (London: Palgrave Macmillan, 2009), 4.

24. Van Buskirk, *Generous Enemies: Patriots and Loyalists in Revolutionary New York* (Philadelphia: University of Pennsylvania Press, 2002), 2–6, 37–38.

25. Sullivan, "Uncommon Cause," in *The American Revolution Reborn*, ed. Patrick Spero and Michael Zuckerman (Philadelphia: University of Pennsylvania Press, 2016), 53.

26. Yokota, *Unbecoming British: How Revolutionary America Became a Postcolonial Nation* (Oxford: Oxford University Press, 2011), 63.

27. McConville, *The Brethren: A Story of Faith and Conspiracy in Revolutionary America* (Cambridge: Harvard University Press, 2021), 7.

28. "An Act More effectually to prevent the Mischiefs, arising from the Influence and Example of Persons of equivocal and suspected Characters, in this State. Passed the 30th of June 1778," in *The Minutes of the Commissioners for Detecting and Defeating Conspiracies in the State of New York: Albany County Sessions, 1778–1781*, ed. Victor Hugo Paltsits, 3 vols. (Albany: State of New York, 1909–10), 1:17.

29. Among those arrested for neutrality in Pennsylvania was Charles Brockden Brown's father, Elijah Brown. It is possible that this had something to do with Brown's later writings on neutrality in the Port of New Orleans affair.

30. Van Buskirk, *Generous Enemies*, 38.

31. New York, *Sir. By virtue of the authority vested in us by certain resolutions of the Congress of the Colony of New-York of the Fifth day of June...* New York, 1776. https://www.loc.gov/item/2020774912/. Holger Hoock reports that over one thousand people were tried by these committees by 1779; see *Scars of Independence: America's Violent Birth* (New York: Crown, 2017), 118–19.

32. *Minutes of The Committee and of the First Commission for Detecting and Defeating Conspiracies in the State of New York December 11, 1776—September 23, 1778 with Collateral Documents*. Vol. 1 (New York: New York Historical Society, 1924), 13. (Emphasis mine).

33. For example, in a law passed 30 June 1778, the New York legislature linked the inaction or abstention of neutrals to the "mischiefs" that might arise from "the Influence and Example of Persons of equivocal and suspected Characters." *Laws of the State of New-York* (Poughkeepsie, 1782), 43–44.

34. "Valerius," *Aurora*, 21 October 1795; "Pittachus," *Aurora*, 13 November 1795.

35. In a letter of 16 August 1793 to Gouverneur Morris, the minister plenipotentiary to France, Thomas Jefferson stated that "we have produced proofs from the most enlightened and approved writers on the subject, that a neutral nation must, in all things relating to the war, observe an exact impartiality toward the parties; that favors to the one to the prejudice of the other, would import a fraudulent neutrality, of which no nation would be the dupe" (*The Writings of Thomas Jefferson*, ed. H. A. Washington, 9 vols. (New York, 1861), 4:34.

36. Neff, *Rights and Duties of Neutrals*, 13.

37. Morgenthau, "The Problem of Neutrality," *University of Kansas City Law Review* 7, no. 2 (1938): 112.

38. Moats, *Navigating Neutrality: Early American Governance in the Turbulent Atlantic* (Charlottesville: University of Virginia Press, 2021), 66.

39. Jefferson to Jean-Baptiste Ternant, 27 August 1792, in *The Papers of Thomas Jefferson*, ed. Julian P. Boyd et al., 47 vols. to date (Princeton: Princeton University Press, 1950–), 24:328–29.

40. Writing as "Pacificus," Alexander Hamilton explained that a neutrality proclamation was not needed when the war involved only Austria and Prussia because they "are not Maritime Powers. Contraventions of neutrality as against them were not likely to take place to any extent or in a shape that would attract their notice. It would therefore have been useless, if not ridiculous, to have made formal Declaration on the subject, while they were the only parties opposed to France": *Gazette of the United States*, 27 July 1793, Founders Online, National Archives, https://founders.archives.gov/documents/Hamilton/01-15-02-0111.

41. Washington to the cabinet, 18 April 1793, Founders Online, National Archives, https://founders.archives.gov/documents/Washington/05-12-02-0358.

42. "Cabinet Opinion on Washington's Questions on Neutrality and the Alliance with France," 19 April 1793, Founders Online, National Archives, https://founders.archives.gov/documents/Jefferson/01-25-02-0530.

43. "Neutrality Proclamation," 22 April 1793, Founders Online, National Archives, https://founders.archives.gov/documents/Washington/05-12-02-0371.

44. For a description of these activities, see Phillip C. Jessup, "Historical Development of the Law of Neutrality," *World Peace Foundation Pamphlet Series* 1 (1928): 355–85.

45. Anonymous to Washington, in *National Gazette*, 15 May 1793, Founders Online, National Archives, https://founders.archives.gov/documents/Washington/05-12-02-0409.

46. Veritas to Washington, *National Gazette*, 1 June 1793, Founders Online, National Archives, https://founders.archives.gov/documents/Washington/05-12-02-0516.

47. "Opinion on the Treaties with France," 28 April 1793, Founders Online, National Archives, https://founders.archives.gov/documents/Jefferson/01-25-02-0562-0005.

48. Fauchet to Edmund Randolph, 18 June 1794, https://founders.archives.gov/documents/Washington/05-16-02-0220-0002, .

49. Elbert D. Thomas, "Theory of Neutrality," *The Annals of the American Academy of Political and Social Science* 186 (1936): 166.

50. "Neutrality Proclamation."

51. Washington to Jefferson, 12 April 1793, Founders Online, National Archives, https://founders.archives.gov/documents/Washington/05-12-02-0353.

52. *Henfield's Case*, Circuit Court, D. Pennsylvania, 1 January 1793; Whart. St. Tr. 4911 F. Cas. 1099.

53. "Memorial from George Hammond," 8 May 1793, Founders Online, National Archives, https://founders.archives.gov/documents/Jefferson/01-25-02-0626. See also Scott Ingram, "Replacing the 'Sword of War' with the 'Scales of Justice': Henfield's Case and the Origins of Lawfare in the United States," *Journal of National Security Law and Policy* 9, no. 3 (2018): 483–508.

54. For more on these questions, see Lindsay M. Chervinsky, *The Cabinet: George Washington and the Creation of an American Institution* (Cambridge: Harvard University Press, 2020), 217–18.

55. See Ingram, "Replacing the 'Sword of War' with the 'Scales of Justice.'"

56. *Henfield's Case*, 11 F. Cas. 1099 (C.C.D. Pa. 1793) (No. 6,360), https://law.resource.org/pub/us/case/reporter/F.Cas/0011.f.cas/0011.f.cas.1099.pdf.

57. Randolph to Washington, 21 August 1793, Founders Online, National Archives, http://founders.archives.gov/documents/washington/05-13-02-0347.

58. Friedman, *A History of American Law*, 285. For more on jury nullification, see Steven E. Barkan, "Jury Nullification in Political Trials," *Social Problems* 31, no. 1 (1983): 28–44; and Barbara Clarke Smith, *The Freedoms We Lost: Consent and Resistance in Revolutionary America* (New York: The New Press, 2010), 29–30.

59. Joseph Ellis explains that the purpose of Jay's mission was "to avoid the outbreak of war, which was looming because of Britain's confiscation of American ships and seamen; to restore trade with Britain, which was a vital lifeline of the American economy and the chief source of revenue for the federal government; and to settle the outstanding provisions of the Treaty of Paris ... [including] the removal of British troops from the northwestern frontier and the payment of debts to British creditors, about £2 million, mostly owed by Virginia planters": *American Creation: Triumphs and Tragedies in the Founding of the Republic* (New York: Vintage, 2007), 197.

60. See James D. Tagg, "Benjamin Franklin Bache's Attack on George Washington," *Pennsylvania Magazine of History and Biography* 100, no. 2 (1976): 206.

61. *Debates in the House of Representatives of the United States, during the first session of the Fourth Congress, upon questions involved in the British Treaty of 1794* (Philadelphia, 1808), 314.

62. Washington to the US House of Representatives, 30 March 1796, Founders Online, National Archives, https://founders.archives.gov/documents/Washington/05-19-02-0513

63. Fenster, *Conspiracy Theories: Secrecy and Power in American Culture* (Minneapolis: University of Minnesota Press, 2008), 94.

64. *Debates in the House of Representatives*, 4.

65. *Debates in the House of Representatives*, 4.

66. *Debates in the House of Representatives*, 309.

67. William Duncan's *Elements of Logick*, quoted in Wilbur Samuel Howell, "The Declaration of Independence and Eighteenth-Century Logic," *William and Mary Quarterly* 18, no. 4 (1961): 473.

68. Martin Diamond, "The Revolution of Sober Expectations," in *The American Revolution: Three Views*, Irving Kristol, Martin Diamond, and G. Warren Nutter, eds. (New York: American Brands, 1975), 64.

69. Washington to the US House of Representatives, 30 March 1796, Founders Online, National Archives, https://founders.archives.gov/documents/Washington/05-19-02-0513.

70. George Washington to Edmund Randolph, 22 July 1795, Founders Online, National Archives, https://founders.archives.gov/documents/Washington/05-18-02-0284. For more on Washington's private opinion of the treaty, see Todd Estes, *The Jay Treaty Debate, Public Opinion, and the Evolution of Early American Political Culture* (Amherst: University of Massachusetts Press, 2006).

71. *Debates in the House of Representatives*, 14.

72. *Debates in the House of Representatives*, 18.

73. "Remarks on the Treaty of Amity Commerce and Navigation lately made between the United States and Great Britain," 9–11 July 1795, Founders Online, National Archives, https://founders.archives.gov/documents/Hamilton/01-18-02-0281.

74. Quoted in Todd Estes, "Shaping the Politics of Public Opinion: Federalists and the Jay Treaty Debate," *Journal of the Early Republic* 20, no. 3 (2000): 409.

75. *Debates in the House of Representatives*, 52.

76. George Washington to Alexander Hamilton, 31 August 1795, Founders Online, National Archives, https://founders.archives.gov/documents/Hamilton/01-19-02-0028; *Debates in the House of Representatives*, 174.

77. *Debates in the House of Representatives*, 34.

78. *Debates in the House of Representatives*, 301.

79. Jay to General Henry Lee, 11 July 1795, Papers of John Jay, https://dlc.library.columbia.edu/jay/ldpd:80114/.

80. *The Correspondence and Public Papers of John Jay*, ed. Henry P. Johnston, A.M. (New York: G.P. Putnam's Sons, 1890-93), Vol. 4 (1794-1826). John Jay to James Duane, 16 September 1795, https://oll.libertyfund.org/titles/johnston-the-correspondence-and-public-papers-of-john-jay-vol-4-1794-1826.

81. Dentith, *Philosophy of Conspiracy Theories*, 36.

Contributors to Volume 54

Yan Che is a PhD candidate in English at Princeton University. His dissertation, "Valuing the Evaluator," examines contested forms of value in the long eighteenth century. An earlier version of his contribution to this volume won the 2023 Graduate Student Essay Prize from the Race and Empire Caucus of the American Society for Eighteenth-Century Studies.

Chloe Summers Edmondson is a lecturer in the Department of French and Italian at Stanford University. Her research is situated at the crossroads of literary criticism, cultural history, and media studies, with a focus on seventeenth- and eighteenth-century France. She holds a PhD in French from Stanford University, as well as a MA in Communication and a BA with Honors and Distinction in French. Her work has appeared in the *Journal of Modern History*, *Digital Humanities Quarterly*, and *Digitizing Enlightenment: Digital Humanities and the Transformation of Eighteenth-Century Studies* (Liverpool University Press, 2020). She co-edited, with Dan Edelstein, *Networks of Enlightenment: Digital Approaches to the Republic of Letters* (Liverpool University Press, 2019). She also serves as a member of the Executive Committee of the Modern Language Association's Eighteenth-Century French Forum. This essay is based on research from her current book project, which examines the evolution of practices of epistolary self-presentation in the ancien régime.

Joani Etskovitz is a PhD candidate in English literature at Harvard University. Her dissertation, "The Feminist Adventure Novel: From the Curious Girl to the New Woman," identifies an Anglo-American genre that developed from 1704–1930, empowering female readers to negotiate their identities, rights, and educations between childhood and adulthood. A Marshall and a Beinecke Scholar, Joani holds two Masters degrees from the University of Oxford, in British and European History and English Literature. Her research has been published in *ELH*, the *Los Angeles Review of Books* and *Public Books*. At Harvard, she is also the founding co-director of the Literary Careers Program, which supports humanities students' professional development.

Allison Y. Gibeily is a PhD candidate in English and a Mellon cluster fellow in Middle East and North African Studies at Northwestern University. She studies embodied and oral literary practices in eighteenth- and nineteenth-century Arabic travel writing. She is the former chair of the ASECS Graduate and Early Career Caucus, and has held research fellowships at the Center for Arabic Study Abroad (CASA) in, Jordan, the Newberry Library in Chicago, and the Gotha Research Library in Germany.

Nan Goodman is the author of many articles and three books: *The Puritan Cosmopolis: The Law of Nations and the Early American Imagination* (Oxford University Press, 2018), *Banished: Common Law and the Rhetoric of Social Exclusion in Early New England* (University of Pennsylvania Press, 2012), and *Shifting the Blame: Literature, Law, and the Theory of Accidents in Nineteenth-Century America* (Princeton University Press, 1998). She has co-edited two books—*The Routledge Research Companion to Law and Humanities in Nineteenth-Century America* (2017) and *The Turn around Religion in America: Literature, Culture, and the Work of Sacvan Bercovitch* (Ashgate, 2011)—and two special issues of *English Language Notes*: *Comparative and Critical Mysticisms* (2018) and *Juris-Dictions* (2010). Her current project concerns the legacy of the Jewish messiah, Shabbtai Sevi, over the course of the 350 years of Jewish settlement in the British colonies in North America and the United States.

Brontë Hebdon is a PhD candidate in art history at the Institute of Fine Arts, New York University. She teaches the history of menswear and European fashion at the Fashion Institute of Technology and was the 2022 Veronika Gervers Fellow in Textile and Fashion History at the Royal Ontario Museum in Toronto. Her dissertation uses Napoleonic salon painting, court costumes, and embroidery to consider how clothing from the French court became tools of imperial and cultural conquest in early nineteenth-century Europe. Her most recent publication, "Embroidered Hierarchies: French Civil Uniforms and the *décret du 29 messidor* in Napoleonic Paris and Milan," appeared in *Costume* (2023).

Robert W. Jones is professor of eighteenth-century studies at the University of Leeds. His work focuses on the political and literary culture of Georgian Britain, especially Drury Lane theater and its owner, Richard Brinsley Sheridan. He is currently writing a book entitled *The Theatre of Richard Brinsley Sheridan: Drury Lane, Politics and Performance, 1775–1787*. He is also a co-editor of *The Political Works of Richard Brinsley Sheridan* (to be published by Oxford University Press).

Vincent Pham is an academic lecturer at University of California San Diego. He received his PhD in art history, theory, and criticism from UC San Diego in 2021. His dissertation, "Consuming faces: portraiture, collections, and display in Mid-Georgian Britain 1760-90" addresses authorial canon formation and re-evaluation in a time of cultural resignification. His research interests include institutional critique, artist communities and friendship groups, eighteenth-century portraiture, and collections studies.

Contributors / 265

Wendy Wassyng Roworth is professor emerita of art history, University of Rhode Island. Her recent publications on Kauffman include "Angelica Kauffman's Portraits of Americans in Rome and a Self-Portrait in Philadelphia," in *American Latium: American Artists and Travelers in and around Rome in the Age of the Grand Tour* (Accademia Nazionale di San Luca, 2023); "An Artist's Bedrooms: Angelica Kauffman in London and Rome," in *Intimate Interiors: Sex, Politics, and Material Culture in the Eighteenth-Century Bedroom and Boudoir* (Bloomsbury Visual Arts, 2023); "Angelica Kauffman: The Acquisition and Dispersal of an Artist's Collection, 1782–1825," in *London and the Emergence of a European Art Market, 1780–1820* (Getty Research Institute, 2019); and "A Celebrity Artist's Studio: Angelica Kauffman in Rome," in *Studies in Eighteenth-Century Culture* (2018). Her contribution to this volume derives from her Presidential Address at the 2023 Annual Meeting of the American Society for Eighteenth-Century Studies.

Robert Stearn received his PhD in 2022 from Birkbeck, University of London, where he also worked as a postdoctoral research associate on the project "Written Worlds: Non-Elite Writing in Seventeenth-Century England." He is currently working on his first book, *Managing Skill: Domestic Service and the Forms of Practical Knowledge, 1650–1750*, and was recently awarded a travel grant by the Lewis Walpole Library to undertake research toward this project. An essay on affect, form, and information management in the diaries of Sarah Cowper is forthcoming in *ABO: Interactive Journal for Women in the Arts, 1640–1830*.

Sanjay Subrahmanyam, FBA, FAAAS, is Distinguished Professor and Irving and Jean Stone Chair of History at UCLA. He is the author and editor of a number of books, including *Europe's India: Words, People, Empires, 1500–1800* (Harvard University Press, 2017) and *Empires between Islam and Christianity, 1500–1800* (Permanent Black, 2018). His contribution to this volume originated as the Clifford Lecture at the 2023 Annual Meeting of the American Society for Eighteenth-Century Studies.

Fauve Vandenberghe is a PhD candidate in literary studies at Ghent University, where her dissertation is funded by the Flemish Research Council. It examines the deeply intertwined and reciprocal relationship between satiric theory and conceptualizations of womanhood in the eighteenth century. Her work has appeared in or is forthcoming from *Eighteenth-Century Fiction*; *Restoration: Studies in English Literary Culture, 1660–1700*; *Women's Writing*; and *Tulsa Studies in Women's Literature*. An earlier version of her contribution to this volume won the 2023 Catharine Macaulay Graduate Student Prize from the Women's Caucus of the American Society for Eighteenth-Century Studies.

ASECS Executive Board, 2024-25

President
Paola Bertucci
Yale University

First Vice President
Misty Anderson
University of Tennessee, Knoxville

Second Vice President
Elena Deanda Camacho
Washington College

Past President
Lisa A. Freeman
University of Illinois, Chicago

Treasurer
Joseph Bartolomeo
University of Massachusetts, Amherst

Parliamentarian
Manushag "Nush" Powell
Arizona State University

Executive Director
Benita Blessing

Members-at-Large
Barbara Abrams, Suffolk University
Brian Cowan, McGill University
Emily Friedman, Auburn University
Meghan Roberts, Bowdoin College
Olivia Sabee, Swarthmore College
Karen Stolley, Emory University

**For information about the
American Society for Eighteenth-Century Studies, please contact:**

ASECS
2397 Northwest Kings Boulevard
PMB 114
Corvallis, Oregon 97330
Telephone: (845) 202-0672
Email: asecsoffice@gmail.com
Website: https://www.asecs.org

American Society for Eighteenth-Century Studies

Sponsor and Lifetime Sponsor Members, 2024-25

Richard Shane Agin
Stanford Anderson
Samuel Baker
Joseph F. Bartolomeo
Robert Bernasconi
Martha F. Bowden
Jane K. Brown
Laura Brown
Marshall Brown
Vincent Carretta
Robert DeMaria, Jr.
Jan Fergus
Lisa A. Freeman
Gordon Fulton
Charles E. Gobin
Susan E. Gustafson
Catherine Ingrassia

Margaret C. Jacob
George Justice
Deborah Kennedy
Heather King
Jocelyne Kolb
Sue Lanser
Elizabeth Liebman
Devoney K. Looser
Elizabeth Mansfield
Jean I. Marsden
David Mazella
Paula McDowell
Heather McPherson
Maureen E. Mulvihill
Melvyn New
Daniel O'Quinn
Douglas Lane Patey

Jane Perry-Camp
Adam Potkay
Joseph R. Roach
Treadwell Ruml, II
Peter Sabor
Harold Schiffman
William C. Schrader
Volker Schroder
Juliet Shields
John Sitter
Karen Stolley
Ann T. Straulman
Randolph Trumbach
Raymond D. Tumbleson
Kathleen Wilson
William J. Zachs
Linda Zionkowski

Institutional Members, 2024-25

American Antiquarian Society
Colonial Williamsburg Foundation
Stanford University
University of Kentucky

Lifetime Institution

Newberry Library